BRITISH EXPORT PERFORMANCE

BRITISH
EXPORT PERFORMANCE

A COMPARATIVE STUDY

BY

S. J. WELLS

*Lecturer in Economics in the
University of Sussex*

CAMBRIDGE
AT THE UNIVERSITY PRESS
1964

CAMBRIDGE UNIVERSITY PRESS
Cambridge, New York, Melbourne, Madrid, Cape Town, Singapore,
São Paulo, Delhi, Dubai, Tokyo, Mexico City

Cambridge University Press
The Edinburgh Building, Cambridge CB2 8RU, UK

Published in the United States of America by Cambridge University Press, New York

www.cambridge.org
Information on this title: www.cambridge.org/9780521174299

© Cambridge University Press 1964

First published 1964
First paperback edition 2011

A catalogue record for this publication is available from the British Library

ISBN 978-0-521-06767-6 Hardback
ISBN 978-0-521-17429-9 Paperback

TO
MY WIFE

CONTENTS

TABLES

APPENDIX TABLES

Import Market Shares Held by Leading Manufacturing Countries

CHARTS

ACKNOWLEDGEMENTS

IN carrying out this Study I owe a very great debt to many individuals and firms who have so cheerfully given their time and knowledge in providing the necessary information and background. Representatives of almost all the major industries covered in the Tables have been consulted for their comments on the facts which emerge from this Survey. This is especially true of those industries analysed in Part II where I have benefited from correspondence and personal discussion with a large number of individuals and firms representing the industries examined. Without their courtesy and patience the Study would have been quite impossible.

It is impossible here to mention the names of individuals who have helped in this way. Below, however, is a list of Companies and Trade Associations whom I visited or with whom I corresponded in connexion with this work. It is hoped that those concerned will accept this as adequate acknowledgement of my debt to them.

This Study was carried out while I was a member of the University of Cambridge Department of Applied Economics, and I am conscious of the considerable debt I owe to the Management Committee of the Department who made the Study possible, and to my colleagues at the Department for their interest and help. In particular, I am deeply indebted to Mr W. B. Reddaway, Director of the Department, for his encouragement and help throughout the period when I was engaged on the Study. Mr Reddaway, Miss Phyllis Deane, Mr J. E. G. Utting, and Mr C. F. Pratten read and commented on earlier drafts. I am also grateful to Sir Donald MacDougall who read a draft and gave me the benefit of his wide experience of international trade problems.

I should like to place on record my appreciation of the assistance I received from the staff of the Department of Applied Economics; Mrs E. Lawrie who drew up many of the Tables, Mr Gilbert Warren and his colleagues who shouldered the burden of computing, Mrs L. Silk who typed most of the text and Tables, and Miss Olga Hickson, Department Librarian.

While I have been greatly helped by many people I accept responsibility for all the conclusions drawn from the Study, and also for any errors of fact which have escaped detection.

I am indebted to the following trade associations and firms for considerable help in the writing of this book. Neither the firms nor their individual representatives with whom I have spoken or corresponded are in any way responsible for the judgments passed or opinions expressed in any part of the Study.

Chemicals and Allied Industries: The Association of British Chemical Manufacturers; The Distillers Company Ltd (Chemical Division); Imperial Chemical Industries

Ltd; Laporte Industries Limited; Shell International Chemical Co. Ltd; Thomas Hedley and Co. Ltd.

Electrical Engineering: Associated Electrical Industries Ltd; Associated Electrical Industries Export Ltd., Cable Division; Belling and Lee, Ltd; British Insulated Callender's Cables Ltd; Burco Ltd; Chloride Electrical Storage Co. Ltd; E. K. Cole Ltd; Crompton Parkinson Ltd; Electrical and Musical Industries Ltd; Electrolux Ltd; Enfield Cables Ltd; Ferranti Ltd; General Electric Company Ltd; Isopad Ltd; Johnson and Phillips Ltd; Lancashire Dynamo and Crypto Ltd; Joseph Lucas (Export) Ltd; Morphy-Richards (Cray) Ltd; Prestcold Division of Pressed Steel Company Ltd; Pye Ltd; Radiation Ltd, Electrical Division; Telegraph Construction and Maintenance Company Ltd.

Engineering and Scientific Instruments: Barford (Agricultural) Limited; E. H. Rentall and Co., Ltd; Bristol-Siddeley Engines Limited; William Cotton and Co. Ltd; Crossley-Premier Engines Ltd; Davey, Paxman and Co. Ltd; HML (Engineering) Ltd; R. A. Lister and Co. Ltd; Ransomes Sims and Jefferies, Ltd; Rolls Royce Limited, International Division; Rustons' Engineering Co., Ltd; The Scientific Instrument Manufacturers' Association; Scientific Exports (Great Britain) Ltd; Short and Mason Ltd.

Hosiery, Knitwear, and other clothing: Aquascutum Ltd; Ashers (Hosiery) Ltd; Atkins Brothers (Hinckley) Ltd; Ballito Hosiery Mills Ltd; Bennet Bros. (Hosiery Manufacturers and Dyers) Ltd; Bonsoir Ltd; British Nylon Spinners Ltd; British Van Heusen Company Ltd; D. Byford and Co. Ltd; Cherub Ltd; N. Corah Ltd; Cumberland Childwear Ltd; Dent, Allcroft and Co. Ltd; Hall and Earl Ltd; F. W. Harmer and Co. Ltd; Hosiery and Knitwear Export Group; The Jaeger Co. Ltd; Johnson and Barnes Ltd; Kayser Bondor Ltd; Montfort (Knitting Mills) Ltd; I. and R. Morley Ltd; Nottingham and District Hosiery Manufacturers Association Ltd; W. and H. Pownall Ltd; Taylor Woods Hosiery Ltd; Webb and Company Ltd; Wolsey Ltd.

Motor Vehicles: The British Motor Corporation Ltd; Ford Motor Company Ltd, Dagenham; Jaguar Cars Ltd; Leyland Motors Ltd; The Society of Motor Manufacturers and Traders; Vauxhall Motors Ltd.

Paints: Ashead Ratcliffe and Co. Ltd; Atlas Preservative Company Ltd; Lewis Berger (Great Britain) Limited; Firwood Paint and Varnish Company Ltd; British Paints Limited; Export Group of the Paint Industry; Arthur Holden and Sons; Imperial Chemical Industries Ltd, Paints Division; International Paints Exports Ltd; Pinchin, Johnson and Company; The Starline Varnish and Enamel Co., Limited; The United Paint Company Ltd.

Pharmaceuticals: Allen and Hanburys Ltd; The Association of British Pharmaceutical Industry; The Beecham Group Ltd; Boots Pure Drug Company Ltd, International Division; British Drug Houses Ltd; Calmic Ltd; Arthur H. Cox and Co. Ltd; The Crookes Laboratories Ltd; The Distillers Company (Biochemicals) Ltd; Evans Medical Ltd; Glaxo Laboratories Ltd; Merck, Sharp and Dohme Ltd; Norgine Pharmaceutical Products (London) Ltd; Roche Products Ltd; Scott and Bourne Ltd; The Wellcome Foundation Ltd.

Pottery: The British Pottery Manufacturers' Federation; The Crown Staffordshire China Company Ltd; The Lawley Group Ltd; Mintons Ltd; Ridgway Potteries Limited; Josiah Wedgwood and Sons Ltd.

Rubber Goods: The Avon India Rubber Co. Ltd; The Cannon Rubber Manufacturers Ltd; Federation of British Rubber and Allied Manufacturers; Pirelli Ltd; The Poppe Rubber and Tyre Company Ltd.

Textiles: The Cotton Board; John Crowther and Sons (Milnsbridge) Ltd; Fothergill and Harvey Ltd; George Fraser Son and Co., Ltd; The National Wool Textile Export Corporation.

INTRODUCTION

THE object of this Study is to analyse on a commodity and country market basis the decline in the United Kingdom share of world trade in manufactures—a decline which went on uninterruptedly during the nineteen-fifties.

In 1951 the United Kingdom share of world trade in manufactures was 22·0%; in 1953 it was 21·3%. By 1959 it had fallen to 17·3%.

During this period it became more and more apparent that the key to the future solvency of the United Kingdom lay in a successful export performance. Indeed, a high and growing level of exports has now come to be regarded as a *sine qua non* of Britain's very existence as an influential trading nation. Without it, the country is certain to have to face recurrent balance-of-payments crises, entailing a continuing threat to the exchange rate, and culminating in either a devaluation or a return to physical controls on imports.

Now there is nothing particularly meritorious about maintaining for all time a given share of world trade. In the case of the United Kingdom there would have been no special virtue in maintaining throughout the nineteen-fifties the share of world trade which happened to have been held in 1951 or 1953. In order to maintain equilibrium in the balance of payments, all that matters is that enough foreign exchange is earned from exports, visible and invisible, to meet international obligations and to finance whatever level of imports and capital investment overseas is deemed desirable. It is indeed conceivable that the United Kingdom share in world trade could go on declining without any serious long-term balance-of-payments problem arising. Such might well be the case if the volume of manufactured imports into Great Britain failed to grow as fast as world imports of manufactures; if there were a long-term movement of the terms of trade in favour of the United Kingdom, or there were a curtailment of overseas investment by the United Kingdom—for example to the under-developed countries. But if the volume of imports and of capital outflow achieved at the end of the nineteen-fifties is to be maintained, or better still increased, during the nineteen-sixties, the United Kingdom simply cannot afford to see her share of world trade continue to decline. The brutal truth is that by 1959 and 1960 receipts from exports were not sufficient to finance outgoings on current and long-term capital account.

Although exports from the United Kingdom continued to grow after 1951—indeed they grew strikingly in some sectors—they did not grow fast enough. For this state of affairs, many explanations have been advanced. It is sometimes urged that a number of Britain's traditional markets, especially in the Sterling Area, have since the war become more and more self-sufficient. In some cases these markets did not grow as fast as those to which German, French and Italian export effort was directed. In other cases, it has been suggested, the United Kingdom has been too dependent upon the export of types of goods, e.g. textiles, the world demand for which in the post-war period has grown less rapidly than for other products. Both these aspects of British export performance are clearly worth considering and we shall examine them in Chapter I (pp. 3–20).

It is alleged by some commentators that in the case of the United Kingdom's trade rivals Government policies, e.g. in regard to tax rebates and concealed export subsidies, have given exporters 'unfair' assistance. In the case of some industries it is held that foreign exporters have enjoyed more favourable credit terms than have been available to British exports. The subject of export aids is one which has been widely discussed, but upon which relatively little factual information is available. We shall, however, look briefly at this topic, particularly as it has concerned Anglo-German competition, in Chapter VI (pp. 78–81).

Sometimes the view is put that, especially in the early nineteen-fifties, the displacement of British goods by exports from Germany, Italy and Japan should be viewed as little more than the inevitable effect of the return of ex-enemy countries to world trade. But this view of the United Kingdom's relatively weak export performance became less acceptable as the war receded into the past. Perhaps a more fundamental view of the failure of United Kingdom exports to hold their own is one that concentrates on prices, costs and productivity. Those who take this view point out that after 1953 United Kingdom prices and production costs rose faster than in most other manufacturing countries. Sometimes this is seen as the result of the wickedness of the trade unions in extracting undeserved money wage increases from their employers; sometimes as the consequence of the slackness of industrialists in failing to keep abreast of new ideas and new techniques or of the Government in failing to ensure an adequate rate of capital investment in industry. The plain fact is that, for whatever reason, United Kingdom exports did not hold their own in the nineteen-fifties in competition with exports from other manufacturing countries, and it is to analyse this problem in a little more detail that this book is offered.

While our Survey does not exclude earlier and later years, in general the Tables and the descriptive sections are limited to the period from 1953 to 1959, one in which the United Kingdom's share in world trade declined by four percentage points, from 21·3% to 17·3% of world trade in manufactures. This period is relatively well covered by published statistics: it is sufficiently long to enable legitimate conclusions to be drawn, and most important of all, it was during this critical period that Great Britain gave place to western Germany as the world's leading exporting country, after the United States, of manufactures.

Throughout the book we confine our attention to exports of manufactures, that is, goods included in Sections 5, 6, 7, 8 of the Standard International Trade Classification.

Most of the Tables and calculations relating to trade are based on the Standard International Trade Classification (S.I.T.C.), and the source most frequently used is the United Nations Commodity Trade Statistics Series D (Annual Volumes). This source is supplemented by O.E.E.C. statistical publications and also by the trade returns of various importing and exporting countries. Trade figures published by the Board of Trade are also used in a number of places.

The Study is in two Parts, the first of which is a general survey, while in the second a more detailed investigation is attempted of exports of selected groups of products.

Generally speaking, in most of the Tables in Part I and in the Appendix Tables, by 'share of the import market' is meant the share obtained by an exporting country of exports of manufactures from the following eleven leading manufacturing countries: the United Kingdom, the United States, Canada, western Germany, France, Italy, the Belgium-Luxembourg Economic Union, the Netherlands, Sweden, Switzerland and Japan.

Ideally, it would have been desirable to have derived 'market shares' from the statistics of the various importing countries. This would have ensured that a consistent classification was adopted for goods imported into a given market from various supplying countries, and would also have accounted for imports from all sources. Unfortunately, in very many cases the trade statistics published by importing countries are not continuous, and differences of classification and presentation as between countries are such that it is virtually impossible to make a comparative analysis on this basis. Accordingly it was decided to base our calculations on figures derived from the export statistics of the eleven leading manufacturing countries. It was particularly convenient to do this, since all eleven exporting countries, with the single exception of Switzerland, make returns at commodity group level to the United Nations on a S.I.T.C. basis. In the case of Switzerland it proved necessary to convert figures published in the Swiss Trade Returns to an S.I.T.C. basis. Where this was not possible, Switzerland is omitted as an exporting country, and the Tables are annotated accordingly.

In Part II, where we are dealing with a more limited field of commodities, it was often possible to supplement the data obtainable from the export side by Tables based on the import statistics of the countries whose markets we examine.

Chapters I and II are largely factual. In them we examine the change in the United Kingdom share in trade in manufactures in a number of commodity, area, and country markets. The chapters are built around a number of detailed Tables which, together with the Appendix Tables, portray the fortunes of the more important British export industries in selected import markets. From the point of view of the United Kingdom the picture is a gloomy one—in the case of almost every group of commodities in the vast majority of the import markets we look at the share of the U.K. fell between 1953 and 1959.

In chapters III and IV some very general explanations for this trend are attempted. In chapter III we draw attention to a movement which is often neglected in studies of export trends, namely the growing tendency in recent years for British (and also American) firms to transfer manufacturing operations from the home country to overseas countries. Usually the effect of this, at any rate in the short term, is to depress commodity export figures, and possibly to bring about a fall in the share of the exporting country in the export market concerned. While in the case of any given commodity it is clearly impossible to establish any direct relationship between changes in import market shares obtained by the U.K. and the establishment by British firms of overseas manufacture in the importing country, it is evident that some connexion between the two does exist. Accordingly an attempt is made in chapter III to draw attention to the scale of overseas direct investment by British firms in recent years.

In chapter IV the importance of price differentials in post-war international trade in manufactures is examined. This leads on to a discussion in chapters V, VI, VII and VIII of the effects of internal domestic economic conditions and policies upon the export performance of the United Kingdom and other leading manufacturing countries—the Federal Republic of Germany and Japan in chapters VI and VII respectively, and France and Italy in chapter VIII. In these chapters an attempt is made to compare the general economic 'climate' in which exporters in the countries concerned worked with that of the United Kingdom.

In general the view taken in this book is that throughout the period we are considering domestic economic conditions fostered export performance more successfully in some competing countries than in the United Kingdom. We shall maintain that this was largely due to a more rapid rate of growth of their economies. Industrial production in the United Kingdom grew less rapidly than in the countries of western Europe. It is, we shall argue, no coincidence that exports grew most successfully in those countries where industrial output also grew most quickly. Accordingly, we shall take a somewhat critical view of the effect of the restrictive economic policies followed by successive British Governments during the period. Undoubtedly there have been times since the war when some deliberate damping down of home demand was necessary to ward off inflation, but a long-drawn-out period of restrictive measures, such as that enforced in the United Kingdom between 1955 and 1958, not only had the effect of making the domestic economy grow less rapidly; it also decreased the spending power of some of the most important potential overseas buyers of U.K. exports. The case against restrictive measures seems particularly strong when these have been discriminatory, e.g. when they have been directed against domestic sales of consumer durables. All too often it has proved difficult to switch sales of these goods from home to foreign markets. Moreover, the industries concerned were often the very ones which should have expanded to satisfy the needs of an increasingly affluent society.

Clearly a country with international reserves as inadequate as those of the United Kingdom since the war must have some means of protecting the balance of payments. In the period we are surveying, when it became necessary to defend the established parity of sterling the policies adopted entailed a damping down of domestic demand. Interest rates were raised, the banks were requested to curtail advances, indirect taxes increased, and restrictions were imposed upon hire purchase transactions. The adoption of these policies, we argue, resulted in a slowing-down of the rate of growth of the United Kingdom economy; this relatively slow rate of growth might well have had an adverse effect upon the capacity and will of British industry to export. Accordingly, we plead for serious consideration to be given to the problem of finding an alternative regulator for the balance of payments, and this leads us to advocate the adoption by the British Government of a flexible exchange rate.

Powerful arguments can be advanced for and against a flexible exchange rate; we are not concerned in this book with the theoretical arguments as such, but rather to argue that the steadfast refusal of the British authorities to adopt a more flexible exchange rate policy, and their decision to rely instead upon restrictive financial policies for external equilibrium, placed a heavy burden upon the rate of growth of the British economy and accordingly had an adverse effect upon exports.

Some of the ideas thus discussed in the first part of this book are in Part II applied to the problems of certain selected export industries. Chapters IX to XIII consist of case studies of U.K. competitive efficiency in five separate and generally diverse industries. The industries were chosen partly because of their intrinsic interest, and partly because they illustrate different aspects of the U.K. export problem.

In chapters IX and X respectively we analyse some of the export achievements of the Motor Vehicle and Electrical Engineering industries. These industries are not only in themselves extremely important to the domestic economy and to the overall export effort of the United Kingdom, but also they illustrate some of the possible effects of domestic restrictions, especially discriminatory ones, upon export performance. The experience of these industries also emphasizes the vulnerability of United Kingdom exports to changes in overseas market conditions—for example, to the tightening of trade controls in the Sterling Area. We shall suggest that in so far as such controls were associated with the difficulties of overseas countries resulting from the adoption of restrictive policies in the United Kingdom, the financial policies pursued by the U.K. authorities hindered rather than helped exports to certain markets.

The industries whose export performances are examined in chapters XI to XIII are Pharmaceuticals—in which overseas manufacture by parent companies and the need for rapid rate of development of new products make the industry a fascinating one to examine; Hosiery and Knitwear, which is a fairly homogeneous part of the clothing industry and where fashion changes are highly important, and finally, in chapter XIII, Pottery, an export industry which well illustrates some of those aspects of Japanese competition discussed in more general terms in chapter VII.

Chapter XIV is a concluding chapter. In it we draw together some of the lessons to be drawn from this Study; we plead for (a) a much more cautious use of restrictive measures in the United Kingdom domestic economy than was the case in the nineteen-fifties; (b) the acceptance of a policy for industrial growth as perhaps the most urgent prerequisite for the long-term expansion of British exports; (c) a substantial reform of international currency arrangements so as to make domestic restrictions even less necessary than in the nineteen-fifties; (d) a willingness on the part of the British Government to consider a flexible exchange rate as a desirable alternative to internal restrictions as the regulator of the balance of payments.

Many people will not, of course, accept this diagnosis of the United Kingdom export problem. It is, however, hoped that they will find the factual part of this Study valuable, especially as the greater part of the book consists of the setting out of facts and problems rather than a detailed attempt at their solution.

PART I
GENERAL SURVEY

CHAPTER I

SOME FACTS AND FIGURES

IN each year from 1953 to 1959 the share of the United Kingdom in the world market in manufactures was smaller than in the preceding year, and in 1958 the United Kingdom surrendered to western Germany her position as the world's second largest exporter of manufactures. These facts are brought out in Table 1.1, which gives a bird's-eye view of the export performance of leading manufacturing countries in recent years.

Comparison with the pre-war pattern of trade in manufactures is difficult to make. Not only were many countries' trade statistics discontinuous between 1938 and 1953, but the percentage share of world trade shown for Germany for 1938 was for the whole of the Reich, whereas for the post-war period the percentage shares relate only to the Federal Republic. Nevertheless the Table suggests that by the middle of the nineteen-fifties the industries of western Germany had more than regained the share in world trade they held in 1938. The exports of the present Federal Republic area accounted for about two-thirds of the share of the exports of manufactures from the whole of pre-war Germany; this implies that in 1938 the share of the present Federal Republic would have been between 15% and 16% of world trade in manufactures—a share which the Federal Republic regained as long ago as 1955.

After 1953, the gains of western Germany, a number of other European countries, and Japan, were largely at the expense not only of the United Kingdom but of the U.S.A. With the exception of 1956 the decline in the United States share was continuous during nineteen-fifties. Indeed, as Table 1.1 shows, the overall decline in the U.S.A. share between 1953 and 1959 was actually greater than in the case of the United Kingdom—and this in spite of the progress made in dollar trade liberalisation in so many countries after 1953. It has been pointed out that during the nineteen-fifties the geographical—but not the commodity—pattern of United States export trade in manufactures was unfavourable.[1] A part of the decline in the United States share can be attributed to relatively unfavourable movements in the cost structure of American industry; part, too, can be explained by the rapid expansion in Europe and other countries of capacity to produce goods which in 1953 and 1954 could readily be purchased only from the U.S.A. The rapid growth in Europe of output of the kind of goods which in early post-war years were perforce purchased (even at high prices)

---

[1] On the subject of the decline of the U.S.A. share in world trade in manufactures between 1953 and 1959 see Sir Donald MacDougall, 'The Dollar Problem: A Reappraisal', *Princeton Essays in International Finance*, No. 35, November 1960.

from the United States offset the effects of dollar trade liberalisation. This is especially true of capital equipment, and in the machinery and transport equipment sector (S.I.T.C. Section 7), where the U.S.A. share in world trade fell particularly steeply—by 13·2 percentage points, from 35·8% of world trade in 1953 to 22·6% in 1959.

To a considerable extent the United Kingdom suffered from the same difficulty as the U.S. in this respect. The sheer capacity of Europe to supply overseas markets was much less in 1953 than in 1959 and the U.K. was able to take full advantage of this—especially in the Sterling Commonwealth countries where social and economic ties gave British exporters a marked advantage over their trade rivals. On the other hand, one must not exaggerate the strength of this argument. It is true that in the early nineteen-fifties the expansion of German exports at the expense of those of the U.S.A. and the United Kingdom could be looked upon as in some measure the inevitable result of the return of defeated ex-enemy countries to markets where they had been well established before the war. Writing in 1957, Sir Donald MacDougall suggested that 'Britain's steadily declining share in the world export market for manufactures between 1950 and 1956 may be largely a temporary phenomenon reflecting, among other things, the delayed recovery from the war of Germany and Japan'.[1] While this explanation might have been acceptable for the period 1951 to 1953, or even 1955, it becomes less and less convincing as the years pass. It is extremely doubtful whether much of the rise in the West German share in world trade between 1957 and 1959 can be explained along these lines. Looking at the figures in Table 1.1 one has grounds for thinking that much more fundamental influences have been at work.

Another interesting fact which emerges from Table 1.1 is the increase in the share of the world trade held from about 1957 onwards by a number of European exporting countries other than Germany. Although the share of France in the world trade in manufactures in the years immediately following 1955 fell quite substantially, her share recovered markedly between 1956 and 1959—from 7·8% to 9·2%, as compared with 6·5% in 1938. In the case of Italy the rise between 1956 and 1959 was from 3·6% to 4·5%. The share of the Netherlands also rose during these years, from 3·5% to 4·2%. All these exporting countries held larger shares in 1959 than in 1958. As regards Japan, her share of world trade in manufactures in 1959 had just passed her estimated 1938 share (6·6%), but as we shall see later, the kind of goods exported by Japan in 1959 were markedly different in type and quality from pre-war Japanese exports—more so than in the case of other manufacturing countries.

Before discussing the other Tables in this chapter, it is perhaps worth

[1] D. MacDougall, *The World Dollar Problem* (London, 1957), p. 355. MacDougall goes on to suggest however (footnote 3, p. 355) that an additional reason for the decline in the U.K. share in manufactures was the fact that Britain's wage costs per unit of output had in recent years risen more rapidly than those of her industrial rivals.

looking at one question which always arises when overall export performance figures are being discussed—namely the extent to which the decline in the U.K. share of the world market can be explained by an adverse commodity or area pattern of U.K. trade. This would have been the case if during the period which we are reviewing the U.K. specialised in those manufactures, the value of world trade in which grew less rapidly than that for manufactures as a whole; alternatively, or perhaps additionally, the regional markets to which U.K. exports were orientated might have been those which expanded less rapidly than the world market taken as a whole. Both of these influences might have been at work together, if U.K. exports were heavily weighted in favour of, say, textiles, in which world trade was declining, and if the U.K. relied heavily upon those overseas import markets, e.g. Australia and the Union of South Africa, which were growing relatively slowly.

In order to examine this question a little more closely—and indeed to grasp the historical background to other U.K. export trends during our period—it is worth going back a half-century or so, to see how far developments in the nineteen-fifties may be regarded as conforming to a long-term pattern, and how far they exhibit characteristics which were peculiar to the circumstances of the decade.

EXPORTS: LONG-TERM TRENDS

1899 to 1950

As the result of a very detailed and laborious study carried out by the late Dr H. Tyszynski at Manchester University it is possible to obtain a fairly accurate picture of the changing pattern of world trade in manufactures over the last half-century and of the share in that trade held by the leading manufacturing countries.[1] Some of the results of Tyszynski's analysis are reproduced as Table 1.2. This Table shows that the United Kingdom share of world trade in manufactures fell from 32·5% in 1899 to 29·9% in 1913, 23·6% in 1929, and 22·4% in 1937. The 1950 share (25·5%) was higher than in 1929 or 1937, but this of course was in a great measure due to the partial elimination of Germany and Japan from world trade in the years immediately following the Second World War.

In Table 1.2 the major exporting countries are arranged in three groups—in the upper part of the Table those whose share of world trade rose more than one percentage point between 1899 and 1937, in the middle part, those whose shares were more or less the same at the beginning and at the end of the period, and in the lower part countries

[1] It will be obvious from the following paragraphs that I owe a considerable debt to Tyszynski's article 'World Trade in Manufactured Commodities, 1899 to 1950' in *The Manchester School of Economic and Social Studies*, September 1951. Also relevant to this section is Professor E. A. G. Robinson's article 'The Changing Structure of the British Economy', *Economic Journal* (September 1954), and a paper by Professor W. Arthur Lewis, 'International Competition in Manufactures', *American Economic Review, Papers and Proceedings* (1957), p. 578.

whose shares decreased substantially. The United Kingdom and France are both found in this latter group. It will be seen that, perhaps rather surprisingly, the German share of world trade in manufactures did not rise very much in the first three or four decades of the century—indeed, according to Table 1.2, it was almost the same in 1937 as it was in 1899. The German share rose quite substantially up to 1913, probably at the expense of the U.K., but it fell back after the 1918 defeat and at the outbreak of the Second World War Germany held the same share as that of the United Kingdom.

The Table shows that few European countries increased their share of world trade in the first four decades of the century—countries which substantially expanded their shares were the United States, Japan and Canada. In 1899 the share of the U.S.A. in world trade was smaller than the share of France; by 1937 it was three times as great. Japan's share rose steadily in the first quarter of the twentieth century, but it was only after the military adventures and the export drive of the nineteen-thirties that Japan outstripped most European industrial countries as a world exporter.

In view of the heavy dependence of the United Kingdom upon textiles and the relative decline in the importance of these products in world trade in the twentieth century, it might be thought that part of the decline in the U.K. share even before the Second World War was due to an adverse pattern of commodity trade. In fact, Tyszynski has shown that in the case of the United Kingdom (and indeed of Japan and France), the change in the position of the country as an exporter between 1899 and 1937 was due rather to ability or inability to compete *within* commodity groups than to the particular pattern of its commodity export trade. If the United Kingdom had retained its competitive position within each group of manufactures between 1899 and 1937, the U.K. share of world trade in manufactures as a whole in 1937 would have been 31·0%, a decline of only 1·5 percentage points. Accordingly, of the decline of 10·1 percentage points sustained by the U.K. between 1899 and 1937, less than one-sixth could be explained as being due to an unfavourable commodity pattern of exports. During this period the percentage share of the United Kingdom fell in textiles (which were declining in relative importance in world trade) but her share also fell heavily in iron and steel and industrial equipment, which were of course among the most rapidly expanding commodity sectors during the period.

By contrast, the commodity pattern of Japan's trade was highly unfavourable up to (and after) the Second World War; her exports were heavily weighted by textiles and clothing. But in spite of this Japan secured a larger share of world trade in 1937 than she held at the beginning of the century, increasing her share both in declining and—more significantly—in expanding categories of exports.

Owing to war and its aftermath, great significance should not be attached to export trends in the period 1937 to 1950. Western Germany,

Japan and many of the occupied countries of Europe were in 1950 still at a relatively early stage of recovery from the war. Nevertheless, even in this period, the decline in the United Kingdom share appears to have been due to lack of competitiveness rather than to an adverse pattern of export trade. If (for this period) western Germany and Japan are eliminated as exporters of manufactures, Tyszynski showed the U.K. share would have fallen from 31·9% to 27·9% of 'world' trade, but of this only 0·1% was attributable to changes in the commodity structure of world trade. During this period France staged something of a recovery as an exporter of manufactures, her share rising from 9·1% in 1937 to 11·4% in 1950 (Germany and Japan again being excluded from both years). This improvement in the position of France was in spite of the adverse effect upon her share in world trade due to the commodity pattern of her exports.

In view of the foregoing it seems that up to 1950 the decline in the U.K. share of world trade was in general due to her inability to compete successfully within each commodity group rather than to her traditional specialisation in what were now the wrong commodities. As for the more recent period, in 1957 the Board of Trade published the results of an Inter-Departmental Working Party Survey on U.K. Export Trends.[1] This survey suggested that only about one-quarter of the decline in the U.K. share in world trade manufactures between 1951 and 1955 could be attributed to an unfavourable commodity/area pattern of trade. For this period changes in the area pattern were more significant than changes in the commodity pattern of British exports, that is to say, the U.K. lost more by exporting to the wrong places than by exporting the wrong goods. But in any case, the importance of both was fairly slight. During this period Germany was helped only slightly by a favourable commodity/area trade pattern. Most interesting of all is Japan which increased her share of world trade quite substantially, as in the first part of the century, although she was adversely affected by both area and commodity pattern of trade (especially the latter).

There is evidence that in the more recent past the 'commodity and area' explanation of the decline in the U.K. share of world trade has even less relevance than in earlier years.

COMMODITY AND AREA PATTERN, 1953–59

Area Pattern

If we assume that in each of the main trading areas of the world the U.K. had in 1959 held her 1953 share, then the total value of U.K. exports of manufactures in 1959 would have been $9,637 million. If the U.K. share in the world market as a whole had been maintained, but not necessarily the U.K. share in each *area* the total value of U.K.

[1] 'Trends in Exports of United Kingdom Compared with Other Countries', *Board of Trade Journal* (30 March 1957).

manufactured exports would have been $9,661 million. In other words the United Kingdom lost only about $24 million of trade as the result of exporting to countries whose import markets grew less rapidly than the value of world trade as a whole. Incidentally it is interesting, and in one sense reassuring, to note than so much of British export effort in recent years has been directed to markets which were clearly expanding. Although British exports were still closely orientated to the Sterling Area market which in 1953 and 1959 took 50·4% and 43·1% respectively of U.K. exports of manufactures, Table 1.3 shows that the market of the United States was in 1959 one of the United Kingdom's most important outlets (in 1953 the U.S. accounted for 5.5% of U.K. exports and in 1959 for 10·5%). Between 1953 and 1959 the United States was one of the world's most rapidly growing import markets. Apart from the U.S.A., an obvious case where the U.K. took advantage of a rapidly growing market was western Germany; imports of manufactures into the Federal Republic from the eleven leading manufacturing countries more than trebled between 1953 and 1959.

As regards the commodity pattern of U.K. export trade, much the same conclusions apply.

If the United Kingdom had held its share of *each* of the broad commodity groupings, then total commodity exports in 1959 would have been $9,600m., that is only $61m. less than if the U.K. share in world trade in manufactures as a whole had been held. In fact the value of British manufactures exported in 1959 was only $7,864m.; by far the greater part of the short fall from $9,661m. was accordingly to be accounted for by the inability of the United Kingdom to hold its own *within* commodity groups.

Commodity Pattern

One of the most rapidly growing export groups from the leading manufacturing countries was machinery and transport equipment; between 1953 and 1959 the value of world trade in these products increased by 75% (as against 64% for manufactures as a whole). Table 1.4 shows that in 1953, 45·0% of the total value of all British manufactured exports consisted of these products. By 1959 the percentage had risen to 50·8. Chemicals in 1953 accounted for 8·5% of U.K. exports of manufactures; world trade in these commodities increased even more—88%—than was the case in engineering products. The share of textiles in U.K. exports of manufactures fell considerably after 1953 and by 1959 they were less important as a group to the U.K. than chemicals; in 1959 textiles accounted for only 8·8% of manufactured exports. Thus the fact that exports of textiles from the eleven leading manufacturing countries rose by only 15% between 1953 and 1959, as compared with an increase of 64% for manufactures as a whole, had less effect upon the overall share of the U.K. in world trade in manufactures than might have been the case in an earlier period. With textiles accounting for less than one-twelfth of total manufactures of all kinds from the U.K. it was a far cry from the middle nineteenth century when they made up about two-thirds of total British exports.

From this discussion it should be clear that U.K. exports have secured a smaller share of world trade in the last fifty years or so largely because they have been becoming less competitive, either within commodity groups, or within particular country markets. Accordingly, to be fruitful, our analysis should try to ask the question why particular exports have failed in particular country markets. Much of the rest of the present chapter is taken up with providing the necessary data for this analysis.

THE CHANGING U.K. SHARE: BY AREA

Table 1.5 shows changes in the shares of area and selected country import markets in manufactures held by various exporting countries.

Western Europe

Table 1.5 shows a decline in the U.K. share in west European and Sterling Commonwealth import markets for manufactures. The United Kingdom share of the west European market fell from 18·7% in 1953 to 13·1% in 1959. The year 1959 was in no way an exceptionally bad one for U.K. exports to Continental western Europe; in fact the decline in the U.K. share of this market was fairly continuous from 1953 onwards. Within western Europe the United Kingdom did less badly in the European Economic Community as a whole than in other countries, but this was largely due to the United Kingdom sustaining only a small decrease in her share of the west German import market. The Federal Republic is easily the United Kingdom's largest European market for manufactures; in 1959 the value of U.K. exports of manufactures to western Germany exceeded the value of exports to New Zealand. They reached just on U.S. $300m., about one-third of U.K. exports to the European Economic Community. Hence the relatively fair U.K. performance in western Germany (where the U.K. share dropped only a little over 1 percentage point, from 12·8% to 11·7%) helped to prevent the U.K. share in the E.E.C. import market from falling as much as it did in western Europe as a whole. The second largest U.K. market in western Europe was the Netherlands. Here U.K. performance was not so good—the share of the import market declining from 19·1% in 1953 to 12·7% in 1959. In 1959 France and Italy were roughly of equal importance to the U.K. as export outlets, but the U.K. share in France had fallen more steeply than in Italy.

If we look at the exporting countries which gained in western Germany and the rest of the E.E.C. we find that both Italy and France increased their share, the gain of Italy being especially marked in western Germany. The U.S. gained in no E.E.C. country except the Federal Republic (in the Community as a whole the U.S. share de-

C

clined), and the gains of Japan were very small indeed. Broadly
speaking the tendency was for the six Common Market countries to
trade more closely with one another, but it should be noted that this
trend goes back to 1953 and in some measure would have occurred
whether or not the Common Market had been formed. Looking at the
changes in market shares obtained by western Germany, Italy and
France (Table 1.5), it is evident that with only one exception (the
French share of the Netherlands market), each of these exporting
countries increased its share of the import market of every other E.E.C.
country.

The Sterling Area

The Non-O.E.E.C. Sterling Area in 1953 still accounted for 50% of
U.K. exports of manufactures and in this very important trading area
the U.K. failed to hold her position as an exporter, her share of the
area import market for manufactures declining by over 14 percentage
points between 1953 and 1959. The U.S. share in the Sterling Area
did not rise much in spite of a considerable degree of dollar trade liberalisation. The Italian and French shares were very small and together
increased only slightly; it was the rise in the German and Japanese
shares which largely offset the U.K. decline. Between 1953 and 1959 the
German and Japanese shares rose respectively by 5·5 and 6·9 percentage points, but whereas the German share in 1953 was already
6·9%, that of Japan was only 3·8% in that year.

Japan's most substantial gains in the Sterling Area were in fact in
British East Africa (+15·4 percentage points), Malaya (+13·6 percentage points), Nigeria (+10·5 percentage points) and Australia
(+5·5 percentage points). In each of these cases the expansion of the
Japanese share was in part due to the removal of restrictions on Japanese
imports after 1953, but it would be wrong to regard the increase in the
Japanese share as a once-for-all development which need not be
repeated. Japan's share of the Sterling Area market has in fact increased
steadily even in the Union of South Africa where discrimination against
Japan was abandoned as early as 1954.

The increase in the German share of the Sterling Area market has
been more evenly spread as regards both country markets and commodities than that of Japan, although it has been especially dramatic
in the case of India, which by 1959 was buying more than one-sixth
of its manufactured imports from western Germany. The Federal
Republic had by 1959 become next to the U.K. the major supplier of
Pakistan, and in the case of the Union of South Africa, over 15% of
imported manufactures were being obtained from western Germany.
Whereas it is possible to explain some of Japan's gains in Commonwealth countries—especially in Australia—by the easing of discrimination, this is likely to be less true of imports from western Germany,
whose exports have been treated on equal terms with those of the U.K.
since well before 1953.

Latin America

In Latin America the United Kingdom actually increased her share of the import market between 1953 and 1959, from 7·6% to 8·2%. Indeed western Germany did no better than the U.K. in this market, and not as well as Japan, whose share rose from 1·2% to 4·5%, or Italy whose share rose from 2·4% to 4·9%. The U.S.A. lost over 6 percentage points of its share of the Latin American market, but in 1959 it still held just on 56% of the import market. As regards individual country markets in Latin America, the pattern of U.K. performance was a varied one. In Argentina, for example, which was the United Kingdom's largest market, the U.K. share between 1953 and 1959 rose by 6·4 percentage points. The German share of this market *fell* between these years. The U.K. sustained losses in the two other Latin American markets in which her share in 1953 was over 10% (in Peru and Venezuela). The United States too lost heavily in these markets, where both Germany and Japan made substantial gains.

The general pattern, then, is of the U.K. losing to western Germany in most (but not all) country markets; to Japan in sterling markets, and to France and Italy in western Europe.

THE CHANGING U.K. SHARE: BY COMMODITY GROUPS

As well as looking at *changes* in the share held by the U.K. in various commodity groups we shall in this section pay some attention to the absolute share of a given market held by the U.K. After all, although the U.K. share of world trade in textiles fell from 27·2% in 1953 to 18·0% in 1959, while the share of the U.K. in glass and glassware fell by only 1·3 percentage points over the same period, the British share of the world market in textiles was still 18·0% in 1959, as compared with 12·3% held by the glass industry. It would accordingly be misleading to infer that the greater fall in terms of percentage points of the textile industry of itself shows that the export performance of the latter industry was inferior to that of the glass industry.

In the remainder of this chapter we shall take, as it were, a bird's-eye view of the export performance of some more important British industries in the world market as a whole; in the following chapter we shall analyse their performance in particular country markets in a little more detail.

Textiles

While the U.K. share of the world market in textiles fell steeply between 1953 and 1959, the share of western Germany rose—but only slightly—from 6·5% to 8·9% of the world market (Table 1.6). The Italian share rose from 8·3% to 9·4%, while the share of the United States fell from 14·2% to 11·6%. A substantial increase in the share of world trade in textiles took place in the case of Japan, whose share rose

8·4 percentage points to 19·6%. The gains of Japan were concentrated in the Commonwealth and the U.S.A., and this almost certainly applied to textiles as a whole.

Within the textile section, the most important group of products is non-cotton fabrics. In this group the U.K. share fell nearly 14 percentage points between 1953 and 1959, and with 20·4% of world trade in this group in 1959, the U.K. held a share of the world market smaller than that of Japan. In cotton fabrics the Japanese share in 1959 was 30·7%, very much greater than that of the U.K. (13·7%). Between 1953 and 1959 the share of Japan rose by 13·1 percentage points, that of the United Kingdom fell by 10·7 percentage points. The United States share fell, but by a very modest amount compared with that of the U.K., while the German share increased slightly. Clearly, this is a case where some concern ought to be felt by British interests.

The Japanese share of the world market in made-up textiles rose from 8·5% to 14·0% between 1953 and 1959, while the share of the United Kingdom fell from 21·7% to 15·2%.

Clothing is very closely allied to the textile industry in many respects (although not included in the S.I.T.C. group 65), and here the U.K. lost ground, not only to Japan, whose share of the world market rose dramatically from 8·9% to 24·8%, but also to Italy and possibly to Germany. Nevertheless the United States clothing industry lost even more ground than the United Kingdom; by 1959 the U.K., the U.S.A., and Germany each held about 10% of the world market, while the share of Japan was a little under 25%. The performance of the U.K. hosiery and knitwear industry, which constitutes an important part of the clothing sector, will be analysed in more detail in chapter XII.

Metals and Engineering

Metals and engineering products together (S.I.T.C. Section 7 and groups 68 and 69 of Section 6) in 1959 accounted for well over half the value of British exports of manufactures. In metals the U.K. held in 1959 some 15·5% of the world market; in machinery and transport equipment the share was greater—21·1%. However, by 1959 the share of western Germany was in both these fields greater than that of the United Kingdom—19·3% and 27·0% respectively. In metals the U.K. share of world trade was in 1959 substantially greater than that of the U.S.A., but in machinery and transport equipment the U.S. share was slightly greater. The shares of both Japan and Italy in these sectors were still relatively small in 1959, but Table 1.6 shows that both countries had increased their share of world trade since 1953.

A sector of the engineering industry in which the U.K. share fell particularly steeply was electrical engineering (S.I.T.C. 721). This sector will be examined in more detail in chapter X—here we content ourselves with remarking that western Germany made substantial gains while both the United Kingdom and the U.S.A. lost ground.

The only S.I.T.C. group in the engineering sector where the U.K.

share in world trade actually rose was power machinery. This was one of the few groups where an initial U.K. share (in 1953) of over 30% was actually improved upon in our period.

In engineering the U.K. and the U.S.A. shares of the world market fell, and the western German share rose, with almost monotonous regularity. Table 1.6 shows that in most cases Japan and Italy increased their shares of world trade in engineering products, but whereas the gains of Italy were largely concentrated in two groups—motor vehicles and office machinery—those of Japan were more evenly spread over the whole engineering sector. Nevertheless, the only row of Table 1.6 relating to engineering in which Japan held in 1959 more than 5% of the world market was in the one showing shares of world trade in the quantitatively relatively unimportant sector—non-motorised road vehicles (mostly bicycles).

Chemicals

In the chemical sector (S.I.T.C. Section 5) the U.K. held her own rather better than in engineering. However, in 1959, the value of chemicals exported by western Germany far exceeded that of the United Kingdom. Within Section 5, U.K. performance was variable, ranging from an almost insignificant increase in the U.K. share in paints and dyes to a decrease of some 6 percentage points (from 33·9% to 28·0%) in soaps and cosmetics.

The gains of western Germany were not as dramatic in chemicals as in metals and machinery, but it was only in paints and dyes that the German share actually declined. The U.K. share in world trade in organic and inorganic chemicals was in 1959 considerably less than that of either western Germany or the U.S.A., but the 'switch' in world trade in these commodities had been relatively small since 1953. Taking organic and inorganic chemicals together, the U.K. share had fallen by 3·7 percentage points; that of western Germany had risen by 1·7 percentage points. Even by 1959 Japan held only a tiny share of world trade in chemicals (3·1%) and in some branches her share was very small indeed.

Other Manufactures

The share of the United Kingdom in each of the commodity groups in the lower part of Table 1.6 (rubber manufactures, glass and glassware, pottery and scientific instruments) declined. This part of the Table draws attention to two fields in which the gains of Japan (almost certainly at the expense of the U.K.) were very substantial—pottery, where the share of Japan rose from 26·1% to 36·6% of world trade, making her the world's leading exporter, and scientific instruments. Japan almost doubled her share of the world market in scientific instruments between 1953 and 1959; holding 10·6% of the market, her exports were almost exactly equal in value to those of the U.K.

In terms of market shares, Germany's record in the case of the commodities in the lower part of Table 1.6 is not particularly noteworthy —indeed in scientific instruments and in rubber products her share actually fell. The Italian shares in trade in these commodities did not increase very much, and in no case were they at all significant in 1959.

Conclusions

Summarising our conclusions from Table 1.6 we can say that, commodity-wise, U.K. export performance was uneven. In some quite important sectors of world trade the U.K. share actually increased; in others, and the majority, it fell, but the magnitude of the decline in the U.K. share varied considerably between groups of commodities. The United States lost in nearly all sectors (but note the increase in the U.S. share of the world market in inorganic chemicals); western Germany has almost—but not quite—always gained where the U.K. has lost. As for Japan, just as we noted from Table 1.5 that her gains had been largely concentrated in the Sterling Area and in North America, so we find that commodity-wise her gains were mostly in textiles and in certain miscellaneous groups of commodities—pottery, scientific instruments and, to a very much less extent, electrical engineering.

Table 1.1. *Share of world market in manufactures, 1938, 1953–59*

Percentage Shares of Principal Manufacturing
Countries

	1938*	1953	1954	1955	1956	1957	1958	1959	Change 1953–59
United Kingdom	22·1	21·3	20·4	19·7	19·1	18·1	17·9	17·3	−4·0
United States†	20·0	25·9	25·1	24·5	25·2	25·4	23·3	21·3	−4·6
Western Germany‡	22·7	13·3	14·8	15·5	16·4	17·5	18·5	19·1	+5·8
Belgium-Luxembourg	5·9	6·5	6·2	6·5	6·7	6·0	5·9	6·0	−0·5
France	6·5	9·0	9·0	9·3	7·8	8·0	8·6	9·2	+0·2
Italy and Trieste	2·9	3·3	3·2	3·4	3·6	3·8	4·1	4·5	+1·2
Netherlands	3·1	3·7	3·8	3·8	3·5	3·5	3·9	4·2	+0·5
Sweden	2·3	2·6	2·8	2·7	2·8	2·9	3·1	3·1	+0·5
Switzerland	2·7	4·0	3·8	3·5	3·4	3·4	3·4	3·4	−0·6
Canada	5·1	6·8	6·3	6·1	5·8	5·5	5·3	5·2	−1·6
Japan	6·6	3·8	4·7	5·1	5·7	6·0	6·0	6·7	+2·9

Notes: * 1938 percentages based on estimates made by Board of Trade.
   † Percentages are based on figures which up to 1957 exclude U.S. Special Category exports. Certain items valued at approximately $185m. in 1957 were in 1958 removed from the Special Category list, and percentages for 1958 are not, therefore, strictly comparable with previous periods. Assuming that these items were valued in 1958 at $185m., the effect of excluding them for that year would be to reduce the U.S.A. share to 22·9, and raise the U.K. and west German shares to 18·0% and 18·6% respectively.
   ‡ 1938, All Germany; 1953–59, German Federal Republic only. Before the war, exports of the present Federal Republic area were roughly two-thirds of those of the pre-war Germany.

Table 1.2. *Percentage shares of trade* in manufactures,† 1899–1937*

	1899	1913	1929	1937	Change 1899 to 1937
U.S.A.	11·2	12·6	20·7	19·6	+ 8·4
Japan	1·5	2·4	3·9	7·2	+ 5·7
Canada	0·3	0·6	3·5	5·0	+ 4·7
Sweden	1·0	1·2	1·7	2·5	+ 1·5
Belgium	5·6	4·9	5·5	5·9	+ 0·3
Germany	22·2	26·4	21·0	22·4	+ 0·2
Italy	3·7	3·6	3·7	3·6	− 0·1
India	2·3	2·4	2·4	2·1	− 0·2
Switzerland	3·9	3·1	2·8	2·9	− 1·0
France	15·8	12·9	11·2	6·4	− 9·4
United Kingdom	32·5	29·9	23·6	22·4	−10·1
	100·0	100·0	100·0	100·0	

Source: H. Tyszynski, *Manchester School of Economic and Social Studies*, vol. 19, p. 286.
   * Exports of manufactures from the countries listed (note that these do not include the Netherlands), consistently accounted for 80 to 85% of world trade in manufactures in the period 1901 to 1938.
   † Manufactures here include those in Class III ('Articles Wholly or Mainly Manufactured') of the British Export List 1950, with the addition of alcoholic drink and manufactured tobacco and the exclusion of coke and refined petroleum. For details, see Appendix I of Tyszynski's article cited in footnote, p. 5. It will be seen that the definition of 'manufactures' used in this Table does not exactly correspond with the one adopted in Table 1.1 and most other Tables in this book.

Table 1.3. *Area distribution of U.K. exports of manufactures, 1953 and 1959*

$m.

	Value of Exports		Percentage of Total	
Area	1953	1959	1953	1959
Continental western Europe	1371	1833	23·3	23·3
United States of America	321	823	5·5	10·5
Canada	375	511	6·4	6·5
Sterling Area	2963	3393	50·4	43·1
Latin America	278	404	4·7	5·1
Rest of World	567	900	9·7	11·4
To World	5875	7864	100·0	100·0

Source: U.N. Commodity Trade Statistics.

Table 1.4. *Commodity structure of U.K. exports of manufactures, 1953 and 1959*

$m.

Commodity	S.I.T.C. Classification	Value of Exports		Percentage of Total	
		1953	1959	1953	1959
Chemicals	5	499	821	8·5	10·4
Textiles	65	912	695	15·5	8·8
Metals and metal manufactures	68/69	956	1261	16·3	16·0
Machinery and transport equipment	7	2643	3997	45·0	50·8
Other manufactures	Rest of 6 and 8	866	1090	14·7	13·9
All manufactures		5876	7864	100·0	100·0

Source: U.N. Commodity Trade Statistics.

Table 1.5. *Changes in shares of area import markets in manufactures held by leading exporting countries, 1953–59*

Market Import	Value of Exports from '11' 1959 $m.	U.K. Share 1953	U.K. Share 1959	U.S.A. Share 1953	U.S.A. Share 1959	W. German Share 1953	W. German Share 1959	Japan Share 1953	Japan Share 1959	Italy Share 1953	Italy Share 1959	France Share 1953	France Share 1959
1. Western Europe*	14039	18.7	13.1	12.5	10.6	25.7	30.6	0.6	1.1	4.2	5.5	7.8	10.0
2. Western Europe Sample**	11818	20.1	13.8	11.9	10.8	23.5	27.5	0.6	1.0	2.9	4.9	7.7	9.9
3. E.E.C.	8597	16.7	14.9	14.1	12.1	21.3	24.3	0.5	0.8	3.2	5.7	9.0	11.4
4. Non-O.E.E.C. Sterling Area	6350	62.4	48.2	11.9	12.8	6.9	12.2	3.8	10.7	2.6	2.6	2.2	2.6
5. Sterling Commonwealth Sample†	4947	62.9	50.4	11.9	12.6	6.5	13.2	3.6	8.8	2.4	2.2	1.8	2.5
6. Latin America	5048	7.6	8.2	62.2	55.9	11.6	12.1	1.2	4.5	2.4	4.9	4.9	4.4
7. Canada	3707	14.2	13.8	80.8	74.9	1.1	3.5	0.4	2.9	0.3	0.7	0.6	1.3
8. U.S.A.	5736	11.1	14.4	—	—	9.0	15.1	5.5	15.8	3.5	4.8	4.5	7.1
9. Belgium-Luxembourg	1450	14.9	9.5	14.2	11.6	25.1	29.7	0.4	0.8	2.8	4.0	14.1	15.3
10. Denmark	814	29.0	20.2	3.2	4.3	29.8	36.0	0.8	1.7	2.3	2.8	3.5	5.7
11. Finland	434	24.0	20.5	10.3	7.1	19.2	31.9	0.9	0.3	1.7	2.3	9.2	7.9
12. France	1467	18.4	11.5	24.1	13.7	20.4	36.8	0.4	0.2	5.2	7.6	—	—
13. Western Germany	2540	12.8	11.7	7.7	13.4	—	—	1.1	1.2	7.1	10.7	17.5	19.7
14. Italy	1149	17.4	14.1	18.5	14.6	29.5	36.4	0.3	0.6	—	—	9.7	13.0
15. Netherlands	1990	19.1	12.7	8.2	8.2	28.0	35.1	0.5	0.9	1.4	2.5	5.4	5.2
16. Norway	761	27.7	15.7	6.4	4.5	25.9	31.0	0.4	1.4	1.3	1.8	3.7	4.5
17. Sweden	1243	27.2	19.1	9.2	11.0	32.0	40.6	1.0	1.5	3.3	3.4	5.4	6.8
18. Australia	1143	70.7	52.0	11.5	17.5	4.5	10.2	0.9	6.4	1.6	1.4	2.1	1.9
19. British East Africa‡	175	81.6	58.9	3.7	3.5	4.4	9.2	0.5	15.9	3.2	2.8	0.6	neg.
20. Ceylon	137	64.2	57.7	4.8	4.1	6.1	9.2	14.9	17.6	0.9	1.3	1.7	2.3
21. Ghana	166	74.4	60.0	2.4	3.3	4.6	14.1	8.4	13.0	neg.	1.3	neg.	1.5
22. India	1027	49.8	44.3	14.0	10.6	11.5	21.6	4.7	7.0	3.7	2.9	3.4	3.9
23. Malaya	308	60.3	40.3	9.9	8.8	5.9	9.3	13.8	27.4	1.8	0.8	1.1	2.3
24. New Zealand	366	84.5	72.2	5.9	9.2	1.9	4.8	5.9	3.1	0.4	0.9	0.2	0.9
25. Nigeria	284	70.0	61.4	2.0	2.4	10.0	9.4	6.1	16.6	6.3	2.7	neg.	1.6
26. Pakistan	246	61.4	35.9	10.2	17.0	11.2	18.8	8.1	10.0	5.0	3.9	4.9	neg.
27. Rhodesia and Nyasaland	166	43.2	74.3	6.0	5.4	1.1	7.1	neg.	1.9	0.2	2.0	neg.	4.2
28. Union of South Africa	944	90.0	42.0	20.9	19.3	8.8	15.4	3.4	5.3	2.3	3.9	1.8	2.3
29. Iraq	185	50.5	42.8	13.3	13.0	6.7	16.3	11.0	11.5	5.2	2.0	3.1	2.7
30. Iran	476	52.6	21.8	20.4	21.9	27.4	25.3	15.3	10.3	5.8	3.1	2.6	1.0
31. Argentina	702	13.3	15.6	27.0	30.7	29.4	20.4	4.4	2.8	9.7	4.1	5.5	7.4
32. Brazil	729	9.2	4.8	39.4	44.1	17.0	19.6	2.7	5.0	3.5	9.9	13.7	6.8
33. Peru	178	7.5	9.0	61.2	47.9	9.2	16.4	1.6	4.1	1.0	2.2	2.0	6.7
34. Mexico	806	3.1	4.5	79.0	70.6	5.2	9.0	neg.	1.9	1.5	2.3	1.3	2.8
35. Colombia	278	5.0	5.3	63.8	60.0	9.2	13.2	0.7	3.3	1.1	1.3	7.7	2.4
36. Venezuela	1066	10.7	8.1	69.1	56.9	5.6	11.6	1.2	4.5	2.0	5.9	1.6	2.6

Source: U.N. Commodity Trade Statistics.   * Western Europe excludes the U.K.   ** Rows 9–17.   † Rows 18–28.
‡ Kenya, Uganda, Tanganyika.   neg. = imports from 'eleven' negligible.

Table 1.5. *Changes in shares of area import markets in manufactures held by leading exporting countries, 1953–59*

Import Market	U.K.	U.S.A.	Changes 1953–59 W.G.	Japan	Italy	France
1. Western Europe	− 5·6	− 1·9	+ 4·9	+ 0·5	+1·3	+2·2
2. Western Europe Sample*	− 6·3	− 1·1	+ 4·0	+ 0·4	+2·0	+2·2
3. E.E.C.	− 4·8	− 2·0	+ 3·0	+ 0·3	+2·5	+2·4
4. Non-O.E.E.C. Sterling Area	−14·2	+ 0·9	+ 5·5	+ 6·9	0.0	+0·4
5. Sterling Commonwealth Sample†	−12·5	− 1·3	+ 6·7	+ 5·2	−0·2	+0·7
6. Latin America	+ 0·6	− 6·3	+ 0·5	+ 3·3	+2·5	−0·5
7. Canada	− 0·4	− 5·9	+ 2·4	+ 2·5	+0·4	+0·7
8. U.S.A.	+ 3·3	—	+ 6·1	+10·3	+1·3	+2·6
9. Belgium-Luxembourg	− 5·4	− 2·6	+ 4·6	+ 0·4	+1·2	+1·2
10. Denmark	− 8·8	+ 1·1	+ 6·2	+ 0·9	+0·5	+2·2
11. Finland	− 3·5	− 3·2	+12·7	− 0·6	+0·6	−1·3
12. France	− 6·9	−10·4	+16·4	− 0·2	+2·4	—
13. Western Germany	− 1·1	+ 5·7	—	+ 0·1	+3·6	+2·2
14. Italy	− 3·3	− 3·9	+ 6·9	+ 0·3	—	+3·3
15. Netherlands	− 6·4	—	+ 7·1	+ 0·4	+1·1	−0·2
16. Norway	−12·0	− 1·9	+ 5·1	+ 1·0	+0·5	+0·8
17. Sweden	− 8·1	+ 1·8	+ 8·6	+ 0·5	+0·1	+1·4
18. Australia	−18·7	+ 6·0	+ 4·5	+ 5·5	−0·2	−0·2
19. British East Africa‡	−22·7	− 0·2	+ 5·8	+15·4	−0·4	−0·6
20. Ceylon	− 6·5	− 0·7	+ 3·1	+ 2·1	+0·4	+0·6
21. Ghana	−14·4	+ 0·9	+ 9·5	+ 4·6	+1·3	+1·5
22. India	− 5·5	− 3·4	+10·1	+ 2·3	−0·8	+0·5
23. Malaya	−20·0	− 1·1	+ 3·4	+13·6	−1·0	+1·2
24. New Zealand	−12·3	+ 3·3	+ 2·9	+ 2·9	+0·5	+0·7
25. Nigeria	− 8·6	+ 0·4	− 0·6	+10·5	−3·6	+1·6
26. Pakistan	− 7·3	+ 6·8	+ 7·6	+ 1·9	−1·1	−0·7
27. Rhodesia and Nyasaland	−15·7	− 0·6	+ 6·0	+ 1·9	+1·8	+2·3
28. Union of South Africa	− 8·5	− 1·6	+ 6·6	+ 1·9	+0·8	+0·9
29. Iraq	− 9·8	− 0·3	+ 9·6	+ 0·5	−4·0	−2·1
30. Iran	+ 8·5	+ 1·5	− 2·1	− 5·0	−1·7	+4·8
31. Argentina	+ 6·4	+ 3·7	− 9·0	− 1·6	+0·2	+1·3
32. Brazil	− 2·7	+ 4·7	+ 2·6	+ 2·3	+0·6	−7·0
33. Peru	− 1·8	−13·3	+ 7·2	+ 2·5	+1·2	+0·8
34. Mexico	+ 1·4	− 8·4	+ 3·8	+ 1·9	+0·8	+1·1
35. Colombia	+ 0·3	− 3·8	+ 4·0	+ 2·6	+0·2	−5·1
36. Venezuela	− 2·6	−12·2	+ 6·0	+ 3·3	+3·9	+1·1

Source: U.N. Commodity Trade Statistics.

* Rows 9–17.

† Rows 18–28.

‡ Kenya, Uganda, Tanganyika.

Note: U.S. Special Category exports are included in the case of country and sample markets, but are excluded for Western Europe and Latin America (rows 1 and 6).

Table 1.6. *Changes in shares* of import markets in selected manufactures, held by leading exporting countries, 1953–59*

Category	S.I.T.C.	Value of Exports from 'Eleven' $m. 1959	U.K. Share 1953	U.K. Share 1959	U.S.A. Share 1953	U.S.A. Share 1959	W. Germany Share 1953	W. Germany Share 1959	Japan Share 1953	Japan Share 1959	Italy Share 1953	Italy Share 1959
1. All Manufactures	5–8	45,359	21·3	17·3	25·9	21·3	13·3	19·1	3·8	6·7	3·3	4·5
2. Chemicals	5	5,470	17·2	15·0	28·1	27·5	16·4	20·2	2·1	3·1	3·0	3·8
3. Textiles	65	3,861	27·2	18·0	14·2	11·6	6·5	8·9	11·2	19·6	8·3	9·4
4. Metal and metal manufactures	68/69	8,161	18·1	15·5	16·9	12·1	12·9	19·3	3·5	4·9	1·7	3·4
5. Machinery and transport equipment	7	18,941	24·4	21·1	35·8	22·6	15·4	27·0	1·7	4·3	2·6	4·0
6. Inorganic chemicals	511	669	19·7	16·1	18·6	26·4	18·6	20·1	0·9	2·2	3·9	4·6
7. Organic chemicals	512	810	14·8	11·0	39·0	30·4	27·5	29·3	0·5	1·0	2·8	5·2
8. Paints, dyes, etc.	53	362	20·0	20·4	29·7	29·9	18·9	11·5	1·1	0·8	2·0	0·8
9. Drugs, etc.	54	839	16·2	14·3	42·0	34·0	7·9	12·1	1·2	1·8	2·5	3·0
10. Soaps, cosmetics	552	262	33·9	28·0	23·9	23·8	5·5	10·6	neg.	1·5	neg.	1·5
11. Yarn thread	651	876	24·3	17·7	8·1	9·8	5·4	9·6	7·1	8·1	10·3	11·9
12. Cotton fabrics	652	949	24·4	13·7	18·9	16·1	6·5	8·5	17·6	30·7	4·4	3·3
13. Non-cotton fabrics	653	1,237	34·3	20·4	12·5	8·2	8·4	9·2	9·9	23·9	12·6	13·7
14. Made-up textiles	656	229	21·7	15·2	30·2	27·5	3·1	5·6	8·5	14·0	7·4	7·4
15. Clothing	84	831	22·7	12·6	23·5	10·5	6·8	10·2	8·9	24·8	8·8	12·6
16. Iron and steel	681†	4,284	14·6	12·6	19·9	9·6	13·0	21·7	5·4	5·9	1·4	3·5
17. Power machinery	711	1,320	31·1	33·3	27·2	22·9	17·4	15·8	0·7	1·1	3·4	4·8
18. Agricultural machinery	712	431	12·2	10·3	39·7	33·4	8·7	17·8	0·3	0·5	0·6	0·5
19. Office machinery	714	489	14·6	12·3	43·2	32·0	12·4	18·9	0·0	0·8	7·1	10·2
20. Metal working machinery	715	925	12·0	11·9	39·2	32·2	27·3	36·2	0·3	0·3	3·2	3·8
21. Mining machinery, etc.	716†	4,672	22·2	18·1	40·6	35·7	19·7	24·7	1·7	3·1	2·4	3·6
22. Electrical engineering and equipment	721	3,206	26·0	19·2	30·5	22·5	14·9	24·3	0·8	3·4	2·1	1·8
23. Railway vehicles	731	348	28·0	27·3	25·2	22·5	14·2	22·1	2·1	4·3	2·6	1·7
24. Road motor vehicles	732	4,658	23·4	23·0	51·9	25·8	9·9	25·2	0·2	1·2	2·3	5·7
25. Non-motor road vehicles	733	183	48·0	33·7	13·2	15·7	11·2	20·3	4·4	6·0	2·5	4·4
26. Rubber manufactures	62	537	24·7	20·7	34·0	26·7	8·4	5·2	1·8	3·5	5·1	3·0
27. Glass and glassware	664/5	422	13·6	12·3	32·4	19·3	13·0	17·2	3·7	5·0	2·5	3·1
28. Pottery	666	160	32·1	24·6	2·6	1·8	23·0	23·6	26·1	36·6	3·7	4·4
29. Scientific instruments	861	669	14·2	10·6	25·5	28·9	34·8	30·0	5·6	10·6	2·2	1·9

Sources: U.N. Commodity Trade Statistics   * For list of exporting countries, see Table 1.1.   † Excluding Switzerland.

Table 1.6. *Changes in shares* of import markets in selected manufactures, held by leading exporting countries, 1953–59*

	Category	U.K.	U.S.A.	W. Germany	Japan	Italy
				Changes, 1953–59		
1.	All Manufactures	− 4·0	− 4·6	+ 5·8	+ 2·9	+1·2
2.	Chemicals	− 2·2	− 0·6	+ 3·8	+ 1·0	+0·8
3.	Textiles	− 9·2	− 2·6	+ 2·4	+ 8·4	+1·1
4.	Metal and metal manufactures	− 2·6	− 4·8	+ 6·4	+ 1·4	+1·7
5.	Machinery & transport equipment	− 3·3	−13·2	+11·6	+ 2·6	+1·4
6.	Inorganic chemicals	− 3·6	+ 7·8	+ 1·5	+ 1·3	+0·7
7.	Organic chemicals	− 3·8	− 8·6	+ 1·8	+ 0·5	+2·4
8.	Paints, dyes, etc.	+ 0·4	+ 0·2	− 7·4	− 0·3	−1·2
9.	Drugs, etc.	− 1·9	− 8·0	+ 4·2	+ 0·6	+0·5
10.	Soaps, cosmetics	− 5·9	− 0·1	+ 5·1	+ 1·5	+1·5
11.	Yarn thread	− 6·6	+ 1·7	+ 4·2	+ 1·0	+1·6
12.	Cotton fabrics	−10·7	− 2·8	+ 2·0	+13·1	−1·1
13.	Non-cotton fabrics	−13·9	− 4·3	+ 0·8	+14·0	+1·1
14.	Made-up textiles	− 6·5	− 2·7	+ 2·5	+ 5·5	0·0
15.	Clothing	−12·5	−13·0	+ 3·4	+15·9	+3·8
16.	Iron and steel	− 2·0	−10·3	+ 8·7	+ 0·5	+2·1
17.	Power machinery	+ 2·2	− 4·3	− 1·6	+ 0·4	+1·4
18.	Agricultural machinery	− 1·9	− 6·3	+ 9·1	+ 0·2	−0·1
19.	Office machinery	− 2·3	−11·2	+ 6·5	+ 0·8	+3·1
20.	Metal working machinery	− 0·1	− 7·0	+ 8·9	0·0	+0·6
21.	Mining machinery, etc.	− 4·1	− 4·9	+ 5·0	+ 1·4	+1·2
22.	Electrical engineering & equipment	− 6·8	− 8·0	+ 9·4	+ 2·6	−0·3
23.	Railway vehicles	− 0·7	− 1·3	+ 7·9	+ 2·2	−0·9
24.	Road motor vehicles	− 0·4	−26·1	+15·3	+ 1·0	+3·4
25.	Non-motor road vehicles	−14·3	+ 2·5	+ 9·1	+ 1·6	+1·9
26.	Rubber manufactures	− 4·0	− 7·3	− 3·2	− 1·7	−2·1
27.	Glass and glassware	− 1·3	−13·1	+ 4·2	+ 1·3	+0·6
28.	Pottery	− 7·5	− 0·8	+ 0·6	+10·5	+0·7
29.	Scientific instruments	− 3·6	+ 3·4	− 4·8	+ 5·0	−0·3

Sources: U.N. Commodity Trade Statistics.
* For list of exporting countries, see Table 1.1.

Note: In this and following Tables U.S. Special Category exports are included (following the practice of the U.N. in Commodity Trade Statistics) unless otherwise specified.

CHAPTER II

BRITISH EXPORT INDUSTRIES:
A COMPARATIVE SURVEY

USING THE BASIC TABLES

WE come now to the Tables which in a sense form the central core of the analysis of this study—Tables 2.1 and 2.2, together with Appendix Tables A—X. These Tables provide a cross-classification which makes it possible to analyse the performance of a group of United Kingdom manufactured exports in any one of the selected markets. Table 2.1 shows the share of U.K. commodity exports in country and sample regional markets in 1953, and Table 2.2 shows the change in the percentage share of the U.K. in the commodity/country import markets between 1953 and 1959. Table 2.1 is included in order to relate the *changes* shown in Table 2.2 to the initial shares held by the United Kingdom, but our main interest at present is the latter Table. This Table makes gloomy reading. Out of the 720 commodity/country markets shown in the Table, the U.K. lost in 512 and gained in 199. In nine markets the U.K. share did not change. In fact, changes of less than 1·0 in either direction are probably not very meaningful, and if we eliminate these we find that the United Kingdom lost in 479 commodity/country markets, gained in 188 and broke even in 53.

Table 2.3 classifies U.K. commodity exports according to their performance in country markets. In group A are exports which improved their performance in more country markets than they lost in; in group B are exports which broadly speaking either improved their position or held their own in as many markets as they lost in. Group C consists of exports whose losses were more numerous than gains or 'stable' market shares but less than twice as numerous; in group D are exports whose losses were more than twice as numerous as gains or stable markets. Too much should not be made of the results of this classification. It is, for example, possible for an industry to lose in a very large number of minor markets but to gain in a substantial one, so that its share in world trade is maintained. Road motor vehicles, for example, fall into category D of Table 2.3, but the U.K. share in the world market in these goods declined much less than in the case of clothing, which falls into category C. But the Table does help to establish whether an industry whose overall performance we know to have been 'good'—e.g. agricultural machinery—achieved this result by an outstanding performance in a few markets, or by an evenly spread advance in a large number of countries. In the case of agricultural machinery it is clear that the increase in the U.K. share took place in a number of markets. The distinction between an increase in the share of the world market which is due almost entirely to success in a few limited markets and one which is more broadly based is important. There is great danger in an industry having too many eggs in one export market—as the experience of the motor industry in 1960 clearly showed. Before discussing these Tables further it is perhaps worth reminding the reader of the *caveat* made on page 11, where we pointed out the importance of taking into account the absolute share of the market in a given product held by the United Kingdom either at the beginning or the end of the period, as well as the *change* in that share over the period.

A further word of warning is necessary at this point. Some of the changes in market shares shown in Table 2.2 appear quite dramatic, but where the entire country import market for the commodity in question is a small one a change in the U.K. share of 30 or 40 percentage points is not very significant. Thus between 1953 and 1959 the U.K. share of the Nigerian import market for organic chemicals fell by over 26 percentage points. But in 1953 the Nigerian market for exports of organic chemicals by the entire group of eleven manufacturing countries was only $613 thousand—accounting for about 0·1 % of world trade in these products. Accordingly, where a country import market for a given commodity represents only a tiny fraction of world trade in that commodity in any year (less than 0·2 %), percentage shares have been placed in brackets in our Appendix Tables. On the basis of the same criterion an asterisk against a figure in Table 2.2 indicates that either in 1953 or 1959 the import of a commodity into a particular market was relatively insignificant.

By looking down the rows in Table 2.2 and comparing the performance of various commodities in the same market it is possible to see which industries progressed better or worse than manufactures as a whole in a given import market. It is also possible to note how the performance of certain categories of goods compared with that of similar ones in the same markets. We can, for example, take the import market of Australia. The United Kingdom lost ground to Germany and Japan in this market. In Table 2.2 we can see in which commodities the decline of the U.K. share of the Australian import market from 70·7 % to 52·0 % was concentrated. The commodity groups whose losses were heaviest can readily be identified from this Table—they were cotton fabrics (a decline of 46·4 percentage points), non-cotton fabrics, made-up textiles, rubber manufactures, pottery, and railway vehicles. In all these sectors losses were heavier than in manufactures taken as a whole (row 1).

TEXTILES AND CLOTHING

Textiles

Within the textile sector it is instructive to enquire why, for example, cotton fabrics fared much worse than non-cotton fabrics in the Australian import market or why there should have been such a striking contrast between the performance of fabrics and that of yarn thread. Further light on the problem is shed by Tables F, G, H and I in the Appendix. These show the shares of the U.K., Germany, the U.S.A. and Japan in the selected markets for various types of textiles for 1953, 1957 and 1959. In the case of cotton fabrics in the Australian market it is clear from Table G that the loss of the U.K. was almost entirely due to vigorous competition from Japan, whose share of the import market increased from 10·2% in 1953 to 52·8% in 1959. In non-cotton fabrics (mostly of wool and of man-made fibres), Japanese competition only became really severe after 1957, but by 1959 the Japanese share of the import market had more than doubled. In strong contrast to the piece goods sector is the Australian import market for yarn, where the Japanese made virtually no impression at all until 1959.

Of course the great upsurge in Japanese piece goods imports into Australia can be explained in large part by the progressive removal after 1953 of restrictions on imports of Japanese fabrics into the Dominion, culminating in the Trade Agreement of 1957, but the fact that the removal of physical controls was followed by imports of such magnitude —and at the expense of the United Kingdom—suggests that Japanese products were cheaper, quality for quality, than those from the United Kingdom. It has been reliably reported that prices of Japanese fabrics of man-made fibres imported into Australia were in 1959 between 40% and 80% of U.K. prices for broadly comparable fabrics, according to whether these were pure or mixture, plain or printed. Early in 1960 the Australian Tariff Board enquired into overseas production costs of fabrics of man-made fibres, and this enquiry shed some light on the absolute cost advantages enjoyed by Japanese textile firms. The enquiry showed, for example, that the price of yarn in Japan was between 50% and 75% of that in Australia. In Japan unit labour costs in textiles were less than half those in the Australian textile industry.

The Tariff Board also elicited the information that Japanese exporters generally were content with a much lower profit margin than Australian mills or wholesalers. This almost certainly applied to British as well as Australian textile houses. Another factor of importance in comparing Japanese and U.K. export performance in textiles is the extent to which the Japanese industry—often helped by American 'know-how'—installed some of the most up-to-date textile machinery in the world.

Now by looking along the commodity rows of Table 2.1 it is possible to see whether the decline of the share of the U.K. in imports of textile piece goods into Australia was an isolated phenomenon, or whether it was repeated in other markets, e.g. in those where discrimination against Japanese textiles had already been relaxed or abandoned in the early nineteen-fifties. The right-hand columns of the Table suggest that the biggest losses of the U.K. in both cotton and non-cotton goods were in the Sterling Commonwealth—but then, of course, the U.K. held a higher absolute share of these markets than she did in Europe. In our western

Europe sample of countries between 1953 and 1959 the U.K. share in cotton and non-cotton fabrics imports declined by 10·1 percentage points and 5·6 percentage points respectively; in the E.E.C. the decline in the U.K. share was less. Indeed, in the case of non-cotton fabrics in the community market the U.K. share declined *less* than for manufactures as a whole. In Europe Britain was helped by the absence of Japan as a major exporter to that market. This is brought out in Table H, from which it appears that Japan in 1959 held only 4% of the E.E.C. import market in non-cotton fabrics. Clearly, if we wish to shed much light upon U.K. performance in textiles we shall have to look at the conditions under which Japanese industries work, and this is attempted in chapter VII.

Clothing

Closely allied with textiles is the clothing sector. It appears from Table 2.2 that in the world market as a whole the U.K. share decreased more in clothing—by 12·5 percentage points—than in all manufactures taken together, and fell more sharply than in other made-up textiles, yarn thread or cotton fabrics. Here again, the area in which performance was worst was the Sterling Commonwealth. Table J shows that, as in other textile sectors, the losses of the U.K. in most country markets were matched by the gains of Japan. The Table also shows that in 1959 the U.S.A. was easily the largest U.K. market for clothing. The value of U.K. clothing exports to the U.S.A. in 1959 was $16·8m.— greater by nearly 3m. dollars than the value of her clothing exports to the entire European Economic Community and not far short of the value of exports to all the Sterling Commonwealth countries included in our sample. In fact, however, the U.K. share of the United States import market fell more in clothing than in any other commodity groups shown in our Table, with but three exceptions—non-cotton piece goods, motorised and non-motorised road vehicles. Within Europe, the British clothing industry fared markedly less badly in the Common Market countries than in the E.F.T.A. countries listed. Whereas in Norway, Sweden and Denmark the U.K. share fell quite steeply in clothing, in some E.E.C. countries the record was fair. By far the largest import market for clothing in western Europe is Germany. Here the fall in the U.K. share was relatively modest. In the Belgium-Luxembourg Economic Union and in Italy the U.K. actually increased its market shares. In most of the markets of the world, however, the U.K. share in clothing fell quite sharply.

The clothing sector as defined by the Standard International Trade Classification is a somewhat heterogeneous one and it is quite possible that there were differences in performance between the various parts which make up the industry. Accordingly, in chapter XII we have chosen an important part of the industry—hosiery and knitwear—and looked at the performance of this part in some detail.

In clothing and textiles it will be generally agreed that the failure of the U.K. to hold overseas markets was not due to inability to supply.

At no time between 1953 and 1959 was there any question of U.K. exporters being unable to meet foreign demand, except perhaps in the case of a few high quality specialist clothing lines. British clothes and textiles failed to be sold abroad, not because home demand pre-empted scarce supplies, but because either the prices quoted by U.K. firms in foreign markets were not competitive with those of other manufacturers, or because the styles and colours of British products were not those required in overseas markets. This subject will be dealt with more fully in chapters VII and VIII where we discuss Japanese and Italian export performance.

MACHINERY

Table 2.2 can be used to investigate whether British exports which were known to have expanded most rapidly in the nineteen-fifties were also the ones in which the U.K. shares of foreign import markets rose or at least were held fairly stable. Unfortunately, this does not seem to have been the case. United Kingdom exports of machinery, for example, rose enormously in value after 1953, but the evidence of our Tables is that machinery exports from other countries rose even more rapidly. Of the S.I.T.C. groups of the engineering sector (S.I.T.C. Section 7), the U.K. share of the world market increased only in power machinery. It remained more or less stable in metal-working machinery, road motor vehicles, and railway vehicles; it fell in 'mining and other' machinery by 4·1 percentage points, in electrical machinery and equipment by 6·8 percentage points and non-motorised road vehicles by 14·3 percentage points.

Electrical Machinery and Equipment

The most striking feature of the engineering section of Table 2.2 is the fair performance in a large number of markets of some of the non-electrical machinery sectors as compared with electrical machinery and equipment. Both electrical and non-electrical exports of the engineering industry grew rapidly after 1953, but there was clearly a very marked falling away in terms of market shares in the electrical sector. Exports of electrical products are of great importance in their own right—especially as they include many consumer durables upon which domestic restrictions have been imposed, and the export performance of the industry is accordingly analysed in more detail in chapter x. It is, however, worth noting at this stage that in the case of Common Market countries the U.K. share of electrical exports fell less than for manufactures as a whole, and in North America the industry actually improved its position between 1953 and 1959. The performance of the electrical industry in the U.S.A. import market was better than that of any other industry, except power and metal-working machinery and glassware. Electrical equipment more than held its own in some of the leading Latin American markets for U.K. exports.

D

Power Machinery

Clearly the best performance in the engineering sector during the period 1953 to 1959 was that of power machinery (Appendix Table L), which improved its share of the world market (+2·2 percentage points), of the western European sample, and also of the European Economic Community. In some country import markets, e.g. the Netherlands and Finland, power machinery was the only, or almost the only, group to improve its position. In the U.S.A. its performance was far better than that of any other industry, the U.K. share rising from 26·4% of the import market in 1953 to 48·7% in 1959. This achievement was particularly noteworthy in view of the importance of the U.S. market for these goods to the United Kingdom; in 1959, the U.S. market accounted for U.K. exports of power machinery worth over $50m.—about one-ninth of total U.K. exports of these goods. Inspection of Appendix Table L will show that, in most non-European markets in this group, competition from western Germany was singularly absent. Even in some European countries the U.K. secured a higher share than western Germany.

Within the power machinery group there was a marked divergence between the experience of the aircraft engine industry and that of some other sectors. Exports of gas turbines from the U.K. compared favourably with those from competing countries, but in diesel engines the U.K. share of the world market decreased from 25·3% in 1953 to 22·8% in 1959, whereas the West German share increased from 22·5% to 25·0% over the period. Thus the U.K. lost to western Germany her position as the leading exporter of diesel engines.

The reason for the poor performance of western Germany in this commodity group as a whole is in part to be found in the fact that in the years we have been reviewing western Germany played practically no part at all in the world's aircraft engine industry—the industry which produced a substantial part of U.K. exports of power machinery.

Exports of aircraft engines and parts accounted for well over one-third by value of U.K. power machinery exports in 1959. Moreover, between 1953 and 1959 the value of U.K. aircraft engine exports more than trebled. The high share of the U.K. in the United States import market in power machinery was largely due to the success of the British aircraft engine industry in that market; in 1959, over two-thirds of the value of all U.K. power machinery exports to the U.S. consisted of aircraft engines and parts.[1]

There were in the period under review only two firms engaged in large-scale manufacture of aircraft engines in the United Kingdom—Bristol Siddeley and Rolls-Royce Aircraft Division. Both these organisations have since the war spent vast sums on research and technical development and have world-wide selling and servicing networks.

[1] Other markets which took substantial quantities of British aircraft engine exports in 1959 were Canada, £5·6m., France £6·5m., Italy £4·1m.

The success of the aircraft engine industry is of course bound up with that of the whole aircraft industry, especially as some aircraft are designed to take only a specific engine, and in these cases the success of the firms making the engines is tied in with that of the firms producing the aircraft. Thus the Viscount can be fitted only with the Rolls-Royce Dart engine, and the Comet with the Avon engine. Accordingly, the successful sale of a Viscount to a foreign airline almost inevitably involves subsequent sale of replacement engines—and provides the engine-exporting firm with the opportunity of substantial earnings on overhauls, the cost of which can amount to something approaching 25% of the cost of a new engine. Not all engines, however, are specific to particular aircraft and where alternative engines can be fitted there is, of course, a greater element of competition between the world's aircraft engine manufacturers. There was during the nineteen-fifties a growing tendency for countries to build up their own aircraft engine industries, but the cost of research and development is such (and the scarcity of qualified aircraft engineers so acute), that in most countries manufacturers produced under licence granted by the U.K. or the U.S. The European aircraft engine industry concentrated on lighter engines, which are not so expensive to produce as the massive power units developed in Britain and the United States. As regards these larger engines virtually the only competition faced by Bristol Siddeley and Rolls-Royce came from American firms. The British firms seemed able to hold their own against the Americans in non-American airlines, but when competing for contracts with the U.S. airlines, the American import duty offset the price advantage of the U.K. industry.

Metal-Working Machinery

Metal-working machinery (S.I.T.C. 715) is another field where the United Kingdom held her share of world trade. In 1959 a high proportion of British exports of metal-working machinery consisted of machine tools. Appendix Table O shows that in the Common Market the U.K. share of the import market in metal-working machinery actually rose; this was largely due to a very good U.K. export performance in France, to which market in 1959 U.K. metal-working machinery exports was almost as large as to the rest of the E.E.C. countries put together. The U.K. share of the fairly rapidly growing Italian market also rose during the period, from 6·8% to 10·2% of the import market.

As in power machinery, substantial gains were made by the United Kingdom in the U.S.A. The U.K. also made gains in some smaller markets—Colombia and Iran, but the performance of the industry in the Sterling Commonwealth sample was disappointing. In some countries (e.g. Malaya and Nigeria) the import market for these products is very small indeed and in these cases too much attention should not be paid to changes in market shares. On the other hand, two of the markets where the U.K. share declined most steeply, India (by 22·9 percentage points) and Australia (by 19·1 percentage points), were the United Kingdom's largest overseas markets for these goods and the obvious switch in demand from U.K. to German sources in supply must be regarded with concern. It is true that other types of machinery lost to western Germany in both Australia and India, but in the case of Australia metal-working machinery fared worse than any other category of machinery.

Although the British machine tools industry held its share fairly well in many overseas markets, better results would probably have been obtained if supply difficulties had been fewer. In the middle nineteen-fifties—when Germany was capturing from the U.K. a large share of her export trade to many markets—there were many complaints about the delivery dates quoted by British firms. It cannot be denied that there was substance in these complaints. The main reason for poor supply service at this time seems to have been the limited capacity of the industry, this being the direct consequence of an inadequate rate of growth of capacity in the early nineteen-fifties. It has been remarked of the industry that much of it 'remained convinced that the post-war demand for machine tools was something quite exceptional and that demand was bound to slacken off in the fairly near future'.[1]

The machine tools industry had particularly unhappy memories of the pre-war depression and it persistently acted on the belief that 'good times cannot last'. By its very nature the industry is exposed to sharp oscillations in demand which accompany cyclical changes in industrial output. Moreover, a large part of it consists of smallish firms and the tendency has been for these firms to sub-contract orders[2] or to allow order books to lengthen in times of buoyant demand rather than permanently to expand capacity. Thus from the point of view of easing supply difficulties, both at home and abroad, the industry might have done well to have increased its capacity. Unfortunately, the very nature of modern demand for machine tools makes general expansion of the industry difficult. Since the war, and indeed since 1930, domestic demand was increasing for tools which were highly complex, very expensive and 'specific' to a particular purpose. There was, for example, a more rapid growth of demand (in the home market) for automatic than for capstan lathes. Accordingly there is a limit to the size of the typical production batch of a tool used specifically in, let us say, the radio industry. Nevertheless, a significant part of the total output of the industry in the nineteen-fifties still consisted of general purpose tools and these made up the bulk of exports, especially to countries at a relatively early stage of industrial development.

Although technically the German industry in the nineteen-fifties was no more efficient than the best British machine-tool-making firms,

[1] Economic Intelligence Unit, *Britain and Europe* (London), p. 106.
[2] Only about three-quarters of the peak war-time production was made by the established industry. See footnote 2, p. 363, M. E. Beesley and G. W. Troup, 'Machine Tools' in *The Structure of British Industry*, ed. D. Burn.

before the war it underwent forced rationalisation, and the deliberate limitation of numbers of types of machine undoubtedly enabled the industry to expand capacity, output and exports. While, for reasons we have stated, there is a limit to the possibility of rapid expansion of output of machine tools, it would seem likely that a steadier rate of growth of industrial output in the British economy in the last ten years would have gone a long way towards giving the machine tools industry that confidence which was so necessary for a permanent increase in capacity. Such an increase would have made possible an even better export performance than was in fact achieved by the industry.

Agricultural Machinery

Two branches of engineering which held their own against German competition in most markets were agricultural machinery and office machinery (Appendix Tables M and N respectively). Although results in the Commonwealth were good (in contrast to metal-working machinery), British farm machinery did not show a very encouraging performance in western Europe, where its share fell in the import markets of all the countries listed in Table 2.2 with the single exception of Italy. The reason for the inability of the British industry to hold its own in western Europe is partly to be found in the differences between British and Continental methods of cultivation. In 1953 the West German farm machinery industry had hardly recovered from the war; as time went on, German industry was built up, and Continental farmers reverted to buying machines from Germany and other west European producers. On the Continent farms tend to be smaller than in Britain and German agricultural machinery is naturally more closely geared to the requirements of agriculture in neighbouring countries than is the U.K. industry. In many parts of western Europe—in Belgium, for example—light, easy, soils predominate and European manufacturers accordingly developed lightweight and cheap ploughs which are perfectly adequate for the requirements of these kinds of soils. Some United Kingdom manufacturers were in the nineteen-fifties able to sell medium and heavy ploughs for use on larger Belgian farms, but such exports were relatively few. From almost all the European markets the story seemed to be roughly the same—U.K. farm machinery exports were unsuitable for local requirements and were too expensive. The chief hope for the United Kingdom in Europe is probably in farm tractors.

Mining and other Machinery

On the whole, rather less successful than the types of machinery we have been looking at was the S.I.T.C. group 716, which is described in Table 2.2 and Appendix Table P as 'Mining Machinery, etc.'. As we have seen this is in fact a group comprising all kinds of non-electrical machinery which cannot conveniently be included under any other heading. It includes mining, pumping, constructional and excavating machinery; paper mill and pulp machinery; printing, textile and air-conditioning machinery, roller bearings, sewing machines and pneumatic tools. In view of the varied nature of these products it would clearly be wrong to deduce any substantial conclusions from percentage share changes in the group as a whole. The inclusion of the group in the Table does, however, help to throw into bolder relief the achievements of those engineering sectors like power machinery which did well in particular markets.

In 1959 over one-eighth of the total value of U.K. exports under the S.I.T.C. heading 716 consisted of textile machinery. It is worth investigating exports of these items to see whether to any marked extent they took the place of U.K. exports of textiles. Unfortunately this does not seem to have been the case for British textile machinery exports were valued at £41·1m. in 1959, only a little above the figure of £40·8m. for 1953. Two of the markets where the decline of the U.K. share in textiles and clothing was particularly marked between 1953 and 1959 were Australia and the Union of South Africa. In neither case did the United Kingdom increase its share of the respective import markets in any important type of textile machinery. For example, if we look at textile machinery imports into the Union of South Africa the U.K. share of the import market in 1953 was 67·1%, the U.S. share 6·9%, and that of western Germany 10·1%. By 1958, the respective shares were 36·6%, 15·4%, and 23·3%. There was one field, however, where U.K. textile machinery manufactures turned to good account the rapid development of overseas manufacture of finished products. Between 1953 and 1960 U.K. exports of circular knit machinery for the making of seamless stockings increased from £8·0m. to just under £40m. In this way the textile machinery industry to some extent made up for the loss the British hosiery industry sustained in export markets as the result of the fashion trend towards non-fully fashioned ladies' stockings.

Now in one sense an export of a piece of textile machinery can be looked upon as a once-for-all item on the credit side of the balance of trade. Moreover such machines have a fairly long life, and there is probably a relatively small replacement demand; hence the export of a machine is not usually as beneficial to the country as the export of goods made by that machine. Nevertheless, so often in practice the choice faced by the U.K. was not between exporting textile machinery or finished textile products. It was between exporting machinery or nothing at all. In these circumstances it is important that other sectors of the textile machinery industry should do as well as the hosiery machinery industry in the export field; in this way there is *some* compensation for the losses sustained by the United Kingdom in the textile sector.

Reviewing the machinery sector as a whole, the United Kingdom had a varied experience over the years covered by our survey. Some parts of the industry—power machinery and machine tools, for example, did better than others. Even within the S.I.T.C. groups into which we have broken down engineering exports there were wide divergencies in performance between products, and in the case of products, between markets. This suggests that the study of U.K. export performance is much more complex than it at first appears. There is clearly room for much more detailed analysis of the comparative performance of various products within and between markets.

CHEMICALS AND ALLIED PRODUCTS

In chapter XI we examine the export performance of the pharmaceutical industry. This is a highly specialised part of the much broader 'chemical industry', and has peculiar export problems of its own. There are, however, other branches of chemicals the export performance of which it is convenient to look at in the present chapter.

In few other industries is the problem of definition so difficult as in chemicals. In this respect the Standard International Trade Classification is not ideal. Dyestuffs, for example, are placed along with water colours and printers' ink. Perfumery is lumped in with polishes, and an arbitrary line is drawn between organic and inorganic chemicals. Nevertheless, it is clear that certain very broad conclusions can be drawn from Table 2.2. Paints and dyestuffs held their share of world markets more successfully than other chemical groups. Drugs and pharmaceuticals did better than either S.I.T.C. Section 5 as a whole, or 'all manufactures' (S.I.T.C. 5–8).

Organic and Inorganic Chemicals

Although there are differences between their relative performance in certain markets (e.g. the U.S.A.) the overall change in the percentage shares of world trade obtained by organic and inorganic chemicals respectively were almost identical.

While the U.K. lost in inorganic and organic chemicals in most markets (Appendix Tables A and B), it is by no means true that wherever the U.K. lost, western Germany gained. In some cases in inorganic chemicals, it was the U.S.A. which gained at the expense of the U.K., especially in E.E.C. markets. In Italy, the United Kingdom's largest European market for inorganic chemicals in 1959, the U.K. lost to both western Germany and the U.S.A. Indeed, the U.K. share of the import markets declined in each of the west European countries and in almost all Commonwealth countries in our sample. The only large markets in which there were gains were the U.S.A., the Argentine and Brazil. In organic chemicals the pattern was similar, except that in this group the U.K. actually increased its share of the import market of India, but the share declined substantially in the U.S.A.

Wages play a relatively small part in total production costs of chemicals—this is perhaps why the U.S.A. and the U.K. held their share of the world market in chemicals more successfully than in some other sectors where labour costs are relatively more important. The two cost items which really matter are raw materials and overheads. In respect of raw material costs there could have been relatively little difference, product for product, between costs in the major manufacturing countries, but a direct comparison is difficult to make, since in the organic chemicals group it was only after about 1955 that the Germans used a petroleum base. For many years after the war, the German industry was based largely on acetylene, produced either from calcium carbide or from natural or coke oven gas. Later, the major German firms switched over to the use of a petroleum base for their chemical products. Much of the German plant coming into use towards the end of the nineteen-fifties was therefore extremely up to date and technically highly efficient.

It has been suggested that a considerable part of the German chemical industry was using particularly obsolescent plant at the end of the war, and the cost of capital development in the industry was such that there was probably a longer delay in the re-equipping of the chemical industry than in the case of some other branches of manufacture. Nevertheless, taking the period from 1953 to 1959, output from the German chemical industry grew faster than in the case of the U.K. The average annual rate of increase of production was about twice as fast in Germany as in the U.K. (11% per annum as against 5% per annum). In many branches of chemicals the Germans appear deliberately to have established more plants than were necessary to satisfy home demand; thus exporting has been an integral part of the industry's activities. In 1958, about 23·2% of the output of the chemical industry of the Federal Republic was exported; for the U.K. the proportion was about 20·3%. In an industry where overheads are so important, a rapid rate of growth is essential if U.K. prices are to keep competitive. However, the cost of plant is so great that firms are reluctant to plan expensive development programmes unless they feel assured of an adequate long-term demand. In this respect, of course, the chemical industry depends upon the growth of the large number of industries which purchases its products. Accordingly, it is essential for the efficiency of this important basic industry and thus for its export success, that the whole United Kingdom economy maintains a steady and consistent rate of growth.

Paints and Dyes

One of the S.I.T.C. divisions where the United Kingdom share was held between 1953 and 1959 was division 53, paints and dyestuffs (Appendix Table C).

The amount of capital required to start a paint industry in a developing country is quite small and accordingly this is one of the fields where indigenous manufacture has naturally tended to oust imports at a relatively early stage of a country's development. Several British companies to a small extent compensated themselves for these losses by setting up overseas factories or by concluding licensing agreements with foreign companies in developing countries. Some firms have been able in this way actually to increase export sales from the United Kingdom of high quality specialist products—e.g. paint for decoration and food cans, crown caps and corks used in the food industry; weather and rust-resistant paints required in tropical areas, road line paints and other specialist products. Such firms, however, found great difficulty in selling ordinary decorative paints, especially in the more developed countries.

Both in the industrial and decorative sectors, competition came from the Netherlands and Denmark rather than western Germany. As regards the high quality specialist lines, price was generally a secondary consideration to the prospective purchaser. In any major operation like the painting of a new factory, the cost of the paint is usually but a fraction of the wages paid to the workmen applying it; quality and reliability are accordingly of more importance than any slight price differential.

The U.K. was probably at a less marked cost disadvantage in paints than in many other industries. This is partly because in paint manufacture wage costs are a relatively small part of total costs,[1] and on the whole there is a world price for the raw materials of the industry. There are, of course, many very small firms in the U.K. industry, but most of the export trade is in the hands of a relatively few firms. Most of the major exporting firms treat their overseas markets very seriously, exporting anything up to 30% of their total output. Although labour costs are low, overhead costs in this industry can be quite high (e.g. expensive advertising is essential), and in some cases a buoyant export trade is necessary in order to cover these costs and keep down prices. It is also true that home demand tends to be seasonal and, in view of the high cost of storage, this probably provides another incentive for building up exports.

In the paint industry, changes in home demand have little influence on overseas sales. It is quite out of the question to market in Brussels or Hamburg tins of paint which cannot be sold at home. On the other hand, overseas requirements for 'specialist' products are unlikely to be similar to those of the home market, and in the short run it is not easy to divert to overseas markets lines intended for domestic use. The technical organisation of the plant should, however, permit a fairly extensive switch from 'home' to 'export' type products in the longer run.

IRON AND STEEL

We are now left with a small number of industries, the export performance of which we have not yet looked at. The most important of these

---

[1] Wages account for about 10 % of the wholesale selling price in the U.K., while raw material costs account for almost half the total costs of manufacturing paint.

is iron and steel. Appendix Table K shows that U.K. exports of iron and steel did not quite hold their own in the world market, especially in Africa, but on the whole the industry maintained its export position better than most other manufactures. In fact, of course, it would be misleading to pay too much attention to the percentage changes shown in Table K, for the work of the British iron and steel industry is essentially to provide the raw materials for many other U.K. export industries, notably those in the engineering sector. For this reason, exports of steel were officially discouraged in the early post-war years, and a given decline —or increase—in the share of the world market in steel held by the U.K. is not a satisfactory measure of the relative efficiency of the industry. Moreover, many sterling area countries regard imports of steel from sources other than U.K. as marginal, and these imports will therefore fluctuate with changing domestic requirements. It is, however, instructive to notice the way in which some European competitors—and Japan—encroached more or less permanently upon certain U.K. markets. By 1959 Germany was supplying 17·7% of the Pakistan import market and 15·5% of the import market of India. By 1959 Japan held 42·1% of the Malayan market, 15·9% of the market of British East Africa, and 16·1% of the Nigerian import market. The U.K., on the other hand (with western Germany and Japan), had weakened the hold of the U.S.A. in the Canadian import market. In the case of the member countries of the European Coal and Steel Community, by 1959 each member was importing at least two-thirds of its iron and steel requirements from other member countries. The U.K. share, never large, had fallen to 4·5% of the import market of the Community; the United States share had fallen even more sharply Japan singularly failed to capture more than a minute share of the market in any of the E.C.S.C. countries. Clearly, in iron and steel there was a tendency for E.C.S.C. member countries to trade more and more with one another, at the expense of the outside world.

RUBBER MANUFACTURES

Exports of rubber goods from the 'eleven' grew about as rapidly as all manufactures, and the United Kingdom share fell by the same number of percentage points (four) as in S.I.T.C. Sections 5–8 as a whole (Appendix Table U). One of the interesting facts thrown up by Table U is the growing importance of the Netherlands as an exporter of these products during the nineteen-fifties. The Netherlands effort was concentrated in western Europe where gains were clearly made at the expense of the United Kingdom. This was especially true of the market of the Belgium-Luxembourg Economic Union.

Rubber Tyres

Nearly two-thirds of the value of U.K. exports of rubber manufactures in 1959 consisted of rubber tyres. Easily the largest single country market for United Kingdom tyres was Denmark, which imported just under £2m. worth of British tyres in that year. Denmark was the only Scandinavian country without a major tyre factory and this accounts for the relatively large size of the import market. As long as 1955 the Monopolies Commission[1] pointed out that current production in North America, India, Japan, South Africa, Australia, New Zealand and certain European countries was wholly, or nearly, sufficient for domestic needs. Since then the rubber tyre industry has developed rapidly in very many countries of the world. Normally countries which have their own tyre-making industries import only a fraction of their requirements —usually these are specialist products designed to fit foreign-made vehicles.

The rubber tyre industry is in fact a highly international one and from the export figures it is extremely difficult to draw any conclusions as to the real competitive ability of a country's exports. A number of British firms are foreign-controlled, and do not export freely to tyre markets where the overseas parent company has a subsidiary company or an agency agreement. Pirelli Ltd of the United Kingdom has selling rights in certain territories only—mainly in the Commonwealth. Goodyear and Firestone deal with orders forwarded to them by their parent companies in the United States. Some overseas-owned U.K. organisations in Britain are little more than shipping points for their parent firms in the U.S.A.

The 'international' nature of the industry means that a parent company which has been supplying a given market from a factory in the U.K. might well at some point decide to supply from one elsewhere. In one case a manufacturer suddenly switched his exports to the Danish market from the British factory to one in Sweden. In another case, exports to Ghana were switched from the U.K. to Switzerland. Most South African tyre manufacturers are associated with British firms and it is often more economical to supply the Rhodesian market from these Union factories than from the U.K.

In the Far East some firms encountered growing competition in tyres from Japan. There were in 1959 three major tyre-producing firms in Japan and the quality of their output was said to be good. Their prices were at that time some 15% to 20% below European prices of similar products.

As the result of local manufacture, U.K. exports of tyres tend to be confined more and more to specialist lines, e.g. very large tyres used on heavy road-building vehicles. For these products, of course, price tends to be of secondary importance to the prospective buyer, but it is said that in the more 'standard' lines, a price differential of much over 5% usually meant the loss of business.

---

[1] *Report on the Supply and Export of Pneumatic Tyres* (H.M.S.O., London), p. 48.

Other Rubber Goods

As regards rubber goods other than tyres, the most severe competition encountered by the U.K. came from western Europe, and often from European subsidiaries of American companies. These establishments enjoy the benefits of research and technical developments carried out by their parent companies in the U.S. (with which, of course, they share many of their overhead costs). They also benefited from the relatively low production costs—especially labour costs—of western Europe.

The Dutch exported rubber goods at lower prices than the British—or even the Germans. In the early nineteen-fifties Dutch wages were among the lowest in Europe. A very large part of their productive equipment was of the most up-to-date design. Although the Netherlands rubber industry is an old-established one, its growth having been closely associated with the raw material production in the Dutch-controlled Indies, much of the equipment in the Dutch factories was destroyed during the war and its replacement received high priority in the Netherlands post-war Recovery Programme.

In many instances the fortunes of the U.K. rubber industry exports are tied up with those of other industries. For example, an overseas authority putting out tenders for rubber hose for its fire service will tend to buy the piping from the countries from which it purchases fire-engines. If the fire-engines have been bought from the Federal Republic, for example, it is only to be expected that hose-pipes will be purchased from the same source. In other cases the sale of rubber products is closely connected with major capital developments in overseas countries. In 1959 the U.K. sold overseas £1·5m. worth of rubber conveyor and elevator belting, much of it destined for use in mining. In the South African and other Commonwealth mining industries the U.K. still had a strong hold, but in Latin-American countries the development of mines with United States capital, often through the Export-Import Bank, meant that conveyor belts used in the mines were almost always of United States manufacture.

CONCLUSIONS

So far our analysis of U.K. exports from a variety of industries has been an outline one. We have tried to build up a bird's-eye view of the performance of a number of these industries in some of their more important overseas markets. Although we have been trying to establish facts rather than search for explanations, certain broad conclusions have already begun to emerge from our discussion. Firstly, we have noted the very wide differences in the experience of various industries and even commodities in overseas markets. Clearly a great deal of attention must be paid to the problem of deciding which exports are likely to be successful in the economic conditions of the sixties and seventies. It is essential, too, to know which markets are likely to be of the greatest potential value to U.K. exporters.

Secondly, it is obvious that during the period 1953–59 U.K. prices often rose more rapidly than those of other countries. This was especially true of labour-intensive industries. The re-equipment and modernisation of industry proceeded more rapidly and wage-increases more slowly on the Continent and Japan than in the United Kingdom; this meant lower prices and greater availability of export supplies in the countries which were the United Kingdom's strongest competitors.

Thirdly, we have already come across several cases where overseas manufacture by parent firms in the U.K. and the U.S.A. was on such a scale as to create real difficulties in the interpretation of export figures.

In our export case studies in Part II of this volume we shall try to see how the three considerations we have just outlined apply to certain selected industries. Before doing so, we shall look a little more closely at these considerations and into the export performance and domestic economic conditions of some of the countries which increased their share of world trade in manufactures at the expense of the United Kingdom. The remaining chapters of Part I are devoted to this investigation.

Table 2.1. *Shares of import markets in manufactures held by the United Kingdom in 1953*

Commodity and S.I.T.C. Description		Belgium-Luxembourg	Denmark	Finland	France	W. Germany	Italy	Netherlands	Norway	Sweden	Australia	British East Africa	Ceylon	Ghana	India	Malaya	New Zealand	Nigeria
5-8	ALL MANUFACTURES	14·9	29·0	24·0	18·4	12·8	17·4	19·1	27·7	27·2	70·7	81·6	64·2	74·4	49·8	60·3	84·5	70·0*
511	Inorganic chemicals	13·7	28·9	48·1	20·8	20·9	27·9	12·8	27·5	19·2	61·2	88·7*	74·4*	83·9*	71·0	94·7*	87·7	96·8*
512	Organic chemicals	11·9	27·6	33·9	16·9	12·8	13·3	36·3	30·1	30·2	49·5	75·6*	46·2*	86·4*	35·9	63·7	65·8	88·9
53	Paints, dyes, etc.	13·8	26·4	34·3	10·4	4·1	12·5	27·9	23·5	24·4	51·5	98·5	96·2	97·5	36·5	87·3	70·5	89·1
54	Drugs and pharmaceuticals	5·9	27·8	32·4	7·0	4·9	10·2	23·1	33·4	22·6	71·7	97·6	55·4	97·2	38·7	77·6	91·9	98·1
552	Soaps, cosmetics	28·3	29·2	28·8*	13·8	45·3	18·7	22·0	33·3	27·4	77·2	99·2*	94·2	98·8	78·4	61·7	89·1	99·3
651	Yarn thread	8·9	34·8	36·9	8·8	16·6	25·3	8·3	29·5	21·4	73·4	77·1*	12·9	63·5	26·2	45·8	96·6	49·2
652	Cotton fabrics	9·0	27·4	32·2	8·0	4·0	23·4	10·2	34·5	13·6	70·5	88·7	77·8	54·3	94·0	29·0	91·2	68·6
653	Non-cotton fabrics	10·4	33·2	29·5	29·9	19·4	58·5	11·2	29·7	25·1	65·4	73·1	20·1	65·3	49·5	45·9	90·7	25·9
656	Made-up textiles	14·7	36·3	52·0*	16·5	22·6	31·8	9·8	23·6	16·8	84·9	44·0	86·4*	67·8	37·0	39·9	99·0	58·6
84	Clothing	3·0	20·4	53·1*	32·0	14·0	17·1	8·0	34·7	35·9	71·8	68·5	32·1	38·7	74·2	32·8	94·2	28·9
681	Iron and steel	8·3	29·8	24·8	9·2	0·9	15·3	12·2	21·2	16·3	69·1	76·7	63·0*	71·3	30·2	73·8	90·6	82·9
711	Power machinery	25·5	28·0	13·7	32·2	17·8	23·8	22·1	19·3	16·3	83·6	94·1	59·7*	91·3	59·7	84·5*	93·3	90·7*
712	Agricultural machinery	16·2	19·8	62·9*	29·3	35·4	14·4	20·4	33·4	47·4	58·8	44·7*	73·6*	80·3*	44·8	24·9	60·2	72·8*
714	Office machinery	9·1	17·5	6·7	8·0	6·8	8·6	14·8	32·2	14·9	62·6	45·5*	45·5*	82·4*	54·0	82·8*	54·0	83·3*
715	Metal working machinery	9·4	12·7	10·6	8·0	13·2	6·8	10·3	32·2	18·7	69·0	84·5*	74·1*	90·7*	59·4	58·9	83·7	90·4
716	Mining machinery, etc.	18·6	22·6	20·7	19·8	27·0	24·1	24·4	27·8	29·9	60·8	75·6	74·6	80·3	57·1	84·6	72·5	82·9
72	Electrical equipment	14·2	16·2	14·7	13·3	12·2	12·6	18·9	22·5	24·7	80·0	92·9	85·2	94·0*	71·4	99·2	90·8	93·4
731	Railway vehicles	28·5	15·6	4·6	19·2	46·5	11·2	34·7	17·0	4·5	81·9	96·9	82·6	95·3	38·1	92·7	99·7	98·2
732	Road motor vehicles	20·8	41·3	53·5	31·9	28·6	29·2	28·6	32·1	40·2	76·9	87·1	84·4	90·3	45·9	92·2	95·8	81·7
733	Non-motor vehicles	26·8	23·4	8·0	38·0	33·8	25·6	25·4	19·1	18·3	94·5	97·4	97·8	93·4	90·5	85·3	99·1	96·6
62	Rubber manufactures	17·6	52·3	67·2	28·0	20·9	41·5	20·1	46·4	42·0	78·4	70·6	33·3	82·3	61·9	41·7	90·7	24·1
664/5	Glass and glassware	3·0	27·6	60·3*	8·5	6·2	3·2	6·1	24·6	18·6	53·4	67·5	54·3	80·1*	46·4	17·4	80·3	53·4
666	Pottery	3·7	21·3	3·7	11·5	50·4	2·8	5·8	29·6	12·0	97·2	62·5	41·8	48·1*	29·1*	48·8	91·3	49·0
861	Scientific instruments	11·6	16·7	26·7	20·4	9·9	11·2	20·1	19·8	11·3	63·5	64·1	62·0	77·9	44·0		67·0	77·0

Table 2.1. *Shares of import markets in manufactures held by the United Kingdom in 1953*

Commodity and S.I.T.C. Description	S.I.T.C.	World	S. Cmmwealth Sample	E.E.C.	W. Europe Sample	U.S.A.	Canada	Mexico	Venezuela	Peru	Colombia	Brazil	Argentine	Iraq	Iran	Union of South Africa	Rhodesia and Nyasaland	Pakistan
ALL MANUFACTURES	5–8	21·3	62·9	16·7	20·1	11·1	14·2	3·1	10·7	11·2	5·0	7·5	9·2	52·6	13·3	50·5	90·0	43·2*
Inorganic chemicals	511	19·7	72·2	18·2	20·8	5·7	18·1	14·3	22·4	37·4	16·8	0·8	13·3	86·2*	20·7*	66·3	99·7*	66·7*
Organic chemicals	512	14·8	48·8	18·9	21·0	25·6	3·2	0·8	6·4	5·4	1·4	1·4	17·3	68·0*	12·8*	56·6	35·6*	45·4
Paints, dyes, etc.	53	20·0	54·6	13·6	16·1	20·2	16·9	3·6	7·6	14·3	3·1	0·1	19·6	70·7	11·3	52·7	100·0*	49·5
Drugs and pharmaceuticals	54	16·2	61·7	8·8	12·1	9·5	8·6	1·6	3·2	18·1	8·2	0·3	5·8*	40·9	11·6	48·9	92·3*	65·4
Soaps, cosmetics	552	33·9	89·8	27·7	27·9	12·4	4·4	4·7	8·9	32·3	20·0	7·5	6·3*	89·9	8·9	68·9	100·0	93·4
Yarn thread	651	24·3	51·3	12·7	18·1	12·6	53·0	26·8	16·2	17·1	5·3	18·7	26·0*	50·9	11·7	62·7	81·8*	12·3
Cotton fabrics	652	24·4	66·0	9·0	16·5	29·0	11·5	3·3*	7·4	40·9	2·1	1·9*	11·0*	18·8	7·8	52·6	99·3	74·3*
Non-cotton fabrics	653	34·3	51·6	19·9	23·6	52·7	61·0	7·3	38·7	8·1	5·1	76·1	7·3*	24·6	20·1	39·7	99·5	60·0*
Made-up textiles	656	21·7	65·0	19·3	21·2	34·4	11·9	0·0	3·5	3·6	5·2	12·7*	0·0*	39·5	0·0	52·7	94·8	43·1
Clothing	84	22·7	57·6	11·6	19·2	30·9	32·2	0·6	3·2	8·4	9·6	7·5*	0·0	44·9	0·0*	50·1	99·8	67·5*
Iron and steel	681	14·6	53·9	8·9	13·1	6·1	13·9	0·8	12·5	9·5	3·1	0·9	5·7	79·1	6·2	35·1	95·9	30·4
Power machinery	711	31·1	75·1	25·4	23·2	26·4	25·8	2·8	8·4	3·6	1·1	6·3	9·6	32·9	13·3	72·3	98·6	53·6
Agricultural machinery	712	12·2	49·8	23·0	24·2	3·1	1·7	1·9	2·6	1·4	1·7	3·6	1·9	61·9*	3·4	27·8	71·0	26·2*
Office machinery	714	14·6	51·6	9·6	11·8	22·8	8·9	1·1	2·0	8·9	3·8	0·5	0·0	70·8*	0·0*	36·4	87·6	44·1*
Metal working machinery	715	12·0	61·2	8·5	10·2	10·9	11·7	2·2	3·7	8·5	4·9	4·8	7·8	54·0	9·9*	48·0	96·4*	51·6
Mining machinery, etc.	716	22·2	58·4	22·1	23·2	30·5	6·4	4·4	8·6	7·9	2·7	11·8	8·8	73·8	10·3	45·6	48·0	52·1
Electrical equipment	72	26·0	79·7	14·8	16·8	16·3	11·3	1·9	9·4		4·3	5·6	10·1	100·0	10·7	78·4	74·7	60·9
Railway vehicles	731	28·0	55·8			1·0	23·3	0·0	2·4	70·2		4·2	9·7		56·6	37·0	93·8	11·7
Road motor vehicles	732	23·4	70·9	31·3	22·4	73·9	11·7	1·2	5·9	1·7	48·0	5·6	7·7	48·9	15·3*	44·6	94·2	41·7
Non-motor vehicles	733	48·0	94·3	24·8	31·3	68·5	18·4	46·8	45·6	50·6	7·0	18·7	20·3*	85·5	83·6	85·4	96·3	73·5
Rubber manufactures	62	24·7	75·4	27·7	24·8	14·5	4·1	2·9	8·2	18·6	4·7	5·6*	13·8	71·3	17·8	51·7	100·0	79·6
Glass and glassware	664/5	13·6	59·0	22·7	32·1	1·3	2·2	0·4	1·2	4·2	11·0	0·0	14·2	26·7	0·0*	65·6	98·7	29·1
Pottery	666	32·1	77·3	5·3	8·0	22·7	77·5	5·3	33·4	36·3		10·2*	43·6*	5·6*	0·0*	64·1	100·0	63·0*
Scientific instruments	861	14·2	56·1	15·1	15·1	4·9	7·3	1·6	7·3	2·7	4·2	3·4	9·8	60·0	5·9*	48·0	85·8	51·8

Note. Total imports of the commodity accounted for less than 0·2% of total exports of the commodity from the eleven manufacturing countries.

* Total imports of the commodity accounted for less than 0·2% of total exports of the commodity from the eleven manufacturing countries.

Table 2.2. *Changes in shares of selected import markets held by United Kingdom, 1953–59*

(Percentage Points)

Commodity and S.I.T.C. Description		Belgium-Luxembourg	Denmark	Finland	France	W. Germany	Italy	Netherlands	Norway	Sweden	Australia	British East Africa	Ceylon
ALL MANUFACTURES	5–8	— 5·4	— 8·8	— 3·5	— 6·9	— 1·1	— 3·3	— 6·4	— 12·0	— 8·1	— 18·7	— 22·7	— 6·5
Inorganic chemicals	511	— 7·7	— 14·4	— 33·6	— 13·5	— 6·5	— 5·4	— 3·4	— 6·9	— 4·3	— 11·3	— 51·4*	— 8·2*
Organic chemicals	512	— 4·4	— 10·5	— 20·5	— 11·3	— 2·1	— 4·0	— 24·4	— 16·5	— 12·9	— 10·1	— 34·1*	— 7·5*
Paints, dyes, etc.	53	— 0·3	— 0·5	— 6·5	+ 1·1	+ 6·9	— 0·9	+ 0·4	+ 12·6	+ 3·3	+ 6·4	— 4·0	+ 3·8*
Drugs and pharmaceuticals	54	0·0	— 13·7	— 15·9	+ 1·6	+ 0·6	+ 3·9	— 15·1	— 2·9	+ 8·5	— 13·1	— 9·9	+ 0·5
Soaps, cosmetics	552	— 12·5	— 6·7	— 11·4	— 3·0	— 17·4	— 1·7	— 6·7	— 7·3	+ 12·5	— 20·4	— 8·1	— 2·5
Yarn thread	651	— 3·5	— 16·0	— 11·6	+ 11·6	— 1·8	— 0·1	— 2·6	— 6·2	— 1·1	— 1·5	+ 3·0*	+ 80·8
Cotton fabrics	652	— 6·0	— 16·6	— 25·3	— 0·8	— 1·4	— 13·0	— 8·5	— 17·0	— 5·2	— 46·4	— 44·7	— 57·8
Non-cotton fabrics	653	— 0·9	— 7·1	— 14·0	+ 0·7	— 1·4	— 19·1	— 2·0	— 9·6	— 1·2	— 21·7	— 62·9	— 11·0
Made-up textiles	656	— 10·7	— 8·0	— 44·4*	— 4·5	— 2·4	— 8·3	— 13·7	— 8·4	— 10·2	— 24·4	— 12·5	— 39·3
Clothing	84	+ 1·1	— 12·7	— 42·6	— 18·2	— 15·7	— 2·9	— 2·9	— 21·7	— 17·2	— 11·7	— 51·3	+ 11·2*
Iron and steel	681	— 1·7	— 11·6	— 9·1	+ 8·2	+ 4·6	+ 8·8	+ 4·5	+ 1·6	+ 1·9	— 2·4	— 27·3	— 8·0
Power machinery	711	— 10·8	+ 7·0	+ 2·4	+ 6·5	+ 2·3	+ 18·7	+ 4·2	+ 2·8	+ 21·5	+ 7·9	+ 5·0	+ 26·9*
Agricultural machinery	712	— 4·3	— 8·9	— 50·3*	— 22·7	— 15·2	— 2·5	— 3·0	— 3·9	— 21·6	— 11·4	+ 27·0*	— 1·2*
Office machinery	714	+ 2·3	— 7·0	— 1·9	+ 2·5	— 1·0	— 2·7	— 6·0	— 23·2	+ 3·0	— 9·0	— 22·8	— 8·6*
Metal working machinery	715	— 1·3	— 2·7	— 5·8	— 2·9	+ 7·6	— 3·4	— 1·2	— 15·3	— 14·2	— 19·1	— 1·7*	+ 1·7*
Mining machinery, etc.	716	— 5·7	— 3·5	— 4·7	— 6·6	— 4·8	— 8·7	— 5·5	— 5·5	+ 8·0	— 13·5	— 5·2	— 2·0*
Electrical equipment	72	— 6·0	— 0·2	— 4·4	— 2·0	+ 4·0	— 2·1	— 7·1	— 5·7	— 13·4	— 16·6	— 13·8	— 17·3
Railway vehicles	731	— 24·8	— 8·0*	+ 10·7	— 18·8	— 29·4	— 5·0	— 30·8	+ 3·8	+ 7·6	— 29·7	+ 0·2	— 57·0
Road motor vehicles	732	— 8·6	— 14·9	— 19·3	— 16·4	— 22·0	— 16·0	— 14·9	— 13·5	— 17·0	— 13·2	— 26·4	— 13·0
Non-motor vehicles	733	— 7·7	— 9·1	— 3·5	— 16·8	— 16·5	— 10·4	— 4·3	— 9·7	+ 8·9	— 36·1	— 23·9	— 9·4
Rubber manufactures	62	— 7·9	— 14·4	— 42·4	— 13·3	— 4·7	— 11·5	— 5·4	— 17·7	— 14·8	— 23·5	— 5·8	— 19·9
Glass and glassware	664/5	+ 0·4	— 12·4	— 30·6*	— 2·9	— 0·8	+ 0·3	+ 1·2	— 9·6	— 6·1	— 15·5	— 18·7	+ 11·4
Pottery	666	— 1·6	— 13·5	0·0*	— 2·2	— 31·0	+ 4·4	+ 0·5	— 17·1	+ 1·3	— 33·7	— 23·6	+ 1·8*
Scientific instruments	861	— 4·9	— 4·3	— 16·1	— 5·5	+ 2·1	— 0·9	— 4·4	— 6·8	— 1·2	— 24·9	— 5·1	— 14·9

Table 2.2. *Changes in shares of selected import markets held by United Kingdom, 1953–59*

(Percentage Points)

Commodity and S.I.T.C. Description		Ghana	India	Malaya	New Zealand	Nigeria	Pakistan	Rhodesia and Nyasaland	Union of South Africa	Iran	Iraq	Argentine	Brazil
ALL MANUFACTURES	5–8	− 14·4	− 5·5	− 20·0	− 12·3	− 8·6	− 7·3	− 15·7	− 8·5	+ 8·5	− 9·8	+ 6·4	− 2·7
Inorganic chemicals	511	+ 1·8*	+ 6·5	− 46·9*	− 26·4	− 22·9*	− 13·7*	− 60·5*	− 31·2	+ 29·9*	− 46·9*	+ 13·4	+ 19·3
Organic chemicals	512	− 70·6*	+ 1·9	− 13·0	− 30·0	− 26·3*	− 15·6*	− 19·1*	− 32·9	+ 8·7*	− 36·7*	− 2·8	− 3·2
Paints, dyes, etc.	53	− 2·5	+ 4·3	− 4·7	+ 2·1	− 0·8	− 13·1	− 10·6*	− 0·4	+ 9·0	− 19·1	− 0·4	+ 10·0
Drugs and pharmaceuticals	54	− 18·5	− 12·6	− 11·0	− 4·5	− 9·3	− 21·3	− 14·7	− 13·6	− 2·1	− 9·8	+ 1·2	− 4·4
Soaps, cosmetics	552	− 2·6	− 5·2	− 19·1	− 29·9	− 8·5	− 29·6	− 6·7	− 16·3	+ 2·1	− 20·1		− 1·0
Yarn thread	651	+ 12·3	− 0·3	+ 2·7	− 9·3	+ 26·0	+ 1·8	− 11·0*	− 16·0	+ 11·6	− 10·6	+ 16·1*	− 7·9
Cotton fabrics	652	+ 1·6	+ 12·3	− 33·3	− 31·9	− 25·8	− 62·7*	− 32·8	− 22·2	− 8·2	− 18·0	− 22·8*	− 6·7*
Non-cotton fabrics	653	− 58·6	− 32·3	− 24·8	− 17·2	− 18·5	− 42·4*	− 48·4*	− 17·6	+ 0·6		+ 24·2*	+ 6·7*
Made-up textiles	656	− 17·3	− 32·1	− 16·0	− 19·0	− 24·9	− 33·9	− 0·8	− 21·1	+ 4·8	− 4·4	− 5·2*	+ 11·5
Clothing	84	− 19·9	+ 7·0	− 23·4	− 14·4	− 9·6	− 13·2*	− 27·3	− 21·0	+ 45·1	− 18·7	0·0*	− 12·7*
Iron and steel	681	− 8·8*	+ 2·6	− 8·9	+ 1·8	− 20·2	− 8·3	− 9·6*	+ 11·8	+ 23·5	− 3·7	+ 1·8*	+ 3·5*
Power machinery	711	− 3·0	+ 4·9	− 3·8	− 25·2	+ 1·9	+ 10·9	+ 6·2	+ 4·4*	+ 7·1	− 17·6	+ 12·8	+ 6·6
Agricultural machinery	712	+ 13·8*	+ 1·8	− 16·3*	− 13·0	+ 20·6*	+ 18·5*	+ 6·5	+ 3·5	+ 40·0	− 5·5*	+ 11·0	+ 1·5
Office machinery	714	− 17·5*	+ 6·8	+ 13·3	+ 20·0	+ 10·3*	− 10·8*	− 17·7	+ 20·7	+ 28·5	− 11·5*	+ 5·6	+ 3·8
Metal working machinery	715	− 4·4	− 2·9	− 33·6*	− 15·7	− 10·0*	− 21·3	+ 2·5	− 31·2	+ 16·0*	− 30·4*	+ 6·1	+ 4·6
Mining machinery, etc.	716	− 15·6	− 8·4	− 10·3	− 12·3	− 8·7	− 23·1	+ 6·2	− 17·9	+ 4·9*	− 26·6	+ 2·0	+ 1·7
Electrical equipment	72	− 11·3*	− 24·9	− 26·1	− 13·7	− 8·9	− 31·0	+ 4·6	+ 32·9	+ 17·2		+ 4·6	− 6·7
Railway vehicles	731	− 73·9*	+ 1·4	− 13·3	− 3·1	− 15·6	+ 20·8	+ 4·0	− 7·1	+ 10·4	− 83·0	+ 14·7	+ 3·2
Road motor vehicles	732	− 33·4	− 7·4	− 30·9	− 6·1	− 20·1	− 5·2	− 18·1	− 27·5	− 56·4	− 6·5	+ 4·3	+ 5·2
Non-motor vehicles	733	− 12·7	− 1·0	− 25·2	− 6·8	− 16·2	− 10·4	− 3·8	− 8·6	+ 5·1*	− 13·9	− 14·1*	+ 6·9*
Rubber manufactures	62	− 24·8	+ 2·9	− 19·8	− 23·4	+ 40·8	− 26·8	− 20·6	+ 2·2	− 14·9	− 42·9	+ 2·0	+ 6·5*
Glass and glassware	664/5	− 35·5*	− 6·4	− 15·4	− 24·4	+ 3·8	+ 12·9	− 16·4*	+ 3·6	+ 3·2	− 6·7	+ 0·5	+ 15·0*
Pottery	666	+ 3·4*	+ 61·2*	+ 0·8	− 15·9	+ 3·5	− 50·9*	− 4·0	− 21·2	+ 9·8*	− 0·0*	− 31·3*	− 10·2
Scientific instruments	861	− 15·5*	+ 0·3	− 15·5	− 20·9	− 18·3	− 19·7	− 36·1		+ 24·0*	− 11·0	+ 4·2	+ 0·7

* These figures are of limited significance: either in 1953 or 1959 imports of the commodity group in question into a particular import market accounted for less than 0·2 % of total exports of the commodity group for the eleven manufacturing countries.

Table 2.2. Changes in shares of selected import markets held by United Kingdom, 1953–59

(Percentage Points)

Commodity and S.I.T.C. Description	S.I.T.C.	Colombia	Peru	Venezuela	Mexico	Canada	U.S.A.	W.E. Sample	E.E.C.	S. Cmmwealth Sample	World
ALL MANUFACTURES	5–8	+ 0·3	— 1·8	— 2·6	+ 1·4	— 0·4	+ 3·3	— 6·3	— 4·8	— 12·5	— 4·0
Inorganic chemicals	511	— 14·2	— 14·6	— 14·6	— 10·8	— 10·2	+ 2·9	— 7·8	— 6·9	— 18·1	— 3·6
Organic chemicals	512	+ 2·0	+ 1·0	+ 5·2	+ 2·1	+ 3·9	— 10·0	— 10·7	— 9·6	— 13·7	— 3·8
Paints, dyes, etc.	53	+ 2·4	— 0·6	+ 2·6	+ 6·6	+ 8·5	+ 0·2	+ 1·1	+ 1·3	+ 4·7	+ 0·4
Drugs and pharmaceuticals	54	+ 0·5	— 1·9	— 0·7	+ 0·4	+ 4·9	+ 4·0	— 3·9	— 2·7	— 5·1	— 1·9
Soaps, cosmetics	552	+ 2·3	— 13·6	+ 9·4	+ 0·0	— 1·8	+ 4·7	— 6·1	— 8·6	— 3·0	— 5·9
Yarn thread	651	— 17·5	— 23·8	— 6·8	— 25·2	— 12·8	+ 1·6	+ 4·2	+ 0·9	+ 3·3	— 6·6
Cotton fabrics	652	+ 6·9	— 12·7	+ 6·2	+ 0·5*	— 5·6	— 18·3	— 10·1	— 5·8	— 31·2	— 10·7
Non-cotton fabrics	653	+ 32·2	— 8·6	+ 0·0	+ 2·2	— 9·0	— 28·7	— 5·6	+ 3·6	— 26·7	— 13·9
Made-up textiles	656	+ 3·9	— 2·0	+ 0·7	+ 0·0	— 2·7	— 7·9	— 12·1	— 11·9	— 16·1	— 6·5
Clothing	84	— 5·1	+ 2·6	+ 1·5	— 0·6	+ 3·0	— 21·4	— 9·8	+ 4·0	— 25·6	— 12·5
Iron and steel	681	+ 0·0	+ 4·4	+ 0·4	+ 4·7	+ 5·8	+ 1·1	+ 5·1	+ 4·6	+ 6·6	+ 2·0
Power machinery	711	+ 4·9	+ 6·9	+ 6·7	+ 9·6	+ 5·8	+ 22·3	+ 5·9	+ 10·7	+ 4·6	+ 2·2
Agricultural machinery	712	+ 3·7	+ 18·9*	+ 6·9	+ 7·3	+ 0·4	+ 0·8	+ 11·5	+ 0·3	+ 0·6	+ 1·9
Office machinery	714	+ 8·5	+ 11·4	+ 8·1	+ 8·9	+ 0·2	— 13·9	+ 1·6	+ 0·5	+ 4·0	— 2·3
Metal working machinery	715	+ 5·6	+ 6·8	+ 3·0	+ 0·1	+ 1·1	— 7·9	+ 1·9	+ 5·7	— 23·9	+ 0·1
Mining machinery, etc.	716	+ 2·2	+ 1·9	+ 3·3	+ 0·0	+ 0·9	— 13·7	+ 5·8	+ 5·8	— 8·3	— 4·1
Electrical equipment	72	— 0·2	+ 2·0	+ 3·2	+ 1·0	+ 3·6	+ 5·4	— 4·8	+ 3·2	— 19·4	— 6·8
Railway vehicles	731	+ 1·4	— 60·1	+ 2·4	+ 4·3	+ 13·7	+ 4·4	— 15·5	— 25·7	— 2·3	— 0·7
Road motor vehicles	732	+ 2·1	+ 2·5	+ 2·2	+ 4·3	+ 8·1	— 42·8	— 14·4	— 13·2	— 15·3	— 0·4
Non-motor vehicles	733	— 33·0	— 17·6	+ 4·0	— 32·1	+ 2·7	— 33·8	— 7·7	— 7·9	— 16·7	— 14·3
Rubber manufactures	62	+ 0·4	— 9·1	+ 1·6	+ 0·7	+ 5·9	+ 1·9	— 10·8	— 7·0	— 15·1	— 4·0
Glass and glassware	664/5	+ 3·6	+ 2·4	+ 0·4	+ 2·5	+ 10·3	+ 9·3	+ 2·5	+ 0·5	— 11·7	— 1·3
Pottery	666	— 11·0	+ 1·8	— 21·5	+ 1·0	+ 4·6	+ 6·2	+ 0·1	+ 2·4	— 18·9	— 7·5
Scientific instruments	861	+ 2·7	— 0·3	— 3·7	+ 0·9	+ 2·8	+ 0·8	+ 3·1	+ 2·8	— 16·9	— 3·6

* These figures are of limited significance: either in 1953 or 1959 imports of the commodity group in question into a particular import market accounted for less than 0·2% of the commodity group for the eleven manufacturing countries.

Table 2.3. *Country import market gains and losses by United Kingdom manufactures*

Grade	Commodity Group	S.I.T.C.	No. of Markets where U.K. share rose	No. of Markets where U.K. share fell	Where change was less than 1 percentage point	U.K. Share 1953	U.K. Share 1959
A	Power machinery	711	18	12	0	31·1	33·3
	Agricultural machinery	712	16	12	2	12·2	10·3
B	Office machinery	714	14	15	1	14·6	12·3
	Metal working machinery	715	14	15	1	12·0	11·9
	Iron and steel	681	13	15	2	14·6	12·6
	Glass and glassware	664/5	10	15	5	13·6	12·3
	Paints and dyestuffs	53	10	15	5	20·0	20·4
C	Railway vehicles	731	13	16	1	28·0	27·3
	Clothing	84	9	20	1	22·7	10·2
	Yarn thread	651	8	20	2	24·3	17·7
	Pottery	666	6	20	4	32·1	24·6
	Drugs and pharmaceuticals	54	4	20	6	16·2	14·3
D	Electrical equipment	72	7	21	2	26·0	19·2
	Scientific instruments	861	3	21	6	14·2	10·6
	Organic chemicals	512	8	22	0	14·8	11·0
	Soaps and cosmetics	552	7	22	1	33·9	28·0
	Rubber manufactures	62	5	23	2	24·7	20·7
	Made-up textiles	656	3	23	4	21·7	15·2
	Cotton fabrics	652	3	24	3	24·4	13·7
	Inorganic chemicals	511	5	25	0	19·7	16·1
	Road motor vehicles	732	5	25	0	23·4	23·0
	Non-cotton fabrics	653	2	25	3	34·3	20·4
	Non-motorised road vehicles	733	1	29	0	48·0	33·7

CHAPTER III

DIRECT INVESTMENT OVERSEAS

ONE aspect of U.K. export performance to which relatively little attention has been paid in recent years is the very widespread practice of the setting up by firms of subsidiaries and branches in overseas territories—often in the very countries which were previously their markets. If this process takes place on an extensive scale in any industry, it might well have adverse effects upon the export figures for the industry concerned since goods manufactured locally at overseas factories do not appear as British exports in the trade returns. Thus, in recent years, Australia, for example, has almost ceased to import fully made-up motor cars from the U.K. as firms which hitherto exported vehicles to the Dominion find themselves engaged in local manufacture, often passing through the intermediary stage of local licensing and local assembly (see p. 120). This trend towards overseas assembly and manufacture has since the war been particularly widespread in Commonwealth countries, especially in Australia and the Union of South Africa, but in the late fifties the process took place more and more on the Continent, too. Indeed, a number of British companies took steps to establish manufacturing or assembly plants with the European Economic Community, after the failure of the European Free Trade Area negotiations in 1958.

DIRECT INVESTMENT AND EXPORTS

In general, if direct investment by the U.K. in manufacturing industry in a particular country is on a more extensive scale than that of export-competing countries, the overall result might well be a fall in the U.K. share of the import trade of that country. On the other hand, the very fact that a United Kingdom firm has established an assembly or manufacturing base in an overseas market will almost certainly bring with it additional trade—trade which might even offset the effect of a diversion of sales of a particular product from the U.K. parent firm to the overseas manufacturing unit.

Almost invariably the substitution of local for British manufacture of a given product takes several years. At first almost all parts will be imported from the U.K.; only gradually will local manufacture of components take place. Moreover, a British firm in the process of developing overseas manufacture will usually purchase machinery and spare parts from the mother country. There will often be a time lag in cases where a British firm grants a licence to enable an overseas manufacturer to produce locally a product previously exported from the United Kingdom. Thus for a considerable period a number of the parts required for manufacture will continue to be supplied from the United Kingdom and the level of imports from the mother country will accordingly fall off only slowly. In some industries—the aircraft engine industry, for example—the gestation period for the complete building under licence overseas of an engine originally designed and manufactured in the United Kingdom might be several years. Thus the immediate impact of a switch from domestic to overseas manufacture should not be exaggerated. It is rather in the long run that the effect might be seen upon the export figures. But even then there are compensating advantages. An overseas branch or subsidiary provides a ready-made sales organisation. Even if the transaction takes the form of the sale of a licence to a foreign firm to manufacture locally, and no components at all are supplied from the U.K. the British firm often continues to keep its name in front of buyers in the overseas market. When a directly-controlled branch or company is established certain distributive economies are likely to be reaped, for example, the saving of the cost of employing agents. In some markets agents are extremely difficult to find and this fact alone might help tip the scale in favour of a decision to establish local manufacture.[1] A firm operating abroad will derive advantages from being in close touch with overseas tastes and fashions, and will be able to send back to its parent company first-hand reports of consumer reaction to goods still exported from the United Kingdom. This is especially helpful where the parent company continues to export some specialist products from the U.K.—often those which cannot be manufactured on a sufficiently large scale in the overseas country. Indeed in the case of multi-product firms the local firm or branch seldom manufactures as wide a range of products as the parent. Sales of the locally made product, often a bread-and-butter line, thus help to advertise the specialist products made by the parent.

On balance, however, most British firms do not engage in local overseas manufacture in order to reap benefits such as these. They do so because they have to. Although there are clearly the compensating advantages we have outlined, it is probably true to say that most firms look upon the substitution of overseas for domestic manufacture as a necessary evil rather than as a means of reaping economies.

There is no doubt that since the war in the majority of cases United Kingdom firms decided to commence overseas activities in order to overcome some trade obstacle put there by the overseas governments. Such decisions represent an attempt by British firms to swim with, rather than against, the tide of world economic developments, one of the most important of which has been the determination of governments of many primary producing countries to diversify their economies by deliberately encouraging indigenous secondary industries.

In some cases the motive of overseas governments is the safeguarding

[1] For a discussion of the effect of direct investment on distributive costs in Canada, see T. E. Penrie, 'The Influence of Distributive Costs and Direct Investments on British Exports to Canada', *Oxford Economic Papers* (October 1956).

of the balance of payments; in others, the creation of wider employment opportunities. Occasionally the desire for self-sufficiency in certain essential economic fields (e.g. pharmaceuticals) is an important factor. Whatever the motive, the decision to encourage domestic secondary industries invariably entails high tariffs, the imposition of quantitative import restrictions, or exchange controls. Sometimes these barriers are almost prohibitive. Faced with such obstacles to exporting to their traditional markets, British firms have, especially since the war, tended to get round them by setting up branches or subsidiary companies in the countries concerned. Thus although a number of advantages have accrued to certain companies who have developed overseas organisations (often these are highly profitable) in many cases the decision to transfer production abroad has been forced upon British firms. Often the choice has been either acceptance of overseas manufacture or the more or less complete loss of a market.

Unfortunately, statistics relating to the scale of direct investment overseas by U.K. companies are notoriously thin. Portfolio investment has been documented by the Bank of England for a number of years, but only since 1960 have any official estimates of the current scale of direct investment become available, and these go back only to 1958. It has, of course, been possible to obtain some rough idea of the scale of direct investment by reference to estimates made in some of the capital receiving countries, but even this information is fragmentary, and an industry-wise breakdown of the figures is seldom available.

Accordingly, we cannot hope to relate the change in the United Kingdom share of any import market with the scale of direct U.K. investment in the country concerned. All we can do is to point out that in a number of traditional United Kingdom markets a considerable amount of direct investment by British firms took place in the nineteen-fifties, and suggest that this undoubtedly had some effect—possibly a significant effect—upon the United Kingdom share of those import markets. Clearly this is a subject upon which a great deal of fruitful research might be done.

U.K. DIRECT INVESTMENT REVIEWED

The Form of Investment

Direct investment can take many forms. The most obvious of these is a straightforward transfer of funds from the United Kingdom, either for the finance of an entirely new enterprise, or for the acquisition of shares in an existing company. The investment might take the form either of the establishment of a wholly-owned branch or company, or alternatively of a subsidiary company with the participation of local investors. The distinguishing feature of direct, as opposed to portfolio, overseas investment is that the U.K. company becomes involved in active participation in the organisation, in both general policy matters and also in policy in regard to profit distribution.

It is by no means necessary that direct investment be financed from the United Kingdom. An alternative is the reinvestment of locally earned profits in the overseas branch or company. In fact, this appears to have been the most important means of financing U.K. direct investment during the nineteen-fifties.

The 1961 Balance of Payments White Paper[1] gave some idea of the scale of U.K. direct investment overseas in the preceding three years, compared with direct investment by overseas companies in the United Kingdom. It showed that the level of direct overseas investment by the U.K. grew between 1958 and 1960 at the expense of 'other' investment, namely portfolio investment and investment by the oil and insurance industries. For these three years (1958–60) total private investment abroad by U.K. residents amounted to £914m. and of this £508m. was classified as direct investment.

The White Paper estimates of direct investment were based upon an Enquiry directed by the Board of Trade in 1959. Some four thousand companies were requested to provide details of direct investment overseas undertaken in 1958 (and later 1959 and 1960).[2] The Enquiry excluded oil and insurance companies. Although no indication of the number of firms which failed to respond to the questionnaire was published it was claimed by the Board of Trade that the amount of investment left out in this way must have been small. Direct investment as defined in the Enquiry covers investment in overseas branches, subsidiaries and associated companies; associated companies being those in which there is a trade investment of a substantial continuing nature. The Enquiry revealed that in both 1958 and 1959 approximately half the direct investment undertaken overseas by U.K. residents consisted of the unremitted profits of U.K. subsidiaries.

Area Pattern of Investment

Almost exactly one-half of the total direct investment of £172·7m. in 1959 was in the overseas Sterling Area; this was an absolute increase over the level of investment in the OSA in 1958, but as a proportion of the total it was somewhat less than in that year. Within the Sterling Area the most important recipient in both years was Australia (£19·4m. in 1958 and £24·4m. in 1959). For 1959 the second largest outflow took place to the Federation of Rhodesia and Nyasaland, (£13·3m.), but it is worth noting that in 1958 there had been a net disinvestment of British capital in the Federation. In 1959, India came third on the list with U.K. direct investment amounting to £10·2m., and the Union of South Africa fourth with £7·0m. In 1958, however, this order had been reversed; India received £5·9m. and South Africa £19·9m. New Zealand received £3·4m. in 1959 and £4·0m. in 1958.

In the case of North America, the level of direct investment in

[1] 'United Kingdom Balance of Payments, 1958 to 1960', Cmd. 1329, H.M.S.O.
[2] 'United Kingdom Direct Investment Overseas, 1958 and 1959', *Board of Trade Journal*, 7th October 1960 and 17th February 1961.

Canada was higher than in the U.S.A. in both years (in 1959, £32·6m. in Canada as against £17·4m. in the U.S.A).

In western Europe, the rate of direct investment by the U.K. increased by one-third between 1958 and 1959. By far the greater volume of the investment was in the countries of the European Economic Community (£15·6m. in 1959). In 1959 western Germany received £6·5m. of this, and Belgium and France with their Dependencies received £4·5m. and £3·4m. respectively. In comparison direct investment by the U.K. in European Free Trade Association countries was small in both years. Another country in which it was significant in 1959 was Brazil (£5·3m.).

Unfortunately no detailed industry breakdown of these figures is available at country level. Even within very broad areas only a very general classification is possible. The Board of Trade Survey showed that in 1958 well over one-half the total volume of U.K. direct investment was in the manufacturing sector. In the case of North America and western Europe the proportions were higher. Although in the OSA the level of investment in manufacturing industries was less than in the non-manufacturing sectors, it was still significant (£30m. out of a total of nearly £80m.).

In spite of the scantiness of the statistics available, the general picture provided by the Board of Trade Survey is fairly clear; firstly, the scale of direct investment by the United Kingdom towards the end of the nineteen-fifties was significant, both as a proportion of total private capital outflow and as a direct burden on the Balance of Payments. Secondly, the traditional investment in mines and plantations was no longer so predominant, even if we include oil; direct investment included the taking by United Kingdom companies of controlling interests in a large range of manufacturing interests in all parts of the world. Such a process must have had a marked impact upon the volume of physical exports from the United Kingdom.

The Board of Trade Survey we have been discussing relates only to the years 1958 and 1959. Thus, although it gives us a useful indication of what has been going on in and after 1958, it provides no information at all on the magnitude and direction of direct investment before 1958. In this book we are, of course, interested in the developments affecting U.K. exports over a longer period—back to 1953 at least. Now although the figures for 1958–60 give no direct measurement of the scale of investment in U.K. companies and branches abroad in the earlier nineteen-fifties, they do at least suggest the general pattern of development. It is, for example, extremely unlikely that the growth in direct investment in manufacturing establishments occurred suddenly in 1958. We can safely assume that the trend was one which became increasingly important since the end of the war. This conclusion is borne out by conversations we have had with British firms in a number of different industries which have carried out overseas development on a large scale. It is corroborated, too, by the picture shown in a number of publications in the capital-receiving countries, especially the more developed Commonwealth countries. We shall now examine in a little more detail the pattern of U.K. direct investment in some of these countries. On the whole, we shall confine our attention to Commonwealth markets, but this is not to suggest that the volume of U.K. investment in the U.S.A. and in western Europe has been insignificant. Indeed, in the future the growing point of British direct investment in manufacturing is likely to be the Continent of Europe rather than the Commonwealth.

THE STERLING COMMONWEALTH

Australia

We have noted already that Australia is the Sterling Area country where by far the greatest amount of direct U.K. investment has taken place since the war. In Australia, up to 1958–59, overseas investment of various kinds accounted for about 30% of all new investment in manufacturing industry since the war, and at least up to 1959 the value of direct investment far exceeded that of portfolio investment. Direct investment in Australia usually took one or more of three forms: (a) the remittance of cash from the United Kingdom; (b) the provision of plant, etc., without full payment; and (c) the reinvestment of locally-earned profits in the subsidiary company. In the case of the United Kingdom, direct investment in Australia largely consisted of the ploughing back of profits made locally.

Since the war there has been an absolute decrease in the value of foreign-held, especially British-held, Australian public debt, but a considerable increase in direct investment in Australian industry. In this connexion it has been estimated that whereas in 1938 the value of British-held Australian public debt was £455m. and of British investments in Australian business only £200m., by 1958 the amounts were £253m. and £600m. respectively.[1]

Some idea of the growth of the inflow of direct capital investment and the stake of the United Kingdom in Australian industry is given in Table 3.1. This Table shows that in each financial year between 1947–48 and 1957–58 well over half overseas private investment in Australian companies came from the United Kingdom. For the eleven-year period, the total inflow of U.K. private direct investment amounted to no less than £241m. out of a total of £416m. from all overseas sources.[2]

Although these figures include investments in the banks and insurance

[1] A. R. Conan, 'Britain's Investment Stake', *The Times* (London, 19th August 1959).

[2] Department of Trade, Melbourne. The scale of foreign investment in Australia has been so great that it has provoked opposition in certain quarters; thus in December 1959, Mr. Arthur Calwell, Deputy leader of the Federal Labour Party in Australia, pointed out that the motor car assembly and manufacturing plants of the Dominion were completely foreign owned, agricultural implement manufacturing was almost entirely owned by overseas interests, and the field of chemicals was occupied almost wholly by three overseas companies; food processing was substantially owned overseas, and although textiles were mainly controlled by Australians they were being threatened by overseas companies. *Financial Times* (London, 14th December 1959).

companies, secondary industry in fact attracted by far the greater part of overseas capital. There were, by 1960, over 400 companies established for manufacture which were United Kingdom-owned or which were financially associated with British concerns; this figure excludes companies which had only licensing, royalty, and similar arrangements with British firms. Of the 400 companies, 40% were engineering firms, 30% supplied processed material for further manufacture; 10% made consumer durables including motor cars. In engineering, the most important single category (comprising about fifty firms) was the electrical sector. Unfortunately, year by year figures are not available for particular industries, but the vast majority of assembly and manufacturing establishments were either set up or considerably expanded in the years following the war and it seems reasonable to assume that the main impact of this development made itself felt on the volume of U.K. exports during the period under review.

Certainly the goods which become widely used in the post-war years figure prominently in the lists of items made in overseas-owned Australian factories; diesel electric locomotives, jet aircraft, synthetic fibres, nylon yarn, electronic equipment, penicillin, plastics, and fungicides.[1] Often the product concerned had not previously been made at all in Australia, and in many cases had been imported from the very firms which by 1959 were manufacturing it locally. Since so many of these firms were British owned, it is hardly surprising that the United Kingdom share of physical exports of these goods into the Australian market fell considerably. In several fields where United Kingdom exports appear to have done worse in Australia than in the rest of the world there was a widespread establishment of United Kingdom-owned plants and factories. This has happened in road motor vehicles, pharmaceuticals, electrical machinery, and, to a lesser extent, in synthetic fibres.

New Zealand

There can be no doubt that apart from direct export losses in Australia the setting up of British-owned manufacturers in that Dominion had an adverse effect upon British exports of manufactures to New Zealand and South-East Asia. The share of Australia in the New Zealand import market in manufactures rose from 10·3% in 1951 to 17·3% in 1958, while between these years the percentage which came from the United Kingdom fell from 53·6% to 52·3%. There was, for example, a switch from British to Australian unassembled motor cars and trucks, iron and steel products and penicillin.[2]

[1] For a complete list of British firms which at the time had Australian subsidiaries and the products made in Australia, see Commonwealth of Australia, Department of Trade, *British Manufacturers in Australia*, 1959.

[2] In general, firms set up in Australia have the right to export freely, but sometimes overseas principals impose restrictions on these rights. In 1959 it was known that 60 companies with British affiliations were allowed only a limited export franchise. Some (usually members of world-wide chains) had been established to cater for the local market only and were not allowed to export at all. See 'Export Franchises of Australian Companies with Overseas Affiliations', *Economic Record* (August 1959).

The difficulty with establishing local manufacture in New Zealand itself is that owing to the relatively small market (the population is only two million) large-scale production is seldom possible.

Of the 8,515 factory establishments in New Zealand recorded in the factory production statistics for 1955–56, which cover all establishments employing two or more persons, only 255 employed over 100 persons and as many as 5,396 employed 10 or less. Transport difficulties are a further hindrance to the development of large-scale output. There has been too a recurrent threat of a shortage of electric power. The cost of imported materials and fuels is significantly increased by freight charged on the long haul between New Zealand and producing centres.[1]

On purely costs grounds the establishment of branches and subsidiaries of U.K. companies in New Zealand was seldom desirable. On the other hand, since the war successive New Zealand Governments aimed at the encouragement of local manufacture, partly on balance-of-payments grounds, partly to reduce the dependence of the economy on primary products. Accordingly import restrictions were deliberately designed as a means of encouraging local industry, and while in many sectors imports of foreign goods were discouraged or even banned, overseas capital and know-how was extremely welcome.

In New Zealand the level of private United Kingdom investment since the war was relatively high, in the period 1950–51 to 1958–59 amounting to £60m.[2] In most years increases in branch assets and inter-company debts largely accounted for this substantial volume of U.K. investment.

During this period, twenty-six subsidiary or branch companies were opened by United Kingdom firms in New Zealand. Twelve of these were set up in 1959. Three of them were in electrical engineering, one in chemicals, and eight in base metal products.

South Africa

In other Commonwealth countries the extent of U.K. direct capital investment is more difficult to gauge. In the Union of South Africa, as in Australia and New Zealand, there has been since the war an emphasis on direct investment rather than on investment in portfolio securities. By 1956 accumulated direct investment in the Union private sector amounted to £762·1m. or 63% of the total foreign investment in this sector.[3] Within the manufacturing sector, 88% of foreign investment took the form of direct investment. There was a switch of interest in South Africa from mining to manufacturing—direct investments in manufactures being by the end of the nineteen-fifties greater than mining. The trend towards direct investment in the Union was especially marked in the case of United States and United Kingdom investors. As

[1] Economist Intelligence Unit, *The Commonwealth and Europe*, p. 309.
[2] Reports on official estimates of the Balance of Payments.
[3] South African Reserve Bank: Foreign Liabilities and Assets of the Union of South Africa.

in Australia, investment generally took the form of the retention in the Union of undistributed profits. Out of accumulated direct investment of over £800m. at the end of 1956, the U.K. held £556m.; U.K. holdings of long-term portfolio investments were less than this, and amounted to about £300m.[1]

Unfortunately, no collected information is available as to the number of South African companies which are British-owned, and it is even more difficult to find out when these companies started operations. It is, however, widely known that in the nineteen-fifties several U.K. manufacturers of motor car components entered into arrangements with South African engineering firms for production of vehicles in the Union. In the electrical cable industry several of the largest producers were affiliated to British companies. I.C.I. also established important chemical plant in the Union.

India

In the case of India, too, much overseas investment since the war has been direct, and has been concentrated in manufacturing industry. Between 1948 and 1953, branches and foreign subsidiaries accounted for over 80% of total foreign investment which took place in India and three-quarters of this was in manufacturing. By the end of 1955 there were 971 foreign-controlled companies, comprising 430 branches and 541 joint stock companies (including subsidiaries, managed companies, and controlled companies). The lion's share of the finance for these concerns came from the United Kingdom. The scale of United States investment was also growing but was largely in petroleum.

Within the manufacturing sector, the capital inflow was concentrated especially in pharmaceuticals, electrical goods, cigarettes and tobacco.

It is hardly likely that United Kingdom direct investments of this magnitude could fail to result in some rearrangement of the import pattern of India's import trade and some decline in the United Kingdom share of visible imports into the Republic between the early and late nineteen-fifties is hardly surprising.

As regards other Commonwealth countries it is extremely difficult to obtain any adequate data regarding United Kingdom direct investment. It is widely known that there was a considerable growth of secondary industries in the Federation of Rhodesia and Nyasaland and many of the companies which have been set up in recent years have direct associations with United Kingdom firms.

CANADA

We have already noted the importance of Canada as an outlet for U.K. private investment. Indeed in both 1958 and 1959 the level of U.K.

[1] South African Reserve Bank: *Foreign Liabilities and Assets of the Union of South Africa*, 1957.

direct investment was higher in Canada than in any other country, amounting to £27·7m. in 1958 and £32·6m. in 1959.[1]

At the end of the war, the value of U.K. direct investment assets in Canada had fallen to £348m.; in the early post-war years the Treasury scrutinised carefully all requests for dollars for investment in Canada and the United States, and the capital outflow from the U.K. to Canadian industry did not become really significant until the nineteen-fifties. By the end of 1958, however, it was estimated that direct U.K. investment in Canada had reached some £1,250m., having doubled in the preceding five years. This rapid growth of U.K. assets largely represented heavy investment in oil, aluminium and other minerals, but a significant part was also devoted to manufacturing industry, notably iron and steel, chemicals, and aircraft. Messrs. Hawker Siddeley, through A. V. Roe Canada Limited, acquired the Victory aircraft plant in Ontario at a fairly early stage after the war; between 1945 and 1953 some $16m. is said to have been invested in the Canadian aircraft industry by the group. Hawker Siddeley by 1959 controlled a large number of Canadian establishments which manufactured items as diverse as railway rolling stock, steel castings, and aircraft.[2]

It was reported in the autumn of 1958[3] that since the war British investors had gained control of some thirty-five Canadian companies; apart from this many U.K. firms have set up their own subsidiaries— there were said to be 950 of these in Canada in 1958.

DIRECT INVESTMENT BY THE U.S.A.

In order to get the scale of U.K. direct investment in correct perspective it is worth looking at the volume of direct investment by the other great capital-exporting country—the United States. In 1959, total U.S. direct investment, that is, investment expenditure by U.S. companies, including undistributed subsidiary earnings in their foreign branches and subsidiaries, amounted to $2,520m. This figure is not strictly comparable with the one of $483m. (£172m.) we have quoted for United Kingdom direct investment in 1959, since the U.S. figures include direct investment in oil and insurance, which is excluded in the Board of Trade estimates. In 1959 over $600m. of total current direct investment by the United States was in petroleum; for the preceding five or six years about one-quarter of all direct U.S. overseas investment had been in this industry.

If we take account only of manufacturing industry, U.S. direct investment in 1959 was $1,034m., as compared with the equivalent of $243m. (1958) for the United Kingdom. Thus in manufacturing industry the scale of United States direct investment at the end of the

[1] H.M. Treasury, *Bulletin for Industry* (August 1959).
[2] *The Times* (London, 14th May 1959).
[3] *Toronto Financial Post.*

nineteen-fifties was about four times as great as in the case of the United Kingdom.

Although the scale of U.S.A. investment was greater than that of the U.K., much of it was in markets where the U.K. had a relatively small interest as an exporter. For example, U.S. direct investment in the Latin American republics was running at about half a billion dollars a year. In the overseas Sterling Area, on the other hand, the flow of American funds into direct investment was quite small—except perhaps in Australia—Table 3.2. In the Union of South Africa very little American investment was in manufacturing and had it not been for the retained profits of the non-manufacturing sector, there would in 1959 have been an overall net disinvestment. In western Europe, especially in European Economic Community countries, the Americans were ahead of the British in developing local manufacture. Between 1950 and 1958, the direct investment stake in Europe of American firms rose from $1,733m. to $5,300m. In 1959 alone, three-quarters of a billion dollars were added; one-quarter of a billion dollars of this was in the European Economic Community.[1] United Kingdom direct investment in the Community countries was just under $53m.—about one-fifth of the level of American investment.

The motives behind the expansion of U.S. industry into Europe are many. A U.S. survey in 1956 and the first half of 1957 showed that there was a decided cost advantage in producing in western Europe, especially in Common Market countries. Labour costs were lower and material costs, although somewhat higher than in the U.S., were not sufficiently high to offset this. Overhead costs were generally lower in the Community than in the United States.[2]

More important than these cost advantages, however, American firms found during the nineteen-fifties that there were very substantial marketing advantages to be reaped from setting up manufacturing units in Europe.

The scope for regional specialisation and the high expectation of an expanding market within the European Economic Community are undoubtedly a powerful attraction; and there is reason to think that this is a more potent factor than relatively low unit labour costs. Market advantages which stimulate the migration of American enterprise into manufacturing in Canada (where cost differences are not inviting) are now making themselves increasingly felt on the Continent of Europe.[3]

Whether or not the United Kingdom ultimately becomes a full

[1] For a discussion of several aspects of American overseas investment in recent years, see U.S. Department of Commerce, 'United States Foreign Investments: Measures of Growth and Economic Effects', *Survey of Current Business* (September 1960).

[2] T. R. Gates, 'Production Costs Here and Abroad: A Comparative Study of the Experience of American Manufacturers', *National Industrial Conference Board* (New York, 1958); quoted by Brinley Thomas, 'Recent Trends in American Investment in Western Europe', *Three Banks Review* (September 1960). Professor Thomas's article provides a useful survey of trends in U.S. capital outflows since the war.

[3] Brinley Thomas, cited above, p. 13.

member of the E.E.C., there is no doubt that in a growing market like that of the Community there is a very great deal of scope for a considerable expansion of United Kingdom direct investment.

One further point is worth making in connexion with British and United States investment. Although the scale of direct U.S. investment in most United Kingdom export markets was limited, there are countries where it was quite important—notably Australia, Canada and western Germany. In these countries we must be on our guard against too facile an acceptance of the view that the switch from U.K. exports to local manufacture in overseas-owned plant over a given period necessarily means that the plant was owned by United Kingdom interests. Sometimes exports were lost, not because a U.K. firm had set up local manufacture, but because an American firm had done so. In Australia, for example, imports of motor vehicles from the United Kingdom substantially declined between 1953 and 1959. This is partly because many British firms were engaged in local assembly and manufacture; it is also in part due to the fact that United States-owned subsidiary companies were by 1959 operating on a large scale in the Dominion, and these secured part of the market previously held by the United Kingdom.

THE YIELD OF DIRECT INVESTMENT

It seems likely that U.K. invisible earnings increased as the result of the process we have been describing in this chapter, and in the long run these earnings might offset a significant part of the deterioration in the visible trade balance which almost certainly results from overseas manufacture, assembly and licensing.

United Kingdom earnings from direct investments overseas rose substantially in 1959 and 1960; this increase undoubtedly reflected in some measure the growing volume of direct investment engaged in by British firms in the preceding years. Income from direct investment overseas increased from £196m. in 1958 to £240m. in 1960, while receipts from portfolio investment remained almost stationary, at around £120m.[1] On the other hand, payments to overseas parent companies of subsidiaries and branches located in the United Kingdom rose even more steeply.

According to Board of Trade estimates, in 1959 48% of the income from overseas direct investment by the U.K. came from manufacturing; 25% from agriculture and mining; and 10% from distribution. Of the £200m. received by U.K. companies from overseas activities, £41m. came from North America; nearly £129m. from the Overseas Sterling Area; £27m. was earned in western Europe. The increase in earnings between 1958 and 1959 from direct investment was especially marked in the case of E.E.C. countries.

In a time of depression, a switch from visible to invisible earnings in the balance of payments can have unfortunate consequences for employ-

[1] Cmd. 1329, 'United Kingdom Balance of Payments, 1956–1960 (H.M.S.O., 1961).

ment. But when domestic resources, of men and capital, are being fully utilized, there is much to be said for the substitution of overseas for home production. There is some advantage even in the export of 'know-how' rather than of physical goods. For example, the British electrical industry has since the war in many instances provided the essential technical experience and 'know-how' for many overseas developing countries. The provision of these services has no import content and in many cases makes a substantial contribution to the balance of payments. Accordingly no survey of export performance would be complete without paying some attention to these invisible, yet very real, earnings. Whether, in view of U.K. balance-of-payments difficulties, the scale of direct investment which took place in the nineteen-fifties was from the point of view of the U.K. economy a 'good thing' is however another matter which cannot here be discussed. Our purpose in the present chapter has been rather to point out that direct private investment has taken place on a scale greater than is often realised, and to suggest that in a number of country and commodity markets this almost certainly reduced the level of British visible exports below what they would otherwise have been, and at the same time reduced the share of the import market held by U.K. exporters. We must, however, now return to our analysis of some of the other causes for the decline in the U.K. share of world trade in visibles. Although the switch from domestic to overseas assembly and manufacture helps to explain part of this decline there is no doubt that other factors were at work, too, and in the following chapter we turn to an analysis of relative export prices. The United Kingdom repeatedly found herself losing orders on this account.

Table 3.1. *Annual inflow of private overseas investment in companies in Australia, 1947–48 to 1957–58*

£m.

From	U.K.	U.S.A.+ Canada	Other Countries
1947–48	23	5	2
1948–49	28	3	3
1949–50	42	8	4
1950–51	34	16	4
1951–52	38	24	7
1952–53*	17	1	2
1953–54*	36	14	6
1954–55*	44	32	7
1955–56*	58	26	11
1956–57*	48	22	12
1957–58*	48	20	12

* Includes holdings by Australian nominees of overseas investors, and by overseas investors using Australian addresses.

Source: Department of Trade, Melbourne.

Table 3.2. *Direct investment by the U.S.A., 1957-59*

$m.

Area and Country	I New Net Capital Outflow			II Undistributed Subsidiary Earnings			I+II
	1957	1958	1959	1957	1958	1959	1959
All areas, total	2482	1181	1439	1363	945	1081	2520
Canada	718	421	409	357	279	393	802
Latin America	1163	299	338	239	143	202	540
Europe	287	190	466	294	238	258	724
E.E.C.	96	106	171	116	113	99	270
of which W. Germany	75	24	77	39	57	52	129
France	15	37	45	34	39	23	68
United Kingdom	172	63	190	160	109	138	328
Other Countries							
Union of S. Africa	—21	5	—12	24	15	15	3
India	4	—2	5	7	9	11	16
Japan	16	—11	15	8	7	14	29
Australia	—3	21	24	47	50	60	84
New Zealand	—1	*	1	1	2	2	3

* Less than $500,000.

Source: U.S. Department of Commerce, Survey of Current Business, Sept. 1960.

F

CHAPTER IV

COMPARATIVE EXPORT PRICES

IT has often been alleged that part of the advantage which German and other trading competitors enjoyed over the United Kingdom exporters in the nineteen-fifties was due to their ability and willingness to quote prices which were more competitive than those of the United Kingdom. Undoubtedly this was so, but there are difficulties in trying to relate export prices to export performance.

THE PROBLEM OF COMPARISON

There are two aspects to the relationship between prices and exports. On the one hand, it might be possible to compare British and other export prices at any one point in time—if we had the necessary data we might, for example, establish that the United Kingdom had a smaller share than western Germany in a particular import market and show that in that market British goods were more expensive than comparable German ones. On the other hand, we could examine the *change* in the shares of the market held by the United Kingdom and western Germany and relate this to *changes* in the export price levels of the two countries. In either case it would of course be wrong to argue that because the export price level of British goods compared unfavourably with that of German goods, and because the German share of a market was greater than, or had increased at the expense of, the United Kingdom, the one was *necessarily* the result of the other. In both cases, too, there are serious difficulties in comparing prices, or changes in prices, between countries.

There are obvious problems in comparing the prices of, for example, German or Italian motor cars, with those of British vehicles. Even within a country motor cars are far from homogeneous. As between countries they are likely to be even more distinctive in regard to size, style and performance.[1] In the chapters on the export performance of particular countries and again in the export case studies of this book we shall have occasion to make direct comparisons between price levels of the exports of various countries, and while some of the conclusions drawn from these comparisons shed light on the export performance of the countries concerned, such comparisons should be treated with considerable reserve.

The difficulty of international comparison is even more acute when we are analysing changes over time. Not only might commodities themselves change more rapidly in one country than in another, but the statistical series showing the change in relative price levels are often

---

[1] These problems are discussed fully by Milton Gilbert and Irving B. Kravis, *An International Comparison of National Products and the Purchasing Power of Currencies* (O.E.E.C.).

discontinuous. In fact, in regard to export price indices for manufactured goods, there is very little published material to work on. The O.E.E.C. publish regularly an average value index for total exports for member countries, Canada and the United States of America.[1] Periodically the Board of Trade has published an index showing unit values of exports of manufactures for five leading manufacturing countries separately, and also one, calculated by the United Nations,[2] for aggregate exports of manufactures for the twelve leading manufacturing countries taken as a group (see Table 4.1). These are, however, omnibus indices and in the case of each country within the category 'manufactures', a number of divergent trends are almost certainly concealed. Accordingly, in Table 4.2 a more detailed breakdown of exports has been given for the years for which adequate data are available.

At commodity level, it is sometimes possible to compare export price movements in various supplying countries by inspection of import unit values, derived from the importing country's commodity trade returns.[3] Such estimates should, however, be used with caution, for it is unlikely that the quality, styling, or even coverage of goods included under a particular heading in the import trade returns will remain unchanged if a period sufficiently long to make any trend meaningful is adopted.

Before looking at Tables 4.1 and 4.2 one further point should be borne in mind by the reader: the fact that the market 'shares' given in chapters I and II and in most of the rest of this book are by value, not volume. Thus in cases where the United Kingdom export prices rose relatively to those of other exporting countries, the United Kingdom share of a market in terms of volume fell more than is suggested by the estimates in our Tables.

THE UNITED KINGDOM AND HER COMPETITORS

Chart 1 (on p. 60) shows that between 1953 and 1959, United Kingdom export unit values of manufactures rose by about 10%; for western Germany the index rose to 102 in 1958, but fell back to 100 in 1959. The United Nations index for manufactured goods from the twelve leading manufacturing countries (the 'World' in Table 4.1) shows a rise of about 6% between 1953 and 1959. The countries whose export unit values rose most were the United Kingdom (10%) and the U.S.A. (14%). Although in the case of France export unit values rose considerably up to 1957, the combined effect of the devaluation of the franc and of the adoption of the 'New' economic policy (see pp. 108–12) led to a substantial fall in export prices in 1959. For 1959 the index for France stood at 94 (1953 = 100): this was more favourable than in the case of any other major exporting nation, except Japan.

---

[1] O.E.E.C. General Statistics.
[2] U.N. Monthly Bulletin of Statistics.
[3] For an example see B. Vitkovitch, 'The U.K. Cotton Industry: 1937–54', *Journal of Industrial Economics* (July 1955), where import unit values are compared for cloth imported into Sweden from the United Kingdom, Germany, the Netherlands and Belgium.

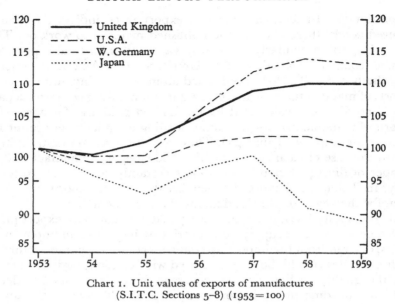

Chart 1. Unit values of exports of manufactures
(S.I.T.C. Sections 5–8) (1953 = 100)

The U.S.A.

Reference to Table 4.1 will show that after 1953 United States export prices appear to have risen more than those of her European trade competitors. In a study of the United States domestic and export price levels, Sir Donald MacDougall suggests that between 1953 and 1959 labour costs per unit probably rose more quickly in the United States than in Italy, Japan and France (after allowing for devaluation), but more slowly than in the United Kingdom.[1] Possibly labour costs rose at about the same rate in Germany, Belgium and Canada, as in the United States. MacDougall suggests that the reason why United States export prices rose much more sharply than those of Germany in spite of the fact that labour costs rose about equally in the two countries is partly to be found in statistical deficiencies; partly in the fact that the basic price data do not take full account of improvements in 'quality' —this might have affected the United States more than Germany— and partly in the fact that raw material prices rose more in the United States than in other countries. Moreover, the metal and engineering industries are especially important in United States exports, and it does seem that in the United States labour costs per unit in these sectors increased more than in manufacturing as a whole. The fact that United States exports are heavily weighted in this way might well account in part for the rise in United States export price level for manufactures as a whole. Certainly, as Table 4.2 shows, export prices of United States engineering products rose substantially more than prices of other products.

[1] G. D. A. MacDougall, 'The Dollar Problem: A Re-appraisal', *Essays in International Finance* (Princeton University, 1960), pp. 16–21.

Japan

In contrast to the United States the export price level of Japanese manufactures fell steeply between 1953 and 1959. In 1959 the unit export value index stood at 90, indicating a considerable fall even since 1957. Of course, Japanese exports were heavily weighted in terms of textiles and changes in the world price of these markedly affected the index for Japan. Indeed, the case of Japan illustrates the danger of an over-emphasis on tables showing aggregate unit value trends. Where a country exports a substantial volume of goods the world price of which is falling (and the export unit values of which are declining), its aggregate export price level will show a fall, but this will not reflect a higher degree of competitiveness so much as the fact that the country concerned is selling a high proportion of goods which are less important than before in world trade.

Commodity break-down

Table 4.2 shows that in almost all manufacturing sectors United Kingdom export unit values increased as much as, or more often more than, those of Germany, France and Japan. In most branches of manufacturing the United Kingdom export price index was outstripped only by that of the United States, and not always by that country, e.g. in chemicals and textiles United Kingdom products appeared less competitive than those of the U.S.A. when compared with 1953.

As regards the connexion between relative United Kingdom price trends and the comparative performance of various United Kingdom industries in world markets, the evidence is not at all clear. From Table 4.2 it can be seen that in textiles (where between 1953 and 1958 the U.K. share by value of the world market fell from 27·2% to 19·9% and the West German share rose from 6·5% to 8·4%), United Kingdom prices after 1953 rose very little more than those of western Germany. As compared with Japan, however, British textile export prices clearly became less competitive and this is confirmed by general observation and the trend of some unit import costs in particular markets. In one broad field where we have already noted that the United Kingdom lost considerable ground to western Germany—electrical machinery and equipment—British export prices rose by 19% between 1953 and 1958; those of western Germany by almost as much—17%. In this sector then, prices alone could hardly have accounted for the decline in the United Kingdom share of world trade. In the machinery sector as a whole (S.I.T.C. Section 7) where the United Kingdom performance was better than in the electrical division, the gap in the export price index between Britain and western Germany was greater than in the case of electrical products. In transport equipment, by 1958 British export prices had since 1953 risen by 9 per cent, while German export unit values had risen by only 3%. Yet in spite of the unfavourable movement of British export prices, transport equipment was one of those sectors in which the export performance of the United Kingdom was, as measured by the decline in the U.K. share of the world market, better than in many other sectors. Thus the evidence, such as it is, points to a possibility—we can put it no higher than that—that British export performance reflected a tendency for prices of U.K. export products to rise distinctly more rapidly than in other countries, but it is difficult to draw conclusions relating to particular industries.

PRICE FLEXIBILITY

Now not only did German export prices rise more slowly than those of the United Kingdom; there is also evidence that they were more flexible. German exporters were almost certainly more sensitive to changes in world demand than their British rivals. Whereas British exporters are said often to have priced their export goods simply by adding a more or less constant profit margin to costs, and thus allowed changes in costs to affect export prices, the Germans have on the whole paid much more attention to demand changes in export markets and have not hesitated to adjust their prices—upwards or downwards—to these changes. Indeed it has been concluded by one student of inflation[1] in the United Kingdom that 'prices of our manufactured exports . . . have probably been uniquely insensitive to fluctuation in world demand'.

If we look a little more closely at Table 4.1 it will become clear that in the nineteen-fifties the increase in British export prices of manufactures outstripped that of western Germany only after 1953. Between 1950 and 1953 German export prices actually rose more rapidly than those of the United Kingdom. During those years the Germans were taking advantage of the sellers' market which persisted in the case of many commodities in the boom period following the outbreak of the Korean war. The gap between U.K. and German export price increases was particularly wide in the case of engineering products—goods for which world demand was especially buoyant after the middle of 1950. By the end of 1953, German export prices of engineering products had risen by 37% (average of 1950 = 100); United Kingdom export prices of these goods had risen by only 29%.

By contrast, when in 1958 world demand for manufactures was sagging, we find German export prices falling—in line with changed world demand conditions;[2] British export prices of manufactures, on the other hand, remained virtually stationary (Table 4.3). Incidentally, U.K. export prices were also less flexible than those of competitors other than western Germany. In 1958, both French and Japanese

[1] J. C. R. Dow, 'Why Do Prices Rise?', *Bankers' Magazine* (March 1957). See also Mr. Dow's article in *Oxford Economic Papers* (October 1956), 'Analysis of the Generation of Inflation'.
[2] This was part of conscious German policy. See *Deutsche Bundesbank*, Annual Report for 1958.

export prices of manufactures were lower than in 1957; in the case of the United Kingdom (and incidentally of the United States too) export unit values of manufactures rose by one point between the two years. There is no doubt that the unwillingness of British exporters to 'tailor' their prices to conditions of overseas demand had an adverse effect upon their sales.[1] We shall find this especially true of certain branches of industry, for example, electrical engineering (see pp. 145–6).

A further point of interest, particularly in regard to Anglo-Continental competition, is the relationship between wholesale price trends in the two countries; and also the relationship between internal wholesale prices and export prices within each country. In the case of West Germany, the United Kingdom's foremost competitor between 1953 and 1959, internal wholesale prices rose less than in the case of the United Kingdom. Not only did German wholesale prices of finished manufactured goods rise less than those of the United Kingdom—7% as against 13%—there is also evidence that, as in the case of export prices, German wholesale prices were more flexible than those of the United Kingdom. There was, for example, a slight fall in the West German index of wholesale prices, and of consumer goods, in 1954 and again in 1958 and 1959. In the United Kingdom, wholesale prices showed a steady upwards movement throughout the period.

As regards the relationship between domestic wholesale prices and export prices in West Germany, export and domestic prices kept more closely in step after 1953 than was the case in the very early nineteen-fifties. After 1958 they moved in close harmony. Probably the gap before 1953 indicated that some German exporters were selling abroad at a little below internal prices in order to be competitive in the many export markets they were beginning to attack for the first time since the war.[2] Since 1953, there has been less price incentive for German manufacturers to sell abroad rather than at home except perhaps in 1954. In regard to the United Kingdom, between 1953 and 1959, domestic wholesale prices tended to rise slightly faster than prices obtainable on the export market, and this might have had the effect of directing marginal supplies from the export to the home market. The general conclusion must be, however, that in the United Kingdom and western Germany, at any rate, export prices moved more or less in line with domestic prices, but that both tended to rise more slowly and to be more flexible in the case of western Germany than the United Kingdom. There is, however, no doubt that the relative price movements in the United Kingdom and her competitors were themselves particular aspects of differences in broader economic conditions and policies and these more general considerations will be examined in the following chapter.

[1] See F. Brechling, 'Anglo-German Export Competition', *Three Banks Review* (March 1959).

[2] On this subject, see H. Liesner, 'Relative Costs and Prices in British, United States, and German Manufacturing Industry', *London and Cambridge Economic Service Bulletin* (September 1956).

Table 4.1. *Unit values of exports of manufactures
(S.I.T.C. Sections 5–8)*

(1953=100)

	1950	1951	1952	1953	1954	1955	1956	1957	1958	1959
United Kingdom	84	98	105	100	99	101	105	109	110	110
U.S.A.*	84	98	105	100	99	99	106	112	114	114
W. Germany	81	98	106	100	98	98	101	102	102	100
France	81	98	106	100	98	99	104	107	103	94
Japan	n.a.	n.a.	109	100	96	93	97	99	91	90
'World'†	n.a.	n.a.	n.a.	100	98	99	103	107	107	106

* Excluding Special Category exports.

† United Nations Unit Value index for aggregate exports of manufactured goods (S.I.T.C. 5–8) based on official indices of the twelve principal exporting countries: Belgium-Luxembourg, Canada, France, W. Germany, India, Japan, Netherlands, Sweden, Switzerland, United Kingdom, United States.

Note: Figures are compiled from national statistics and caution should be exercised in using them.

Table 4.2. *Unit values of exports of groups of manufactures*

(1953=100)

S.I.T.C. Section or Division	1953	1954	1955	1956	1957	1958
Chemicals(5)						
U.K.	100	100	101	101	103	100
U.S.A.	100	99	97	99	99	93
W. Germany	100	100	98	96	95	90
France	100	103	100	98	99	94
Japan	100	101	105	100	97	87
Textiles(65)						
U.K.	100	101	101	101	103	102
U.S.A.	100	96	99	97	97	96
W. Germany	100	101	101	100	101	101
France	100	99	96	99	102	94
Japan	100	96	91	93	92	86
Machinery and Transport Equipment(7)						
U.K.	100	100	102	107	112	115
U.S.A.	100	99	98	106	115	118
W. Germany	100	98	97	100	103	108
France	100	101	102	105	111	109
Japan	100	97	95	94	96	94
Electrical Equipment (72)						
U.K.	100	100	103	106	114	119
U.S.A.	100	100	99	109	118	120
W. Germany	100	102	101	105	110	117
France	100	103	102	106	114	119
Japan	100	100	97	98	102	n.a.
Transport Equipment(73)						
U.K.	100	100	105	108	109	109
U.S.A.	100	98	96	99	107	112
W. Germany	100	94	93	96	98	103
France	100	100	111	116	121	121
Japan	100	92	81	80	80	n.a.

See note to Table 4.1.

Table 4.3. *Unit values of manufactures, 1956–58*
Quarterly Series

Quarterly Series (1953 = 100)

All Manufactures	1956				1957				1958			
	I	II	III	IV	I	II	III	IV	I	II	III	IV
United Kingdom	104	104	105	106	107	108	109	110	110	110	110	110
U.S.A.	107	107	107	110	112	112	112	113	114	114	113	113
W. Germany	99	100	101	101	102	103	103	103	103	103	102	101
France	105	104	105	106	106	107	109	103	104	104	103	101
Japan	95	97	98	98	99	99	98	97	93	91	90	89

See note to Table 4.1.

Table 4.4. *Wholesale and export prices, U.K. and West Germany*

(1953 = 100)

	United Kingdom			West Germany*†			
	Wholesale Prices		Export Prices‡	Producer Prices for Industrial Products			Export Prices
	All Manfd. Products	Basic Industrial Materials	Manfd. Products	All Products	Raw Materials and Producers goods	Consumer goods	Finished Products
1950	85	95	84	85	76	103	80
1951	100	135	98	101	96	126	93
1952	102	111	105	103	105	108	98
1953	100	100	100	100	100	100	100
1954	100	98	99	98	98	99	99
1955	103	101	101	101	103	99	99
1956	107	105	105	103	104	101	101
1957	111	106	108	105	105	105	103
1958	111	99	110	106	105	104	106
1959	112	100	110	105	104	102	105
1960	113	100	113	107	105	106	107

* Includes W. Berlin.

† To 1952 computed from old index (basis 1950 = 100); from 1952 onwards, new index (original basis 1954 = 100).

‡ Base weighted value index computed originally on base 1954.

— indicates break in the series.

Source: O.E.E.C. General Statistics.

CHAPTER V

DOMESTIC ECONOMIC CONDITIONS
AND EXPORT PERFORMANCE:

THE UNITED KINGDOM

EXPORTS cannot be looked upon in isolation. Both the prices and the volume of exports from a country depend to some extent upon the economic conditions in that country and upon its internal economic policies as well as upon conditions in foreign markets. Thus a country might fail to export on an adequate scale on account of a high level of domestic demand which makes it less necessary or profitable for manufacturers to sell their products abroad. When all that can be produced can be sold at home, manufacturers have little incentive to export—partly because the cost of selling (e.g. transport, distribution and advertising) is usually lower at home, and partly because most firms are reluctant to give up any opportunity of building up a large and growing domestic market. Almost always, a home market is more secure than an export market; there is no danger of its collapsing as the result of some arbitrary act of a foreign Government, as, for example, the sudden imposition of quantitative restrictions on imports. Usually, changes in demand and tastes can be foreseen more quickly and accurately in the home market than in foreign ones. In a time of full employment, therefore, firms might require some special tangible encouragement to export rather than to sell at home.

The Government and Exports

This encouragement can take several forms. Taxation might be adjusted so as deliberately to encourage firms to sell abroad. Export subsidies might be granted. The exchange rate might be kept at such a level that goods can be sold abroad at higher domestic currency prices (or more easily) than at home. A differential exchange rate for certain export commodities is a variant of the arrangement. In a time of raw material shortage, an allocation to a firm of its raw materials might be made to depend upon its exporting a given percentage of its output. The Government might remove some of the risks of exporting by providing (usually through an agency set up for the purpose) export finance and insurance on especially favourable terms. Most of these measures involve some kind of 'bribe', encouraging firms to export; they are measures involving the 'carrot' rather than the 'stick'. But the stick is often used too. The Government might, for example, impose drastic restrictions on domestic sales in order to force firms the more diligently to seek for markets abroad. A policy of general monetary and fiscal stringency might be employed to damp down home demand and deflect supplies abroad.

On the other hand, discriminatory restrictions, aimed at concentrating the contraction of demand on particular industries, e.g. those using substantial quantities of steel, might be imposed.

Now these restrictive measures, whether general or discriminatory in their application, might be directed primarily to improving the balance of payments by reducing or containing the level of imports rather than by directly stimulating exports. Nevertheless, when such measures are suggested, their advocates usually think of them as having, on the whole, a favourable effect upon exports. Certainly it was the intention of the British Government when it imposed various disinflationary measures in 1955–58 that these should directly stimulate the flow of exports.

Undoubtedly there are times when an overall 'tough' financial policy, possibly supported by discriminatory restrictions directed against certain industries which are heavy users of some scarce raw material, will result in a short-term improvement in the balance of payments on both the import and export side. This might well be the case at a time when there is a definite physical limit to the volume of output which can be produced, for example in the immediate aftermath of the war. There is no doubt that in the case of Great Britain, the ten-year period following the war was one when there was such a physical limit to industrial output, and the deliberate curtailment of domestic demand was accordingly necessary in order to encourage the export drive.

On the other hand, it is equally true that the supply situation changed after 1955 and the restrictive policies followed after that year in the United Kingdom had an adverse long-term effect upon the level of industrial output, upon productivity, and hence upon exports. While restrictions upon domestic demand, whether general or discriminatory, might have had a dampening effect upon imports, the experience of 1955 to 1959 suggests that it is extremely doubtful whether they had a correspondingly favourable effect upon exports. Indeed, we suggest that after 1956, in regard to exports, the balance of payments might well have been harmed, rather than helped, by some of the controls imposed. Before that date, it is true, there was a considerable degree of excess demand in the economy. In many industries there was a substantial back-log of orders; the sale of another motor car on the home market often resulted in one less motor car being available for export. But the argument for restrictions became very much weaker in 1956 and 1957. By this time, excess capacity was becoming evident on the home market. In many industries the export problem was not, as hitherto, to find goods; it was to find markets.

We suggest that it is possible that the restrictive policies followed in the United Kingdom in the second half of the nineteen-fifties had at least two unfortunate results. Firstly, the slowing down of the rate of growth of the British economy adversely affected the purchasing power of some of Britain's most important overseas customers, especially those in the Commonwealth. Secondly, domestic restrictions kept down the level of investment in the British economy, and this reacted unfavourably upon productivity, costs, and the will to export—an improvement in all three of which was essential if the U.K. was to retain its share of world trade.

Effects upon British Export Markets

Some of the fruits of the restrictive policies accepted in London were to be seen in the Sterling Area in 1957 and 1958. In many sterling countries—and these together accounted for about 50% of the United Kingdom exports of manufactures—sales of British exports began to flag. The irony of the situation in 1957 and 1958 was that the very policies which were intended to encourage United Kingdom manufacturers to export more vigorously were in fact making it extremely difficult for some of Britain's largest overseas customers to buy their products. Not only did many sterling countries raise their own interest rates in 1958 in order to keep in step with money rates in London,[1] they were also adversely affected by the deterioration in their terms of trade associated with the slowing down of the rate of growth of the United Kingdom economy. Table 5.1 shows the fall in the volume of United Kingdom imports of certain basic materials which took place between 1955 and 1956, and again between 1957 and 1958. This fall, especially in 1958, can be looked upon as in part the result of the failure of the British economy to grow as fast as hitherto.

Table 5.2 shows the effect of recession in Europe and North America upon Sterling Area commodity prices. Here it should be remembered that United Kingdom demand plays an important role in determining these prices. Table 5.3 indicates the effect of declining prices and export sales upon the reserves of the Overseas Sterling Area. These reserves fell by 23% between the end of 1954 and the end of 1958.

Productivity

Apart altogether from the adverse short-term effect of restrictive financial policies upon the Overseas Sterling Area (especially when the weapon of a high interest rate was used), the long continuance of restrictive measures in the United Kingdom had adverse long-term effects upon the level of investment in the British economy, and hence upon industrial productivity and unit costs. Although we are not denying that in *some* industries and in *some* markets, domestic restrictions in the United Kingdom had a favourable effect upon export sales, we

---

[1] In, for example, Northern Rhodesia, where the general raising of interest rates, superimposed upon the fall in incomes resulting from the drop in the price of copper had a direct effect on domestic spending. The reduction in the level of domestic expenditure resulted in a curtailment of imports, especially of manufactures, which were largely supplied by the United Kingdom. For a discussion of the effect of changes in the London Bank Rate upon the level of activity in overseas Commonwealth countries see Memoranda (Part V, No. 6) and Minutes of Evidence of the Committee on the Working of the Monetary System, (Radcliffe Report), Qu. 4327 ff.

are suggesting that in the long run the policies adopted so confidently in and after 1956 had a damaging effect upon the ability of many British manufacturing industries to compete successfully abroad. It is significant that countries whose share of world trade in manufactures increased most rapidly in the later nineteen-fifties—Japan, Italy, western Germany and France—were also the ones where real output per head increased most (Table 5.4). Table 5.5 draws attention to the fact that as regards industrial output, this grew more rapidly in all the major European countries listed than in either the United Kingdom or the United States—the two countries whose export performance left so much to be desired over the period.

There can be little doubt that the lowly position occupied by the United Kingdom in the international league table of industrial production in large measure reflects a failure to attain a sufficiently high level of fixed investment, and this was of course part of the price paid by Britain for the reliance placed upon restrictive financial policies.

There is good reason for believing that the absence of a sufficiently high level of investment in industry has been the Achilles heel of British economic policy since the war. It is this failure which denied to Britain that surplus of capacity of plant and equipment which could have been such a powerful stimulus to businessmen in their search for overseas markets. As Mr Andrew Shonfield has expressed the point—'the combination of fat order books and static productive capacity is a wonderful formula for making a salesman lackadaisical . . . the prospect of a surplus is a great cleanser of the businessman's spirit'.[1] By means of restrictive policies the authorities have from time to time tried to get rid of the 'fat order books'. In some industries, notably in the consumer durable goods industries, they succeeded, but since the approach was essentially negative, there was a lack of vigour in the British economy which inhibited a really aggressive export drive. As we shall see in our case studies, the damping down of home demand repeatedly failed to lead to any significant long-term increase in exports.[2]

In an economy which is consistently working at full capacity and where that capacity is not increasing, businessmen will have little direct incentive to export. But merely to deny them the full benefit of the home market is likely to be self-defeating. The restriction of home demand, especially when the restrictions are discriminatory, is almost certain to discourage long-term investment planning and to diminish the willingness of firms to take risks by installing extra capacity.

Clearly we cannot state categorically that if there had been a higher level of capital investment in British industry after 1955, export performance would have been better than it was. Such a proposition cannot be 'proved', but we are suggesting that there is substantial evidence that the kind of policies adopted in Britain after 1955 failed to create

[1] Andrew Shonfield, *British Economic Policy Since the War*, Penguin Special, Revised Edition, p. 84.
[2] See especially pp. 131–5 and pp. 150–7.

that atmosphere of expansion, enterprise, and optimism in which, *because* capacity was increasing, firms had a positive incentive to seek out foreign markets in order to sell goods which were being produced in ever-increasing quantities.

A survey of the domestic policies and export achievements of some of Britain's leading rivals in the export field suggests that in these countries —in Germany, Japan, Italy and later in France as well—successful export performance occurred alongside a rapid growth of domestic output. Goods were produced in such increasing quantities that producers who wished to increase their scale of output (and to enjoy the economies of scale) had a positive incentive to sell abroad, often at prices which were substantially lower than those ruling the domestic market. The artificial restriction of demand, on the other hand, especially when achieved by means of selective restrictions, almost inevitably curtails the level of output of individual firms, and in this way denies them economies of large-scale production.

Long-term Planning

The uncertainty as to the future, engendered by the ease with which these particular restrictions can be switched on and off, lowers the confidence of firms in their future prospects. Thus a further adverse effect of the various restrictions imposed by H.M. Government upon consumer spending was the uncertainty which the prospect of the imposition of these restrictions created in many industries. Firms cannot be expected to look ahead and install very expensive capital equipment if they know that they are likely to be faced by recurrent periods of officially-induced recession in the home market. The somewhat demoralising effect which Government policy had upon certain industries is exemplified by the evidence submitted to the Radcliffe Committee by the Engineering Industries Association.[1] Referring to the increase in Bank Rate to 7% in September 1957, the Association submitted that '. . . the increase has been taken as a clear signal that the modernisation of basic industrial equipment, long overdue, must again be postponed. The doubts about expansion which arose because of restricted bank advances have been converted into certainties.' The memorandum went on to aver that 'The interest rate of 8–10% makes many new projects impossible: such a high rate may make price increases inevitable, or give overseas markets away to foreign competitors'. Undoubtedly many businessmen used the existence of domestic restrictions as the excuse for their own failure to remain competitive, and many of the investment 'plans' which they alleged were frustrated by the high rate of interest in 1956–58, and by other restrictions, probably consisted of little more than vague intentions to expand plant and equipment at some future date. Nevertheless, the one fact that stands out from all this discussion is the fact that after 1953 investment in British industry lagged behind that in German, Italian, French, Dutch and Japanese

[1] Memoranda of Evidence, part vii, no. 6, and Minutes of Evidence, Qns. 6308 to 6411.

industry and, to say the least, the credit squeeze and associated measures of 1957–58 did nothing to help close this gap. Bearing in mind these considerations we shall now look briefly at the kind of domestic economic climates in which the export successes of some of Britain's leading competitors were achieved.

Table 5.1. *Volume of U.K. imports of certain basic materials*

	Total	1954=100 Textile Materials	Wood	Pulp	Ores and Scrap
1954	100	100	100	100	100
1955	106	98	114	118	112
1956	102	100	92	113	114
1957	106	101	101	112	126
1958	94	89	89	111	94
1959	100	103	98	120	91
1960	109	92	119	146	134

Source: National Institute Economic Review.

Table 5.2. *Overseas Sterling Area exports, commodity prices, 1957–59*

		1957=100
1957	I	103·7
	II	102·6
	III	99·6
	IV	94·1
1958	I	93·0
	II	93·4
	III	92·2
	IV	91·4
1959	I	91·4
	II	96·6
	III	97·2
	IV	99·1

Source: National Institute Economic Review.

Table 5.3. *Sterling Area countries gold and exchange reserves, 1954–59*

		\$b. at end of period
1954		5·71
1955		5·40
1956		5·14
1957		4·73
1958		4·36
1959	I	4·55
	II	4·64
	III	4·74
	IV	4·93

Source: National Institute Economic Review.

Table 5.4. *Growth rates in national product per man-year,*
1954–59

Japan	7·6
Italy	3·8
Germany	3·6
France	3·3
Netherlands	2·9
Norway	2·5
Sweden	3·0
United States	2·2
Canada	1·8
Denmark	2·5
United Kingdom	1·6

Source: National Institute Economic Review, July 1961.

Table 5.5. *Index numbers of industrial production,*
1954–60

	1954	1955	1956	1957	1958	1959	1960
			1953 = 100				
Belgium	106	116	123	124	116	122	129
Canada	100	110	120	120	120	129	130
France	110	120	133	144	150	156	174
West Germany	112	128	138	147	151	162	180
Italy	109	120	128	137	142	158	180
Japan	108	116	144	167	168	208	261
Netherlands	110	118	123	126	127	139	157
Sweden	104	111	114	117	120	124	134
United Kingdom	106	112	113	115	113	120	128
United States	94	106	109	110	102	116	119

Source: United Nations.

CHAPTER VI

DOMESTIC ECONOMIC CONDITIONS AND EXPORT PERFORMANCE:

WESTERN GERMANY

THE exporting country which in size, population, industrial structure and commodity, although not market, pattern of foreign trade was most similar to the United Kingdom in the nineteen-fifties was, of course, western Germany. At the end of 1959, the population of the United Kingdom was 52,348,000: that of West Germany (including the Saar), 53,373,000. In both countries manufacturing was by far the most important sector of the economy—in the Federal Republic in 1959 manufacturing accounted for 41·2% of gross domestic product at market prices; in the United Kingdom it accounted for 36·3% of gross domestic product at factor cost. For western Germany, manufactures (S.I.T.C. Sections 5–8) made up 88·3% of total exports; in the case of the United Kingdom the percentage was 83·8%. Within the manufacturing export sector, both countries leaned heavily on exports of engineering products. As regards the geographical pattern of export trade, however, there were substantial differences between the two countries. Whereas about one-half of British exports of manufactures were destined for Sterling Area countries, in the case of the Federal Republic there was a heavy dependence upon western Europe. Indeed, in 1957, well over half by value of German exports of both engineering products and other manufactures were exported to O.E.E.C. countries. About one-quarter were sold in the other five European Economic Community markets.

Whatever similarities there may have been in population and in industrial structure between the Federal Republic and the United Kingdom, however, in other ways the two countries followed quite divergent economic paths after 1948 when, following the Monetary Reform, western Germany began to develop once more into an economic power to be reckoned with.

Costs and Prices

In chapter IV we drew attention to the fact that in the case of Germany, both wholesale and export prices after 1953 rose less than in the case of the United Kingdom. Now it is worth noting that this happened in spite of the fact that prices of some of the major industrial 'input' materials, notably steel and coal, rose less in the U.K. than in western Germany during the early nineteen-fifties.[1] Thus although raw materials

[1] See F. Brechling, 'Inflation in the United Kingdom and W. Germany', *Bankers' Magazine* December 1957).

G

had become relatively more expensive to German producers than to their competitors in the United Kingdom, these higher costs were not reflected in correspondingly higher output prices. How can we account for this?

It is extremely difficult to compare movements in profit margins per unit of output between the two countries, but on the basis of such estimates as are available Dr Brechling has suggested that up to 1953 profits per unit of output rose faster in western Germany than in the United Kingdom. After that date they rose more rapidly in the U.K., but the gap was hardly great enough to have had any marked effect upon relative output prices.

Labour Costs

Up to 1956, but not after that year, hourly wages in manufacturing industry increased at about the same rate as in the United Kingdom (Table 6.1), but after 1956, German wages actually rose faster. It should, however, be remembered that although between 1956 and 1959 hourly earnings in western Germany increased more rapidly than in the United Kingdom, in the earlier years of the decade (up to 1954) when the Federal Republic was pioneering her post-war export drive, money wages were almost certainly substantially lower in western Germany than in the United Kingdom. Even in 1959, hourly earnings in manufacturing were higher in the United Kingdom (see Table 6.2), but as Table 6.3 shows, social charges levied on the employer accounted in 1959 for a much larger addition to wage rates in Germany than in the United Kingdom. In western Germany they were equivalent to about 44% of wages, as against 14% in the United Kingdom.

Table 6.3 suggests that the money wage burden carried by employers for an hour's work was, towards the end of the period, about equal in both countries. This was not necessarily true of separate industries. For instance, in some sectors where the Germans made gains in export markets at the expense of the United Kingdom, notably in engineering, German labour costs were either below the average for manufacturing as a whole, or more commonly, not as much above the average as in the case of the United Kingdom. Thus it has been estimated that in vehicles and aircraft German labour costs were in 1959 about 6% above the average for manufacturing as a whole; in the British vehicle and aircraft industry they were as much as 20% above the average. In electronics German labour costs were 7% below the average for German industry, in Britain labour costs were equal to the average. In the new industry of plastics processing, German costs were 9% below the average, in the United Kingdom they were 3% below. On the other hand, in iron and steel, German labour costs were 14% above the average, whereas for the U.K. they were only 7% above.

In the early years of the export race, rather more restraint in regard to wage claims was exercised in western Germany than in the United Kingdom. This was partly due to a lack of unity in the German Trade Union movement—in 1955 the Christian Democrat Trade Unions seceded from the Deutscher Gewerkschaftsbund. It was however more likely due to the generally weaker bargaining position of German labour, this being itself the consequence of a considerable influx of refugees from eastern Germany and other communist countries, together with a natural increase resulting from the high war-time birth-rate.

Table 6.4 shows that although in earlier years the average length of the actual working week in western Germany was about two hours greater than in the United Kingdom, by 1959 there was little difference between the two countries in this respect. By the end of 1958, a six-day, forty-five-hour week was common in a number of major industries in the Federal Republic. When considering the relative lengths of the working week in Germany and the United Kingdom, it should also be remembered that there are more public holidays in the Federal Republic than in Great Britain. The number varies from state to state, but in general there are about twelve a year.

Thus, except perhaps to some limited extent in the earlier years of the decade, it would be wrong to attribute the increasingly competitive prices of German goods, domestic and exports, simply to greater wage restraint or to longer hours of work in the Federal Republic. The really important point in this connexion is not that German labour was becoming cheaper, but that its productivity was increasing more rapidly than was the case in the United Kingdom. The rate of growth of output per head in western Germany was more rapid than in the case of any other country—the United Kingdom being easily outstripped by western Germany in this respect (see Tables 5.4 and 5.5). Indeed, the gap between the rates of growth of the level of output per head for the two countries has become steadily greater.

Domestic Policies

Fixed Investment

Now there are many possible explanations for the rapid growth of labour productivity in Germany. One of the most obvious is perhaps the extent of fixed industrial investment which took place in the nineteen-fifties. From 1952 to 1959 the amount of domestic capital investment was higher in Germany than in the United Kingdom; this is especially true of investment in machinery and equipment (Table 6.5). In each year, from 1952 onwards, the Federal Republic invested substantially more in this sector than was the case in the United Kingdom —and up to 1959 at least, the gap showed no sign of narrowing. Between 1953 and 1959 (inclusive), fixed capital investment in machinery and equipment amounted to the equivalent of $28,000m. in the United Kingdom and $35,000m. in Germany (at 1954 prices).

According to a study carried out by Professor T. E. Barna, between 1948 and 1956 the net value of fixed capital in manufacturing assets rose by 25% in the U.S., by 50% in the United Kingdom and by no less than 110% in western Germany.[1] The significance of this difference should

---

[1] T. E. Barna, 'Investment in Industry: Has Britain Lagged?', *The Banker* (April 1957).

not be exaggerated, for as Barna points out, the relative difference in rates of growth of capital in these years did no more than just about offset the different fortunes of the respective countries during the war years. Moreover, apart altogether from the question of war damage, there was in the post-war period probably a smaller proportionate need to create capital in the United Kingdom than in either the U.S.A. or the Federal Republic. But whatever the precise 'need' for capital creation in the early nineteen-fifties, the fact is that German manufacturing firms did install more machinery than British firms. This machinery, since it was installed later than was the case in Great Britain, was up to date and almost certainly for that reason relatively more efficient than much machinery still being used in the United Kingdom. Thus although, owing to war-time destruction and population increase, German manufacturers felt a greater urgency about installing capital than has been the case with British manufacturers, the very fact that the machinery was installed has given them a substantial advantage over many British firms which tended to go on operating obsolescent equipment. Now it is true that in spite of the installation of new plant in the nineteen-fifties, by 1959 Germany probably still had less plant per worker than Great Britain, but the really important factor was the psychological one. German employers and workers were conscious all the time that physical capacity was expanding—and often very rapidly. In this atmosphere both sides in industry had an interest in expanding sales—if only to keep the growing capacity fully utilised.

In a further discussion,[1] Professor Barna has suggested that not only did the volume of German investment exceed that of the United Kingdom in manufacturing industry as a whole, but it was concentrated much more in what we might call the export-oriented industries—iron and steel, non-ferrous metals, mechanical and electrical engineering. After 1953, western Germany also secured a clear lead over the United Kingdom in investment in the chemicals sector. The United Kingdom, on the other hand, in the post-war period spent more than western Germany on investments in textiles, clothing, food, drink and tobacco—industries which in the twentieth century have become less and less significant in world trade.[2] Accordingly, the pattern of West German investment in manufacturing was clearly more appropriate than that of the United Kingdom to the change in the pattern of world trade, and it may well be that this fact itself had something to do with the overall performance of the Federal Republic in the export field.

Population Growth

As we have already noted, closely linked with the growth of invest-

---

[1] T. E. Barna, 'Industrial Investment in Britain and in Germany', *The Banker* (January 1958).

[2] For a discussion of the changes in the pattern of world trade in the twentieth century, see H. Tyszynski, 'World Trade in Manufactured Commodities, 1899 to 1950,' cited above.

ment in western Germany was a steady expansion of the population. Between 1950 and 1957, the number of people gainfully employed in the Federal Republic increased by 16%. Much of this increase was due to the inflow of refugees from the east. By July 1959, western Germany had received 3·2m. refugees from the Soviet Zone, and 9·4m. from East Germany beyond the Oder-Neisse line, the Sudeten area, and South-East Europe. Altogether these refugees in 1959 accounted for 25% of the total population of the Federal Republic.[1] At first this level of immigration was a burden on the labour market and was reflected in high unemployment figures. In 1951 the percentage of the working population unemployed was as high as 7·7%, but after 1953 the level of unemployment in the Federal Republic dropped sharply and by 1958 the percentage of the working population unemployed was actually higher in the United Kingdom (2·2%) than in western Germany (1·7%). And yet Germany continued to capture export markets from the United Kingdom. Whatever the position in earlier years, by 1954–55 it cannot possibly have been true that the success of German exports was significantly due to there having been built up a pool of unemployed labour, willing to accept employment at low wages. Moreover, much of the unemployment at any time in the Federal Republic was temporary, and was in large measure due to the inevitable delay in the immigrants finding themselves suitable jobs. It was, too (for the same reason), largely localised, and tended to be concentrated in the eastern frontier zone.

Now the influx of refugee labour, so far from leading to further unemployment, was actually a powerful influence in creating fresh employment opportunities. The expansion of population enabled full advantage to be taken of improved manufacturing techniques; economies of scale became possible over a much wider field. At any rate in the latter half of the nineteen-fifties, it seems quite clear that it was the rapid growth of demand—for all kinds of consumer and capital goods—that led to rationalisation of production, the adoption of new techniques and ultimately to the lower unit costs which enabled German firms to sell abroad so cheaply.

Because industrial output grew so rapidly in the Federal Republic the volume of private consumption was able to grow along with rising domestic investment. In each year after 1950 the percentage increase in private consumption was greater in western Germany than in the United Kingdom. Of course the initial level of real consumption per head in 1950 was substantially lower in western Germany, but by the end of the decade the Federal Republic could not have been far behind the United Kingdom in this respect.

Financial Policies

So far as the Federal Government was concerned, relatively few measures were taken to reduce the level of domestic consumption

[1] Quoted in *Growth in the British Economy*, PEP (London, 1960), p. 239.

demand. There was no credit squeeze; hire purchase restrictions were relatively mild and there was no discriminatory purchase tax. On the other hand, the broad financial policies of the Bonn Government were fairly stringent during the decade we are reviewing. The German bank rate was, on the whole, fairly high—although (after 1952) only for a few months in 1956 did it stand at a level higher than 5%.

The relatively high level of investment in the Federal Republic was not achieved by a cheap money policy. Indeed in the earlier years of the period we are reviewing, credit was extremely difficult to get and only by the most vigorous ploughing back of profits was it possible for firms to obtain the finance they needed for essential re-equipment. Thus in the early nineteen-fifties both businessmen and the public accepted the need for restraint. As time passed, however, both budgetary and monetary policies were relaxed; these relaxations had a profound psychological impact. They created an atmosphere of confidence and expansion; the general easing of credit in particular encouraged firms to commence and often speed up investment plans in order to reap the full advantage of the relaxations. It was this rapid expansion of capacity which gave firms an incentive to export. Indeed in many cases investment decisions were taken on the assumption that a considerable part of production would in fact be exported, and the very fact that the capacity was there made the export successes of the Germans possible.

Taking into account the shortage of capital and reductions in direct taxation, monetary policy in Germany in later years cannot be said to have been deflationary. Certainly, monetary policy can in no way be regarded as having been of itself so 'tough' that domestic demand after 1955 was to any significant extent deliberately damped down in favour of exports.

Export Aids

It has sometimes been suggested that the Federal Government has aided German exporters through relatively favourable export credit and insurance arrangements.[1] There is no doubt that, particularly during the early nineteen-fifties, the German exporter was helped to a considerable extent in securing new markets by the export credit and insurance schemes available to him. This is not, however, the same thing as saying that he received export subsidies, paid for from the proceeds of taxation of the community at large.

Favourable Credit Arrangements

The whole question of export credit and insurance is regularly watched over by the International Association of Credit Insurers known as the Berne Union. When this Association met at Lugano in 1955, each member submitted his trading accounts and these showed

[1] For a very full discussion of this subject, see C. Segre, 'Medium-Term Export Finance', Banca Nazionale de Lavoro, *Quarterly Review* (June 1958). This article has been drawn on extensively in the paragraphs which follow.

that almost without exception members' operations were free from subsidy; a comparison of credit terms showed that most members were in step.[1] It is, however, probably true that in the earlier nineteen-fifties German exporters had been helped in their efforts to develop the Middle East and Latin American markets by the deliberate offer of highly favourable credit terms, and in this they were assisted by institutional arrangements made in the Federal Republic. Certainly in the case of Brazil and the Argentine, specially favourable exchange rates were given by their respective Governments to importers who could secure deferred payment terms and in 1953 and 1954 such terms could often be secured more readily from German than from British exporters.

In particular, German exporters were helped in their efforts to penetrate new markets, or rather to recapture some of their pre-war markets, by receiving preferential terms on bills discounted at the *Bank deutscher Länder* when these were drawn on foreign customers. A draft drawn on a foreign importer could be rediscounted at the *BdL* at the rate obtaining in the importing country (plus a small commission), if this rate were more favourable than the corresponding rate in the Federal Republic. Moreover, rediscount could take place whatever 'ceilings' were being currently imposed on the rediscount of domestic paper; since, moreover, the exporter could discount at the rate ruling on the day of discount, exchange risks were also eliminated. This system of export drafts, or *Exporttraten*, as they were called, was very popular and was widely used up to August 1957, when it was discontinued in view of the balance-of-payments surplus. Not only could the pre-shipment period be covered in this way; even after the export goods had been shipped, an importer's acceptance could be discounted at favourable rates. In fact it was possible to dovetail the credits covering both the pre-shipment and post-shipment periods in such a way that a credit on favourable terms was obtainable for a longer period than was normally the case in short-term finance.

As regards medium-term finance, in 1951, a credit line of DM 400m., based on ERP counterpart funds, was put at the disposal of the Reconstruction Loan Corporation by the *BdL* for medium-term export financing.

In 1952, an organisation known as *Ausfuhrkredit AG (AKA)* was formed and took over and managed this line of credit, together with further funds provided by a bankers' consortium. In extending credit from the original Reconstruction Loan Corporation line (known as credit line B), *AKA* was able to make loans from twelve months to four years, but in granting a loan under credit line A (which was derived from the funds provided by the consortium), the credit period dated only from the first *use* of the funds. Since the permitted time-lag between the making of an agreement between *AKA* and the exporter and the utilisation of funds might be anything up to a year, the effective period of credit could thus be extended to five years. The Reconstruction

[1] See the *Economist* (London, 21st May 1955).

Loan Corporation, the *Kreditanstalt für Wiederaufbau*, concentrated on long-term export finance—sometimes for finance of periods of eight years or more. The *KfW* has, for example, helped finance the import of capital equipment for steel mills in India and Iran.

Export Insurance

The provision of credit is, of course, very closely linked with insurance. Here there were substantial differences between United Kingdom and German practice. The British Export Credit Guarantee Department required an exporter wishing to cover any credit of up to three years to insure the whole of his short-term turnover with all countries (or at any rate with an agreed group of countries). Although medium-term credits were not restricted in this way, it is known that the Export Credit Guarantee Department looked with greater favour upon applicants for insurance cover who normally used the facilities of the Department for the bulk of their transactions. This 'blanket' cover, of course, enabled a much greater spreading of risks, and hence lower premiums, than would otherwise have been the case. Where the ECGD arrangement covered only an agreed group of markets, as opposed to all the exporters' markets, the premium was higher. In either case, payment terms could be varied to suit the requirements of the exporters, but the normal limit was five years. Wherever it could be shown, however, that the terms offered by the ECGD were insufficient to enable the British exporters to match those offered by foreign competitors, the Department was prepared to make special arrangements with the exporter to ensure that he was not at a disadvantage *vis-à-vis* foreign competitors.[1]

British firms which deal in stable markets and with foreign importers who can be relied upon to meet their obligations tend to resent the blanket cover arrangements insisted upon by the Department. They point out that in western Germany, the corresponding institution—*Hermes*—has never imposed such restrictions. In fact, when an exporter does insure all his transactions through *Hermes* he obtains policies at cheaper rates, but no pressure is put upon him to do this. He can, if he wishes, insure a single transaction. He can insure all his trade with a particular country or customer, or whatever proportion of it he wishes. Since 1953 he has been able, if he so wishes, to insure only against transfer and conversion risks. This limited cover can be obtained at considerably cheaper rates than in the case of cover against all risks.

There is no doubt that the British Export Credit Guarantee Department has become considerably more flexible in recent years, but over the period we have been discussing as a whole, the German exporter probably gained slightly over his United Kingdom competitor from the relatively greater flexibility in credit and insurance arrangements in the Federal Republic.

---

[1] A feature of the Budget of 1954 was the general permission given by the Chancellor to the ECGD to grant longer-term loans, in order to remain competitive with overseas credit insurance institutions. Subsequently, even greater freedom has been permitted the ECGD.

Between 1953 and 1959,[1] neither the Federal German nor the United Kingdom Governments gave much direct assistance to exporters by means of discriminatory taxation devices. In the early nineteen-fifties the German exporter enjoyed a rebate on income tax amounting to up to $3\frac{1}{2}\%$ of his export turnover, but following talks between the British Chancellor and the German Federal Minister for Economic Affairs, it was announced that the Federal Government would not renew this concession when it expired at the end of 1955. It is clear that no substantial part of the success of the German export effort can be explained in terms of specific Government fiscal aid.

Tariff Policy

There is one quite different field where Government action seems to have had a far reaching and beneficial effect upon productivity and exports, and this in regard to tariffs. Since the war, western Germany has been a low tariff country—that is, in regard to manufactures—but in 1956 and 1957 very substantial reductions were made in the already low tariff structure.[2] In 1956, duties on industrial products which were between 1% and 16% *ad valorem* were lowered by 20%; those between 17% and 25% were lowered by 25%. All other tariffs were reduced to 21%. In 1957 a further round of reductions took place. This time it took the form of a general lowering of 25% on all items. Now the effect of these reductions was to raise substantially the level of imports of goods subject to the tariff modifications. There was a marked substitution effect upon home demand. But—and this is the interesting point—German exports of these goods rose substantially in 1957 and 1958. Indeed they rose so much that together with the effects of the normal rate of growth of demand, the adverse effect of increased imports upon domestic production of the products concerned was more than offset. Here we have yet another example of the favourable effects on exports of the removal of restrictions—this time by letting in imports more freely. Not only did the reduction of tariffs have a price-effect, causing German producers to drop their prices, it undoubtedly also had the effect of stimulating greater efficiency and productivity in German industry. Perhaps there is a lesson here for the United Kingdom.

Psychological Factors

A survey of the influences which have helped German exports would not be complete without some reference to the psychological factors which have been operative in post-war Germany. There may be some truth in the psychological explanation of German export successes—

---

[1] For assistance given by some European Governments (including the United Kingdom and western Germany) in the early nineteen-fifties, see *Les Avantages Spéciaux Accordés Aux Exportateurs En France, En Allemagne, En Grande-Bretagne, Et Aux Pays-Bas*, Bulletin D'Information et de Documentation, Banque Nationale de Belgique, June 1953.

[2] For an interesting discussion of the economic effect of these tariff adjustments see J. Wemelsfelder, 'Effect of the Lowering of Import Duties in Germany', *Economic Journal*, March 1960.

namely that following defeat in war the German people were determined once more to restore themselves to a position of world leadership. Thwarted in their attempt to achieve this by war they turned to trade as a means of asserting their superiority. It might well be true that the German businessman derives more satisfaction than his British counterpart from successful selling abroad. Perhaps the German worker does feel a sense of elation at striving for higher productivity and successful export achievement. It would be wrong to omit entirely these subjective factors in our assessment of German performance, especially in view of the fact that after about 1953 the environmental factors were just right for full advantage to be taken of these factors. Growing employment, physical reconstruction, lower taxes, all these contrasted with the dismal experiences of 1945–48, and made for an atmosphere of hope and expansion.

It is, too, salutary to remember that the mere installation of machinery without ensuring that it is used efficiently will not get a firm or country very far. But when due account is taken of this, the fact remains that the most striking single difference between the German and the U.K. economies in the late nineteen-fifties has been in rates of growth. It is here that the secret of German success undoubtedly lies. All the important German export industries grew rapidly after 1950—this rate of growth enabled both home market and export demand to be satisfied. This was in marked contrast to the United Kingdom where, due in part to the imposition of restrictions on domestic demand, industrial output grew very much less rapidly.

Table 6.1. *Hourly wages in manufacturing,*
1951–59

	U.K.	West Germany	U.S.A.	France	Italy
		1953 = 100			
1951	88	89	90	84	93
1952	96	96	94	97	98
1953	100	100	100	100	100
1954	104	103	102	106	104
1955	111	109	107	114	110
1956	119	119	112	123	117
1957	126	131	117	132	123
1958	130	140	121	150	128
1959	133	148	125	158	130

Source: O.E.E.C. Statistical Bulletin.

Table 6.2. *Hourly earnings in manufacturing industry,*
1950–59

(in pence)

	West Germany	United Kingdom
1950	27	35·5
1951	31·3	36·8
1952	33·7	39·8
1953	35·2	41·7
1954	36·1	44·3
1955	38·5	48·0
1956	41·9	51·8
1957	46·9	55·3
1958	50·2	57·0
1959	52·8	58·6

Source: O.E.E.C. Statistical Bulletin.

Table 6.3. *Hourly earnings and social charges in manufacturing*
industry, April 1959

$

	Hourly Earnings	Fringe Benefits Oct. 1958	Total Cost per hour	Fringe Benefits as Percentage of hourly earnings
Netherlands	·44	·13	·57	30·1
Italy	·35	·26	·61	74·0
France	·47	·24	·71	51·5
Belgium	·56	·17	·73	31·0
Switzerland	·67	·10	·77	15·4
United Kingdom	·68	·10	·78	14·0
West Germany	·54	·24	·78	44·3
Sweden	·94	·14	1·08	15·3
United States	2·22	·46	2·68	20·5

Source: First City National Bank, based on calculations made by Institut National de la Statistique et des Etudes Economiques, published in *Etudes et Conjuncture,* March 1960.

Table 6.4. *Hours of work per week in manufacturing*

(averages)

	U.K.	West Germany	U.S.A.	France	Italy
1951	45·7	47·4	40·7	44·8	39·3
1952	45·4	47·5	40·7	44·0	38·3
1953	45·8	47·9	40·5	44·2	38·8
1954	46·2	48·5	39·7	44·6	39·8
1955	46·4	48·8	40·7	44·8	39·9
1956	46·0	48·0	40·5	45·4	39·4
1957	45·9	46·5	39·8	45·7	39·3
1958	45·4	45·7	39·2	45·0	38·5
1959	45·9	45·7	40·3	45·0	39·4

Source: O.E.E.C. Statistical Bulletin.

Table 6.5. *Fixed capital formation in machinery and equipment*

Year	at 1954 prices West Germany		United Kingdom	
	DM m.	$m.	£m.	$m.
1950	11360	2707	1154	3231
1951	12500	2979	1185	3318
1952	13400	3193	1106	3097
1953	14800	3527	1162	3254
1954	17450	4158	1287	3604
1955	21450	5112	1416	3965
1956	22400	5328	1465	4102
1957	22100	5266	1562	4374
1958	23300	5552	1584	4435
1959	25700	6124	1602	4486

Source: O.E.E.C. General Statistics.

CHAPTER VII

DOMESTIC ECONOMIC CONDITIONS AND EXPORT PERFORMANCE:

JAPAN

IT is difficult to realise that Japan, one of the countries whose share of many import markets had risen so dramatically by 1959, had a mere fourteen years earlier been an economic shambles. In 1945 Japan lay in ruins. One-quarter of all the houses in the country had been totally destroyed; sixty-six cities had been subject to air bombardment of the heaviest kind—a bombardment so severe that half the houses and an enormous number of factories and commercial undertakings in these cities were completely wiped out. The physical destruction suffered by Japan during the war is said to have been equivalent to twice the national income for the fiscal year 1948–49.[1] Even by 1949, the volume of industrial output was little more than 37% of the 1934–36 level. The Japanese merchant fleet, the third largest in the world before the war, was reduced to a handful of coasting vessels, and the nation's export trade was virtually at a standstill. Indeed, Japan's export trade was more adversely affected by the war and its immediate aftermath than that of any other belligerent.

Before the war, and partly with the aid of the great trading houses, the *Zaibatsu*, the Japanese built up a vast network of overseas trade. In spite of the fact that the volume of world trade was declining in the nineteen-thirties, the volume of Japanese trade actually increased, rising by 83% between 1929 and 1937. By 1938 Japan was the fourth largest exporter in the world. The war shattered this, and even three years after the ending of hostilities in the Far East, the quantum index of Japanese exports stood at a mere 7·5% of what it had been in 1934–36. Japanese exports were particularly badly hit by the break up of the old empire, the loss of her position in Manchuria and above all by her expulsion from Occupied China. In 1934–36 China and Japan's colonies together took over two-thirds of Japanese exports. In the early post-war years these markets had almost entirely disappeared. For the time being Japan earned part of her essential flow of foreign exchange mainly by sales to American troops stationed in Japan or in Korea, and received a further part as aid from the U.S.A.

Growth of the Economy

Although industrial production in Japan recovered only slowly in the early post-war years, the picture in this field changed rapidly after 1950. The recovery in exports, however, was longer delayed and did

[1] *Japan Economic Yearbook* (1954).

not really get under way until after 1953. In fact, in Japan the recovery in industrial output preceded (and was an essential prerequisite of) the recovery in export trade.

The Occupation

The turning-point in Japanese internal economic affairs came in 1949, when the Dodge plan for economic stability was adopted. This nine-point plan, imposed on Japan by the Supreme Commander of the Allied Powers (S.C.A.P.) provided for a balanced budget, tight credit restrictions and a vigorous attempt to curb price increases. The Stabilisation Plan had a similar effect upon Japan as the 1948 Currency Reform had in the Federal Republic of Germany. It restored confidence in the yen, discouraged the black market and put a much needed emphasis upon increasing physical output.

A further impetus to recovery was provided shortly afterwards by the outbreak of the Korean War. Japan became the Far Eastern arsenal of the Free World. Expenditure in Japan on account of the United Nations forces stimulated the entire economy; by 1951 industrial production had reached the pre-war level; by 1954 it was 70% higher than in the nineteen-thirties. From 1950 onwards, Japan never looked back, and in the decade following enjoyed a more rapid rate of industrial expansion than any other manufacturing country, including western Germany (see Table 5.5, p. 72).

Apart from the 'shock' effect of the Dodge Plan in 1949 and the outbreak of the Korean War in the following year, several other factors played an important part in the recovery process.[1] Foremost among these was the financial and physical assistance provided by the Americans. After a somewhat hesitant start, during which the United States Government seemed reluctant to do much to get the ex-enemy on her feet again, money and supplies were poured into Japan on a scale which no conquering nation can ever before have provided for its vanquished enemy. Between 1946 and 1950 alone, the U.S. gave Japan direct aid amounting to $2 billion. This was apart from U.S. special procurement expenditures in Japan, on account of purchase of supplies, equipment, and entertainment of American occupying troops.[2] The United States supplied foodstuffs for yen, thereby enabling the Japanese authorities to conserve valuable dollars; through the Export–Import Bank substantial revolving dollar credits were made available.

Real Investment

A second factor behind the recovery of Japan was the consistently high level of capital investment in the economy—even in years when financial policies were stringent. Between 1950 and 1959 the amount

---

[1] For a discussion of some of these factors, see chapter II of J. B. Cohen's study: *Japan's Post-War Economy* (Indiana, 1957).

[2] See also G. C. Allen, 'Industrial Production and Productivity in Japan', *Westminster Bank Review* (August 1955).

of capital accumulation was in most years higher in Japan than in any of the other great manufacturing nations—including western Germany. Especially in the earlier post-war years, Japan had an advantage over the United States and the United Kingdom in that she made virtually no expenditure on armaments. The fact that throughout the decade on an average about one-quarter of Japan's national product was devoted to capital investment had a profound effect upon her ability to modernise and hence to export. In the early years much of the investment was devoted to the replacement of plant destroyed or damaged by war; the extension of capital followed in later years, and towards the end of the nineteen-fifties there took place in some industries the rapid replacement of even fairly new plant in order to reap full advantage of the most recent technological developments. Much of the capital development was channelled into the appropriate industries by the Reconstruction Finance Bank and by the Japan Development Bank.[1] There was some ploughing-back of profits, but not nearly enough to finance the capital needs of business and most firms relied heavily upon external finance. The Japanese commercial banks after the war tended to favour the larger enterprises in making loans—it is said that they were only too willing to lend to 'safe' borrowers, and these were usually the larger concerns which spent substantial sums on new techniques for rationalisation purposes.[2]

It has been suggested that a further cause of the rapid recovery of industrial output in Japan was the strength of domestic demand. The average Japanese citizen enjoyed very much greater purchasing power than he had before the war and this resulted in a buoyancy of demand for all kinds of goods and services. In part this was brought about by the substantial redistribution of wealth which took place in Japan after the war. Thus, in 1934, the employees' share of the National Income was only 38·9%; by 1955 it was 47·6%. This improvement in the relative position of the worker *vis-à-vis* the landlord and rentier reflects not only the increased bargaining power of the labour unions,[3] but also the effect of the post-war Land Reforms. It has been estimated that as the result of reforms in the system of land tenure, the real purchasing power of the average farmer was in 1954 twice what it was in 1934.[4]

It would be wrong to claim that official policy in the post-war period was deliberately expansionist. Indeed, in 1949, 1953, and again in

---

[1] See *Oriental Economist* (July 1957), for a discussion of the finance of capital development in Japan.

[2] Ministry of Foreign Affairs, Japan, *Exports and Wages. The Case of Japan* (1960).

[3] This bargaining power was of course largely conferred upon the Japanese workers by deliberate American policy in the early post-war occupation period. Before the war membership of trade unions never exceeded 5% of the total labour force in industry, and the right of collective bargaining had, in the nineteen-thirties, been conceded only in a very few industries. In July 1940, the Government dissolved all independent trade unions. For a discussion of trade unionism in Japan, see the chapter 'Industrial Relations and the Rise of Trade Unions' in G. C. Allen, *Japan's Economic Recovery*, Royal Institute of Economic Affairs (London, 1957).

[4] *Oriental Economist* (July 1957).

1956, financial policies were clearly disinflationary. Throughout the period the bank rate was high, and for most firms bank loans were difficult to get. Taxation, too, was markedly higher than it had been before the war.[1] Nevertheless, after 1950 Gross National Product in real terms increased rapidly, if somewhat erratically. Table 7.1 shows how rapidly industrial production rose in each year. In spite of recourse to austerity programmes at various times, the Japanese economy, unlike that of the United Kingdom, continued to expand. In this of course lies an important difference in the policies pursued in the two countries. In the United Kingdom, the authorities were imposing restrictions on an economy which was expanding only slowly. In Japan the restrictions, however stringent, did singularly little to damp down the rate of real growth. Certainly, a dear money policy failed to slow down the great technological developments taking place in Japan's newer industries. It is by no means so certain that this was the case in the United Kingdom. Japanese industrialists, too, seem to have had a vision of growth and its attendant advantages which British businessmen lacked. Perhaps the lesson to be learned from Japanese experience is that occasional recourse to disinflationary policies can be salutary, providing these take place against a background of long-term advance. It was the absence of such a growth policy, coupled with the frequent falling back on 'tough' monetary policies, which caused the British economy to grow relatively slowly in the nineteen-fifties while that of Japan—and of Germany—forged ahead.

Not only did overall industrial output in Japan rise rapidly, but the components of output were substantially different from what they were before the war. In the nineteen-thirties, over one-half of the total Japanese labour force was engaged in textiles manufacture; in the middle nineteen-fifties, the proportion had dropped to one-quarter. By 1956 textiles contributed only 18% of current industrial output. Whereas textiles had become relatively less significant, heavy industry (this includes metals, metal products and machinery) had increased in importance, and accounted for 50% of industrial output as against about 35% before the war. Clearly, the Japanese economy has shown a considerable degree of adaptability in adjusting itself to the changing pattern both of domestic and overseas demand. This is to be seen even within the broad sectors we have mentioned; for instance, within textiles there has been since the war a substantial switch of world demand away from cotton to synthetics. In 1955 Japanese output of cotton yarn and fabrics was 58% and 63% respectively of the 1937 level. Silk output was less than one-third of the 1938 level. On the other hand, by 1956 Japan had become the world's largest producer of rayon staple. In fact there was at Government level a deliberate policy of fostering synthetic textiles at the expense of cotton and silk. Government loans at favourable rates were granted to firms making

---

[1] In 1955, national taxes amounted to 13·8% of National Income, as compared with 8·5% in 1934–36.

synthetic fibres or fabrics, taxation concessions being granted to enterprises expanding their synthetics capacity.

Both the newer branches of the textile industry and also the older-established natural fibres sector installed a large volume of up-to-date machinery. It was estimated in 1956 that '75% of Japan's cotton spindles have been installed since the war; 91% of spun rayon spindles and 78% of worsted spindles are new, as is 81% of the rayon capacity'.[1] As we shall note later, Japan has had since the war substantial absolute cost advantages over Western countries in producing both natural and artificial textiles, especially the former.

In regard to some of the 'newer' branches of heavy engineering Japan has fewer of the cost advantages she enjoys in textiles. On the contrary, despite low wages, Japanese manufacturers of iron, steel and heavy engineering products are high cost producers. This is partly due to the heavy dependence of Japanese steel mills on imported coking coal and scrap.

In many sectors of the engineering industry, material costs tend to be more significant than labour costs in determining final prices, and in these fields Japan's comparative cost advantage is less than in textiles. There have been cases on record of Japan being underbid by German firms in tendering for heavy plant. On the other hand, especially after 1955, there was a marked improvement in productivity in Japanese heavy industry, and this helped to offset high raw material costs. While heavy industry—notably shipbuilding—played an essential part both in the recovery of domestic output and the development of export trade, it is perhaps in lighter industry that the greatest advance in productivity when compared with before the war was made. Typical of these light industries are the making of scientific instruments, cameras and transistor radios.

The Pattern of Export Trade

The change of emphasis in production from textiles to engineering (and changes within these industries) has been reflected in developments in the pattern of Japanese exports. Whereas before the war textiles accounted for over 58% of total exports from Japan, by 1956 the share of textiles was only 34·8%. Metals and metal products in 1956 accounted for 13·6% of exports, as compared with 8·2% for 1934–36. In 1956 13·6% of exports consisted of machinery; before the war the proportion was only 7·1%.

Alongside these changes in the commodity pattern of her export trade, there took place a substantial change in the country markets to which these goods were sent.[2] Before the war most of Japan's exports

---

[1] See J. B. Cohen, cited above, p. 65.

[2] Japan gained slightly from a favourable area pattern of trade after the war, but the commodity pattern of her trade was unfavourable, so that she did not reap the full benefit from the expansion of world trade which took place after 1953. For a statistical evaluation of this disadvantage, see P. R. Narvekar, 'The Role of Competitiveness in Japan's Export Performance, 1954–58', IMF Staff Papers (November 1960).

were taken by the countries of North-East Asia. After the war, Japan lost many of these markets and the United States, Africa[1] and India, became relatively more important. South-East Asia (and this includes the traditional British markets of India, Ceylon, Malaya and Hong Kong) was in the middle nineteen-fifties taking well over a quarter of total Japanese exports, as compared with under one-fifth in 1934–36. So far as the United Kingdom was concerned, the strongest challenge from Japan was undoubtedly felt in these newer Japanese export markets, especially the western U.S.A., India, and Malaya. By 1959, the Japanese share of the U.S.A. market in manufactured imports was 15·8%—an increase of over 10 percentage points since 1953. In India, Japan held 7·0% of the import market in 1959; in Malaya the percentage share was 27·4%, and in Pakistan 10%.

Export Successes

As for commodities, the United Kingdom felt the impact of Japanese competition especially in textiles, shipbuilding, scientific instruments and pottery. In made-up textiles (S.I.T.C. 656) between 1953 and 1959 the U.K. share of world trade fell by 6·5 percentage points; that of Japan rose by 5·5 percentage points. In fabrics other than cotton— that is, largely woollen, nylon, rayon and silk fabrics—the Japanese share in world trade rose by 14 percentage points, the U.K. share fell by 13·9 percentage points. In this S.I.T.C. group, the Japanese share of our Sterling Commonwealth Sample (see Table H) rose from 13·3% in 1953 to 49·2% in 1959. In cotton fabrics (Table G), Japan's share of world trade rose by 13·1 percentage points, the U.K. share fell by 10·7 percentage points. Taking the Sterling Commonwealth Sample alone, the Japanese share rose by 31·4 and the U.K. share fell by 31·2 percentage points. By 1959 Japan held about half Australia's import market in nylon fabrics; her share of nylon fabric imports into South Africa, although still much less than that of the United States, was by 1959 greater than the United Kingdom share.

Another commodity group in which Japan made substantial gains at the expense of the United Kingdom was pottery (Table W). Between 1953 and 1959 the Japanese share of the world import market rose from 26·1% to 36·6%. The U.K. share fell from 32·1% to 24·6% over the same period. Again, the advance of Japan was particularly marked in the Sterling Commonwealth—and in this case also in the U.S.A. and Canada. Very substantial gains were made by Japan in scientific instruments, transistor radios and cameras.

In scientific instruments, for example, the Japanese share of world trade rose by 5 percentage points between 1953 and 1959; in the Sterling Commonwealth Sample, Japan's share rose from 2·4% to 11·8%.

In transistors, the Japanese pioneered what was in fact almost a new

---

[1] The largest country export market for Japan in Africa is Liberia, but trade with this country is accounted for almost entirely by the export of Japanese-built ships to companies registered in Liberia.

world market; in cameras they not only broke new ground by developing a hitherto unexplored market for medium-priced products in South-East Asia; they also captured a quite substantial proportion of the old-established markets previously supplied by western Germany.

Japanese radios and scientific appliances are in no way inferior to products of other countries in similar price ranges. The Government of Japan has tried to ensure that quality standards are rigidly maintained in all exports; trade associations and the larger firms are particularly jealous of these standards. In 1954 the Japan Camera Inspection Association was established in order to secure an improvement in the quality and the reputation of Japanese cameras. The Association inspects all cameras for export according to standards laid down by the Japanese Government. In these and other ways Government and industry have combined together to kill the widely-held notion that Japanese goods are 'cheap but shoddy'.

There is no doubt that the war and the American Occupation played an important part in stimulating the camera and scientific instrument industries. Before the war, these industries were small, and their products of indifferent quality. The necessities of war gave an impetus to the development of all types of scientific instruments and the presence of the United States forces after the ending of hostilities gave a further incentive, particularly in the development of cameras and binoculars.

By 1955 about three-quarters of a million cameras were being made each year in Japan; about a quarter of this number were exported. The value of optical instruments exported was in 1958 ten times as great as in 1950 (Table 7.2). Cameras lend themselves to mass production but skill, manual dexterity, and patience in testing are enormously important in this industry and these are qualities with which the Japanese operative is abundantly endowed.[1] Accordingly, first-class workmanship and moderate prices have been the essence of the success of the Japanese in exporting these goods. A large part of their success, too, must be accounted for by the willingness of Japanese light industry to keep abreast of all technical developments, and by its speed in embodying in its products as standard features the kind of refinements which in many producing countries are regarded as 'luxuries'.

Wages, Costs and Productivity

Now there is no doubt that in certain industries—especially those we have been discussing—labour productivity in Japan in post-war years compared very favourably with Western standards. But money wages in Japan were still relatively low—and this was especially true of some of the most successful export industries, e.g. precision instruments, clothing and textiles (Table 7.3). The whole question of Japanese wage rates and their effect upon exports is, however, extremely complex and it would be quite wrong to draw too sweeping a conclusion from the bare figures in this Table.

[1] See G. C. Allen, *Japan's Economic Recovery*, p. 125.

Money Wages

Table 7.4, based on figures published by the International Labour Office, suggests that in 1957 Japanese money wages were about one-eighth of those paid in the U.S.A., and about half those of western Germany. This kind of comparison is, however, in the case of Japan, extremely misleading. Japanese wage rates were in 1957 almost certainly very much less out of line with those in other manufacturing countries than these estimates imply. In the first place, the monthly cash wage, upon which the I.L.O. calculations are based, takes no account of a number of supplementary benefits received by the workers and paid for by the employer. These supplementary, or fringe, benefits are extremely important in Japanese industry, especially in the larger, modern factories—which are the very ones which make the major contribution to exports.

In some cases workers live at very low rents in houses owned by their employers; where they live away from the factory it is common for fares to and from work to be paid, or for transport to be provided by the employer. Companies frequently provide medical treatment for the employee and his family in their own hospital; they run seaside homes for recuperation holidays and week-end breaks. One firm actually arranges for the installation of television at reduced rates in the homes of its workpeople.

Another difficulty in forming an accurate picture of wage rates in Japanese export industries arises from the great disparity in wage rates paid in establishments of varying size. Table 7.5 shows that wages in firms employing between 50 and 100 persons were in 1957 only slightly over half those paid in firms employing over 1,000. In firms employing less than 50 workpeople wages were less than half those in the largest firms. The most striking feature of Table 7.5 is the very substantial gap between wage rates of firms employing *less* than and those employing *more* than 1,000 people. Now the vast bulk of exports of all kinds comes from the larger firms, where wages are so much higher than in the small enterprises. This is brought out in Table 7.6, which shows that in 1957, in the case of almost all export commodities, well over two-thirds of total exports were produced by firms employing more than 500 workers. This weighting in favour of the larger unit was especially marked in some of the quantitatively most important export sectors—transport equipment (93% of exports in 1957 from firms employing over 500), steel and non-ferrous metals (83% from these larger firms), and chemicals and products (81%). Even in textiles, where concentration was less than average for Japanese manufacturing industry, over 60% of the value of exports was produced in the larger units.

Many Japanese toy exports are made by small firms, but for manufacturing industry as a whole this is the exception rather than the rule. Certainly almost all exports of transistor radios, metal goods, china ware, clocks and watches are products of the larger establishments.

Accordingly, an 'average wage' for any particular industry such as those shown in Table 7.3 might give little real indication of the money costs incurred by the exporting firms of that industry. On the other hand, while wages during our period were higher in the larger, export-oriented Japanese firms, it is also true that labour productivity in these firms was substantially greater than in the smaller firms which cater mostly for domestic requirements. Accordingly, real wage costs per unit of output in these export enterprises might in fact have been lower than in the less efficient firms serving the home market.

A study undertaken in Japan showed that although wages paid in larger firms were two to three times as high as those paid in smaller ones, the gap between productivity in the large and small firms was even greater (Table 7.7).[1]

Certainly the amount of machinery per worker was higher in the larger firms—as indeed one would expect (Table 7.8). What is perhaps even more revealing is the very much higher level of productivity per worker in the larger organisations. Table 7.9 suggests that the 'value added' per worker in the largest enterprises of all (those employing over 1,000 people) was in 1957 over three times what it was in the smallest firms. Reference to the United Kingdom Census Returns will show that in the case of the U.K. the gap in productivity between the largest (over 1,000 employed) and the smallest firms (10–24 employed) was very much less than this. Perhaps it was of the order of 10%. For the U.S.A. it was probably about 30%.[2]

Japan: Two Economies

In analysing the Japanese economy we are really looking at two quite distinct economies—on the one hand a highly efficient modern mechanised economy, geared to the requirements of world trade, and on the other a semi-feudal economy where money wages and productivity are low, and where modern methods of production have not yet penetrated. The situation in regard to exports is even more complicated, in that wages are not uniformly high in all export sectors. In steel and shipbuilding, for example, productivity and wages are high; in some lighter export industries productivity is also high, but wages are somewhat lower than in heavier industry. This is largely on account of the high proportion of young female workers employed in Japanese light industry. Traditionally, one of the most important causes of wage differentials in Japan has been the practice of paying women very much less than men and, in the case of both men and women, of paying by age and length of service. The pay of young workers—especially girls—is regarded as being little more than pocket money.[3] Accordingly, industries which by their very nature employ large numbers of

[1] K. Ohkawa, 'The Differential Employment Structure of Japan' in Annals of the Hitotsubashi Academy (April 1959).

[2] See Japan Ministry of International Trade and Industry. 'Basic Survey Report on Small and Medium Enterprises, 1957', quoted in Exports and Wages, the Case of Japan.

[3] See 'Japan A Low-Wage Nation?', Oriental Economist (February 1960).

responsible men (e.g. heavy engineering) have a markedly heavier wage burden than those industries—like transistor radios and textiles, where the vast bulk of the labour force consists of women. Throughout the nineteen-fifties the cash earnings of women were estimated to have been less than half those of men in similar industries; when one remembers that probably three-quarters of all the operatives in textiles and clothing are women, it is clear that those Japanese exporters of textiles who enjoy modern large-scale methods of production, a high standard of quality inspection, and relatively cheap labour rates, are in a well-nigh impregnable position, when they come to compete with Western industry.

Export Aids

In 1959 the Japanese Government was giving some direct assistance to exporters by way of tax concessions. A manufacturer of an exported product could claim the following relief in computing his profits for income tax: the lower of (a) 3% of gross export turnover in each account year, or (b) 80% of net profit from export turnover. Additionally, if the total income from export sales during a given accounting period exceeded the amount received in the preceding period, rates of tax allowance were increased by 50%.

Apart from these tax concessions, exporters received also what were known as retention certificates, issued by the Government to the organisation which actually did the exporting. These certificates, which were freely marketable and in fact frequently changed hands (at a premium), permitted the holder to import specified commodities to the value of approximately 3% of the value of the goods exported. The specified commodities included luxuries which could be sold at very high prices within Japan.

The Link Scheme

Apart from this general assistance granted to exporters of all kinds of manufactures, exporters of woollen textiles received an additional subsidy by participation in the 'link' scheme. The object of this scheme, inaugurated for wool in June 1950, was to encourage the export of woollen products by linking the amount of raw wool imported with exports of woollen products. When a manufacturer exported a woollen article, he received an import entitlement which permitted the holder to import a certain quantity of wool, the amount depending upon the total allocation of woollen imports to holders of such rights. Unlike the retention certificates the permit could be used only for the import of wool, and then only by the spinner. In practice the exporter could usually sell the permit to a spinner, or to an intermediary, who paid a price for the import entitlement, depending upon demand and supply conditions. Although the permit was issued in the first instance to the actual exporter, it was in fact shared by all the manufacturers and dealers through whose hands the product in question passed; thus all along the line there was some incentive to divert sales to export, or likely export, outlets.

The link system was important during the nineteen-fifties, although by 1960 there were signs that the Government was moving closer towards a free market policy in wool.

The whole system had in it an element of export subsidy, for a spinner who imported through a link permit tended to reimburse himself by charging a higher price on the domestic market than he received from exports. This was of course one of the reasons for the difference between domestic and export prices of Japanese woollen textiles—and undoubtedly a factor too in the success of the Japanese in overseas markets. The gap between domestic and export prices during the 'fifties was in some branches of the woollen industry as great as 40% or 50%, although in 1958 and 1959 it narrowed somewhat. There is no doubt that the link scheme stimulated competition between Japanese firms to obtain the available export business and this had the effect of encouraging them to quote even lower prices. Indeed, given the high premium at which link certificates changed hands it was often possible for firms to export abroad even when the proceeds did not cover marginal costs.

Table 7.1. *Index of Industrial Production: Japan*

	Manufacturing Industry	Iron and Steel	1955=100 Precision Machinery	Ceramics	Textiles
1946	22·9	9·9	7·4	17·5	14·6
1947	30·1	12·9	15·2	21·4	19·7
1948	36·9	21·7	21·8	32·9	22·4
1949	48·4	37·2	30·0	43·3	29·9
1950	59·2	52·2	27·2	51·1	42·5
1951	69·0	70·5	39·6	70·7	60·3
1952	83·9	71·7	51·4	73·9	68·6
1953	87·4	85·4	74·7	87·0	82·5
1954	96·0	89·4	94·2	99·3	89·6
1955	100·0	100·0	100·0	100·0	100·0
1956	111·9	121·8	124·9	121·6	118·8
1957	117·8	138·7	159·0	143·1	131·2
1958	118·8	130·2	163·3	135·4	117·7

Source: Japan Statistical Yearbook.

Table 7.2. *Growth of exports from Japan*

	Pottery	£m. Optical Instruments	Iron and Steel	Woollen and Worsted Fabrics
1953	10·1	4·8	49·8	2·4
1954	12·4	5·5	59·7	6·0
1955	15·0	7·4	92·7	9·9
1956	17·7	10·7	79·8	11·9
1957	18·2	14·0	74·8	15·9
1958	17·3	16·8	89·3	12·1

Table 7.3. *Average monthly cash earnings in Japan*

Industrial classification	Regular Workers								
	1953			1955			1958		
	£	s.	d.	£	s.	d.	£	s.	d.
All industries	16	11	4	18	9	0	21	0	8
All manufacturing industries	15	3	7	16	11	4	19	0	11
Food processing	14	1	9	15	11	6	16	7	5
Textiles	9	10	6	10	8	4	11	8	2
Clothing	7	16	9	8	14	8	9	12	6
Furniture	10	10	4	11	16	1	13	11	10
Printing, publishing, etc.	17	1	3	19	0	11	22	18	4
Chemicals	17	7	3	20	2	9	23	18	2
Rubber products	13	11	10	14	3	9	14	5	9
Iron and steel	20	6	9	22	14	4	29	5	4
Made-up metal products	14	17	7	16	5	5	17	1	3
Precision instruments	16	7	5	17	3	3	18	5	1
Machinery	15	17	6	16	5	5	20	8	9

Source: Ministry of Labour, Japan.

Table 7.4. *Hourly wages in manufacturing industry*

1957

	Japan	U.S.A.	U.K.	West Germany	Italy
Hourly wage in U.S. $	0.26	2.07	0.65	0.51	0.33
Per cent of U.S. wages	13	100	31	25	16

Source: International Labour Office and Ministry of Labour, Japan.

Table 7.5. *Disparity between wages paid by enterprises of different sizes in manufacturing industry in Japan, 1957*

Number of Employees	Percentage of Wage Rates Paid by Enterprises with 1000+ Employees
1–3	36
4–9	40
10–19	44
20–29	48
30–49	48
50–99	52
100–199	56
200–299	64
300–499	68
500–999	76
1,000+	100

Source: Ministry of International Trade and Industry, Japan. *Basic Survey Report on Small and Medium Enterprises, 1957.*

Table 7.6. *Percentages of Japanese exports of selected commodities originating from enterprises of various sizes, 1957*

Classification	Percentage of Exports from Enterprises of Given Size					
	Total	1–9	10–29	30–99	100–499	500+
Foodstuffs	100	3	5	7	23	62
Textile goods	100	1	6	12	18	63
Timber and wood products	100	3	12	25	30	30
Pulp and paper	100	1	4	6	9	79
Chemicals and products	100	0	1	6	12	81
Stone, clay and glass products	100	2	6	13	18	62
Steel and non-ferrous metals	100	0	1	4	12	83
Machinery, metal goods	100	1	6	15	24	53
Transport equipment	100	0	1	2	4	93
Other	100	6	22	39	22	10
All manufacturers	100	1	5	10	16	68

Source: Ministry of International Trade and Industry, Japan; *Basic Survey Report on Small and Medium Enterprises, 1957.*

Table 7.7. *Wage and productivity differentials in manufacturing industry in Japan, 1955*

Size of firm No. of Employees	Value added Per Worker A	Index (largest class=100)	Wage Earnings Per Worker B	Index (largest class=100)	B as % of A
		yen 1,000			
4–9	197	28	87	32	44
10–19	236	33	107	40	45
20–29	265	37	117	43	44
30–49	303	42	126	47	42
50–99	364	51	141	52	39
100–199	450	63	158	59	35
200–299	532	75	176	65	33
300–499	594	83	199	74	34
500–999	683	96	217	80	32
1,000+	714	100	270	100	37
Average	364	—	144	—	40

Source: Annals of Hitotsubashi Academy, April 1959.

Table 7.8. *Capital equipment per employee in Japanese manufacturing establishments, 1960*

Number of employees	1960 £ Capital per employee	As % of largest enterprises
1–9	68·5	11
10–29	77·4	12
30–49	90·3	14
50–99	119·0	18
100–199	164·7	26
200–299	207·3	32
300–499	306·5	48
500–999	404·8	63
1,000–1,999	593·3	91
2,000–4,999	681·5	106
5,000–9,999	553·6	86
10,000+	645·8	100

Source: Economic Planning Agency, Japan. *Capital Structures and Differences in Enterprises, 1960.*

Table 7.9. *Productivity in enterprises of different sizes in manufacturing industry in Japan, 1957*

Expressed as Percentage of Productivity per head* in enterprises of 1,000+ Employees

Number of Employees	1,000+ = 100
1–3	17
4–9	23
10–19	30
20–29	34
30–49	38
50–99	46
100–199	53
200–299	61
300–499	75
500–999	84
1,000+	100

* Productivity = Value added per worker.

Source: Ministry of International Trade and Industry, Japan. *Basic Survey Report on Small and Medium Enterprises, 1957.*

CHAPTER VIII

DOMESTIC ECONOMIC CONDITIONS AND EXPORT PERFORMANCE:

ITALY

THE share of world trade in manufactures held by Italy has never been large—at no time up to 1960 did it exceed 5%—but it grew quite substantially in the nineteen-fifties. Italy's share in world trade in manufactures rose from 3·3% in 1953 to 3·8% in 1957 and 4·5% in 1959. Although the impact of Italian competition upon United Kingdom exports was not as spectacular as that of western Germany or Japan, in the case of certain commodities Italian exports provided formidable competition to British products. Looking ahead, it seems certain that Italian manufactures will play an increasingly important role in world trade, if only in a limited range of products.

Between 1953 and 1959, the value of Italian manufactured exports rose from $902m. to $2,027m. This represents an annual average rate of growth of over 18%—a rate of growth exceeded only by that of Japan. The expansion of Italian exports was particularly rapid in machinery and transport equipment (S.I.T.C. Section 7); the value of exports of these products more than trebled between 1953 and 1959, from $282m. to $753m. By 1959 transport equipment exports accounted for nearly half the total exports of the engineering sector (S.I.T.C. Section 7), having risen from $94m. in 1953 to $359m. in 1959. Breaking down the transport division further, we find that the value of passenger road vehicles and chassis (S.I.T.C. items 732.01 and 732.04) alone reached $183m. in 1959. This represented a fivefold increase over the value of exports of these goods in 1953.

Exports of electrical machinery (S.I.T.C. division 72) were quantitatively of minor significance to the export trade of Italy and in 1959 accounted for less than 3% of total exports of manufactures. A substantial increase took place in Italian exports of non-electrical machinery throughout the nineteen-fifties, especially machine tools and office equipment. Outside the machinery sector, progress was made in iron and steel, exports of which rose from $35m. in 1953 to $149m. in 1959.

Exports of chemicals more than doubled in value. As regards textiles, the expansion in exports was less than in the case of most other categories of goods (this was true of all manufacturing countries), but whereas Italian exports of cotton and synthetic fabrics remained almost stationary between 1953 and 1959, exports of woollen and worsted piece-goods doubled in value. As regards the increase in Italian exports, engineering, iron and steel, and woollen textiles undoubtedly made the most significant contribution.

If we analyse Italian performance in terms of market shares, it is only in a very limited number of S.I.T.C. commodity groups that Italy held in 1959 a share of the world market greater than 5%. In this connexion much depends upon how a commodity group is defined. For example, in textiles as a whole, the Italian share in world trade was in 1959 less than 10%, but in woollen fabrics it was over 20%. In non-electrical machinery (S.I.T.C. division 71) the Italian share in 1959 was 3·8%; but in office machinery (S.I.T.C. group 714) it was over 10%. Clearly too, the Italian share in world trade in motor cycles was higher than in road motor vehicles as a whole. In footwear (in which Italy in 1959 held over 25% of the world market) the Italian percentage share was higher than in clothing and footwear together. The Italian export effort, unlike that of western Germany, was largely limited to a relatively few products, but in these products the effort was very vigorous indeed.

Nearly 50% of Italian export trade in manufactures is with the countries of western Europe and the United Kingdom. The prosperity of the Italian export industries is, therefore, closely bound up with that of Europe—in marked contrast to Japan. In 1959 the United States was slightly more important to Italy as a market than it was to the United Kingdom, nearly 14% of all Italian exports of manufactures being taken by the U.S.A. Canada, on the other hand, accounted for only a small proportion of Italian exports. Latin America was important to Italy, accounting for just on 12% of manufactured exports; the non-O.E.E.C. Sterling Area took only 8·1% in 1959. Generally speaking, the most vigorous competition offered by the Italians to British exporters was in some European markets—notably western Germany—and in the U.S.A.

Textiles

A good example of the way in which the Italians penetrated into the world market in a particular commodity is to be found in woollen textiles. The value of worsted fabrics exported from Italy doubled between 1953 and 1959. Table 8.3 shows the increase over the last few years in the value of woollen and worsted fabric exports from Italy, the United Kingdom, and Japan. In fact the Table understates the increase in the *volume* of piece-goods exports from Italy, since it is based on values, and U.K. exports consist largely of high quality worsted and woollen cloths; those of Italy are cloths made from shoddy and medium-quality worsted materials. So far as quantity is concerned, Italy became after 1955 the world's largest exporter of woollen and worsted piece-goods.

By far the greater part of Italy's wool cloth exports were sold to Europe—in 1958 as much as 80% by weight and value. The other market for Italian woollens which grew rapidly was the American one. Exports to Africa remained fairly static; exports to Asia actually declined between 1955 and 1959.

It has been estimated[1] that in woollen manufacture Italian hourly wage costs (including social charges) were in 1955 about 72% of those of France. In the United Kingdom, costs were estimated at 88% of French costs. This comparison almost certainly understates the wage cost differential between the Italian and United Kingdom woollen industries, for a substantial part of the Italian output comes from the country's cottage industry, where it is easier for employers to avoid contractual wage rates and the very high social charges levied in Italy.

The Italian woollen industry has been considerably helped (more so than that of Japan) by the progressive liberalisation of O.E.E.C. trade since 1953. But it is also true that since the middle nineteen-fifties the industry has developed in such a way as to take advantage of this freedom. The outstanding position held by the Italian woollen industry is partly due to the enterprise shown by rapid development at Prato, where were to be found in 1959 about half the total woollen spindles and one-third of the looms in Italy. About 70% of total woollen exports from Italy were in 1959 accounted for by the Prato industry.

Since the war, great strides have been made in bringing the whole of the Italian textile industry up to date,[2] but perhaps the greatest progress of all has been in woollens and worsteds. In worsted spinning, for example, there was after 1950 a reduction in the number of spindles employed, but a very marked increase in the industry's efficiency, as self-acting spindles were replaced by ring spindles.

WORSTED SPINNING IN ITALY

	thousands of spindles	
	1st Jan. 1950	1st Jan. 1959
Self-acting spindles	397·5	71·6
Ring spindles	345·0	542·8
	742·5	613·3

Although the total number of spindles decreased, the production of worsted yarns actually increased during the decade.

In woollen spinning, technical developments were less rapid, but the number of ring spindles was in 1959 about five times what it had been in 1950. In 1959 Italian output of woollen yarns was second in Europe, being exceeded only by that of the United Kingdom. Output was greater than that of either France or Germany, and in 1959 was about double that of Japan.

[1] Inquiry undertaken by the French Comité Centrale de la Laine, quoted in 'Britain and Europe', *Economist Intelligence Unit*, p. 210.

[2] See Roberto Dodi, 'Progress and Prospects in the Italian Wool Textile Industry', Banco di Roma, *Review of the Economic Conditions in Italy* (November 1959).

Engineering Products and Steel

Motor Vehicles

A sector in which outstanding successes were achieved by Italian exporters in the late nineteen-fifties was the motor industry. Production of cars in Italy quadrupled between 1950 and 1959, when it reached half a million vehicles. At the end of 1960 output of vehicles was five times as great as in 1950. In 1959, nearly a quarter of a million vehicles were exported—many of them were sold to western Germany, the market next in order of importance being the U.S.A.—a market where Italian cars competed directly with those of the United Kingdom.[1]

The factories of all five leading Italian motor firms—Fiat and Lancia at Turin, Alfa Romeo and Autobianchi near Milan, and OM at Brescia, underwent rapid expansion and modernisation during our period. By the autumn of 1961 Lancia, for example, were expecting to produce 200 vehicles a day from their new plant alone. Fiat were at the end of 1959 already turning out 2,000 daily, and further enlargement of their works was under way. In 1961 over 20,000 models of the Fiat 600 (later the 700) were produced every month.

Closely associated with the motor industry is the now famous Italian motor-scooter industry, the best known products of which are of course the Vespa, and the Lambretta, made by Innocenti. The Innocenti organisation grew out of a tube-making firm whose factory was damaged by war, but which after the ending of hostilities started production in new fields. The early post-war petrol shortage and the high rates of indirect taxation on motor fuels in many countries, followed in later years by the overcrowding of urban roads in all the great cities of Europe gave a great impetus to the motor-scooter industry. The success of the Vespa and Lambretta is almost certainly based on a buoyant home market. As any visitor to Rome or Florence will attest, the Italian streets are crowded with scooters. In the decade following 1950 very many Italians saw their real incomes rise enough for them to afford motor-scooters, but not enough to justify their buying cars. Incidentally, too, the Italian motor vehicle licensing arrangements encourage the use of smaller motorised vehicles.

All Innocenti motor-scooter production is concentrated in one very large and highly efficient plant. The plant was entirely new after the war and was designed for mass production methods. A cast-iron foundry is an integral part of this plant; and all tooling equipment is made locally. Over 1,000 machines, including scooters, mopeds and three-wheel trucks were being produced every day in 1958.[2]

Light Engineering

The way in which Italy has turned to good account her comparative cost advantage in certain fields is exemplified by the expansion of

---

[1] See chapter IX.
[2] *The Statist*, Supplement on Italy (March 1958).

Italian exports of certain light engineering products. Goods which require little steel, but which need for their manufacture the two chief natural resources of Italy—electric power and skilled workmanship and design—are eminently suitable as exports and are found in the light and specialist engineering sector. An example of such a product is office machinery. Reference to Appendix Table N will show that in this S.I.T.C. group the Italian share of the world market (10·2% in 1959) was not much less than that of the United Kingdom (12·3%). In the West European sample the Italian share in office machinery was greater than that of the U.K. By 1959, Italy was supplying over 20% of the French, and over 17% of the German import markets. Italy also held nearly 19% of the U.S. import market, an increase of 4 percentage points over its 1953 share, and was clearly a prominent and increasingly successful supplier of many Latin American markets.

There is no doubt that success in the export field followed the rapid extension of the home market in typewriters and calculating machines after 1953; output of typewriters rose from 183 in 1953 to over 350,000 in 1959. Output of calculators more than doubled over the period.

Much of the credit for the rapid expansion of office machinery production in Italy is due to the well-known firm of Olivetti, which make typewriters and calculating machines of all kinds. Olivetti have always been in the forefront of Italian industry in the modernisation of their factories, the installation of the newest machinery, and the provision of staff welfare facilities.

One reason for the success of Italian office machinery was the styling of the models. The industry has been most careful to combine neatness and efficiency and (like other Italian industries) has paid considerable attention to appearance.

This close attention to style is also to be seen in the very successful production and export figures for domestic sewing machines. Necchi, the largest firm making these products, made it a matter of deliberate policy to produce a domestic sewing machine which was also an attractive piece of furniture. Accordingly, they marketed elegant machines in two-tone colours which in style were vastly superior to machines made anywhere else in the world.[1]

Before leaving the question of the importance of styling in Italian goods, it is perhaps worth noting that this has been, above all else, the reason for the success of the Italian clothing industry.[2] It has, too, been of vital importance in motor vehicle production and export successes. The foremost name in motor car styling in the world is that of the Italian, Farina. The British Motor Corporation have made extensive use of Farina's services and many other motor car firms in various countries have been influenced by Italian ideas and styles—so much so

---

[1] See *The Statist*, Supplement on Italy (March 1958), cited above, where there is a useful discussion of Italian export trends.
[2] See chapter XII.

that half of all the cars being built in Europe in 1960 were said to have been designed by Italian stylists.[1]

Steel

Ten or so years ago, Italian steel output was of little account, either in world trade, or as a direct contribution to Italian exports. In 1953 the Italian share of world trade in iron and steel (S.I.T.C. 681) was only 1·4%. By 1959, Italy accounted for 3·5% of world trade in this S.I.T.C. group, and steel was making a very worth-while addition to the volume of manufactured exports.

When Italy joined the European Coal and Steel Community in 1952 her production of crude steel was a mere 3·5m. tons—as compared with an output of 15·8m. tons in western Germany, 10·9m. tons in France, and 5·2 m. tons in Belgium. By 1959, Italy, with an output of 6·7m. tons, had overtaken Belgium; a further rise in output to 12m. tons is planned for 1965.

The Italian steel industry has undergone a remarkable transformation since the war—indeed it is safe to say that the industry has been almost completely remodelled since the Liberation. Old plants have been extended and some entirely new ones set up. Foremost among the latter is the huge steel plant at Taranto; this plant specialises in steel tubes and already in 1960 had a capacity of 2m. tons. The remodelled Cornigliano plant was one of the biggest in Europe, and accounted for some two-thirds of Italian steel output.

From what has gone before it should be tolerably clear that a remarkable transformation has come over the Italian economy since the war, and this has been largely brought about by extensive factory and plant modernisation. Capital development on a very impressive scale has taken place.

The average income per head in Italy (somewhere in the region of £200 per annum) was in 1960 about half what it was in the United Kingdom. But, as one commentator[2] on the Italian economic *risorgimento* has pointed out, given the rates at which industrial output in the two countries have been rising in recent years, income per head in Italy might well be equal to that in the United Kingdom by about 1980. In fact, as compared with 1953, the index of industrial output of Italy had by 1960 increased by over 80%, about the same increase as for western Germany.

Development of the South

A great impetus has been given to Italian recovery by developments in the south. Since the adoption of the so-called Vanoni Plan in the early nineteen-fifties, the industrialisation of the south has been the declared policy of successive Italian Governments. Originally, it was hoped to bring living standards in the poor, agricultural south up to

[1] *Sunday Times* (1st January 1961).
[2] Paul Bareau, 'Italy's Economic Risorgimento', *Three Banks Review* (June 1961).

those of the industrialised north within ten years—that is by 1964. In fact this will not be achieved. Although the level of income per head in the south has risen significantly, that of the northern 'half' of the country has risen just as rapidly, so that the gap in the standard of living of the 'two economic nations' which make up modern Italy persists.

Much of the finance for the basic development of the south—iron and steel plants, road and agriculture, has been provided by the *Cassa par il Mezzorgiono* ('Fund for the South'), which is financed out of the Budget.[1]

Generally speaking, the authorities have followed a policy of providing in the south the infrastructure necessary for sound economic development, leaving private enterprise to finance the lighter industrial projects which it was hoped would be attracted to the region. However, firms establishing factories or branches in the south are given special tax concessions, cheap transport facilities, and low interest-rate loans.[2]

The industrialisation of the south, limited though it has been, has had two favourable effects upon Italian exports. In the first place a number of the larger industrial firms[3] have established branches and factories in the south; there they have received substantial assistance from the authorities and in this way costs have been reduced. Apart from this, wage rates are substantially lower in the south than in the north. Secondly, capital development and the improvement in living standards in the *Mezzorgiono* have in themselves stimulated industrial development in the already prosperous north.

Over the last few years Italian industries in the Milan–Genoa–Turin belt have enjoyed a steadily rising market in the south. This in itself has helped to create an atmosphere of expansion and growth throughout the whole country.

As in Japan and Germany, the Italian authorities throughout our period resolutely defended the value of their currency, using for this purpose the traditional monetary weapons. But at the same time, by their consistent encouragement of investment, especially in the south, they ensured that the long-term health of the economy was not impaired.

There can be no doubt that the Italian business community as a whole consciously aimed at sales expansion, both at home and abroad.

---

[1] There are several useful accounts of Italian development plans for the south. The question is discussed in the European Economic Commission, *Report on the Economic Situation in Countries of the Community* (1957), p. 356. There is a valuable document in English published by the Association for Industrial Development in Southern Italy, Rome, entitled *Summary of Measures to Promote Industrialisation in Southern Italy*. Another study from an Italian source (but again in English) is by Giuseppe di Nordi, 'The Policy of Regional Development: A Case Study in Southern Italy', Banca Nazionale de Lavoro, *Quarterly Review* (September 1960). A more critical view of the way in which development has taken place is to be found in an article by V. Lutz, 'Italy as a Study in Development', *Lloyds Bank Review* (October 1960).

[2] For details of these arrangements, see the Association for Industrial Development in Southern Italy pamphlet, cited in footnote above.

[3] One of the first of these was Olivetti.

I

The average post-war Italian exporter devoted a considerable amount of time and effort to design and technique; this paid handsome dividends, as the Italian export record clearly shows.

Productivity and Costs

The adoption of new techniques and the general expansion of output in Italy led to a very substantial increase in labour productivity. There were wide differences in productivity as between industry and agriculture in Italy, and part of the increase in productivity in the economy as a whole can be attributed to the movement of workers from agriculture where their productivity was low, to industry, where it was high. In 1957, the level of productivity per worker in industry was estimated to be about 45% higher than for the economy as a whole; in agriculture, it was estimated to be about 43% lower. Likewise rates of growth have diverged. It was estimated that between 1950 and 1957 productivity in agriculture rose by an average of 3·8% per annum, in industry, the rate of increase was 6·7%. But even if we eliminate the contribution to improved productivity resulting merely from a transfer of labour, the record of Italy in regard to labour productivity is still impressive.[1]

Wage rates in Italy were in 1953 probably lower than in almost all other West European countries, and after 1953 they increased less than in most other major manufacturing countries. Whereas in Western Germany hourly wages rose by 48% between 1953 and 1959, hourly wages in Italy rose by 30%. Nevertheless, great care should be exercised in interpreting any wages data for Italy, where social and other charges borne by the employer are perhaps the heaviest in western Europe. An illustration will perhaps emphasise this point. A comparison of hourly wages paid in the electrical engineering industries of various countries in 1957 showed Italian money wages to be 65% of those in Britain; if however, bonuses, paid holidays, family allowances, and other social security benefits paid for by the employer were taken into account, the cost of labour in Britain would have been slightly lower than in Italy.[2] It has been estimated that in the United Kingdom, social benefits added only 9% to the average employer's wage bill in 1958–59. In Italy they added 81%. There are also substantial differences in wage rates as between various regions in Italy. Taking into account the social security levies on the employee (these are lower in the south than in the north), the minimum wage rate for an engineer working a 48-hour week was, in 1958, 25% less in Reggio Calabria than in Milan.

Labour Mobility

There is a high degree of labour mobility between south and north in Italy. Although it has been government policy to take industry to

[1] For a discussion of productivity changes in the three sectors of the Italian economy since 1950 (agriculture, industry, tertiary activities), see E.E.C. Commission Report cited above, pp. 369 ff.

[2] Cesare Varnutelli, 'Topical Aspects and Problems of Italy's Wages Policy', Banco di Roma, *Review of Economic Conditions in Italy* (March 1959).

workers in the south, this has by no means eliminated the general movement of labour in a northward direction. Indeed, the Italian worker is perhaps the most mobile in Europe, both within and outside his own country. Unemployment has been high in most years since 1945—usually around 1·8m. out of a total labour force of 20·1m. There has also been much disguised unemployment in agriculture, petty trading, etc. On the other hand, as in western Germany, a significant part of the unemployment can probably be accounted for by workers on the move—those moving into the northern industrial districts, for example. This was reflected in a fairly high rate of turnover of registered unemployed. In 1959 some half million or so names of unemployed workers were added to the unemployment registers each month, but these were offset by the removal from the roll of approximately the same number.

'Cheap Labour' based on a reservoir of unemployed has possibly had something to do with the success of Italian exports, but this can be only a partial explanation. Also relevant are the considerations we have outlined—the skill of the Italian worker, the care taken by businessmen to think in terms of exports, and perhaps most important of all, an atmosphere of uninterrupted economic growth and advance in which capacity has kept up with home demand and in which home demand has seldom been allowed to flag. Clearly British businessmen and the British Government have much to learn from the enterprising, go-ahead attitude shown by the Italians.

FRANCE

We do not propose to discuss the export performance of France in terms of commodities and markets, but rather to examine the general background against which French exporters worked, especially in terms of domestic economic policies.

Up to and including 1957 French export performance in manufactures was mediocre. Table 1.1 shows that although the share of France in world trade in manufactures was higher in the nineteen-fifties than in 1938, the general tendency was for the French share to decline between 1953–54 and 1956–57. This lack of competitiveness shown by French goods was reflected in the serious balance-of-payments deficits which occurred in the early and middle fifties and which culminated in a severe gold reserve crisis at the time of General de Gaulle's accession to the Presidency in May 1958. There is no doubt, too, that the decline of the French share in world trade in the decade following 1946 would have been even more severe but for the privileged position which French exports enjoyed in the large number of territories which were still politically and economically associated with metropolitan France.[1]

---

[1] In 1959, total French exports of manufactures amounted to $4,176m.: out of this, $1,089m (almost a quarter) were accounted for by exports to French associates. France depends much less than Italy upon European markets. Latin America is less significant to France than to Italy; this is also the case with the U.S.A. market.

In 1959, however, there took place a remarkable transformation in the French balance of payments. From seemingly chronic deficits, the balance of trade swung suddenly into surplus. This improvement was due largely to a dramatic upswing in exports, an upswing which was more than sufficient to offset an increase of some 15% in imports. Exports of machinery and transport equipment, especially of motor vehicles, did extremely well in 1959. With the recovery in the balance of payments in 1959, the French share in world trade in manufactures rose to 9·2%, some 1·4 percentage points higher than at its nadir in 1956.

The December Reforms of 1958

Now the great improvement in the French trade balance in 1959 followed immediately upon a series of economic reforms adopted at the instigation of the special committee set up by General de Gaulle to make recommendations for the solving of the franc crisis of 1958. Some of the proposals of the so-called Rueff Committee which were adopted by the Government had a distinctly deflationary flavour about them. The Committee urged, for example, a drastic reduction in Government borrowing, which it claimed was the prime cause of inflation in France. Accordingly it recommended that the budget deficit be kept to the 1958 level (at the level of expenditure as earlier forecast by the Government the size of the 1959 deficit would have been twice as great as in 1958). This reduction of the deficit was to be achieved by a substantial reduction in subsidies and by an increase in taxation. The index-tie between the cost of living and wage rates was to be abolished, except in the case of legal minimum wages, which were to remain tied to the retail price index.

By themselves, these measures are reminiscent of some of the policies aimed at an overall reduction of demand, the adoption of which in the United Kingdom after 1956 we have criticised in this Study. But the policy measures advocated by the Rueff Committee and implemented by the French Government at the end of 1958 did not end at this point. Indeed, as well as having a 'damping' effect on some forms of spending, the measures had in other respects a decidedly expansionist flavour. It is in these other respects that we see the difference between the Rueff proposals of 1958 and earlier French attempts at disinflation in late 1956 and 1957. These earlier measures, however, had consisted largely of monetary and budgetary restraints.[1]

In 1958, on the other hand, it was decided that so far from being reduced, investment financing from public funds would have to be increased in the interests of adapting the French economy to face foreign competition. Secondly, whereas in June 1957 trade liberalisation had been halted, in the 1958 crisis the Government took the seemingly heroic step of liberalising the O.E.E.C. import quota to 90% and the dollar area quota to 50%. Thirdly, the franc was devalued by 17·5%,

---

[1] The comment of a United Nations source on these earlier credit restrictions was that they had 'failed to work'. *United Nations Economic Survey of Europe in 1959*, chapter VI, p. 26.

at the same time as France joined in the collective European move to non-resident convertibility.

Trade Liberalisation

The importance of the steps towards greater freedom of international trade and payments taken by France at the end of 1958 should not be overlooked. In advocating fewer and not more trade restrictions, the Rueff Committee hoped to create greater flexibility in the French economy. By easing import controls they hoped also to bring some of the healthy winds of competition to blow on the hitherto sheltered industries of France. Perhaps in most countries more attention should be given to the removal of import restrictions and the reduction of tariffs as instruments of disinflationary economic policy than has been the case in recent years. The entry of imports which have previously been obtainable only on quota has a stimulating effect upon a country's industry. Not only does the supply of goods reaching the shops increase and thus help keep down prices; new ranges of goods are introduced from abroad and domestic producers are provided with a powerful incentive to keep up to date in design and fashion. There is no doubt that the liberalisation of clothing imports into the United Kingdom, for example, has had an entirely salutary effect upon the attitude of mind of the British clothing and knitwear industry. In the same way the popularity of the Continental car in the U.K.—the Renault Dauphine, for instance, has helped keep British designers aware of the fact that even at home British styles are no longer accepted simply because they are British.

Moreover, the existence of an open market places a limit on the ability of manufacturers to pass on wage increases to consumers in the form of higher prices. It is wholly desirable that those engaged in wage negotiations should realise that if prices of British goods rise beyond a certain limit, even within the home market, consumers will turn to cheaper imported products. Such a 'long-stop' check to the wage-price spiral would almost certainly be more effective than the weary round of ministerial exhortation to which both sides in industry have become so accustomed since the war. We have noted earlier (p. 81) how Germany carried out considerable reductions in tariffs since the war, and how this was followed by an expansion of exports. The French recovery of 1959, too, suggests that import restrictions can sometimes be removed with salutary effects on the domestic economy. The experience of France and Germany together suggests that the British Government might do well to pay more attention to the whole problem of the tariff than it has done in the past.

The import liberalisation programme carried out by France at the end of 1958 was linked with the devaluation of the franc. While prepared to see the removal of some of the distortions in the economy created by excessive consumer subsidies and also to accept a tougher taxation policy, the French Government—again following the advice of the

Rueff Committee—was not prepared to defend the franc at the expense of the growth of domestic investment. Accordingly, it was decided that the moment had come once more to reduce the value of the franc, but this time it was hoped that the exercise would not need to be repeated. Judging by the recovery of the French domestic economy and the growth of exports in 1959 and early 1960, the franc was in 1961 in a stronger position than it had been at any time since the end of the war.

Modernisation of the Economy

There is one important aspect of the subject which we have not yet discussed, and this is the timing of the French recovery. It would be folly to suggest that all was wrong with France up to 1958 and then suddenly the light dawned; import restrictions were removed, domestic subsidies cut, fiscal arrangements tightened up, the franc devalued (once and for all) and as the result of all these measures the French economy once more became a model for all Europe to admire. In fact it is more realistic to view the French 'miracle' of 1959 as the fruition of the massive programme of domestic investment carried out in France over many years since the war. The chaos of the French public finances, the 'hot-house' protective atmosphere in which so many of her industries lived, and perhaps above all the recurrent political crises of the Republic veiled the very real technical advances which were being made in the French economy.

In order to appreciate the extent of industrial investment and progress in France—and the tenacity of successive French Governments in encouraging this development—it is necessary to go back to the early post-liberation years when the French authorities resolved to make a determined attempt to repair the war-ravaged economy and to make up for the neglect of the pre-war years.[1]

An essential instrument in recovery was the planning organisation set up in 1946, with M. Monnet as *Commissaire Général*, and known as the *Commissariat du Plan de Modernisation et d'Equipement*. The first Modernisation Plan, generally referred to as the Monnet Plan, concentrated on the basic industries of fuel and power, transport, steel, cement and agricultural equipment. The Second Plan which covered the years 1952 to 1957 paid attention to manufacturing industry, housing and agriculture.

The Four Year Plans are drafted by the *Commissariat*, aided by Special Commissions which consist of Government officials, representatives of management, labour and other interests. A draft Plan is submitted through the Economic Council to Parliament. When the Plan is approved, general responsibility for its implementation rests with the *Commissariat*. The *Commissariat* is not a separate Government department but works through the departments. It is charged with watching the progress of the Plan in every aspect—if all is not going as arranged

---

[1] Between 1929 and 1938 the level of industrial production in France fell 5%. For a discussion of the immediate problem faced by France at the end of hostilities, see PEP Study no. 345 (18th August 1952), *France, Reconstruction and Investment*.

it will look into difficulties and inform the Government of any factors which prevent the carrying out of the Plan. Progress reports on the Plans are made annually by the *Commissaire Général* who is empowered to suggest any modification which might be necessary.

The general aim of the Plans has been to ensure not only that an adequate overall level of investment takes place in the economy, but also that such investment is directed into the most appropriate channels. As defined by the law establishing the *Commissariat*, the plans are 'designed to provide an instrument of orientation . . . and the framework for investment programmes'. They are not intended to usurp the powers of any other authority and are certainly not aimed at replacing private enterprise. Their object is rather to ensure that the correct environment is provided for private investment, and that private investment takes account of the overall needs of the economy.[1]

In general the Plans have been a success. In the case of the 1952–57 Plan for investment the target of a 35% increase was exactly achieved. The target for the increase in industrial output was actually exceeded —the increase over the four years being 35%, as against an anticipated increase of 25–30%.[2]

The effect of the Plans was to co-ordinate investment decisions and to ensure that attention was constantly focused on the growth requirements of the whole economy. In one United Nations Study it has been stated of the Plans that 'they have played an important role in shaping not only investment but also overall economic policies. The objectives and policy recommendations have been given high priority in most government programmes.'[3]

Adherence to the investment targets as laid down by the Plans resulted in a consistently high level of domestic investment, particularly in the basic industrial sectors. It resulted, too, in a very much faster rate of growth of industrial production than took place in the United Kingdom, the United States, Belgium or the Netherlands (see Table 5.5, p. 72). Indeed, France maintained her rate of growth in industrial output into 1958, when output in all these countries was falling back.

The French have laid such stress on growth that they have tended to neglect the balance of payments—in this, of course, they have in a sense followed the opposite policy to that of successive British Governments since 1955. Balance-of-payments considerations, although important, do not need to loom quite as large in official decision-taking in France as they do in the United Kingdom. The French economy is much more self-sufficient than that of the U.K., and compared with

---

[1] Representatives of private industry help in drawing up the Plans and this gives them some influence on determining the general policy of the *Commissariat*. In general, the authorities make individual arrangements and contracts with firms who undertake to carry out development in accordance with the Plans. In return for their co-operation industrialists receive raw material allocation and finance. See *Growth in the British Economy*, PEP (1960), p. 222.

[2] PEP Study No. 445, *The Growing Economy—Britain, Western Germany, and France* (17th October 1960), p. 302.

[3] United Nations, *Economic Survey of Europe in 1959*, chapter VI, p. 25.

sterling, the franc is a somewhat parochial currency. Nevertheless, it is difficult to believe that there is nothing which United Kingdom policy-builders can learn from the experience of France. In view of the remarkable recovery in exports in 1959, it is difficult to argue that the French have been entirely wrong-headed in their insistence over the last fifteen years that re-equipment and modernisation must come first in some circumstances—before the balance of payments and before price stability. Perhaps almost everything else was wrong with the French economy in the middle-fifties, but the fact that industrial capacity was all the time expanding and becoming more adapted to the needs of the modern world produced very real dividends when reforms took place in other directions. 'The success of this operation' (the financial reforms of December) 'released a powerful spring that had been coiled during the preceding years of uncertainty, lack of confidence and export of capital.'[1]

Perhaps one of the weaknesses of the United Kingdom position since 1951 has been the lack of such a spring.

Table 8.1. *Italy: exports of selected manufactures by commodity groups*

$m.

	S.I.T.C.	1953		1959	
		Value	%	Value	%
Chemicals	5	87	9·6	210	10·4
Textiles	65	277	30·7	363	17·9
Metals & metal manufactures	68/9	89	9·9	277	13·7
Machinery & transport equipment	7	282	31·3	753	37·1
Cotton fabrics	651	45	5·0	32	1·6
Woollen & worsted fabrics	653: 02	52	5·8	105	5·2
Fabrics of synthetic & artificial fibre	653: 05	56	6·2	42	2·1
Non-electrical machinery	71	148	16·4	334	16·5
Electrical equipment	72	39	4·3	59	2·9
Passenger road motor vehicles	732: 01 and: 04	37	4·1	183	9·0
All manufactures	5–8	902	100	2027	100

Source: Board of Trade, London.

Table 8.2. *Italy: exports of manufactures by area, 1959*

	$m.	%
World	2024	100·0
E.E.C.	493	24·4
E.F.T.A.	350	17·3
O.E.E.C. combined*	931	46·0
United Kingdom	128	6·3
United States	280	13·8
Canada	24	1·2
Non-O.E.E.C. Sterling Area	163	8·1
Latin America	240	11·9
Other Countries	386	19·1

* Including E.E.C. and E.F.T.A.

[1] P. Bareau, 'Economic Miracle in France', *Three Banks Review* (March 1961), p. 9.

Table 8.3. *Exports of woollen and worsted fabrics*

S.I.T.C. 653.02

$m.

	Italy	U.K.	Japan	Belgium-Luxembourg	France
1953	52	188	7	26	31
1954	54	183	17	31	34
1955	71	196	28	29	33
1956	89	198	33	36	33
1957	109	207	45	42	35
1958	92	178	34	37	32
1959	105	180	47	43	34

PART II
INDUSTRY CASE STUDIES

CHAPTER IX

CARS AND COMMERCIAL VEHICLES

EXPORTS of road motor vehicles and parts are extremely important to the U.K. for a number of reasons. Firstly, in absolute value, exports of the motor industry, including components, spares and accessories, amounted in 1959 to £546m., about 15·8% of U.K. exports (including re-exports) for that year.[1] Secondly, both from the U.K. and from other leading manufacturing countries, in the nineteen-fifties exports of motorised road vehicles and parts grew faster than exports of most other manufactures. In the third place, exports of vehicles and parts account for a substantial proportion of the total output of the industry and changes in overseas demand have an important bearing on the level of activity not only of the vehicle industry itself, but also on a very wide range of components industries—the electrical equipment, rubber tyre and sheet metal industries to mention but a few.

A detailed case study of the motor industry is worth while also in that it provides a useful field in which to analyse some of the problems discussed in Part I. For example, one of the most interesting developments in the industry since the war has been the extent to which local manufacturing overseas has been undertaken by—indeed often forced upon—a large number of British companies. This fact has doubtless had a profound effect upon exports of motor vehicles and parts.

Another aspect of vehicle export performance was the way in which domestic demand in the U.K. influenced the exporting ability of the industry. The motor car industry should provide a useful study of the way in which changes in regard to taxation and hire purchase controls affect export performance.

THE BROAD PICTURE

In chapter VIII we noted that towards the end of the nineteen-fifties growing competition from France and Italy was felt by British exporters in certain fields. Especially in Europe and North America the British vehicle industry encountered vigorous French and Italian competition and one of the objects of this case-study is to draw attention to the fact that in the 'sixties competition from both these countries might be quite as serious as from western Germany.

Appendix Table S shows that for the S.I.T.C. Group 'road motor vehicles' as a whole, U.K. performance in the world market was rather better than in the case of most other industries. While the U.K. share of all manufactures declined from 21·3% to 17·3% between 1953 and

---

[1] In 1960 the value of exports and re-exports rose to £639m., which was equivalent to 17·3% of the total.

1959, in the case of road motor vehicles the U.K. share fell only from 23·4% to 23·0%. Looking down the last column of Table S, however, the reader will notice a very large number of minus signs, denoting that in almost all the important European and Sterling commonwealth markets the U.K. share fell quite markedly. In E.E.C. countries the U.K. share was 24·8% in 1953; by 1957 it had fallen to 15·4% and in 1959 was 11·6%. In the Sterling Commonwealth sample the U.K. share of the import market fell from 70·9% in 1953 to 58·5% in 1957 and 55·6% in 1959.

In the large and rapidly expanding import market of North America, however, the U.K. held its own very much better, and this accounts partly for the relatively fair overall performance of the industry in 1958–59. In the case of the U.S.A. the value of imports of road motor vehicles and parts from the eleven leading supplying countries rose from $53m. in 1953 to $865m. in 1959—an increase of such a magnitude that it makes nonsense of any comparison of changes in percentage market shares over the period. In Canada, the increase in the value of vehicles and parts imported was much less but since Canada was one of the most important import markets for U.K. exports of motor vehicles and parts (in 1959 it ranked second to U.S.A. and took U.S. $100m. from the U.K.), the increase in the U.K. share of this import market from 11·7% in 1953 to 16·3% in 1958 and 19·8% in 1959 had an important bearing on the ability of the U.K. to hold its own in these goods in the world market.

Table S is based on the S.I.T.C. group and covers passenger road vehicles, buses, motor cycles, trucks, chassis, engines and parts. Since in this case study we propose to concentrate on cars and commercial vehicles, Table S is supplemented by Tables 9.1, 9.2 and 9.3, which show the number of cars and commercial vehicles exported by the leading manufacturing countries to the world (Table 9.1), and to various important country and regional markets (Tables 9.2 and 9.3). Table 9.1 shows that in contrast to the picture presented by Table S, the U.K. share in the world trade in numbers of completed cars and commercial vehicles fell quite markedly after 1953. This contrast is perhaps an indication of the tendency of many hitherto substantial British markets for completed vehicles to become themselves engaged in the assembly of vehicles and accordingly to substitute imports of chassis, engines and components for imports of completed vehicles.

The trend towards domestic manufacture is well illustrated in the case of Australia which imported fewer cars and commercial vehicles from the U.K. in 1959 than in 1953 (61,000 against 82,000). By number of vehicles the share of the United Kingdom in the Australian import market for completed cars and commercial vehicles fell from 89·4% in 1953 to 60% in 1959 (Table 9.2), a fall of nearly 30 percentage points. The fall in the *value* of all motor vehicles and parts (S.I.T.C. 732), however, was much less pronounced, one of just over 13 percentage points, from 76·9% to 63·7% of the import market.

The World Market

Confining our attention for the moment to Table 9.1, it is clear that the greater part of the decline in the U.K. share of the world market in completed cars and commercial vehicles took place between 1953 and 1956. After 1956 the decline was much less pronounced. Moreover, up to 1956, most of the competition experienced by the U.K. came from western Germany, and there was a definite switch in demand from the U.K. to the Federal Republic. After 1956, however, the pattern of competition changed somewhat. It was now the turn of the United States to fall seriously behind in world trade; the fall in the share of the U.K. was much smaller (the U.S. share fell from 23·0% in 1956 to 10·0% in 1959, that of the U.K. fell from 28·5% to 26·0%).

Before examining the country-market pattern of British vehicle exports in more detail it is perhaps worth making some further general comments on the decline in the U.K. share of the world market in made-up vehicles, as shown by Table 9.1.

The failure of the United Kingdom to hold its share in the world market is partly due to a concentration of exports in the early post-war years on Commonwealth rather than on European markets. Unfortunately, especially since 1955, Commonwealth import markets for cars have grown very much more slowly than the European market. Not only has the rate of growth over the post-war period as a whole been relatively slow, but since most Sterling Commonwealth countries depend upon primary products for the foreign exchange with which to buy imports, their ability to import is subject to the quite violent fluctuations in world price of these goods (see p. 68). The Commonwealth countries, too, are the very markets in which imports have been the most seriously affected by the deliberate encouragement given by Governments to local assembly and mnufacture.

It has been suggested that in the earlier post-war period the Commonwealth was, for the long-term health of the motor industry, far too 'soft' a market. Commonwealth agents and purchasers were, it is alleged, willing to accept poorer service and longer delays in delivery than would have been the case in other markets. Thus reliance upon the Commonwealth lulled the British motor industry into a false sense of security.

THE COMMONWEALTH MARKETS AND LOCAL MANUFACTURE

Table 9.2 which covers the leading Commonwealth markets for made-up cars and commercial vehicles shows that the U.K. share of all these import markets fell steeply, except perhaps in New Zealand.

Throughout the Commonwealth the absolute value of British exports was in the nineteen-fifties frequently limited by overseas Governments' restrictions on the importation of built-up vehicles, often imposed for balance-of-payments reasons. For example, in New Zealand in 1958, the import of built-up vehicles was virtually prohibited; the Indian Government had a few years earlier restricted the number of imported cars to five or six popular makes and insisted on these being imported C.K.D. (Completely Knocked Down). These restrictions almost always act as a deterrent to the import of good quality vehicles in which the United Kingdom can perhaps best hold her own in such markets.[1]

The largest Sterling Commonwealth markets for vehicles from the United Kingdom in 1959 were Australia and the Union of South Africa, but by 1959 three times as many vehicles were being sent by Britain to the United States of America as to Australia. Not only did the number of vehicles exported from the United Kingdom to Australia decrease over this period but the United Kingdom obtained a much smaller share of the import market whether we measure performance on the basis of total value of vehicles and parts (Table 8) or whether we measure it in terms of numbers of complete vehicles (Table 9.2). Both tables show that western Germany made substantial gains at the expense of the United Kingdom.

Australia

By 1958 one-fifth of all cars and commercial vehicles imported into Australia came from western Germany; out of every 100 new cars registered seven were Volkswagen. Table 1.5, however, which enables us to make a comparison of the performance of motor vehicle exports with that of other U.K. exports in Australia, shows that the decline of the U.K. in the share of the Australian import market for motor vehicles and parts between 1953 and 1959 was only 13·2 percentage points, whereas for manufactures as a whole in Australia the decline was 18·7 percentage points.

It will be remembered that earlier we suggested that in some cases the fall in the United Kingdom share of a particular market might not reflect a failure of British manufacturers if identical products to those previously imported from the United Kingdom were being made locally in factories owned or partly owned by British interests (p. 44). The Australian market for motor cars gives us an opportunity for illustrating this point since this is one of the country markets where local assembly has become more important than in almost any other country and this trend has become of particularly great importance in the Australian motor industry.

Official encouragement of local assembly and later of manufacture has been the settled policy of the Commonwealth Government since the First World War, when it was stipulated that two out of every three cars were to be imported without bodies. Tariff action was taken to protect local manufacture at a relatively early stage in Australia, and as early as 1925 and 1926 the Ford Company of Canada and General Motors of the United States respectively had established chassis-assembling plants. Since the Second World War the Australian Govern-

[1] See *Motor Business*, Economist Intelligence Unit, 1960.

ment has deliberately encouraged the production of vehicles from Australian-made parts. In 1950–51, 74,837 fully built-up vehicles were imported; in 1953–54 the number was 26,481; by 1957/58 imports had fallen to 4,455. By 1956–57 only one vehicle in forty was imported in a built-up condition, and even of the chassis assembled in Australia more than 75% can be regarded as of substantially Australian manufacture. Generally vehicles were imported only where there was insufficient demand for a particular model to justify local assembly.

In Australia the sequence of events in the development of local manufacture was as follows.[1]

(a) Assembly from imported components using only a few standardised Australian parts, e.g. tyres, batteries;

(b) the wider use of Australian-made parts such as springs or shock absorbers, radiators;

(c) the local assembly of engines with body panels pressed in Australia, only the chassis components being imported;

(d) the final stage, the whole car being substantially manufactured within Australia.

Although British firms, especially the British Motor Corporation, played a much more active part in this process than their Continental competitors, Britain was a long way behind General Motors Holden Ltd, in which all the ordinary shares were held by the General Motors Corporation of America; 50% of all cars and commercial vehicles registered in Australia in 1958 were made by General Motors Holden Ltd.

The Ford Motor Company of Australia, owned by the Canadian parent company, was next in importance to Holden. For some models this company was still in 1959 importing major components from Dagenham, but locally produced components were being increasingly used and the company planned to produce a new all-Australian car in the near future.[2]

The largest British-owned firm operating in Australia is the British Motor Corporation which is wholly owned by the parent company of the same name in England. The Australian company was formed from the amalgamation of the Austin and Nuffield subsidiaries. The Austin Company had acquired its first Australian assembly plant at Melbourne in 1948, and Nuffield opened its factory at Zetland only in 1950. The company achieved an output of 50,000 vehicles a year in 1960 and sold Austin, Morris, Wolseley and M.G. vehicles and also B.M.C. trucks and Nuffield tractors in Australia. An Associated Company, Fisher and Ludlow, also owned in the United Kingdom, operates the pressed metal shop for the organisation's Zetland plant. Of the other firms with British connexions, Rootes (Australia) Pty Ltd, is controlled by Rootes Motors of England, but Australian interests also hold a

---

[1] See *The Australian Motor Industry*, Department of Trade, Melbourne, 1959, which has been used as a source for much of the material in this section.

[2] The Falcon 'Compact' range was in production in Australia by 1961.

K

substantial number of shares. The Standard Motor Company (Australia) Pty Ltd is a wholly owned subsidiary of the Standard Motor Products Ltd, and although the controlling interest is held in Australia, a minority share holding is held by the Standard Motor Company of England. The company began operations in 1951, with exclusive rights for twenty-five years for the manufacture of Standard and Triumph vehicles. The Australian content of these vehicles was from the outset considerable, and continued to increase.

Leylands Motors Ltd is a direct branch of Leyland Motors of England and commenced operation with the importation of fully built-up vehicles, but by 1959 all vehicles were imported 'fully knocked down' and Australian-made tyres and batteries were supplied to this firm locally.

Volkswagen (Australasia) Pty Ltd came rather late into the field, but assembly of Volkswagen sedans and transporters had commenced in June 1954 by March and King (Pty) Ltd; Volkswagen (Australasia) Pty Ltd, of which the parent organisation at Wolfsburg held 51% of the shares, was by 1959 in the process of taking over the factory and an extensive programme of capital development was being undertaken in order to provide for the local manufacture of Volkswagen vehicles.

It cannot be denied that British firms responded to the challenge of these developments in Australia, but they had little grounds for complacency in this field, any more than in the case of visible exports from the United Kingdom. Only one British-owned company, the British Motor Corporation, had at all a substantial share of the market, and the share of new registrations obtained by companies with British connexions was in 1958 less than 20% as against 32% in 1954. In all cases British companies had a smaller share of new registrations in 1958 than they had in 1955. The evidence, such as it is, does not suggest that the United Kingdom fully compensated for the decline in physical exports by adequately expanding the volume of direct investment in the Australian motor car industry. Indeed it points in the other direction; not only did the United Kingdom share of imported motor cars decline, but the United Kingdom stake in local manufacturing appears to have declined relative to that of the United States.

However, the significance of the sheer volume of direct investment should not be exaggerated; other factors, e.g. model policy, sales organisation, delivery dates also play an important part in determining the share of the market obtained by the overseas subsidiaries of any country.

Furthermore, Australian manufacturers—which of course includes United States, Canadian and German interests in Australia—were in the later nineteen-fifties paying increasing attention to overseas vehicle markets; and the ones where they were most active were the very markets which hitherto had been of first importance to the United Kingdom—the Union of South Africa, New Zealand (to which Australia exported 2,441 cars in 1956) and Malaya. Holden began to export to New Zealand in 1954 and by 1960 sixteen territories were covered by officially-appointed distributors in the Pacific, Asia and Africa. By October 1958 over 10,000 Holden vehicles had been exported from Australia.

New Zealand

In regard to the New Zealand market it is worth noting that although according to our tables the United Kingdom share does not appear to have fallen very much, the percentages are based on the exports of the leading manufacturing countries and these do not include Australia. Indeed, more Holden than Volkswagen vehicles were imported in 1959, and competition from the foreign-owned firms in Australia might well constitute a threat to the traditional hold of the United Kingdom on the New Zealand market.

During the period covered by our survey, local manufacture within New Zealand was not very important, but in 1960 the Department of Industries proposed to encourage production of motor vehicle components so that the New Zealand content of locally assembled vehicles would be raised from the level of about 30% to about 60%.[1]

South Africa

In contrast to Australia, in the Union of South Africa the gains of western Germany since 1956 seem to have been at the expense of the United States rather than the United Kingdom. This might well have been because of the fixing by the South African Government of a ceiling price for the importation of cars; this had the effect of shutting out many of the more expensive United States models. The British motor vehicle industry in the Union appears to have done very much better than most other branches of manufacture; Table 2.2 shows that the record of the industry compared extremely favourably with that of other engineering sectors. In spite of this, South Africa was the only Commonwealth market where western Germany had by 1959 actually replaced the U.K. as the leading supplier of vehicles.

As late as 1960, vehicle production in South Africa was restricted to the assembly of components, which were largely imported from overseas, vehicles assembled locally being much more expensive than similar models manufactured abroad.

The motor car industry has reported particularly vigorous competition by the Germans in other African territories and this is reflected in all the country markets analysed in Table 9.2. In the case of West Africa, the German effort was concentrated largely in one model, the ubiquitous Volkswagen, but in the Federation of Rhodesia and Nyasaland the figures for new registrations in 1958 show that 1,045 vehicles registered were Volkswagen, and 1,472 were Opel. Table 9.2 draws attention to the fact that in the last two or three years the French challenge became serious in West Africa; in Ghana the French share of the market was negligible in 1953 but by 1959 had risen to 11·5%. In

[1] See *The Commonwealth and Europe*, Economist Intelligence Unit, cited above.

Nigeria it had risen from zero to 9·7%. Except perhaps in Kenya, Uganda and Tanganyika, Italian cars had not yet secured a strong hold on the African market, but a serious challenge from this quarter was to come in the early nineteen-sixties.

THE UNITED STATES MARKET

We have already noted the very great increase in U.K. exports to the U.S.A. and Canada, especially between 1956 and 1959. Table 9.2 shows that in 1959 over 45% of the cars and commercial vehicles entering Canada were of British origin; in the case of the U.S.A. the percentage was just over 31%. In both Canada and the U.S.A. the United Kingdom had since 1956 improved its position *vis-à-vis* western Germany. The German share of the United States import market actually fell from 57·0% in 1956 to 31·6% in 1959, and of the Canadian import market it rose by only 3·5 percentage points.

In the United States market there was a striking upsurge in demand for foreign cars between 1956 and 1959. In 1955, only 0·8% of all car registrations were in respect of foreign cars; in 1958 the figure was 8%. The most remarkable aspect of this increasing desire on the part of American citizens to buy imported cars was the growing importance of small car registrations. These grew from 1·8% of all registrations in 1955 to 10·7% in 1958. Table 9.2 shows that the United Kingdom exporters took full advantage of the opening up of these new possibilities and the number of British vehicles exported to the U.S. rose from 38,000 in 1956 to 214,000 in 1959.[1]

Most of these imported 'small' cars which sold so well in the United States in 1958 and 1959 were cheaper than comparable U.S. models and they tended to be bought by American two-car families. They supplemented rather than took the place of the family's first car which was almost invariably an American one. In this connexion it is sometimes difficult for the European to appreciate the spread of car-owning in the U.S.A. The importance of the U.S. market for 'second' cars is easier to realise when one remembers that in the United States there were by 1959 more 'multi-car' than 'no-car' households.[2] Imported cars were generally purchased by households whose incomes were above the average. Before the advent of the American compact car, the imported 'small' car with its convenient size and handling characteristics was superior for town use to the average United States model—although the latter continued to be more popular on week-end and holiday trips.[3] As

---

[1] In the United States a 'small car' does not mean quite the same thing as in most other countries. In the U.S. it may be defined as a car having a wheelbase less than or equal to 108 inches. This formed a distinct sector of the United States market, where there was practically nothing between such a car and one with a 118-inch wheelbase, e.g. the Plymouth. The popular United States Rambler, the 3·4 litre Jaguar and the Mercedes Benz 219 all have a 108-inch wheelbase.

[2] *Fortune* (October 1959).

[3] For a discussion of the U.S. small car market in 1958, see H. Brems, 'The New American Market for Small Cars', *Skandinavinska Banka Quarterly Review* (April 1959).

regards price and performance, United Kingdom small cars compared favourably with their French, Swedish and Italian competitors (see Table 9.4).

Unfortunately, hardly had the 'small car boom' got under way in the United States when the American companies themselves entered the arena. The three manufacturers to produce cars to rival the imported small models were Ford (the Falcon), Chrysler (the Valiant), and General Motors (the Corvair). These are six-cylinder cars, rather larger than European 'small cars', and they compete more immediately with the Austin A99, the Humber Hawk, and the Ford Zephyr than with the Morris Minor size vehicle. The effect of their introduction and also of a changed climate in the American car market was a sharp downturn in imports of cars in 1960.

It should perhaps have been realised that the halcyon days of 1958 and early 1959 in the United States market could not last for ever, and the effect of the curtailment of the U.S. market on the overall export figures of the motor car industry in 1960 showed the danger of an over-dependence upon one particular market. Nevertheless the very substantial achievements of the British motor industry in the United States in 1958 did show what the industry was capable of, given propitious circumstances and sales drive. In this connexion it is worth noting that the British company which in 1959 held the lead[1] in exporting cars to the U.S. market was the British Motor Corporation, which had earlier carried out a radical reorganisation of its distributive network in the United States. As part of this effort, special emphasis was placed upon the development of an efficient spare parts system. It has been claimed by the British Motor Corporation that by 1959 85% availability of spares had been achieved; this might well have had an important bearing upon the success of Morris and Austin vehicles—especially in view of the widely-held belief that a highly efficient spares service was one of the essential ingredients in the early success of Volkswagen in North America.[2]

In spite of the ups and downs of the small car market, sales of larger and faster British cars were well maintained throughout the period. There will always be a buoyant market in the U.S. for high-priced and high-performance saloon cars from any country, e.g. Mercedes, Alfa Romeo, Jaguar saloons, as well as sports cars such as the Austin Healey, M.G.A., and Triumph TR3.[3]

Another field where U.K. performance was consistently good was the commercial vehicle market. United States imports of British commercial vehicles jumped from 361 in 1956 to 6,000 in 1959. Sales of German commercial vehicles were, however, well ahead of this—about 32,000 a year in 1959. As in the case of passenger cars, the American

---

[1] Value of sales of passenger cars to U.S.A. in 1959 was as follows: B.M.C. $663·6m.; Ford (England) $624·4m.; General Motors Vauxhall $330·4m.; Rootes Group $266·0m.; Standard Triumph $238·0m.

[2] *Printers Ink* (New York, 3rd July 1959).

[3] In 1960 some 55,000 sports cars were exported from the U.K. to the U.S.A.

industry supplies the bulk of its own requirements in trucks. The imported commercial vehicle market is a specialised one, into which the American industry is increasingly protruding, with light commercial vehicles derived from the 'compact' cars.

EUROPE

As in North America, the European market for imported motor vehicles has grown rapidly since the war, but here the United Kingdom was not at all successful in maintaining her share of the market. Table S shows that in road motor vehicles and parts (S.I.T.C. 732) her share of nearly all West European country import markets fell dramatically. In almost all cases, the decline of the United Kingdom share in the group was greater than for manufactures as a whole. Table 9.3 tells much the same story. In all eight major West European markets the U.K. share in imports of cars and commercial vehicles fell between 1953 and 1959, in some cases quite steeply.

The largest Continental markets for cars and commercial vehicles in 1959 were Belgium (which had no motor vehicle manufacturing industry although imported vehicles were assembled in the country) and western Germany. The growth of the German import market after 1956 was phenomenal—from little over 11,000 units in 1953 to over 152,000 in 1959. Unfortunately the United Kingdom (like the United States) singularly failed to profit from this enormous growth.

E.E.C. Markets

By 1959 Italy supplied over half the vehicle import requirements of the German market, and France held a share of over a third. In Belgium, on the other hand, Italian manufacturers failed to secure any hold on the market, which was shared by western Germany and France, the French having gained at the expense of the Germans after 1956. In Italy itself France held over one-third of the import market: the Germans held over one-half, and the United Kingdom share in 1959 was as low as 8·6% (as compared with 26·5% in 1953). It is, however, worth noting that in 1960 the U.K. again secured one-quarter of the Italian import market, partly as a result of the British Motor Corporation agreement with Innocenti, who assemble the Austin A40 under a progressive manufacture programme. In absolute size the Netherlands import market was much greater than that of France and Italy combined, the United Kingdom supplying over one-fifth of the 70,000 vehicles imported into the Netherlands in 1959.

Table 9.3 shows that in the Common Market as a whole, the U.K. share fell from 23·9% in 1953 to 10·2% in 1959. The decline in the United Kingdom share can be attributed in part to France whose share in the Common Market imports rose from 14·4% in 1953 to 31·5% in 1959, and to Italy, whose share rose from 6·3% to 24·9%. The seriousness of the decline of the share of the United Kingdom is obvious when we remember that total imports of cars and commercial vehicles into Common Market countries grew more rapidly than into either the European Free Trade Area or into Commonwealth countries.

Although the progressive reduction of tariffs within the Common Market might mean some diversion of trade from the United Kingdom the danger to the U.K. resulting from tariff discrimination should not be exaggerated. Cars are far from homogeneous in quality and specifications, so that of itself a substantial price margin might not be an insuperable barrier to maintaining U.K. vehicles exports to Common Market countries. In this connexion it is worth remembering that the average intending purchaser of a car is influenced by a large number of factors—style, finish and salesmanship as well as price. It is by no means certain that within a given price range roughly comparable cars will have to be priced at the same level.[1] In regard to the Common Market it is also worth noting that Jaguar Ltd, which make exclusively high quality expensive models, reported that in 1959–60 their exports to the E.E.C. had actually risen by about 10%. This firm had still in 1961 a long order book and experienced no difficulty in finding customers in Common Market countries. B.M.C. exports to Common Market countries rose in 1960 by 45% over their 1959 exports. The real danger to the United Kingdom from its exclusion from the Common Market surely lies in the fact that the E.E.C. arrangements will inevitably lead to greater rationalisation and higher efficiency of the motor vehicle industry within the member countries. Thus Germany, Italy and France will assure for themselves a secure and growing market for a very much larger output of vehicles than was the case in 1959, and this will enable them to derive further economies of scale—economies which will be denied to British manufacturers.

E.F.T.A. Markets

As regards European Free Trade Area countries, it is interesting to notice that in three of these countries, Norway, Sweden and Denmark, the United Kingdom share fell sharply. It might well be that freer trade within the area will lead to some diversion of trade in the motor industry from western Germany to the United Kingdom, but it should also be remembered that Sweden herself has a growing motor car industry and the Volvo is becoming a most popular car in export markets. Certainly the Swedish share of the Norwegian market grew considerably in the late nineteen-fifties, and the United Kingdom motor industry might well find herself encountering serious difficulties from this quarter. In 1958, Norway imported over 4,000 cars from Sweden, as against 2,570 from the United Kingdom. In Denmark, Sweden was less strong; in 1958 3,000 cars were imported from Sweden and 7,200 from the U.K.

[1] According to a survey of the highly competitive Belgian car market, the 'cheapest car in two groups of three roughly comparable cars did not have the largest share of the market'. See Economist Intelligence Unit, *Britain and Europe* (London, 1957), p. 139.

In Norway, Sweden and Denmark, western Germany had by 1959 secured the lion's share of the market.

In this country market analysis we have noted repeatedly the strong competition which came from European car manufacturers. This is in marked contrast to the pre-war picture, when the United States and Canada between them supplied 67% of the total motor car exports, as compared with 33% from all European countries.[1] This change was the result not only of dollar restrictions which made import from the United States more difficult in the earlier post-war years, but also of the development of a typical European product—a vehicle which was cheap and economical to run and readily serviced. These three characteristics seem to be essential for success in those growing motor car markets, where among all social classes a car has come to be regarded as a necessity rather than a luxury. These factors undoubtedly account for the relatively greater success achieved by German, French and Italian cars than by American ones in recent years.

There has been a tendency for Continental producers to concentrate on a relatively few mass-produced models—the Volkswagen and the Dauphine, for example. In the United Kingdom British manufacturers continued to produce a very wide range of cars of varying styles and prices, whereas the Continental makers concentrated on cheapness and low running costs. The production of a few relatively stereotyped models by Continental manufacturers enabled a spares service to be streamlined and it is impossible to deny that at least until the late 'fifties the after-sales service provided by Continental suppliers was better than that provided by British firms.[2]

DOMESTIC RESTRICTIONS AND EXPORTS

The motor car industry provides us with a means of testing the idea that Government-imposed restrictions had a favourable effect upon United Kingdom export performance in recent years. Now there is a strong feeling in the motor industry that, so far from helping export performance, Government policies actually hampered the efforts of the industry to expand its exports. It has been suggested that German manufacturers were less hampered by Government intervention than their British counterparts and that this contributed to the export successes of the German motor industry.

[1] See J. M. A. Smith, 'The British Motor Industry', *National Provincial Bank Review* (May 1958).

[2] Herr Thoenissen, President of the German Motor Vehicle Manufacturers, is on record as having stated that the prime reason for the lack of success of the Standard models in Germany since the war was the lack of supporting service. *The Economist* (27th June 1959). There must clearly be something wrong when we remember that in 1951 2,000 Vanguards alone were sold in western Germany and in 1958 the number of British cars of all kinds imported into western Germany was 1,853. Between these years the number of vehicle registrations in western Germany rose from 500,000 in 1951 to nearly three millions in 1958. On the subject of the after-sales service provided by Volkswagen, see *The Guardian* (5th July 1960), and for a discussion of the technical qualities of the vehicle, see *The Economist*, (22nd October 1955).

Up to 1959 the purchase tax on British models was as high as 60%, while in western Germany there was no discriminatory purchase tax on the British pattern, but a general turnover tax of 4% was levied on all internal sales and this, of course, included sales of motor cars. It is arguable that the high level of U.K. purchase tax might have handicapped British producers who, as a result of the tax, lacked a high level of home demand and hence were not able to take advantage of large-scale production. Perhaps, however, a more serious difficulty arose from relatively stringent hire-purchase restrictions imposed on the sale of vehicles in the U.K. over much of the period under discussion.

Now as regards the sizes of the domestic markets in various countries, some indication is given by figures of vehicles in use, which were as follows in 1959: the United Kingdom 5,080,000, western Germany 4,032,000, France 4,360,000, Italy 1,644,000. Using this criterion the size of the German market was smaller than that of the United Kingdom, but German manufacturers produced on a larger scale than was possible for United Kingdom manufacturers. In 1959, 1,719,000 cars and commercial vehicles were produced in western Germany, as against 1,560,000 in the United Kingdom. Figures for France and Italy were 1,283,000 and 501,000 respectively (see Table 9.5).

The motor industries of western Germany, Italy, and France, all grew more rapidly than that of the United Kingdom during the period of our survey, although of course from a much lower level, and psychologically this almost certainly had an influence on the whole attitude of the industry in European countries. The importance of growth psychology among industrialists as a means to spurring them on to new ideas and progressive designing is something which has been overlooked in postwar Britain.

It is, however, debatable whether the Government alone is to be blamed for the fact that the British motor industry did not grow faster during the critical middle nineteen-fifties. The relatively slow growth rate might have been as much due to the lack of appealing designs as to sheer inability to produce on a sufficiently large scale. Nevertheless, firms might have been more willing to lay down bigger plants if the Government had not inhibited long-term growth by having recourse so frequently to discriminatory restrictions—ones which hit the motor industry particularly hard. It is not possible to prove that if the Government had eschewed altogether discriminatory hire purchase restrictions, the motor industry would thereby have sold more vehicles at home, reduced its unit costs, and thereby increased exports. But it is possible to look, as it were, at the negative side of this problem, and to ask whether the restrictions did in fact cause more cars to be exported than would have been the case in the absence of such restrictions. An important justification for the imposition of discriminatory restrictions must surely be that such restrictions do cause supplies to be diverted from the domestic to the export market. The evidence we have assembled in the remainder of this chapter suggests that this was not the case in the period 1953–59.

The Scale of Output

The problem of deciding what is the optimum scale of output in any industry is a complicated one, but it was suggested by Maxcy and Silberston[1] in their study of the motor industry that no British motor firm had attained the fullest possible economies of large-scale production. They suggest that most of the possible technical economies of scale could be obtained with an annual production of 500,000 nearly identical vehicles. At the time of writing they doubted whether any single U.K. model was produced on a scale of over 100,000 per annum; by contrast Volkswagen produced 497,585 vehicles (in 1958) and, of course, all these models were virtually identical. In the same year Renault produced 367,673 models, and of these a very large number were Dauphines.[2]

From these figures it might be inferred that a reduction in the level of purchase tax or an easing of hire purchase restrictions in the nineteen-fifties might have had a favourable effect on the cost structure of the British motor car industry. Undoubtedly the prospect of a large home market might well have encouraged many manufacturers to make development plans on a vaster scale than was in fact the case. This, theoretically, would have enabled many firms to approach more nearly the scale of output enjoyed by Volkswagen in Germany and to a lesser extent by Renault in France. In the circumstances of the nineteen-fifties, however, a reduction in taxation would not *in itself* have created the conditions for such an advance.

At times during the period there was a grave steel shortage, and unless steel development plans had been speeded up to keep step with motor car production schedules a most acute raw material problem would have beset the industry. Moreover, in the traditional vehicle manufacturing Midlands labour was scarce, and a long-term increase in the output of vehicles might well have been held up for shortage of skilled labour. The extension of plant in areas where there was relatively high unemployment, for example Northern Ireland, and in the North-east would undoubtedly have resulted in increasing marginal costs.

Moreover, while purchase tax was higher in the United Kingdom than on the Continent this is not the same thing as saying that in regard to the tax burden as a whole United Kingdom car manufacturers laboured

---

[1] G. Maxcy and A. Silberston, *The Motor Industry*, Allen and Unwin (London, 1959).

[2] Of course the economies of scale obtained by a single company are greater than can be inferred from the number of any particular model they produce, because many parts are common to a number of models. It might also be added that many operations on the conveyor belt are identical, whatever the run of models being produced; for many stages of production it matters little whether sports cars, saloon cars or trucks are being assembled. Indeed on a single B.M.C. assembly line one can usually see a series of four or five different types of vehicles being run off.

under a net disadvantage *vis-à-vis* their Continental rivals. While indirect taxation raised the purchase price of British-built vehicles more
than that of Continental competitors, fuel taxes were substantially
higher in France and Italy than in the United Kingdom, and the total
weight of taxation on motoring was probably at least as high in France,
Italy and western Germany as in Great Britain.[1] Measured like this it
seems unlikely that in the field of taxation the export effort of the British
motor car industry suffered more than that of its Continental counterparts. On the other hand the intending purchaser of a motor car does
not concern himself so much with long-run taxation charges as with
initial purchase tax rates and hire-purchase facilities. There can be no
doubt that under these heads, particularly the latter, British manufacturers suffered more from official discrimination against their industry
than their Continental rivals.

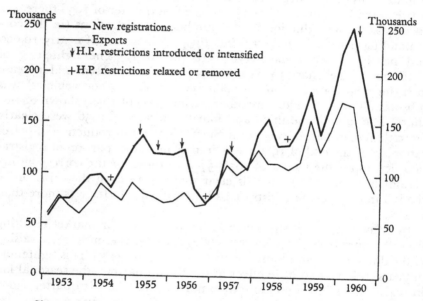

Chart 2. New registrations and exports of passenger cars (quarterly totals)

Hire-Purchase Arrangements

Chart 2 shows that quite apart from the seasonal pattern there were
marked variations in numbers of passenger car registrations in the
United Kingdom. These fluctuations were in part associated with
changes in the hire-purchase arrangements relating to sales of motor cars
(see Table 9.6).

[1] The Society of Motor Manufacturers and Traders estimated that in 1954 the total tax
burden on a 1,500 c.c. car over 80,000 miles with a life of eight years amounted to about
£86 per annum. Comparable figures for the United States were £18, for western Germany
£92 and for Italy £104 (*The Motor Industry in Great Britain*, 1954, p. 298).

At the beginning of 1955 there were no hire-purchase restrictions on passenger cars (earlier restrictions having been removed in July 1954). In February, however, a minimum deposit of 15% was required against hire-purchase transactions in private motor vehicles and the maximum period of repayment was fixed at two years. These requirements were stiffened in July 1955, when the minimum deposit was raised to 33⅓%, and again in February 1956 when it was fixed at 50%. In spite of the February restrictions registrations reached a post-war peak in the second quarter of 1955, and even after the increase in the down-payment requirement in July, the drop in registrations between the second and third quarters might be looked upon as little more than seasonal. However, whereas in 1953 and 1954 the fourth quarter had shown a more favourable pattern than the third quarter, in 1955 there was some falling away in registrations in the final three months. More definite signs of the effectiveness of controls can be seen in the fact that between the last quarter of 1955 and the first quarter of 1956 there was an unmistakable reduction in the number of registrations (in the corresponding periods in 1953–54 and 1954–55 increases of nearly 10,000 and nearly 20,000 respectively were recorded). The tightening of restrictions in February 1956 did not prevent the usual seasonal increase in spring registrations, but the increase (less than 4,000 vehicles) was substantially less than for any other period (except 1954) shown on our chart. The falls in the third and fourth quarters of 1956 were clearly more than seasonal; of course the Suez crisis and introduction of petrol rationing at the end of 1956 make impossible a comparison of registration figures for the winter of 1956–57 with those for the corresponding period in other years, but it is clear that before even the crisis broke the fall in numbers of registrations in the third quarter was more than seasonal.

By May 1957 the disturbance to the passenger car market resulting from the Suez difficulties was largely over and this month saw a raising of the down-payment requirements from 20% to 33⅓%. This tightening appears to have had little effect in the third quarter—the seasonal fall in registrations being no more than normal, but the last quarter shows a quite marked fall—of about 10,000 registrations. Hire-purchase restrictions remained stringent until October 1958 (when they were lifted altogether), but in spite of this, registrations for the second and third quarters were at what was for that time a record level. Presumably, by the spring of 1958 would-be car owners had been able to save enough to put down the required one-third deposit of the purchase price. The reimposition of hire-purchase controls (20% down-payments and a maximum period for repayments of two years) in April 1960 was followed by what was surely a more than seasonal fall in the third and fourth quarters—a fall of 52,000 in the third quarter followed by one of 56,000 in the fourth quarter.

Reviewing the effect of hire-purchase restrictions, it seems clear that between 1953 and 1960 there were three periods when tightening of restrictions led to a fall in registrations: (1) the end of 1955 and most of 1956; (2) the end of 1957; (3) the second half of 1960.[1]

Now the disturbance to production from the imposition of these controls might have been justified if *either* cars which were not saleable on the home market were in fact diverted to the export field *or* if the motor industry had, as the result of restricted home demand, released labour for employment in export industries. In the case of the motor car industry neither of these desired consequences followed the tightening of restrictions.

What we might call the adverse hire-purchase effect on domestic sales was non-existent in the second half of 1954, and at its most stringent in the second half of 1955 and throughout 1956. Exports of new motor cars were, however, higher in both the third and fourth quarters of 1954 than in the corresponding periods in 1955 and 1956! The restrictions imposed in February 1955 cannot have had much effect upon the export figures for the first quarter of 1955 and this period might therefore be regarded as a 'pre-control' one; by the first quarter of 1956 one would expect the effects of domestic restrictions to have done their work in stimulating exports. Yet in the period January–March 1955, 90,630 new motor cars were exported, as against 73,554 in the corresponding period of 1956 and 85,631 in the first quarter of 1957!

It is difficult to interpret the export figures for 1957. The loosening of restrictions at the end of 1956 was made in view of the fall in home demand caused by petrol rationing and the surcharge on motor spirit: exports in the first quarter rose by 15,000 vehicles—an increase of unprecedented magnitude for this quarter; it would be dangerous to draw any substantial conclusion from this fact. The tightening of controls in May 1957 failed to prevent exports falling in accordance with the seasonal pattern between the second and third quarters of 1957, but while there was a more than seasonal fall in home registrations in the fourth quarter of 1957, there was a quite unseasonal increase in exports in this quarter. Possibly we have here a case of hire-purchase restrictions aiding the export effort by the deliberate damping down of home demand and the stimulation of exports. If this is indeed a case of the scissors effect at work (home registrations down, exports up) it must be almost the only case we can find in the period. For the evidence of Chart 2 is that domestic registrations and exports tended to move together. This is clearly seen in the last two years covered by our chart. Throughout 1959 and until April 1960, there were no hire-purchase restrictions on motor vehicles. Home demand rose to record heights—yet so did exports. The highest export figures for the post-war period were achieved in the first two quarters of 1960—yet these were the very

---

[1] It is noteworthy that in each of these three cases restrictions were made more harsh at the beginning of the year, but the effect on registrations was not clearly apparent until after the seasonal spring peaks had been passed. This is, after all, what one might expect for many people who had planned to purchase a car for the holiday season would probably make sacrifices in other directions in order to raise the necessary deposit. With the onset of autumn fewer people would be prepared to put the purchase of a car so high on their list of priorities.

quarters when home registrations too reached record levels. After mid-1960, home demand fell—and so did exports. We have to go back to 1956 to find a year when exports for the second half of the year were lower than they were in the second half of 1960.

The fact is that U.K. export performance in motor vehicles depends very much more on what is going on in overseas markets than on the degree of tightness of domestic restrictions. Thus, in 1956 and again in 1958, U.K. exports of motor vehicles fell away—but this was largely due to import restrictions imposed in some of the United Kingdom's major overseas markets—Australia, New Zealand, the Union of South Africa. The export achievements of the industry in 1959 and early 1960 were largely concentrated in North America and were partly due to a change in U.S.A. demand towards smaller imported cars. It would, of course, be possible to argue that had it not been for restrictions imposed in 1957 British motor manufacturers would never have had the incentive to fight their way into the North American market in 1958 and 1959. There might be something in this, but it should also be remembered that the substantial increase in British sales of cars and commercial vehicles to the U.S.A. took place in 1959—at the very time when hire-purchase controls on the domestic market were entirely absent.[1]

The very striking drop in British exports of cars in the third and fourth quarters of 1960 (almost wholly accounted for by the decrease in sales to the U.S.A.) coincided with an equally severe drop in domestic deliveries. In spite of every incentive to expand sales overseas—sluggish demand at home, reimposition of hire-purchase controls in April 1960, and continued exhortations to export—the motor industry in late 1960 seemed unable to create for itself new openings overseas.

The evidence from this survey of domestic hire-purchase restrictions is clearly limited and ambiguous. But, to say the least, it sheds considerable doubt on the view that by turning the screw on the home market the authorities helped manufacturers to expand exports. Indeed, it could be argued that by artificially limiting home demand on at least three occasions since 1953 the authorities probably on balance hindered rather than helped the industry's export effort. Certainly the curtailment of home demand is likely to have led to a slowing down of innovation in plant and of the development of new manufacturing techniques.

One further point must, however, be considered. Even if discriminatory domestic controls do not actually directly encourage exports, they might, by their effect upon home output, release labour for employment in industries which *can* sell their products overseas. So far as one can see this has not happened in the case of the motor industry, which has been understandably notorious for holding on to its labour force even when seriously affected by recession. Employers, anticipating

[1] British sales of cars to the United States were 20,991 in 1955, rising to 94,867 in 1957, 152,527 in 1958, and 208,139 in 1959.

recovery of demand, are reluctant to part with labour; the workers on their part are prepared to accept occasional short-time working as the price of the high average wages they can earn in the industry.

CONCLUSIONS

Our conclusion must be that high rates of purchase tax and discriminatory hire-purchase restrictions in the nineteen-fifties neither provided a direct stimulus to exports nor brought about a substantial diversion of labour into other industries. Indeed, the 'off-on' nature of fiscal and hire-purchase changes created a wholly undesirable atmosphere of uncertainty in the industry and this almost certainly militated against, rather than aided, that expansion of output which was so essential to successful export effort. As Table 9.5 shows, since 1955 the German motor industry grew faster than that of Great Britain.

In view of the importance of long-term planning in the motor industry it is certain that if the authorities are proposing to resort to discriminatory restrictive measures as frequently as they did in the period we have reviewed, there is less chance of long-term reduction in unit costs being secured than if a steady growth in output takes place. In this connexion difficulties have been created not only by the discriminatory controls directed against the motor industry, but also by the lack of growth of the whole economy in recent years.

If industrial output in the United Kingdom had grown anywhere near as fast and as steadily as in western Germany, France and Italy, the motor industry would have been able to have absorbed rates of purchase tax ruling in the period of 1953–60 (which most people regarded as being necessary for revenue purposes), and still have been able to sell enough cars to reduce costs. On the export side, too, it must not be forgotten that the United Kingdom recession of 1958 had an indisputably adverse effect upon the Outer Sterling Area's earnings and in particular this affected some of the United Kingdom's largest vehicle markets. In the case of the motor industry at least, the effect of the well-meaning attempts to protect the balance of payments in 1957 had a most unfortunate side effect upon export performance. Policies of successive Governments can hardly have helped the British motor industry.

On the other hand, in some important respects domestic economic policies followed by their Governments might well have aided Continental car manufacturers. It has been suggested that the Continental Governments gave more generous export incentives to their motor car manufacturers than was done in Great Britain. In Germany, for example, export goods were not subject to turnover tax but since the tax had already been paid at various points on materials embodied in the final export product, a rebate ranging from 0·5% was payable on all goods exported. In addition the export-merchant had a tax incentive, represented by the export-merchant grant which amounted to between

0·25% and 4% of the sale price of the goods exported. Furthermore a remission of direct taxation amounting to 3·5% of export turnover was allowed to the manufacturer.

In France all manufacturers paid a social security and wage tax, and exporters could claim reimbursement of these taxes paid on export turnover. The taxes were quite substantial and might have amounted to as much as 30% of an employer's wage bill (1959); thus the bounty on export could be quite considerable.

These taxation measures were of themselves unlikely to be of critical importance in determining relative export performance, but they reinforced the generally more favourable export climate which we have described (pp. 73–84 and 99–113) in Continental countries.[1]

While Continental governments almost certainly smoothed the path of exporters by adopting appropriate policies in regard to export, the fact remains that such measures cannot be a substitute for first-class salesmanship and much of the credit for the expansion of Continental exports of motor cars must go to the vigorous salesmanship shown by the larger Continental manufacturers. That this is the case few British manufacturers would deny.

Nevertheless, the long-term export outlook for the British motor industry is not perhaps as gloomy as might appear from this study. We have seen that much of the success of Continental makers was due to their concentration on a very small range of models. These models will not last for ever and sooner or later newer models will have to be introduced, entailing heavy re-tooling costs and creating problems in regard to spares and servicing. Moreover, as incomes rise it is possible that purchasers will lay more stress on novelty and variety in their requirements and less on sheer 'toughness'. In this respect there seems no reason for the products of the motor industry to be different from any other commodity and it would be surprising if the late 'sixties and the 'seventies did not witness a greater profusion of models of varying size, performance and price.

In many countries more and more people are likely to own a second car and it is conceivable that British exporters will be able to repeat in other markets their achievements in North America.

For this to happen certain conditions must be fulfilled:

(a) Car ownership in a country is closely linked with *per-capita* income level,[2] thus for the British motor industry to continue to expand its exports there must be a rapid growth of real incomes throughout the world. This presupposes the pursuit of policies for

---

[1] It has also been suggested that loans granted at Government level and Government-sponsored credit arrangements in Latin America and some Middle Eastern countries have tended to favour German exporters when import licences have been in short supply, but little factual material is available on this point.

[2] See A. Maizels, 'Trends in World Trade in Durable Consumer Goods', *National Institute Economic Review* (November 1959), for a chart showing the relationship between ownership and income for passenger cars.

uninterrupted economic growth by the industrial nations, one of the most important of which is the United Kingdom.

(b) Closely bound up with (a), some solution must be found for the balance-of-payments difficulties of primary producing countries, and the solution must not be one which entails restrictive policies, either monetary, fiscal or commercial. Too often in the past countries like Australia and South Africa have only been able to extricate themselves from balance-of-payments difficulties by shutting out imports of motor cars and other durables.

(c) So far as the motor industry is concerned, in the long run Britain cannot help but gain from freer international trade, and this should encourage the Government to play a full part in international attempts to lower tariffs.

Table 9.1. *Exports of cars and commercial vehicles from leading producing countries, 1953–59*

Number of Vehicles (complete) Exported

Year	U.K.	U.S.A.	West Germany	France	Italy	Sweden	Grand Total†
1953	412,064	288,894	177,493	104,271	31,507	4,782	1,064,233
1954	490,825	357,962	298,154	131,570	44,136	8,150	1,341,790
1955	528,612	388,776	403,963	162,681	74,645	10,920	1,588,028
1956	462,068	372,442	484,598	176,625	87,034	17,143	1,618,944
1957	547,277	335,951	584,274	251,920	119,123	28,092	1,886,757
1958	596,239	269,489	733,392	359,328	169,254	41,716	2,185,852
1959	696,937	267,694	870,957*	561,709	221,195	53,342	2,683,597

Share of World Market

Year	U.K.	U.S.A.	W.G.	France	Italy	Sweden
1953	38·7	27·1	16·7	9·8	3·0	0·4
1954	36·6	26·7	22·2	9·8	3·3	0·6
1955	33·3	24·5	25·4	10·2	4·7	0·7
1956	28·5	23·0	29·9	10·9	5·4	1·1
1957	29·0	17·8	31·0	13·4	6·3	1·5
1958	27·3	12·3	33·6	16·4	7·7	1·9
1959	26·0	10·0	32·5	20·9	8·2	2·0

* Includes 11,121 internal deliveries against foreign currency.
† Includes Canada.

Source: Society of Motor Manufacturers and Traders.

Table 9.2. *Exports of cars and commercial vehicles to Commonwealth and North American markets, 1953–59*

To	Year	Total Exports*	Share of Import Market				
			U.K.	U.S.A.	West Germany	France	Italy
Australia	1953	92,630	89·4	1·8	0·1	0·5	0·5
	1956	94,541	77·4	1·5	14·0	4·1	1·0
	1959	101,854	60·0	2·2	25·8	7·6	2·3
New Zealand	1953	25,637	99·5	0·2	0·1	0·2	neg.
	1956	42,278	88·2	1·0	4·8	0·4	0·3
	1959	31,285	92·4	0·2	4·5	0·5	0·2
British East Africa†	1953	8,726	89·5	1·2	6·6	neg.	2·7
	1956	17,482	64·8	3·3	18·4	11·7	1·9
	1959	16,113	46·4	1·0	24·2	22·5	5·6
Ghana†	1953	7,872	74·2	10·6	14·6	neg.	0·6
	1956	9,539	75·6	1·8	13·5	3·7	5·4
	1959	8,784	51·4	3·4	29·7	11·5	2·5
Nigeria†	1953	5,860	100·0	neg.	neg.	neg.	neg.
	1956	13,676	76·9	2·4	18·5	2·2	neg.
	1959	15,555	58·1	2·2	26·7	9·7	2·7
Union of South Africa	1953	58,849	50·2	19·5	6·7	3·3	1·3
	1956	85,227	39·3	30·0	14·8	3·6	1·4
	1959	103,583	34·2	10·3	36·3	10·3	3·7
Canada	1953	60,144	50·4	46·1	3·4	neg.	neg.
	1956	90,302	23·8	54·6	21·3	0·2	neg.
	1959	170,704	45·2	17·5	24·8	10·3	1·4
U.S.A.	1953	29,353	88·4	—	8·1	2·4	0·6
	1956	112,526	34·2	—	57·0	7·7	1·0
	1959	686,586	31·2	—	31·6	26·3	7·0

* From U.K., U.S.A., W. Germany, France, Italy, Sweden, Canada.
† From U.K., U.S.A., W. Germany, France, Italy.

Source: S.M.M.T.

Table 9.3. *Exports of cars and commercial vehicles to selected European markets, 1953–59*

To	Year	Total Exports*	Share of Import Market				
			U.K.	U.S.A.	W.G.	France	Italy
Belgium-Luxembourg	1953	89,880	18·4	19·9	34·1	17·7	2·1
	1956	148,844	14·3	15·7	45·6	21·8	2·4
	1959	155,218	11·5	5·7	40·7	37·6	3·2
France	1953	8,741	37·7	20·8	33·9	—	4·1
	1956	11,684	24·0	21·3	46·2	—	8·5
	1959	18,497	16·2	3·8	58·9	—	20·4
West Germany	1953	11,174	29·7	1·8	—	17·8	50·6
	1956	30,588	12·2	1·7	—	19·6	66·4
	1959	152,662	3·5	0·3	—	36·6	58·8
Italy	1953	2,868	26·5	13·8	47·3	11·9	—
	1956	5,733	17·4	5·4	51·6	25·0	—
	1959	16,179	8·6	4·1	52·7	34·3	—
Netherlands	1953	40,477	31·3	7·4	47·5	9·5	4·2
	1956	58,863	25·9	4·9	52·6	8·3	8·1
	1959	70,044	20·6	1·5	54·9	14·8	6·0
Combined E.E.C.	1953	153,140	23·9	15·2	35·4	14·4	6·3
	1956	255,712	17·2	11·6	41·9	17·5	11·6
	1959	412,600	10·2	2·8	29·3	31·5	24·9
Norway	1953	13,249	40·7	6·7	47·5	2·7	2·3
	1956	11,659	29·1	4·6	60·6	4·2	1·4
	1959	26,999	21·4	0·7	49·1	6·6	1·1
Sweden	1953	60,915	40·3	9·7	33·8	10·7	5·2
	1956	102,070	18·4	5·6	65·1	6·7	4·0
	1959	117,007	17·9	1·8	68·0	9·3	3·0
Denmark	1953	38,851	44·0	3·2	44·6	5·3	2·5
	1956	39,747	31·9	6·5	51·9	7·1	2·6
	1959	85,228	24·2	1·5	54·0	9·9	3·9

* U.K., U.S.A., West Germany, France, Italy, Sweden, Canada.

Source: S.M.M.T.

Table 9.4. *Price and performance data of small cars in the U.S. market, 1960*

Model	Overall Length ft.	Overall Length in.	Turning Circle ft.	Turning Circle in.	Kerb Weight cwt.	Port of Entry Price N.York U.S. $*	Touring Fuel Consumption m.p.g.	Maximum Speed m.p.h.	Cubic Capacity Litres	Acceleration 0–50 m.p.h. Seconds
European:										
Austin A55	14	10½	35	6	21	2198	31·0	76·6	1·5	15·7
Vauxhall Victor	14	0½	31	9	20⅛	1957	29·1	75·3	1·5	16·0
Hillman Minx	13	7½	35	9	20	1599	31·8	76·9	1·5	16·3
Morris Minor 1,000 2 door	12	5¼	32	9	14¾	1459	39·5	73·2	0·9	16·0
Peugeot 403	14	9½	28	9	21¼	2250	31·3	80·9	1·5	16·9
Renault Dauphine	12	11	28	6	12¾	1385	46·2	66·4	0·8	24·7
Fiat 1200 Gran Luce	12	10	33	0	17¾	1648	35·7	84·9	1·2	13·6
Volva PV444L 2 door	14	6	31	6	21	1895	26·7	89·3	1·6	11·9
Volkswagen 2 door	13	4	33	6	14	1565	30·8	68·2	1·2	18·2
American:										
Ford Falcon	15	0	37	0	22¼	1912	25·0	84·3	2·3	14·3
Chevrolet Corvair	15	1½	36	0	21¾	1920	27·0	85·9	2·4	13·7

Source: The Motor.

* March 1961. *Note:* Prices are in all cases lowest offered, e.g. they do not include optional equipment. Prices exclude dealer preparation charges, state and local taxes.

Table 9.5. *Production of cars and commercial vehicles by countries*

'000s

Country	1953	1954	1955	1956	1957	1958	1959
Belgium	2	2	2	1	neg.	neg.	neg.
France	497	600	725	827	928	1128	1283
West Germany	491	681	909	1073	1212	1495	1719
Italy	174	217	269	316	352	404	501
Netherlands	1	2	2	3	2	2	7
E.E.C.	1165	1502	1906	2221	2494	3028	3510
Austria	4	6	7	5	6	13	14
Sweden	29	45	50	57	72	90	112
Switzerland	1	1	1	1	1	1	1
U.K.	835	1039	1238	1006	1151	1364	1560
E.F.T.A. Countries	869	1089	1296	1068	1227	1469	1687
Canada	484	350	454	474	411	355	369
U.S.A.	7323	6601	9169	6921	7221	5135	6729
Japan	47	61	60	101	175	182	263
Australia	44	55	64	69	95	110	195*
U.S.S.R.	n.a.	n.a.	445	465	486	511	496
Total World	10326	10140	13496	11459	12334	11092	13662

* Not comparable with previous years.

Source: S.M.M.T.

Table 9.6. *Changes in hire purchase controls affecting consumer durables, 1952–60*

Date	Items where change took place	Min. deposit Percentage	Max period for repayment Months
Feb. 1952	Motor vehicles, domestic appliances, radio and television	33$\frac{1}{3}$	18
July 1954	Controls on all the above removed	—	—
Feb. 1955	Private motor vehicles, furniture, domestic appliances, and radio and television	15	24
July 1955	Private motor vehicles	33$\frac{1}{3}$	24
	Furniture	15	24
	Domestic appliances, radio and television	33$\frac{1}{3}$	24
Feb. 1956	All motor vehicles	50	24
	Furniture	20	24
	Domestic appliances	50	24
Dec. 1956	All motor vehicles	20	24
May 1957	All motor vehicles	33$\frac{1}{3}$	24
Sept. 1958	Restrictions removed on the following: heavy vehicles, furniture, motor cycles and bicycles	—	—
	All other controlled items	33$\frac{1}{3}$	24
Oct. 1958	All remaining controls removed	—	—
April 1960	Furniture, floor coverings, watches, jewellery	10	24
	Motor vehicles, radio, television, washing machines, refrigerators, vacuum cleaners	20	24
	Cookers, wash boilers, water heaters	10	48
Jan. 1961	Motor vehicles, radio, television, washing machines, refrigerators, vacuum cleaners	20	36

CHAPTER X

ELECTRICAL ENGINEERING

ELECTRICAL products form one of the largest groups of British exports; in 1959 they accounted for over 8% of the total value of manufactured exports from the U.K. Exports of electrical products of the U.K. grew rapidly between 1953 and 1959, but not as rapidly as from other manufacturing countries, and the United Kingdom share of world trade declined more steeply than in the case of many other industries.

The United Kingdom's largest market for electrical products (as defined by the Standard International Trade Classification[1]) in 1959 was India, followed closely by Australia and the Union of South Africa. Together these countries accounted for nearly one-quarter of the total value of U.K. electrical exports. In each of these countries the U.K. share of the import market fell fairly steadily after the early nineteen-fifties, and this decline showed no signs of easing in 1958–59 (Appendix Table Q). In all three of these Commonwealth markets the strongest competition came from western Germany. In the case of India and South Africa, Germany succeeded in increasing her share of the import markets at the expense of the United States as well as the United Kingdom. The U.K. share of the Canadian import market (14·9% in 1959) was very much less than in New Zealand, but this share greatly exceeded that of western Germany, which for some reason made little headway in Canada. In the United States itself the U.K. share fluctuated widely (in 1959 over one-fifth of the market was held by the United Kingdom), but the German share of this import market increased steadily. The share of Japan in the import market of the United States rose to 34·7% in 1959.

In western Europe the only import market in which the U.K. share increased between 1953 and 1959 was western Germany. In the Common Market as a whole the U.K. and the U.S.A. shares fell; the shares of western Germany and the Netherlands both rose. In most E.F.T.A. countries, western Germany made substantial gains, especially in Sweden.

There is no doubt that in electrical engineering by far the most serious competitor to the United Kingdom was western Germany. Nevertheless, as Table 10.1 shows, the Netherlands too gained at the expense of the U.K. The share of Japan in world trade in electrical products as a whole was fairly small, but as we noted earlier (pp. 90–91) in certain sectors, notably in radios, the Japanese became very important exporters.

[1] The S.I.T.C. definition includes generators, transformers, switchgear, batteries, accumulators, bulbs, radio and telephone equipment, cables and domestic electric appliances.

In heavy electrical engineering, i.e. transformers, electric motors and switchgear, the U.K. probably did less badly than in other branches of the industry. From our survey of the industry as a whole it seems that the U.K. fared worse in wireless equipment and domestic electrical appliances than in heavy equipment. We shall accordingly analyse the wireless and domestic electrical appliance sectors in some detail, not only because these are parts of the industry where the U.K. share fell steeply, but also because together they make up one of the fields where the effect of domestic discriminating restrictions was likely to have been felt most strongly. In the case of domestic electrical appliances the level of purchase tax was higher, and hire-purchase restrictions more stringent than in most other sectors of the economy. One would accordingly expect manufacturers of these goods to have had a strong incentive to search particularly diligently for export markets. Before dealing with this limited sector of electrical engineering, however, we shall survey briefly the export performance of two other parts of the in-dustry—heavy electrical plant and electric cables.

HEAVY ELECTRICAL EQUIPMENT

The Commonwealth

In the category 721.01, which includes generators, transformers and switchgear, the Union of South Africa was the United Kingdom's largest single country market. However, the U.K. share of the South African market in electrical machinery declined to the advantage of the United States. There was a considerable growth of local manufacture in the Union; electrical motors, for example, were by 1959 being made by two large companies (both of which were closely associated with British manufactures). In the Federation of Rhodesia and Nyasaland, the U.K. more than held its own in electrical motors and parts between 1954 and 1959. Although ground was lost to South African exporters in imports of transformers and switchgear into the Federation this might well have been accounted for by the transfer of sales by British companies with South African interests from Great Britain to the Union. It is, moreover, worth noting that by 1958–59 the United King-dom share of the Federation import market in heavy electrical equip-ment was still well over 70%.

In several countries overseas manufacture by U.K. companies was quite extensive in heavy electrical engineering—in Australia, for ex-ample, United Kingdom exporters lost to indigenous manufacture, but with the exception of ASEA (an organisation of Swedish origin), local manufacture in the Dominion was carried out largely by subsidiaries of British firms. Many of the leading United Kingdom manufacturers of motors, switchgear and transformers had associated companies in Australia.

In India, mass-production was also carried out by subsidiaries of British (and to a lesser extent, German) companies, but the tendency in India was towards technical licensing arrangements rather than the setting up of foreign-controlled companies or branches.

North America

Sales of heavy electrical products in North America still in general took the form of direct exports and in both Canada and the U.S.A. the U.K. performance was good (Tables 10.2 and 10.3). In Canada the U.K. gained at the expense of the previously dominating U.S.A. and successfully withstood German competition, especially in dynamos and generators and parts, where the U.K. share rose from 12·3% in 1953 to 13·1% in 1957 and 17·0% in 1959 (Table 10.2). In some years the U.K. achieved good results in exporting heavy electrical products to the United States. Since the greater part of this kind of export consists of very large contracts, e.g. the equipping of a power station, the trade figures show very substantial year-to-year variations. From Table 10.3, for example, it is clear that in generators and parts substantial orders caused the total value of imports into the U.S.A. to swell quite considerably in 1956 and again in 1958; by securing large contracts the U.K. markedly increased its share of the market in each of these years. The United Kingdom also held its share of the U.S. market in converters and dynamos. In this sector, as in generators and transformers, the U.K. was well ahead of western Germany and in many years was the principal supplier of the U.S. import market. Neither were the Germans able to secure more than a moderate share of the market in transformers and parts. In these goods, as in the case of generating plant, there were considerable annual fluctuations in the United Kingdom share, but the U.K. clearly remained the leading supplier.

In heavy electrical goods the U.K. succeeded in holding its share of the market better in North America than in the Sterling Commonwealth. There is no doubt that in tendering for electrical equipment in the Sterling Commonwealth the U.K. lost a number of contracts on account of price, but it is questionable whether these differences in tender quotations really represented basic domestic cost differences. The evidence is that there were not (after 1953) substantial cost differences in producing heavy electrical goods in the United Kingdom and in western Germany. Of course labour costs per hour in the U.K. in electrical engineering were higher than those of most European countries, and since large transformers and generating plant are fairly labour-intensive, wage differentials might have played some part in making British quotations less competitive than those of their foreign rivals. In 1955, for example, it was estimated that British labour costs in electrical engineering were some 69% of those of Sweden, and those of Germany 59% of those of Sweden. The significance of these wage differentials should not however be exaggerated and it should be remembered that in the electrical industry two of the organisations most keenly competitive with the U.K. in Sterling Commonwealth markets (ACEC and ASEA) were domiciled in the European countries where wages were relatively high (Belgium and Sweden respectively).

Relative Costs and Prices

Although the U.K. was at some disadvantage in wages, prices of fuel and raw materials (coal, steel and copper) were probably lower in the U.K. than on the Continent. In heavy electrical engineering fuel and raw materials probably accounted for about 50% to 60% of total costs and thus lower raw material prices probably offset the high labour costs faced by U.K. manufacturers. United Kingdom steel prices were lower in a number of categories than those ruling in Germany, France and Belgium. Between 1953 and 1959 British coal prices were almost certainly lower than European coal prices.

Copper prices tended to be similar throughout Europe, although perhaps slightly higher in France than in Germany or the U.K. Domestic production of the ore is nowhere important in Europe and the world price has to be paid. In refining non-ferrous metallic ores, wages and salaries account for only about 13% of the value of gross output; thus the most important cost elements in the copper supplied to electrical industry were accounted for by materials and fuel. Accordingly copper was probably supplied to U.K. electrical engineering firms at prices which were certainly not higher, and possibly lower, than those ruling on the Continent.

From the facts available it is difficult to know whether, product for product, costs in heavy electrical engineering were higher in western Europe than in the United Kingdom. On the Continent tenders were very seldom invited from outside countries, but it was said that the prices which German manufacturers obtained from their authorities were at least as high as corresponding prices in Great Britain.[1]

British export products tended to be of higher quality and price than those of their Continental competitors. In Britain, too, safety standards were more stringent than on the Continent. British switch-gear and alternators will not fail if loaded 20% to 30% beyond their nominal capacity, but it is said that Continental designs will fail when worked as little as 5% above the limit.[2] More exacting safety standards often entail bigger and heavier machinery and this, too, adds to costs. In general, developing countries probably prefer cheaper and lighter structures, even with slightly lower standards of efficiency. In this respect the United Kingdom is at a disadvantage.

It is also true that in the nineteen-fifties Continental suppliers were more flexible in the prices they quoted when tendering than their U.K. counterparts. Continental tenders are seldom consistent—they move up and down according to the job, the purchaser, and the country. In particular, they aim at securing contracts which will lead to repeat orders. In the British electrical industry, on the other hand, there is a

---

[1] *Britain and Europe*, Economist Intelligence Unit (London, 1957), p. 121.
[2] *Ibid.* p. 121.

tradition that bids should be made for all available contracts and this in itself leads to quite substantial overhead costs. According to the BEAMA annual report for 1958, U.K. firms made tens of thousands of tenders a year to 120 countries; for about four times as many jobs as they won contracts.[1] British firms, unlike their Continental rivals, estimate costs very carefully and are less willing than the Germans to scale down their tenders in order to secure a long-term hold on a particular market.

Cables and Wires

A great deal of what has been written about electrical plant applies also to cables. This again is a sector which was severely hit by competition and by the setting up of indigenous manufacture in many of the United Kingdom's more important overseas markets. Not only did the development of local manufacture have a directly adverse effect upon U.K. export sales, but, with the cutting off of many of their overseas outlets, Britain's competitors themselves intensified their export efforts in other markets. Thus for cables India was by 1958–59 virtually a closed market; United Kingdom and foreign firms which previously sold to that country were accordingly intensifying their efforts elsewhere. With increasing competition in so many markets, prices became of considerable importance, and whatever might have been the case in electrical motors and switchgear, in cables the United Kingdom was at a serious price disadvantage, particularly when competing with German, Dutch and Japanese manufacturers. Continental and Japanese firms enjoyed high prices and profits in their home markets and it is said that they habitually exported at prices which covered little more than their prime costs. The extent to which the United Kingdom share of the market in cables and wires fell is exemplified by the case of South Africa. While supplying nearly 72% of the import market in 1953, the U.K. in 1959 supplied less than half the import requirements of the Union. Western Germany on the other hand, which in 1953 held less than 10% of the market, held over one-third of the import market by 1959.

It is sometimes suggested that foreign governments gave rather more assistance in the form of credits and even subsidies to cable manufacturers than was obtainable in the United Kingdom. British exporters we spoke to criticised the United Kingdom Government for its hesitation in making representation to Continental authorities in regard to these export arrangements, and there is a strong feeling in the industry that German manufacturers were treated rather more generously than the British manufacturers in regard to export credits. No concrete evidence is however available to show that the German industry was being directly subsidised in the export field.

One criticism frequently made by this section of the industry of the British Export Credit Guarantee Department was the Department's insistence that a firm insuring with it should take up a blanket cover

[1] Annual Report, 1958.

relating to all its transactions in a given country market. For many transactions exporters claim that insurance cover was quite unnecessary and they assert that the insistence of the Department on these blanket arrangements merely added to the total cost of the premiums required of them, even though it doubtless enabled the E.C.G.D. to quote lower *average* rates.

It is generally accepted that in cables and wires the setting up by U.K. firms of overseas subsidiaries diverted work overseas which would previously have been entrusted to the U.K. factories. One large manufacturing firm has reported that in 1959 it had substantial expanding interests in the Union of South Africa, Rhodesia, India, Pakistan, Malaya, Australia and New Zealand; this firm had, in recent years, deliberately diverted orders and materials from manufacturing units in Britain to these overseas countries.

RADIO AND RADIO EQUIPMENT

We turn now to a survey of British export performance in radios and wireless equipment. Although quantitatively exports of wireless sets and equipment are relatively small—in 1959 the total value of United Kingdom exports of radio (including radar) equipment was £42m., of domestic radio sets only about £2m.—this is one of the fields where hire-purchase restrictions during the period were quite stringent, and as in the case of vehicles (see pp. 131–135), it is worth asking whether domestic restrictions in any way aided export performance.

Australia

Australia has traditionally been Britain's most important market for radios. Since the war this market has been considerably affected by the changing policies of Commonwealth Governments in regard to quantitative trade controls, but it is clear from Table 10.4 that (apart from the exceptional year 1956–57 when total imports were severely curtailed) the U.K. share of the market in made-up wireless sets fell very markedly after 1953–54. There was an almost phenomenal increase in the Japanese share of the import market in radios after about 1956. By 1959 Japan was supplying twice as many radio sets to Australia as did the U.K. There has also been a falling away in the United Kingdom share of the Australian market in wireless components, but the fall was not as marked as in the case of complete sets. It is worth noting that almost the whole impact of Japanese competition was in sets; very few parts or valves were imported from Japan; in parts and components the most vigorous challenge to the U.K. in the Australian import market came from the United States and from the Netherlands.

Africa

The tendency of the U.K. share of the market in radio sets to fall more than the share in markets for radio equipment is also illustrated in the case of South Africa, where the U.K. share in made-up radios fell from 74·4% of the market in 1951 to 22·6% in 1958, one of the biggest falls for any commodity in the market of the Union. Much of the decline could be accounted for by German competition, but also of considerable significance was a very substantial growth in imports from the neighbouring Federation of Rhodesia and Nyasaland, due presumably to the growth of local manufacture in the Federation. This growth was concentrated in sets rather than in parts. Competition from Japan in the Union became serious only after 1958.

In the Federation itself, in spite of a preferential tariff which was quite favourable to the U.K., prices of Continental and South African radio equipment were very competitive with U.K. exports, and the U.K. share of this market too declined, from two-thirds of the import market (by value) in 1954 to about one-half in 1958–59. It has been said that makers of German radio sets devoted more attention to appearance and to novelty devices than their British rivals and this gave sets a greater sales appeal. Importers of radios into the Federation from South Africa in 1959 were paying duty of 22·5%, on radios from the U.K. and the colonies the duty was only 10%. One would expect this to have given the British exporters some advantage which ought to have outweighed the advantage of proximity enjoyed by South Africa, and indeed the preferential tariff rate probably goes some way to explain why in spite of the *decrease* in the United Kingdom share, that share was still relatively high in 1959.

In contrast to the Federation of Rhodesia and Nyasaland, the countries of British East Africa gave no imperial preference to the United Kingdom and the British share of the total market was accordingly considerably smaller. There was virtually no local production, the market being shared by the United Kingdom, the Netherlands and western Germany. Dollar restrictions tended to keep out the United States models. The Dutch and German shares of the British East African import market rose, and in fact exporters in both countries did especially well in selling radiograms, a market in which the United Kingdom had for some reason virtually no share. Throughout the nineteen-fifties, sales of radiograms were virtually confined to the European population, but with rising standards they should become a worth-while proposition among the coloured people. As in Rhodesia, styling is important—the African likes a set decorated with gilt and ivory. He prefers a large cabinet; advertising is very important and it has been suggested by the Board of Trade that pamphlets and catalogues being issued by Continental firms were more appropriate for African consumption than those distributed by British manufacturers. Up to 1959 Japan had barely entered this market.

Nigeria and Ghana are two other markets where there were no preferential tariff rates on imported radios; in both these markets the Dutch gained at the expense of the United Kingdom.

In general it does not appear that in Africa there was much difference in regard to prices between Dutch, British and German radios, but Dutch and some German models appealed more to African taste because they 'looked expensive'. It is also alleged that British exporters adopted too conservative a policy in Africa. For example, they were reluctant to allow local agents to deal with rival products, whereas German and Dutch exporters welcomed as many agents as possible, even when these also acted for their competitors.

North America

One of the markets for radio sets which grew most rapidly after 1953 was Canada. The value of imports of receiving sets rose from £455,200 in 1953 to £4,305,600 in 1959 (Table 10.5). Now it is sometimes suggested that the Canadian market is (in the case of most products) one where the U.K. can have little hope of success, owing to the strong influence of the United States. In regard to radios, however, this argument must be treated with considerable caution, since it is clear from Table 10.5 that the United States hold on the Canadian market was considerably weakened—but it was not the United Kingdom which caused the fall in the United States share, so much as western Germany and Japan.

There is, however, consolation to British exporters to Canada in that the losses on made-up radio sets were offset by gains in exports of wireless equipment and accessories, the total value of imports of which into Canada was in 1959 very much greater than the value of imports of manufactured radio sets. Table 10.5 shows that the United Kingdom more than held its own in this field. After 1955 Canadian manufacturers probably took over some of the business previously falling to United States suppliers, the value of imports from the United Kingdom remaining fairly stable.

Unfortunately, in the case of the United States Trade Returns, market import values of radio sets and radio parts are not distinguished, but for the group 'radio apparatus and parts' the United Kingdom share fluctuated considerably. It was however never greater than 18% of the total, whereas the share of Japan rose from an almost negligible amount in 1953 to 36·5% and 56·9% in 1957 and 1958 respectively. The German share grew also, but on nothing approaching this scale and, like that of the United Kingdom, fluctuated considerably from year to year.

In our Study of the export trade in radios and equipment over our limited period we have noticed several points which are of long term significance for the health of United Kingdom export trade. Firstly, in spite of the fact that British radio products seldom directly priced themselves out of markets, trade was nevertheless diverted to suppliers from other countries—particularly in the case of the African markets. Britain's Continental and Japanese competitors sold more vigorously in almost all markets of this continent, and they produced sets which met local requirements, however different these might have been from those sold on the home market. Other countries possessed that flexibility which seemed to be lacking in the British radio industry; this is perhaps best seen by the lead taken by the Japanese in developing the transistor radio set and marketing it on a massive scale.

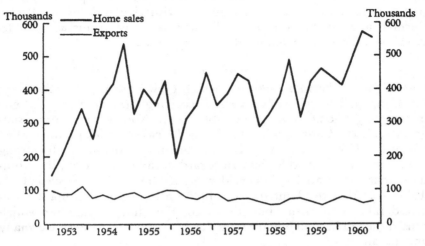

Chart 3. Home sales and exports of radios and radiograms (quarterly totals)

DOMESTIC RESTRICTIONS AND RADIO EXPORTS

In the case of radios it certainly cannot be argued that the home market was so 'soft' between 1953 and 1959 that manufacturers lacked the necessary incentive to export. The evidence, such as it is, points in the opposite direction. There were many periods, after 1955, when there was quite considerable excess capacity in the industry, and firms certainly did not lack the incentive to sell abroad. A substantial degree of under-employment in the industry existed in 1956 and again in the first half of 1958. This is clearly indicated in Chart 3 which suggests that the imposition or the tightening of restrictions on the home market singularly failed to produce any improvement in exports. In our examination of the export performance of the motor industry we noted that changes in requirements relating to hire-purchase transactions had some effect, albeit a delayed one, upon domestic sales of passenger cars (pp. 131–135). There is no doubt that similar restrictions also played a part in bringing about a recession in home demand in the case of radios and other consumer durables.

As we noted above (p. 132) the period when hire-purchase restrictions were most severe was that between July 1955 and September 1958. During these three and a quarter years, domestic sales of radios were affected by the harshness of the controls—the level of sales of radios attained for the fourth quarter of 1954 was not reached again until the corresponding quarter of 1960. But during this time of severe curtailment on the home market, exports of radios did not rise at all.

Indeed they were falling fairly consistently over the whole period between 1955 and 1958. Export sales recovered somewhat in 1959 and 1960, but export trends as shown in our chart seem to bear no relation at all to what was happening in the home market. Certainly the tightening of restrictions was *not* followed by improved export performance.

In fact the radio industry could well argue that discriminatory restrictive policies were particularly harmful in their effect upon the export efforts of the radio industry. Throughout the post-war period purchase tax on products of the industry was high (Table 10.6) and, as we have seen, from time to time stringent hire-purchase controls were imposed. The effect of these changes was to bring about frequent variations in domestic sales, but there was clearly no 'scissors' effect upon exports, which in any case by the very nature of the industry accounted for only a small proportion of total production. The constant ups and downs of the home market create a serious problem for an industry in which designing and tooling is extremely expensive and uneconomical unless done on a relatively large scale—and on the basis of a steadily expanding home market. A radio set specifically designed for the home market cannot easily be switched to the market of the Far East or to western Europe. Accordingly, reductions in domestic demand have brought about periods of excess capacity in the industry rather than variations in quantities exported. Indeed it could be argued that reliance on restrictive measures for encouraging exports was more wrong-headed in the case of the radio industry than in the car industry. The consumption of steel in radios is very much less than in the case of motor cars, and it is difficult to switch plant to making alternative products. Moreover the radio industry gave employment to a relatively large number of women, and a reduction in output brought about under-employment rather than the diversion of the workers released to other expanding industries. And some of the larger radio firms were not located in areas where labour could move easily into those industries where export demand remained buoyant.

REFRIGERATORS AND OTHER DOMESTIC EQUIPMENT

Many of these considerations applied also to other domestic electrical appliances—washing machines, refrigerators, electric stoves and the like.

Domestic electrical appliances are usually produced locally by countries at a relatively early stage in their secondary development. Nevertheless, economies of scale in this sector are extremely important, and there are still very many products for which there is a buoyant import demand in a large number of overseas markets. Even where countries have their own assembly plant, they invariably continue to import parts (e.g. cooling units for refrigerators) on a substantial scale for a number of years. This was the case in Australia, where the value of imports of refrigerators fell from £201,000 in 1950/51 to £43,000 in

1958/59, but where imports of parts of refrigerators were well maintained, in 1958/59 being worth £847,000. Taking refrigerators and parts together, the United Kingdom share of the Australian import market fell quite steeply, and the United States share increased substantially (Table 10.7). The western German share was relatively small; in fact in all but one financial year, the value of imports from Denmark was greater than from the Federal Republic. The development of local manufacture and the deliberate discouragement of imports took place also in the case of the Union of South Africa; although in 1958–59 the U.K. was still the largest supplier, western Germany followed very closely behind.

Table 10.8 shows imports of domestic refrigerators and washing machines into the Federation of Rhodesia and Nyasaland. The Table indicates growing competition from the Union of South Africa in washing machines and from both the Union and, up to 1958, Sweden also in domestic refrigerators. In the case of refrigerators this was largely due to the concentration of South African manufacturers on the popular 6·29 cu. ft. range; in Rhodesia fairly large capacity refrigerators suitable for frozen food storage are essential, the meat storage drawer must be of substantial dimension, and ample space must be available for the storage of vegetables and fruit. Most Rhodesians like to keep on hand bottles of drinks and these must be stored in the refrigerator. It has been suggested that on more than one occasion the U.K. lost ground in this market simply because her refrigerators did not take account of the need for storing a considerably larger number of bottles than was the case in Great Britain.

Demand for washing machines in the Federation rose between 1953 and 1959, but since these machines were operated mainly by African servants and consequently were apt to be somewhat roughly treated, toughness was of greater importance than the proliferation of labour-saving gadgets on the machines. Hot water was usually readily available from kitchen heaters, and a heating element in a machine was therefore regarded as something of a luxury.

These points illustrate the problem of exporting to a market like that of the Federation. Domestic refrigerators need to be a little more complex and embody more refinements, washing machines should be simpler and employ fewer refinements than in the case of the U.K. domestic market. It was partly because South African manufacturers were better able to adapt models to the particular requirements of the Rhodesian markets that their share of them increased at the expense of the United Kingdom.[1]

Again it is arguable that the certainty of a steady expansion of the domestic market in Great Britain would have made possible the adoption of greater varieties of styling and function which are so essential

---

[1] Prices in South Africa were higher ex-factory than corresponding ones in the U.K., but lower at the point of entry into the Federation owing to the fairly heavy transport costs of these larger domestic appliances.

to a successful export trade in domestic electrical appliances. As in the case of radios, the modifications in design which were necessary to enable British manufacturers to capture and hold so many overseas markets, particularly in Africa, were relatively small, but usually only worth making if total output of the appliance in question was considerable. There is little doubt that by 1958 the scale of output of the German refrigerator industry was greater than that of the United Kingdom industry. The German industry enjoyed advantages which were closely associated with the greater size and rate of growth of the home market, partly made possible by the freedom of the industry to cater for the needs of that market.

For many years the United Kingdom was, after the United States, the world's largest exporter of domestic refrigerators. In 1950, practically no domestic refrigerators were being made in western Germany, but in part as the result of the absence of Government restrictions on the German home market (there was virtually no purchase tax and hire-purchase deposits were as low as 10% to 15%), by 1956 German output was 750,000 units. In the United Kingdom, output in 1956 was but 307,000 units. It is perhaps not entirely coincidental that for most of the period between 1950 and 1956 the purchase tax on domestic electrical appliances in the U.K. was 60%, while the Government insisted on hire-purchase deposits being in some years as high as 50%. In this environment of discriminatory and extremely onerous restrictions it is, perhaps, understandable that British industries making consumer durables did not expand as rapidly as in the case of western Germany.

Charts 4, 5, 6, show that, as in the case of cars and radios, the falling domestic demand in the United Kingdom associated with the tightening of restrictions on sales of other consumer durables did not result in any improvement in export sales. In the case of refrigerators, both home sales and export deliveries were low in 1956 and 1957; exports improved somewhat in 1958, but this was when home sales also rose very substantially. The post-war 'peak' for exports of refrigerators from the United Kingdom was the second quarter of 1960—the very time when domestic sales were substantially greater than for any other quarter.

For vacuum cleaners (Chart 6), total export sales were fairly stable in 1956 and 1957, but 1958 saw a marked falling away and the decline continued steadily throughout the year. But the first quarter of 1959 was a good one for exports (as good as any since 1954) and this was the period which almost immediately followed the complete abolition of hire-purchase restrictions in the autumn of 1958. It is true that the reimposition of controls in April 1960 was followed (in the third quarter) by a rise in exports, which must have been more than seasonal, and this improvement in exports was accompanied by a fall in home demand. But home demand recovered in the last quarter (presumably this was largely seasonal) and exports also increased.

From the chart showing domestic deliveries and exports of washing

M

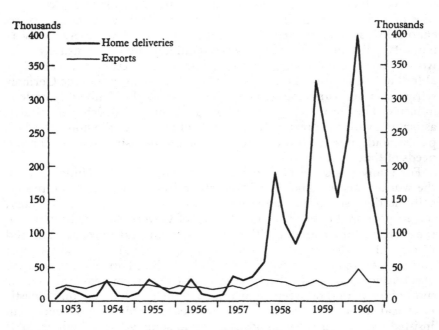

Chart 4. Home deliveries and exports of domestic refrigerators (quarterly totals)

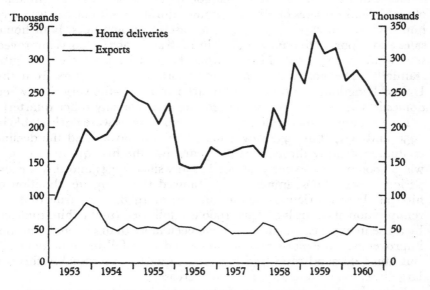

Chart 5. Home deliveries and exports of washing machines (quarterly totals)

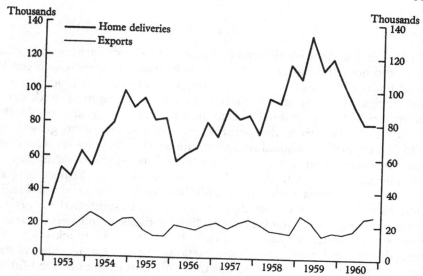

Chart 6. Home deliveries and exports of vacuum cleaners (quarterly totals)

machines (Chart 5) it looks as if the relaxation of hire-purchase controls in the autumn of 1958 permitted a substantial upsurge in demand on the home market. The increase in sales for the last quarter of the year was clearly more than seasonal, and for the second quarter of 1959 sales were greater than for the corresponding quarters in 1957 and 1958 put together. It is possible that washing machines were being diverted from the export market to satisfy home demand at this time (export sales for the second half of 1958 were lower than for any other half-year on our chart), but after the middle of 1959 exports began to climb again and this recovery took place long before restrictions were reimposed in the spring of 1960. The falling away in exports which took place in mid-1960 can hardly have been due to the 'pull' of the home market. This was a time of considerable excess capacity in the industry and the steep fall in home deliveries for the second and third quarters shows that exports were not flagging because home demand was buoyant. They were flagging because overseas buyers were no longer willing to purchase them. The fact is, in the case of consumer durables, it proved extremely difficult for manufacturers to transfer to the export market goods which could not be sold at home. It was perhaps unfortunate that those consumer durables which provided such a ready field for the imposition of discriminatory controls and taxes were among the most difficult to sell overseas. As we shall see in the following section, there were several reasons for this.

CONCLUSIONS

Firstly, in the field of electrical appliances, a very large number of firms did not export at all, and had no organisation for switching goods from home to export markets. In selling overseas mass-produced goods like refrigerators a quite extensive organisation is required, and, even more important, personnel skilled in overseas selling are absolutely essential. Indeed, from the point of view of the long-term growth of national exports, occasional *sorties* into the overseas field by firms lacking the know-how and without a long-term interest in building up a soundly based export trade can be positively harmful. Firms engaged in sporadic overseas selling invariably lack spares and servicing facilities; to a far greater extent than in the case of established exporting firms their products often lack the styling for overseas markets. In some cases even, quality might be sacrificed to the need for quick sales. As regards the regular exporting organisations (usually but not always the larger firms in the industry), it was probable that in the nineteen-fifties most of them were already making a substantial export effort—indeed they had to do so in order to cover the very high overhead costs of exporting such products in the modern world. The bulk of exports of domestic electrical appliances was in the hands of a very few companies, and judging by the proportion of their output exported in recent years, the charge that manufacturers of these goods neglected export opportunities would be difficult to substantiate. As we have seen there was a considerable difficulty in switching from the home to the export market in this field. One obvious difficulty arises from the differences in safety requirements of various countries. Because Scandinavian soils are thin, special care has to be taken over earthing; accordingly the authorities in Denmark, Norway and Sweden insist on higher standards of insulation for domestic electrical appliances (e.g. washing machines) than is the case in the United Kingdom.[1] There is also on record the case of a British firm which once flew loaves of bread to England from all over the world in order to adjust toaster speeds to take account of differences in the texture of flours used in the various markets to which they proposed to export. In the case of electric blankets special types are required for American markets, where electric blankets are commonly put above the bedclothes and not (as in the United Kingdom) under the rest of the bedlinen.

There is some justification for arguing that the long-term effects of repeated changes in internal policies in the United Kingdom had an adverse effect upon export performance in the electrical industry. In the field of domestic electrical appliances overhead costs are very significant; they are much higher than in the case of heavy electrical machinery, where raw materials form the bulk of costs. It has been

[1] *Britain and Europe*, Economist Intelligence Unit, cited above, p. 121.

estimated that in domestic appliances (refrigerators and vacuum cleaners) 60% of total costs are accounted for by overheads, e.g. tooling, research, design, salesmanship; 20% are accounted for by direct labour, and only 20% by raw materials. Any decline in domestic demand is thus likely to have an adverse effect upon marginal costs and upon extension or experimentation with new lines. A steadily expanding home market, on the other hand, such as the Germans have enjoyed since 1950, facilitates forward planning. Apart from temporary interruptions to output caused by the 'off-and-on' nature of direct controls, the alternate damping down and stimulation of demand between 1954 and 1960 made an assessment of long-term demand extremely difficult to make. In the refrigerator industry, for example, many firms made mistakes in 1959, when the fairly drastic removal of controls released a pent-up demand for appliances, which the manufacturers wrongly mistook for a long-term growth in demand. In many cases they drew up over-ambitious development programmes, which were rendered more wasteful by the reimposition of controls in 1960.

It has also been pointed out by members of the industry that in an atmosphere of expansion an export director often finds it easier to persuade a board to tool-up in order to take account of relatively small sales to a particular overseas market, than he would do if future overall demand were less certain. When expansion is going on all around, the capital cost of such a development can be taken in a company's stride. On the other hand, in a time of falling domestic demand and declining company profits, boards are understandably likely to be very much more cautious in undertaking new capital expenditure, even if there is a chance that ultimately substantial rewards might be reaped in the export field as a result of such a venture.

Finally, it should be remembered that as a matter of historical fact whenever hire-purchase restrictions were applied in the United Kingdom many overseas countries deliberately reduced their imports of consumer durables on balance-of-payments grounds. These difficulties had an unhappy habit of coinciding with the adopting of 'tough' policies in the U.K. Indeed, as we pointed out on p. 68, the balance-of-payments difficulties of overseas countries were often made more intractable by these very policies.

There is no doubt that, human nature being what it is, businessmen have exaggerated the difficulties they face as a result of Government interference; but that such difficulties exist cannot be doubted, and it is at least possible that these discriminatory restrictions had on balance a generally adverse effect upon U.K. export performance in the goods we have looked at in this section.

Table 10.1. *Share of world market in electrical products**
(S.I.T.C. 72)

Year	U.K.	U.S.A.	West Germany	Nether-lands	Italy & Trieste	Belgium-Luxembourg	France	Japan
1953	26·0	30·5	14·9	5·9	2·1	3·6	6·2	0·8
1955	24·1	26·1	20·1	8·1	2·0	3·8	6·7	1·4
1957	22·6	26·5	22·8	6·8	1·8	3·6	5·8	2·8
1958	21·3	25·0	22·8	7·7	2·1	3·9	6·8	3·4
1959	19·2	22·5	24·3	8·4	1·8	2·9	6·2	5·9

* Share based on exports of U.K., U.S.A., West Germany, Netherlands, Italy, Belgium-Luxembourg, France, Sweden, Switzerland, Canada, Japan.

Table 10.2. *Imports of dynamos, generators and parts into Canada*

£ 000

	1952	1953	1954	1955	1956	1957	1958	1959
Value of imports	3012	3623	3432	3701	5674	6346	4458	3757
U.K.%	8·6	12·3	9·8	19·5	17·8	13·1	12·9	17·0
U.S.A.%	91·0	87·2	84·0	75·7	80·6	81·5	68·3	74·2
West Germany%	0·2	0·2	3·1	0·3	0·2	2·5	0·4	0·9

Source: Trade of Canada, Volume III.

Table 10.3. *Imports of heavy electrical equipment into the United States*

£ 000

	1952	1953	1954	1955	1956	1957	1958
Generators and Parts							
Value of imports	117·9	123·6	224·3	140·4	1662·9	352·1	1874·6
U.K.%	7·9	1·7	12·4	19·6	65·2	7·4	50·2
West Germany%	1·5	2·3	4·1	10·7	2·9	13·8	39·6
Converters							
Value of imports	45·0	2539·6	107·1	243·9	307·1	426·1	322·1
U.K.%	30·2	3·5	21·3	43·8	36·4	29·0	38·5
West Germany%	11·1	1·6	11·3	8·8	7·1	9·7	12·6
Canada%	11·1	88·9	23·3	30·5	37·7	32·0	14·3
Japan%	neg.	neg.	1·7	2·5	3·6	8·9	21·5
Transformers and Parts							
Value of imports	156·8	368·9	570·7	1219·3	1339·6	1505·0	1742·1
U.K.%	20·0	19·6	43·3	55·8	56·9	49·4	51·1
West Germany%	5·7	1·8	1·4	1·3	9·8	8·6	2·8
Canada%	52·4	5·0	9·6	1·2	1·5	2·5	4·5

Source: United States Imports of Merchandise for Consumption, Commodity by Country of Origin.

Table 10.4. *Imports of radio sets into Australia*

£ 000

	1950–1	1951–2	1952–3	1953–4	1954–5	1955–6	1956–7	1957–8	1958–9
Value of imports	58·4	130·4	35·2	40·0	228·0	188·8	47·2	184·8	359·2
U.K.%	75·2	92·0	68·2	78·0	15·1	45·8	71·2	26·8	25·8
Japan%	neg.	neg.	neg.	neg.	neg.	neg.	9·0	40·6	50·8

Source: Australia *Overseas Trade.*

Table 10.5. *Imports of radio sets and parts into Canada*

£ 000

	1952	1953	1954	1955	1956	1957	1958	1959
Radio & receiving sets								
Value of imports	491·0	455·2	338·0	472·7	787·8	1096·5	2412·4	4305·6
U.K.%	14·1	3·0	4·7	2·8	4·5	5·1	3·4	2·6
U.S.A.%	85·8	96·0	92·5	90·7	74·3	51·7	36·6	19·9
West Germany%	0·1	0·9	2·6	4·5	13·9	16·9	24·2	28·5
Japan%	neg.	neg.	neg.	0·9	6·3	20·0	28·5	43·9
Radio apparatus & Parts								
Value of imports	8021·3	15135·3	21450·5	22078·4	16245·5	12685·8	12245·4	12106·8
U.K.%	7·8	6·7	8·0	7·7	11·5	11·9	13·0	18·8
U.S.A.%	91·6	92·6	91·1	91·6	87·1	85·5	83·4	75·9
Netherlands%	0·6	0·7	0·6	0·6	0·8	1·3	1·4	1·6
Japan%	neg.	neg.	neg.	neg.	1·0	0·3	0·5	1·1

Source: *Trade of Canada*, Vol. III.

Table 10.6. *Purchase tax on radios, radiograms and television sets*

%

From	10th April 1946	33⅓
	13th November 1947	50
	1st April 1948	66⅔
	16th June 1948	33⅓
	14th April 1951	66⅔
	15th April 1953	50
	26th October 1955	60
	8th April 1959	50

Source: H.M. Customs and Excise.

Table 10.7. *Imports of refrigerators and parts into Australia*

£ 000

	1950–1	1951–2	1952–3	1953–4	1954–5	1955–6	1956–7	1957–8	1958–9
Value of imports	1372	2690	334	946	953	856	786	729	726
U.K.%	95·3	94·2	77·0	86·1	79·5	59·8	55·0	63·4	55·1
U.S.A.%	3·6	4·2	14·0	9·4	13·3	14·9	39·1	28·2	36·8

Source: Australia *Overseas Trade*.

Table 10.8. *Imports of domestic refrigerators and washing machines into the Federation of Rhodesia and Nyasaland*

£ 000

	1954	1955	1956	1957	1958	1959
Domestic refrigerators						
Value of imports	469·1	780·1	767·6	816·7	740·3	635·1
U.K.%	51·0	52·8	54·3	35·1	43·3	32·2
West Germany%	neg.	neg.	0·5	1·7	3·1	4·4
South Africa%	41·0	39·4	30·2	38·2	27·3	33·0
Sweden%	0·8	0·9	6·0	13·1	13·1	4·6
U.S.A.%	5·4	4·4	6·8	10·6	8·5	8·1
Washing machines						
Value of imports	93·6	111·6	144·2	166·9	181·5	199·6
U.K.%	86·4	83·8	72·3	58·2	65·1	59·8
South Africa%	9·4	12·2	21·9	36·1	28·3	31·3

Source: Federation of Rhodesia and Nyasaland *Annual Statement of External Trade.*

CHAPTER XI

PHARMACEUTICALS

SINCE before the war the manufacture of drugs and pharmaceuticals has been one of the most rapidly expanding of all British industries, and in 1958 and 1959 about one-quarter by value of the industry's total output was exported. Although in 1959 drugs and pharmaceuticals as defined in the Standard International Trade Classification accounted for only 2% of U.K. exports of all manufactures the industry is one which is full of interest for the student of export performance.

In spite of a considerable increase in total overseas sales in recent years, 'drugs and pharmaceuticals' (S.I.T.C. 54) was a sector where a marked decline in the U.K. share of world trade took place in the period covered by our Study. Even in those import markets, like France, where the U.K. share in most other branches of chemicals rose between 1953 and 1959, pharmaceuticals failed to hold their own.

Sterling Commonwealth countries accounted for over one-half of the total value of U.K. exports of pharmaceuticals in 1959; of these countries Australia and (somewhat surprisingly) Nigeria were the largest export markets for the U.K. Chart 7 shows the increase in sales of British manufactured drugs to the United Kingdom's five major markets between 1953 and 1959. The value of U.K. pharmaceutical exports to all these markets, except perhaps the Union of South Africa, expanded considerably over the period. Unfortunately, in all the more important Commonwealth countries, the U.K. appears to have lost a substantial part of its share in the import markets. In Australia, Nigeria, the Union of South Africa, India and Pakistan, for example, the decline in the U.K. share was in each case over 7 percentage points. Table D shows that in almost all the western hemisphere markets on the other hand (Canada, the U.S., the Argentine and Brazil, for example), there was an improvement of one or more percentage points. Small gains were also made in western Germany.

Now it would be a great mistake to assume that in all branches of pharmaceuticals the U.K. fell behind its competitors. As we shall see later, in a number of country markets certain drugs have clearly held their own although the U.K. share in other drugs has fallen. Moreover, this is a field where the setting up by British firms of branches overseas has been common, and, for reasons which we noted in chapter III (p. 44), in such cases figures relating to visible trade must be treated with great caution.

WORLD TRADE IN PHARMACEUTICALS

Before the war, Germany dominated world trade in pharmaceuticals, France taking second place. Since the war the U.S. has become the world's leading exporter, followed by Switzerland, the U.K. and West Germany in that order. Table D shows that in spite of the progressive easement of restrictions on the import of dollar goods, the United States had by 1959 lost much of her earlier lead. Drugs and pharmaceuticals is one of the fields where the gains made by western Germany in terms of import market shares during the nineteen-fifties were not particularly spectacular.

Although in 1959 France was a substantial world exporter of pharmaceuticals, about one-quarter of the value of her trade was with French overseas possessions and with Vietnam countries where the U.K. had little interest as an exporter. The values of drug exports from the more important O.E.E.C. countries are given below (Table 11.1).

Of greater significance than the gains of western Germany was the remarkable performance of Switzerland which between 1953 and 1959 held or increased her share of all Commonwealth markets, particularly Australia (which was in 1959 still Britain's largest Commonwealth market). The Swiss share of the Australian import market rose from 9·6% in 1953 to 16·0% in 1959, while the United Kingdom share fell from 71·7% to 58·6% over this period. In 1953 Switzerland exported practically no drugs at all to Pakistan; by 1959 she was supplying over 15% of this import market. Swiss exports made advances in the U.S.A. and Canada, and in all Latin American countries in our sample. In western Europe Switzerland gained only in some markets.[1] Switzerland however made such strides in certain European markets that she became the leading foreign supplier in Denmark, France, western Germany and Sweden (see Table D). In 1959 Switzerland supplied over one-quarter of the total pharmaceutical imports into the European Economic Community. The Swiss, however, confined their attention mainly to vitamins and medical specialities. The world-famous firm of Roche Ltd had during our period the monopoly of vitamin manufacture in Switzerland and greatly extended their productive capacity. No antibiotics were made in Switzerland, at any rate before 1960.

Up to 1959 Japan had not made great inroads to any of the markets included in our Table except the U.S.A.; even there she had secured only about one-tenth of the import market. Nevertheless more than

---

[1] The growing share of the Benelux partners in trade with one another may be looked upon as a result of the removal of some of the remaining obstacles to the free circulation of goods within the Benelux union, and some decline in the share of Benelux markets held by other European countries is therefore only to be expected. Thus between 1951 and 1958 the Dutch share of the market of the Belgium-Luxembourg Economic Union in pharmaceuticals grew from 7·5% to 13·6%, and the Belgian share of the Netherlands market grew from 7·9% to 13·5%.

one manufacturer has expressed concern at the threat of Japanese competition, which was by 1959 becoming increasingly serious in the Far East, especially in Hong Kong and Malaya, countries which hitherto had been traditional British markets. Apart from the direct assistance to Japan provided by the U.S. in the early days of reconstruction, a number of large-scale Japanese manufacturers benefited from technical assistance contracts with foreign manufacturers on a royalty basis; this was especially important in the case of antibiotics. In 1955 there were 938 pharmaceutical manufacturing plants in Japan and although 847 of these were extremely small (employing less than 100 each) there were four factories in each of which over 1,000 were employed. Although the Japanese Government did not grant direct export subsidies, exporters were allowed to retain, in the form of a 'retention fund certificate', 3% of the invoice value of all foreign exchange earnings, and these certificates were transferable at a premium (see p. 94). In view of what has happened in other export sectors when British exports have been faced with the combination in Japan of low wage costs and the latest available machinery and techniques one must expect some of Britain's largest Commonwealth markets to be increasingly threatened by Japanese competition. This is likely to be especially true of vitamins, but by 1960 Japan also had large and efficient factories producing significant quantities of penicillin and streptomycin.

INTERNATIONAL INVESTMENT

In the U.K.

The pattern of world trade in pharmaceuticals is extremely complex, and difficult to unravel by reason of the fact that it is one of the most internationally owned and controlled of all industries. From this point of view it is an extremely valuable illustration of the danger of paying too much attention to bare trade figures without taking into account 'invisible' earnings and payments associated with an industry.

A very large number of firms operating in the United Kingdom are foreign-owned. Ciba and Roche are, amongst others, owned by Swiss interests; May and Baker is French-dominated. Almost all the leading U.S. drug firms have subsidiaries in the U.K.; among the twenty-five American subsidiaries manufacturing in this country are Merck, Sharp and Dohme; Parke Davis and Pfizer. It was estimated in 1958 that between one-fifth and one-quarter of the total U.K. output of pharmaceuticals was produced in American-owned manufacturing units. Foreign influence is especially marked in the part of the industry specialising in ethical drugs—that is, drugs which are advertised only to the medical profession and supplied direct to the National Health Service. Of the major U.K. companies which specialize in ethical specialities only seven were in 1959 British-owned; thirteen were

American-owned, several were controlled from Switzerland and one was in part financed by French capital.[1]

American firms have manufacturing interests throughout the world. It is estimated that 45% of Charles Pfizer's net income in 1959 came from overseas activities. For Merck and Co. and for Schering the percentages were thirty-five and forty-two respectively.[2]

Hoechst of Germany had in 1959 a share in the capital of thirty-seven companies in twenty-nine different countries—as diverse as the U.K., Spain, Australia, and Mexico. The great Swiss firms, Ciba, Geigy, Roche and Sandoz have all founded branches or subsidiaries abroad; many of these are now much bigger and more important than the parent firms in Switzerland.

By the U.K. Overseas

As regards U.K. investment overseas, this has been very extensive indeed. Glaxo, who have perhaps done more than any other British pharmaceutical manufacturer in this respect, have established subsidiaries in India, Pakistan, South Africa, Australia, New Zealand, Canada, Nigeria, Ceylon, Malaya, Colombia, Cuba, the Argentine and Brazil. More than half these subsidiaries have been set up since the war. Glaxo have also a very extensive overseas administrative network with regional controllers and sales organisations.

Glaxo is not alone in having developed overseas manufacturing units. One large proprietary medicine manufacturer informed us that while the f.o.b. value of exports from his firm shipped from the U.K. had remained constant between 1951 and 1958, his total overseas *turnover*, that is, the value of exports from the U.K. *plus* the value of output from overseas manufacturing establishments, had risen by one-quarter. Whereas in 1951 the value of this firm's commodity exports represented 30% of its total overseas turnover, by 1958 physical exports accounted for only 22% of its overseas turnover.

Local manufacture by U.K. companies has perhaps developed most rapidly in India, where the Government of the Republic has been very stringent indeed in its willingness to grant import licences for pharmaceuticals. The only drugs imported are those which cannot be manufactured locally; these tend to be the newest specialist drugs. The Indian Government has been particularly anxious to foster the development of an indigenous pharmaceutical industry,[3] and as early as 1951 the Government associated itself with United Nations Agencies W.H.O. and U.N.I.C.E.F. in building a penicillin plant at Pimpri. In 1959 this plant produced 20m. mega units of penicillin.

Both in Australia and in the Union of South Africa the respective Governments have taken positive steps to foster the growth of a local

---

[1] J. H. Dunning, *American Investment in British Manufacturing Industry* (London, 1958), p. 62.

[2] *Outlook* (18th April 1960).

[3] We were told by one firm that they were (in 1960) manufacturing locally some 90% of the value of all products sold by them in India.

pharmaceutical industry. As early as 1946 the Government-owned Commonwealth Serum Laboratories established a penicillin plant in Australia. Since then Glaxo have opened a fermentation plant (1956) and it is alleged by the suppliers that these units together can satisfy the entire domestic demand for penicillin.[1] Indeed, productive capacity in 1960 was such that Glaxo-Allenburys (Australia) Pty Ltd, supported by the Commonwealth Serum Laboratories, petitioned the Australian Tariff Board for protective duties on the importation of penicillin and streptomycin. In the course of this enquiry it was stated that Glaxo-Allenburys (Australia) Pty made no imports whatsoever from their parent company in the United Kingdom of any products manufactured by them in Australia. What is more, in order to maintain employment at Port Fairy the U.K. company had transferred to its Australian associate the whole of its New Zealand orders. The capacity of the Australian penicillin and streptomycin plants was such that when import restrictions were lifted early in 1960 and a substantial rise took place in imports of cheap penicillin and streptomycin, the Commonwealth Serum Laboratories temporarily ceased production of penicillin.

There is no doubt that production costs were higher in Australia than in Britain or on the Continent. In the evidence before the Tariff Board Enquiry it was stated that the price of penicillin and its salts to secondary manufacturers in Australia was 10d. per m.u. while the import price from the U.K., including transport costs, was 2·93d. per m.u. For penicillin V the Australian price was 1s. 3d. per gramme; for imports from the U.K. it was 1s. 0·4d. per gramme and for imports from the Netherlands a price of only 3·68d. was quoted.

There can be no doubt that British and other companies which have established manufacturing units in the Commonwealth invariably find that both the initial costs and actual running costs are high. This is especially true of the antibiotics where elaborate equipment is essential and minute attention must be paid to sterility. An extensive 'sterile area' is absolutely imperative and expensive precautions are required to make sure that products are at no stage contaminated. The Glaxo-Allenburys' plant at Port Fairy made regular losses between 1955 and 1958. As regards running costs Australian industry in general has a notoriously high-cost structure.

On the other hand, production overseas helps a firm to reap the benefits of closeness to markets, lower packaging costs (usually a very high proportion of total manufacturing costs), and relative freedom from exchange and trade restrictions. Additionally there is the advantage of closer links with the medical profession in the consuming country. In the case of American firms establishing overseas organisations, the taxation motive has been very strong; by channelling sales through an overseas country, or by remitting profits from operations in a foreign

[1] Proceedings of Tariff Board Enquiry Regarding Penicillin and Streptomycin, held on 26th January 1961. Evidence given on behalf of Messrs. Glaxo-Allenburys (Australia) Pty Ltd.

country to a third country, the tax burden on American-owned companies is substantially reduced. In fact, however, the determination of Governments to establish their own pharmaceutical industries has been so great that usually British and other firms have had either to establish themselves locally (often at great cost) or to forego entirely the chance of selling their products in a particular market.

In some cases a Government's motive for encouraging local manufacture was to provide employment; often the object was one of national security. Modern life-saving drugs are an essential part of defence and Governments have felt justified in fostering local pharmaceutical industries in the same way that they have fostered a home-grown food supply. Another motive arises from their desire to reduce imports in the interests of the balance of payments. Countries with inadequate exchange reserves and which export mainly primary products, the prices of which fluctuate widely from year to year, have a strong incentive to encourage import-saving industries. In the case of Australia it has been calculated that if the entire domestic demand for penicillin and streptomycin in 1958–59 had been imported it would have cost about £1·4m.

There is, moreover, an element of prestige arising from the acquisition of scientific know-how which goes with a domestic pharmaceutical industry and this should not be underrated, especially in the case of the younger Commonwealth countries.

There is no doubt that the development of manufacture overseas by British companies has had a marked effect upon the U.K. export figures for pharmaceuticals to many markets, and thus some of the decline in the U.K. share of such markets is apparent rather than real. This is a fact which must be firmly borne in mind when conclusions are drawn from our Tables. While the total volume of American direct investment in pharmaceuticals has, since the war, undoubtedly been greater than that of the British or Swiss (the Swiss led the way before the war), in those markets which are most significant to the U.K., e.g. the Commonwealth, the level of investment by U.K. firms has undoubtedly been greater than that of any other country and one would accordingly expect the U.K. share of such import markets to have been affected more than that of the U.S., Switzerland or Germany.

On the other hand the effect of the establishment overseas by American companies upon U.K. exports should not be underestimated. These U.S.-owned companies have all the advantages of American 'know-how' and capital resources and their products have frequently ousted those of British companies. One large British firm gave as a main reason for the decline in their exports to certain foreign markets, not the setting up abroad of *British*, but of *American* subsidiaries.

Bearing in mind what has been said about overseas manufacture, it is worth looking at some of the United Kingdom's overseas markets in more detail.

UNITED KINGDOM EXPORT MARKETS

Australia

Although in pharmaceuticals as a whole the U.K. share of the Australian import market fell fairly sharply between 1953 and 1959 from 71·7% to 58·9% (Table D), as between various kinds of drugs the decline was by no means uniform. In fact in the more modern drugs the U.K. share was retained very well in spite of the extensive development of local manufacture. Up to 1957 the U.K. maintained its share of the sulpha drug import market, and although the value of import of vitamins from all sources fell between 1953 and 1959, the United Kingdom was in 1959 supplying almost half by value of the Dominion's import requirements of vitamins—the U.K. share was substantially greater than that of her closest rival in the vitamin field—Switzerland. The U.K. appears also to have held her own in insulin.

South Africa

In the case of the Union of South Africa there was a contrast between the performance of certain selected drugs and that of other proprietary medicines. Whereas the U.K. share of the South African import market for the latter fell from 52·5% in 1953 to 44·5% in 1958, the United Kingdom share in sera and vaccines was maintained at rather less than one-quarter of the value of the import market; in the case of penicillin and other antibiotics the United Kingdom share of the import market actually rose between 1953 and 1957; it fell back in 1958—largely as the result of growth of low-priced imports from Denmark, but even so the U.K. remained by far the largest single supplying country.

Canada

In Canada, the U.K. has, since the war, secured only a small share of the total import market. Most manufacturing is in the hands of Canadian subsidiaries of the very large U.S.A. concerns and import requirements are usually met by the U.S.A. British pharmaceuticals, whether made in Canada by the twelve or so manufacturing units of the important U.K. firms, or imported direct from the U.K., compared favourably in 1959 in price and quality with those of the U.S.A. American products are, however, very much more widely advertised than those of the U.K. and in this market only intense sales promotion will enable British firms to make their products generally known. In a country like Canada where self-treatment is widely practised a very high level of expenditure on sales promotion, sampling and packaging is essential. In this respect the Americans are said to have been, throughout the nineteen-fifties, well ahead of the British.

Western Europe

Table D shows that during our period, the continent of Europe was not an important market for U.K. pharmaceuticals. This was in part due to fairly high tariffs, but an additional handicap arises from the very strict controls imposed on the marketing of drugs in almost all European countries. The regulations with regard to the sale of pharmaceuticals were especially restrictive in France and Italy, where registration of all drugs was rigidly enforced, and often in such a way as to discourage imports.

In most European countries the United Kingdom share of import markets has always been fairly small. Thus Table D shows that in 1959 the U.K. held only 6·1% of the total import market of the E.E.C. countries. In the Netherlands, the U.K. share was higher (8%), and in Italy it was 6·3%.

Although the share of pharmaceuticals as a whole in the Italian import market cannot be said to have been high (it was in 1959 much less than the share of 'other chemicals'), in the antibiotic field a very substantial proportion of the import market was held by the U.K. There were marked variations in the percentage share of the Italian import market obtained by the U.K. between 1953 and 1959, but for most years the U.K. was the leading foreign supplier of streptomycin; in penicillin, too, the U.K. share tended to rise. Certainly the United Kingdom share (in 1959 one-fifth) of the Italian import market for 'other antibiotics' increased after 1953–54.

In the E.F.T.A. countries the U.K. share of the import markets was generally higher than in the Common Market. This is especially true of Norway, where the U.K. in 1959 held over one-fifth of the total import market for pharmaceuticals. Both in Norway and Sweden fairly vigorous competition in the antibiotic field came from Denmark, as well as from the U.S.A. Danish export prices of antibiotics were, it should be noted, particularly low.

Although the British pharmaceutical industry (e.g. antibiotics) held its own remarkably well in some products and countries, it is probable that the U.K. share in the import markets of most countries fell during the nineteen-fifties, even when account is taken of local manufacture by British subsidiaries. In our search for explanations of this, we shall look first at relative price levels.

BRITISH AND FOREIGN PRICES COMPARED

In the export field, comparative price quotations are difficult to come by, but it is generally accepted that British firms lost exports on account of their price quotations being higher than those of their overseas competition. In the case of the Australian market, although prices of imports of penicillin from the U.K. were lower than Australian domestic prices they were substantially higher than those of the Netherlands.

We were told of the U.K. losing contracts in Ghana, Malaya and Nigeria because lower prices were quoted by other exporting countries. In these particular countries, Government purchases account for a significant proportion of total drug imports and in tendering for such contracts prices are exceedingly important.

Domestic Prices

Paradoxically, although British export price quotations were so often well above those of other countries, the reverse was true of domestic price levels. Thus although the U.K. lost business abroad because the prices British manufacturers asked were too high, those same manufacturers obtained lower prices on the U.K. domestic market than did most of their foreign competitors in their respective domestic markets. In fact, on the home market British drugs were among the cheapest in the world. As always with such price comparisons it is impossible to draw very precise conclusions but, in the case of penicillin 'G', which accounts for a significant proportion of world trade in pharmaceuticals, U.K. domestic prices were relatively low.

Price to Public of Sodium Penicillin G

1959
1 mega vial

	s.	d.
U.K.	2	0
Denmark	3	7
Norway	2	8
Sweden	2	6

It is particularly unsatisfactory to make international comparisons of retail prices of medical specialities, but there is no doubt that of the leading producing countries, U.K. prices were among the lowest. A firm manufacturing medical specialities informed us that whereas the price of a pack of their most important product in the U.K. was 3s. 6d. (without tax), in Germany and France the product would sell for the equivalent of 4s.; in Italy and Belgium the price would be about 5s. 6d., and in the U.S. as much as 7s. These prices included import duties. The retailer's mark-up on the Continent and in America was higher than in the case of the U.K., but only moderately so, and certainly not enough to account for the retail price differences.

An exhaustive survey into international specialist drug prices was conducted in 1959 by Dr V. Valier, an Italian authority on the pharmaceutical industry. The results of this investigation are embodied in Table 11.2. From the survey it is clear that the United Kingdom was classed among those countries where medical specialities were relatively cheap. In the field of antibiotics, U.K. domestic prices were in fact lower than those of Italy. Table 11.2 shows that internal German prices for the range of products covered by the survey were about 50%, Belgian 38% and Swiss 22% higher than those of the United Kingdom.

N

The truth is that the very high prices realised by pharmaceuticals in the domestic markets of most countries enable producers to export at extremely *low* prices. Exports from many countries tend to be marginal and are invariably sold at prices which approximate more to marginal than average costs. This is especially true of the United States where research expenditure is a large element in fixed costs and where exports are looked upon very much as an overflow from domestic output.

Low export prices were on the other hand *sometimes* due to low domestic costs. In the case of Italy, for example, there were in 1959 no patent laws and the commercial drug firms spent relatively little on research. The Italian pharmaceutical industry was able to obtain very cheaply the fruits of research conducted at the State-owned Higher Institute of Health. This institute, originally financed by a Rockefeller Grant, and one of the finest of its kind in Europe, was entirely financed by the State and its annual budget was of the order of £500,000. The paucity of commercial research in Italy is shown by the fact that those companies possessing adequate research facilities were allowed to take this into account when determining production costs for the purpose of the price regulations; in 1959 only fourteen drug houses were able to take advantage of this concession.[1]

Where the United States—and indeed other producing countries—establish overseas manufacturing units, it is usual for research to be concentrated in the parent company's laboratories and to be charged against domestic operations. Although in practice overseas subsidiary companies sometimes pay royalties to their parent organisations in respect of the benefits they derive from research operations,[2] prices of products made by subsidiaries often do not bear the full weight of research costs. This means that exports from an American-owned subsidiary in, say, France, might for this reason be cheaper than similar products manufactured in the States. Products manufactured in this way in third countries might sell at prices much lower than those of U.K. exports.

Price Regulation

Now one reason why domestic prices of British drugs were relatively low is to be seen in the Voluntary Price Regulation Scheme, which applied to all drugs sold under the National Health Service. This Scheme was revised in 1961, after which the position was as follows:

For three years after the introduction of a new preparation, the manufacturer was normally free to fix his own price—this to enable him to recoup his research and development expenditure in respect of the

---

[1] See 'L'organisation de la recherche et la protection de L'invention dans les Etats de la Communauté', in *La Pharmacie Industrielle*, Bulletin de la Chambre Syndicale Nationale des Fabricants de Produits Pharmaceutiques, p. 143.

[2] This was the case with Glaxo-Allenburys Australia (Pty.) Ltd. See Evidence presented to the Tariff Board Enquiry, cited above.

drug. After three years, however, the home price of a drug was related to one of three criteria.

(1) The 'export' criterion, which aimed at linking the domestic wholesale price in the U.K. to prices in the principal export markets.

(2) The 'unbranded standard equivalent' criterion which applied to preparations, the formulae for which were identical to those of standard products described in the British Pharmacopaeia.

(3) The 'trade price formula' criterion which provided for the calculation of retail prices in accordance with standard prices and allowances.

In some cases individual manufacturers could elect to negotiate prices direct with the Ministry of Health. On the other hand, in the case of certain patented drugs, the Ministry had the right to negotiate prices direct with the manufacturer, regardless of the fact that the prices of the drugs in question had already been justified under one or more of the above criteria. There was thus a considerable element of Government price-control in the British pharmaceutical industry—of a degree unique in the peace-time experience of manufacturing industry.

It would be a mistake to assume that pharmaceutical prices have been controlled only in the United Kingdom. Quite rigid control has also been exercised since the war in France,[1] but notwithstanding this, French and other European drug prices were in the nineteen-fifties definitely fixed at higher levels than in the United Kingdom.

The relatively low level of British drug prices had, it is alleged by the industry, two indirect but adverse consequences for U.K. drug exports in the nineteen-fifties. In the first place, manufacturers were unable to cut their profit margins on exports to the same degree as did their overseas trade competitors. In the second place, since profits were relatively restricted, firms were unable to finance research and development on the same scale as their American and Continental rivals. A consistently high level of research expenditure is absolutely essential if a company or nation is to keep abreast of modern developments in this industry. World trade in pharmaceuticals has become more and more a matter of producing and selling abroad drugs which other nations have not yet discovered or developed. As countries develop their own pharmaceutical industries they rapidly cease to require older established preparations and only drugs which cannot easily be manufactured locally are welcome as imports.

RESEARCH

In absolute terms, both the United States and Swiss pharmaceutical industries spend more on research than does the U.K.—the U.S. drug

---

[1] See 'Etudes sur les prix des produits pharmaceutiques specialisés dans les Etats de la Communauté', by J. Roy in *L'Industrie Pharmaceutique dans les Sis Payx de la Communauté Economique Europeenne*.

industry in 1959 spent about £63m., Switzerland about £7½m., and the U.K. about £5½m.

The U.S.A.

It is said that any one of the major U.S. firms probably spends more on research than the whole U.K. industry; in view of the absolute size of the American industry, however, it is only to be expected that both in research expenditure and achievements in terms of new products the U.S. should be ahead of the United Kingdom. Some of the American giants spend a very high proportion of their revenue on research. In view of the intensive research effort of the leading U.S. firms it is hardly surprising that the Americans have been in the forefront in developing new drugs. The broad spectrum antibiotic drugs which were commercially developed after 1957 were almost exclusively of American origin. It has been estimated that about two-thirds of the new ethical drugs prescribed since the war originated in the United States.[1] These developments had a profound effect upon world trade in drugs, especially as the new antibiotics are covered by world patents and in 1959 were still being sold at high introductory prices.

The older types of penicillin and streptomycin were in extremely short supply in the early post-war years and sold at high prices. With the growth of local manufacture, however, and the flooding of export markets by supplies from practically all the European manufacturing countries the world price of these antibiotics dropped sharply during the second half of the 'fifties. Thus although U.K. exports of penicillin in 1954 were 44m. mega units, realising £2·8m., in 1959 they were over twice as great in volume (90m. mega units), but were valued at only £1·7m.; the unit value falling from 1s. 3½d. per mega unit to 4½d. per mega unit. Although the U.K. exported more and more penicillin each year, the foreign exchange earned actually fell. This is a clear reminder that the pharmaceutical industry is not one where a country can afford to rely upon past achievements. New products are absolutely essential—and this means a high level of expenditure on research.

While the research achievements of the British drug industry cannot in aggregate match those of the United States, it would be a mistake to regard the U.K. industry as having failed in this respect. Expenditure on research and development by the industry more than doubled between 1953 and 1959.

The U.K.

Research in the U.K. has resulted in some notable developments in the British drug industry in recent years. It would be invidious to single out particular firms; the following are however mentioned merely as examples. Beechams developed three new penicillins, Broxil, Celbenin, and Penbriten; I.C.I. (Pharmaceuticals Division) developed Palu-

[1] See J. H. Dunning, cited above.

drine and the Wellcome Foundation have antimalarial preparations to their credit. Glaxo and I.C.I. (Pharmaceuticals Division) together developed Griseofulvin an effective antifungal biotic for human use.

Distillers Co. (Biochemicals) Ltd must take the credit for introducing Penicillin V into the United Kingdom. This penicillin, which is not only more convenient to administer but also maintains a higher blood level than the older penicillin G when taken orally was in the first place discovered and patented by an American firm, Lilly. The drug was never developed in the U.S., however, and the real credit for realising its significance must go to an Austrian firm Biochemie, which had worked on similar lines to Lilly. Distillers Co. (Biochemicals), later obtained processing rights and did a great deal of subsequent research on the drug, being the first company to produce Penicillin V in Great Britain.

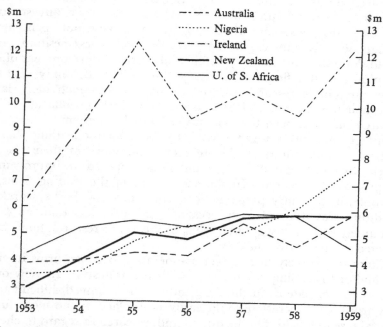

Chart 7. Leading markets for U.K. exports of pharmaceuticals (S.I.T.C. group 541)

In 1958 and 1959, two striking achievements were announced by the National Research Development Corporation. A new drug Cephalosporin 'C', one of a group of antibiotics on which the N.R.D.C. worked for several years in collaboration with the University of Oxford and Medical Research Council scientists, was developed. Cephalosporin is resistant to destruction by the enzyme penicillinase which inactivates penicillin. It was claimed by the N.R.D.C. that the drug, or compounds derived from it, could be the starting point for a new range of antibiotics; by 1960 a number of business arrangements had been entered into with substantial U.K., American and European pharmaceutical houses to permit this development to be carried out; in that year foreign drug houses were already contributing about £280,000 in respect of rights arising from this new preparation.

Another important development supported by the National Research Development Corporation in the late nineteen-fifties was Interferon, a drug produced by the interaction of a virus with living animal tissue which had the important property of limiting the reproduction of a normal virus. It was hoped that its development would lead to the production of a therapeutic agent of wide usefulness against viral diseases.[1]

There is no means of estimating how much is spent by the U.K. Government research agencies and the universities on research in the medical field. A substantial part of the research which is of value to the pharmaceutical industry is in any case a by-product of investigations in quite different fields. Nevertheless by almost any standard it is clear that post-war British Governments have not spent nearly enough on university expansion generally and a less hesitant policy would doubtless have made possible a more rapid development of new techniques in this field—as in many others. It is certainly true that American public research institutions have been much more lavish with their use of funds which have aided medical and pharmaceutical research than has been the case in the United Kingdom.

In fact, the tendency in the U.K. has been for the leading pharmaceutical manufacturers to devote more and more of their research expenditure to 'original' or 'speculative' as opposed to 'improvement' or 'processing' research. In the case of one of the leading firms, for example, in the early post-war years some 90% of their research expenditure was devoted to 'processing'; in 1960, less than 30% was accounted for in this way; over 70% of this firm's research funds being devoted to speculative fields.[2]

There is relatively little direct co-operation between firms in either original or processing research in the British industry. In view of the importance of patents in the drug industry it is indeed difficult to see how fruitful co-operation could easily take place in the more fundamental research field. On the other hand, research in regard to cheaper methods of processing and packaging is probably just as well carried out independently by various firms. Independent research of this kind introduces a valuable element of competition into the cost structures of the firms in the industry. There is however a very great deal of mutual

---

[1] National Research Development Corporation, *Report and Statement of Accounts for Year July 1959–June 1960.*

[2] The less dramatic contribution made by processing and packaging research is not to be despised. Intensive research on processing techniques have helped (1961) to bring down production costs of penicillin in the U.K. to a level as low as 5% of costs when production was first started. Packaging research has brought down costs to such an extent that many preparations which a few years ago were beyond the pockets of the mass of people in the poorer parts of the world can now be bought by them in large quantities.

exchange of knowledge in the purchase and sale of royalties between the leading companies, both at home and abroad, and this should not be overlooked.

THE GOVERNMENT AND THE INDUSTRY

The research effort of the industry during the nineteen-fifties was striking, but in view of the fact that the U.K. was clearly being outstripped by the Americans and possibly the Swiss in this field it is pertinent to ask whether even better research results could have been achieved—and thus export performance improved—if the domestic price level of drugs had not been below that ruling in other countries. The answer can be only speculative, and in the last resort the reader must make his own judgement. Within the industry there is a strong feeling that low domestic prices had a harmful effect upon research and exports.

The Hinchliffe Committee Report

This whole question was examined by the Hinchliffe Committee, which, although criticising high advertising and sales promotion expenditure, realised that manufacturers had to rely largely upon the profits from medical specialities to finance their research expenditure.[1] The Committee accordingly recommended that any pricing arrangements between the Ministry of Health and the British pharmaceutical industry should be designed to make full allowance for genuine research expenditure so as 'to enable a vital industry to make its maximum contribution to the development of drug therapy and also to export trade . . .'.

The Committee further found that the increase in the N.H.S. drug bill in recent years could be largely attributed to inflation and to the discovery of new drugs involving large research expenditure and intricate production facilities. The Committee were clearly right in stressing that the pharmaceutical industry was one where vigorous and expensive research was all important. It must be vigorous since a firm must always keep one step ahead of its rivals in order to secure the necessary product and process patents for the fruits of its research. It is also expensive because in this industry there are so many research 'dead-ends'. The results of a given line of investigation cannot possibly be foretold with any accuracy and many attractive-looking fields of study have to be abandoned without worth-while results being achieved.[2]

[1] *Final Report of the Committee on the Cost of Prescribing* (London, H.M.S.O., 1959), para. 224: 'The pharmaceutical manufacturers have to rely upon the profits of proprietary medicines to finance their research expenditure. If this source of finance were not available to the manufacturers, money for research would have to be found elsewhere. The Ministry of Health does not undertake research into the discovery of new drugs.'

[2] 'If a firm makes one major advance in 10–20 years it is doing very well. . . . There must be very few industries in which it is possible for a firm to lose a market so quickly as in the pharmaceutical industry. The staff and equipment which have been organised to manufacture a successful product may be a source of profit for one year, and a liability the next' (*Final Report on the Cost of Prescribing*, para. 232).

Thus the Hinchliffe Committee emphasised the 'importance of doing nothing to circumscribe the wide range of research activities upon which the discoveries of new drugs depend or the incentive to widen it' (para. 249).

The Size of Firms

Closely linked with the problem of prices is that of the scale of output and the size of the consuming market.

In our period there were some important mergers in the British pharmaceutical industry, but in general the industry remained one where medium-sized firms predominated.

In itself the number of smallish and medium-sized firms is no sign of inefficiency. Many of the remedies and tonics which one finds crowding the shelves of every chemist's shop—Aspirin and Epsom Salts, for example—can be produced quite efficiently by simple machinery in moderate-sized establishments.[1]

In the case of a number of well-known proprietaries, many firms have only a limited range of products and do not require large factories for their manufacture. On the other hand, antibiotics are produced most cheaply on a very large scale. Penicillin is made by only four firms in the United Kingdom and the two largest fermentation plants, those of Distillers Co. (Biochemicals) Ltd and Glaxo Ltd, are said to have cost £1m. each, when originally built. The subsequent extensions have been of immense proportions, dwarfing the original expenditures.

It is probably true, however, that in the British pharmaceutical industry in general, there were in 1959 a number of firms whose scale of operations was too small. In this connexion, much depends upon the size of the market served, and here the U.S.A. and most Continental manufacturers have a distinct advantage. The population of the U.S. is about three times that of the United Kingdom and is almost certainly more health (or drug) conscious, especially in regard to self-treatment with branded proprietaries.

The Domestic Market

Although the population of the U.K. is greater than that of most other European countries, the British domestic market for most drugs is substantially smaller; this is especially true of medical specialities.

The number of proprietary remedies (ethical or non-ethical) in the U.K. might appear to be high—about 6,000—but the total is certainly less than one-third of the number in either the U.S.A., France, or western Germany. In Italy there were in 1960 about 12,000 registered medical specialities on sale.

Table 11.3 shows that expenditure on prescribed drugs per head of the population in Great Britain was in 1960 very substantially less than in the other leading drug manufacturing countries. Moreover, in 1953, the

---

[1] For a discussion of this question, see C. J. Thomas, 'The Pharmaceutical Industry' in *Structure of British Industry*, vol. II, ed. D. Burn.

International Labour Office had shown that expressed as a percentage of National Income the cost of pharmaceutical benefits per head of the population was lower in England and Wales than in almost any other country for which figures were quoted.

All the evidence we have gathered points to the same conclusion— that on the Continent individuals are prepared to consume more drugs per annum than the average Briton. Thus almost all Continental countries' pharmaceutical manufacturers had the advantage of a larger home market than their opposite numbers in the U.K. The one major exception is, of course, Switzerland, where by far the greater part of drug manufacture is exported. It should, however, be remembered that at a very early stage indeed of the development of the medical speciality industry (the first pharmaceutical specialities were introduced about 1890) the Swiss companies were already opening distributing houses abroad and for the last fifty years or more they have regarded foreign markets as being their main concern. Indeed, the Swiss firm regards the foreign market much as most British or U.S. manufacturers regard their respective home markets—as the essential base upon which all operations depend.

It would, of course, be wrong to suggest that the existence of the National Health Service, as such, and as at present constituted in Britain, has had a harmful effect upon the development of new drugs and hence upon the export performance of the industry. Neither does official policy in practice greatly discriminate against proprietary preparations. Certainly the cost of prescribing rose during our period (the cost of drugs and dressings supplied under the N.H.S. rose from £27m. in 1949 to £57m. in 1959), but this takes no account of savings resulting from the greater efficiency of modern drugs and which are reflected in earlier recovery, reduced absenteeism due to illness, and saving on hospital costs. In general, it is doubtful whether the British drug industry has so far suffered serious adverse effects from the pressure exercised by the Ministry of Health. Nevertheless, should the Ministry at any time try to exercise direct pressure on the doctors in the matter of prescribing proprietary drugs, this should be done with great circumspection, for the drug industry is typical of those industries where an atmosphere of expansion and experimentation is absolutely essential to success both at home and overseas.

In this connexion there is a lesson to be learned from France. Before 1939 France was the world's second largest exporter of pharmaceuticals. At the end of the war restrictive regulations were introduced whereby each new pharmaceutical preparation had to be licensed, but a licence was granted only if an application had not already been accepted in respect of a similar preparation. This requirement was interpreted quite rigidly with the result that by 1960 France had fallen even farther than Britain behind the U.S.A. and Switzerland in developing new types and varieties of drugs. This decline was reflected in the fact that France was in 1959 not, as before the war, second, but sixth in importance as an exporter of pharmaceuticals. Indeed, the consequence of rigid controls have been so serious that some relaxation took place in 1960 in the licensing arrangements for new French drugs.

Table 11.1. *Exports of medicinal and pharmaceutical products by U.S.A. and major O.E.E.C. countries*

$m.

	1953	1954	1955	1956	1957	1958	1959
U.S.A.	217·4	244·8	227·6	247·9	286·2	279·0	285·4
Belgium-Luxembourg	9·3	10·4	12·2	15·7	18·4	16·2	18·9
Denmark	12·3	10·9	10·8	11·8	15·2	15·0	18·5
France	57·4	64·8	65·8	73·3	86·6	85·5	85·9
West Germany	40·8	49·0	53·9	68·3	85·0	88·2	101·2
Italy	12·8	16·1	16·6	17·2	21·1	22·5	25·2
Netherlands	12·9	14·4	17·9	23·8	31·8	32·5	40·2
U.K.	83·6	94·0	107·7	108·2	118·7	113·3	120·3
Other O.E.E.C. and Canada	10·9	11·4	11·2	13·5	18·0	20·9	17·9

Source: O.E.E.C., *The Chemical Industry in Europe, 1959–60.*

Table 11.2. *Comparative prices of medical specialities, 1958*

Country	Antibiotics	Vitamins	Sulphona- mides	Hormones	Various Specialities	Total
U.K.	98	108	84	80	114	106
Italy	100	100	100	100	100	100
France	116	78	83	67	83	89
Switzerland	133	104	152	110	130	128
Belgium	163	137	139	139	139	145
West Germany	274	142	114	118	120	159

Source: V. Valier, *Comparazione dei Prezzi delle Specialita Medianali i Italia ed All 'estero.*

Table 11.3. *Expenditure on prescribed drugs per head of population per annum*

	s.	d.
Great Britain	16	0
Netherlands	22	2
Sweden	25	8
West Germany	26	1
U.S.A.	33	0
Italy	47	5
Belgium	55	4

Sources: Winthrop Group Ltd Statistical unit; compiled by them from confidential but reliable sources (1960). The figures are based on manufacturer's prices and do not include profits of pharmacists or wholesale distributors.

CHAPTER XII

HOSIERY AND KNITWEAR

THE world market in many types of clothing grew less fast than for most other commodities after 1953, this being a field where the establishment of domestic manufacture is particularly easy. Generally, in clothing the labour cost element is an important part of total cost and this makes the industry a particularly appropriate one for establishing in the relatively undeveloped countries which have a large potential labour force, and where wage rates are relatively low.

One would have expected some falling away in the total value of the export market secured by the United Kingdom, but what is more disconcerting is the way in which British exports sagged more than those of her competitors. The U.K. share of the world market in clothing, as defined by the S.I.T.C., fell from the quite substantial percentage of 22·7% in 1953 to 14·2% in 1958, and 10·2% in 1959.

The industry is a heterogeneous one and the Standard International Trade Classification (which we have adopted in Table J) includes outerwear, underwear, leather and rubber clothing, hats, ties, gloves, fur clothing, stockings and socks, but excludes footwear.

Unfortunately, in the S.I.T.C. no distinction is made between knitwear on the one hand and woven clothing on the other. In the trade this distinction is quite marked and it is clearly necessary in analysing export performance to distinguish between the two. In this case study we confine our attention to the knitting industry, although much of what will be said in connexion with knitwear applies also to woven clothing.

Even within the knitwear industry there are a number of sectors—sectors which in many instances have in common only the fact that they knit their fabric as opposed to weaving it. In this study we have accordingly analysed in greater detail one item, nylon stockings, an item which is fairly easily defined and for which adequate statistics are available in most importing countries. We shall then examine other sectors of the knitwear industry, but in less detail.

NYLON STOCKINGS

Nylon stockings are essentially an import of more prosperous countries in temperate latitudes. The markets which are of greatest significance in world trade are those of the developed industrial countries of western Europe and North America with the addition perhaps of Australia, New Zealand and the Union of South Africa. West European countries are of greatest importance in this connexion, and it is noteworthy that total imports of nylon socks and stockings from all sources into these West European countries expanded considerably between 1953 and 1959. To a lesser extent the same is true of the southern Dominions.

U.K. Markets

The United Kingdom share of the European import market fell away very considerably after 1953. Whereas in 1953 the U.K. share of the Norwegian import market for nylon stockings was over 32%, by 1959 it had declined to less than 5%. In the case of the Netherlands the U.K. share fell from 10% to almost nothing. Of the major European markets it was only in Sweden that the U.K. retained more than a 10% share of the import market in 1958–59—but here the U.K. share had been as high as 52% in 1953. However, in the case of Australia and New Zealand the U.K. held over 80% of each import market throughout our period. In these markets the strongest competition came from local manufacture rather than from imports. In the Union of South Africa, however, the number of pairs of stockings imported from the U.K. fell year by year, so that the U.K. share of the market, whether measured by volume or by value, declined steeply. The size of the total import market however increased considerably. In terms of the share of the market by value in South Africa British nylon stockings fared worse than most other types of knitwear.

In South Africa the United States made considerable gains at the expense of the U.K. (one of the few country markets in the knitwear sector where this happened). This switch in demand from British to American stockings was associated with a marked divergence in unit values between the two countries. American stockings were dearer than British ones in 1951, but by 1953–54 had become very much cheaper. The effect of this on the competitive position of the two countries can be seen in the dramatic switch which occurred in 1954, when the United States took the place of the U.K. as the leading supplying country.

This general pattern is not, however, repeated in western Europe, for although in all the major European markets the U.K. share of the import market for nylons fell, the United States failed to profit from this and it is to Italy, and in the Italian market itself to western Germany, that we must look for the source of the vigorous competition which seems to have defeated U.K. exporters. By 1958 Italy had captured at least half the import market for nylon stockings in Denmark; she was the leading supplier of Sweden and Norway. In the Scandinavian markets particularly, western Germany, too, had become a powerful competitor. In most cases the main impact of Italian competition came after 1955—ten years after the war and can hardly be explained as simply the result of her recovery from war-time difficulties. Much the same applies to western Germany, whose export of nylon stockings to Norway more than doubled between 1955 and 1957. This is a field where it is not good enough to brush aside the decline of the U.K. share as being the inevitable result of the post-war recovery of ex-enemies.

In regard to nylon stockings, United Kingdom Government restrictions can have had little effect upon sales or export performance in recent years. It is probably true that in the early nineteen-fifties manufacturers were still only just emerging from the period when their raw material allocation depended directly upon their export performance, and the easing of these requirements after 1953 undoubtedly encouraged some firms to relax their export efforts. Yet this can hardly have had more than a marginal impact in the years after 1954.[1]

Some British firms which previously exported established their own subsidiaries in overseas markets. One of the largest clothing manufacturers set up an Australian company for the manufacture of nylon hosiery in 1953 and a factory was opened in South Africa at the end of 1956. The same firm has concluded licence agreements for the manufacture of hosiery under its brand name in (among other countries) Germany, France, Austria and Spain. Overseas manufacture has been significant in the Union of South Africa (largely to avoid payment of the heavy import duty) and British capital has probably played a larger part in this process than, say, American or German capital. We were told by the companies concerned that the setting up of British-owned factories for manufacture of stockings overseas had had some impact upon the U.K. share of the various country markets. Nevertheless the process was not as marked as in the motor car and electrical industries and can hardly explain the down-turn in the U.K. share in so many markets of the world.

Comparative Prices

A more general explanation of the decline in the U.K. share is to be found in the relatively favourable price structure of many foreign countries. We were informed that production costs for fully-fashioned hosiery in a dyed and finished state in the U.K., including packing, overheads, amortisation of machines, but excluding profits, were estimated in 1958 to have been between 37s. and 45s. a dozen pairs. Similar stockings could be bought from western Germany and Italy for prices as low as 20s. a dozen pairs.

In the case of the U.K. the largest items in manufacturing costs are wages and the cost of installing and running machines. The cost of yarn in the making of stockings is low—equivalent to no more than a few pence per pair. In fact U.K. list prices of nylon for the period 1953–59 were comparatively low—for some deniers used in stocking manufacture the lowest in the world. In regard to export trade, however, and also for a large part of internal trade in some countries, these

---

[1] The raw material allocation scheme had one side effect which undoubtedly had an adverse effect upon later export performance. Since there was such a close link between a firm's export returns and its raw material supplies manufacturers tended to export at any price which covered marginal costs. Thus British export prices of stockings were abnormally low in the early nineteen-fifties. This was taken for dumping by the authorities in some importing countries and quite stringent anti-dumping legislation directed specifically against imports from the U.K. was introduced in the Union of South Africa, Australia, and Sweden.

list prices mean very little. For example, the Italian Government imposed a producer's tax on yarn for domestic use, but this tax was not levied on any yarn destined for export. The Italian nylon producers themselves allowed a substantial 'quantity' discount, which could be as high as 25 % and which was itself a valuable aid to the larger exporting firms. This discount was additional to the direct export subsidy allowed by nylon producers. In view of these complicated arrangements it is extremely difficult to compare raw material costs between the United Kingdom and Continental exporters.

Of far greater importance than the difference in nylon yarn prices between the U.K. on the one hand and Continental producers on the other was the very marked differential in wage-costs. The gap between the earnings of British textile operatives on the one hand, and those of Germany and Italy on the other is probably greater in the hosiery industry than in most other industries. We were told by one stocking manufacturer that in 1959 a skilled knitter in his factory could earn up to £25 a week. This was probably exceptional, but the basic wage of a knitter of fully-fashioned hosiery in western Germany was almost certainly only half of that of a knitter in this country.[1] In Italy the wage rate was even lower, but was compensated to a certain extent by extremely high social security taxes, amounting in some cases to over 80 % of the wage bill (see p. 106). On the other hand, there was in Italy a profusion of very small 'manufacturers' who, since they employed only one machine could avoid much of this taxation burden. Such manufacturers worked for wholesalers who supplied the yarn (subsidised if intended to be made into export products), and these quasi-domestic manufacturers, it is said, were prepared to knit stockings for a fee of approximately 10s. per dozen! Dutch stockings were also cheaper than those of Britain and 'Perlon' stockings from Germany made substantial inroads into Britain's European market.

A further point is that on the Continent three-shift working was common, whereas British practice was to limit production to two shifts a day. This consideration is of great importance when one remembers the relatively high level of fixed costs in the hosiery industry.

While the British stocking industry used much more up-to-date machinery than was employed in Italy, this was not necessarily true in the case of Germany. On a visit to German hosiery factories in the spring of 1960 it was reported by a British Productivity Committee that there were more fully-fashioned frames of modern type in use *pro rata* in Germany than in the United Kingdom. The circular knit factories, too, were equipped with the most modern machines.[2]

---

[1] The British hosiery industry was at a disadvantage because its workers were on high piece rates, which were tied to the retail price index. The average male operative's wage in April 1956 was £12 17s. 7d.—well above the average wage in textiles.

[2] Report of Hinckley and District Productivity Committee of the Hosiery Manufacturers' Association visit to Germany. Quoted in *Hosiery Trade Journal*, July 1960.

Importance of Fashion

In the late 'fifties the U.K. nylon stocking industry was particularly badly hit in the fully-fashioned sector. Exports of these stockings were 243,000 dozen pairs in 1957, but only 75,000 dozen pairs in 1959. The reason for this is to be found in the trend towards seamless, circular-knit stockings. This fashion switch occurred in the U.S.A. in 1956, and rapidly spread to western Europe. With this change in demand the Continental manufacturers, and especially the Italians, found themselves with a surplus of fully-fashioned machinery. The consequence was a rapid fall in the price of fully-fashioned stockings on the Continent and a flooding of the export markets with them. In view of her already high costs and heavy dependence upon fully-fashioned stockings in the export sector, the British industry was particularly adversely hit by this movement. In 1955, U.K. exports of seamless stockings were 267,000 dozen pairs; of fully-fashioned 360,000 dozen pairs. By 1959 exports of seamless were 621,000 dozen pairs, of fully-fashioned, as we have noted above, only 75,000 dozen pairs.

In regard to stockings one is almost forced to the conclusion that here is a product in which U.K. prices were so high as to render competition with most Continental suppliers almost hopeless.

Yet even in this field the prospect was not entirely one of unrelieved gloom. By 1959–60 manufacturers could no longer easily sell abroad their medium quality branded products, but in spite of intense Italian and German competition there were two sectors of this industry where selling prospects were extremely good. In the first place little difficulty was encountered in selling the best quality nylons in shades made to the order of the overseas purchaser, and here was a field where British firms could develop a highly remunerative trade. The dyeing side of the industry in the U.K. was far more efficient than that of Germany and Italy, and especially in the darker shades British manufacturers were said to produce a finer article than the Germans and Italians. On the Continent demand for the less common stocking shades has since the war been greater than in the United Kingdom. Possibly a tendency for shades to become more varied in the United Kingdom market would encourage manufacturers to take advantage of their relatively greater technical ability in the dyeing field and so to become much more fashion conscious in suiting their stocking shades to different market conditions.

Secondly, as we have seen, there developed after about 1956 an extensive market for seamless stockings, and here the price and wage differentials we discussed above were much smaller. When this change in fashion occurred, those U.K. firms which had already installed circular knit machinery found that they could export without difficulty. This was especially true where they were prepared to export stockings 'in the grey', that is, worked up into shape, but unfinished and undyed. Overseas buyers like to sell their stockings under their own trade names, and in 1958, for example, were willing to buy as many unfinished stockings as the United Kingdom could supply.

Clearly the nylon stocking market is one where fashion changes are of first importance, and while in the circumstances of the nineteen-sixties there would seem little chance of the U.K. greatly increasing its share of the world market in these products there are fields within the market in which the U.K. need not be at a great disadvantage. This case study certainly exemplifies the lesson that where U.K. exporters have been prepared to tailor their products to the requirements of overseas purchasers they have been able to hold their own. But the foreign importer is no longer prepared to purchase goods simply because they are British and because they are well made.

There is no doubt that in earlier post-war years nylon stockings were the best export proposition of the clothing industry—stocking exports in 1951 were estimated at £15m. By 1959, however, their export value did not exceed £2m., and the place of stockings as currency earners was taken by woollen knitwear.[1]

WOOLLEN KNITWEAR

Costs and Prices

Woollen knitwear is a branch of the clothing industry where labour costs are relatively less important than in the case of nylon stockings. In woollen knitwear generally, it is the weight and price of wool rather than labour costs which determine selling price. One large knitwear firm told us that in manufacturing men's socks of synthetic fibres, their direct material costs comprised 25·6%, and labour 14·2% of total costs. In woollen knitwear the figure for materials varied from 48% to 58% and for labour from 25% to 16·2%, according to the type of garment and the particular factory in which manufacture took place.

The proportion of labour costs to total costs rises with the numbers of hand-operated knitting machines, but since a large part of the export output of hand-made woollen knitwear (e.g. Shetland) is exported to the high-price North American market, this factor cannot much militate against export success.

Unfortunately no international comparisons of wage rates in knit-wear are available, but in clothing generally earnings in the U.K. were during the nineteen-fifties higher than on the Continent—except perhaps in Switzerland, Sweden and Norway. Of these higher labour cost producers, Sweden has one of the largest clothing industries in western Europe, but the Norwegian and Swiss industries are relatively small.

The largest cost item in knitwear is, as we have seen, raw materials, and where this material is wool, the United Kingdom was at no price disadvantage vis-à-vis other countries. Raw wool is sold at auctions

---

[1] It should not be forgotten that a substantial quantity of stockings and other clothing items are sent abroad each year by parcel post. These are not, of course, included in the Trade Returns.

and there is therefore a world price at the ports of the leading producing countries. However, as soon as low cost producers—notably Japan, Hong Kong and perhaps Italy, begin to process the wool, their low wage rates provide them with substantial economies.

U.K. Markets

Nevertheless, the cost disadvantage under which U.K. exporters work is considerably less in knitwear and woollen hosiery than in nylon stockings, and in some import markets the U.K. was able to retain its share of the market quite satisfactorily. In the Union of South Africa, for example, the U.K. share of the knitted outerwear market in 1958 and 1959 was considerably higher than in 1953. In men's and boys' outer-garments the United Kingdom share of the South African import market rose from a very small share in the early nineteen-fifties to 9·7% in 1957 and 13·5% in 1958. In Australia, the U.K. held its share of the import market in men's half hose (98·0% in 1955–56 and 96·6% in 1958–59). In general, however, it must be admitted that the United Kingdom share of the knitwear market in most countries, especially in the Sterling Commonwealth, declined quite substantially between 1953 and 1959. Australia was a typical case and a country where other supplying countries, notably Italy, became important suppliers of woollen garments.

In both Australia and South Africa a great deal of indigenous manufacture of knitwear developed after the war—many leading U.K. manufacturers set up manufacturing plant overseas or entered into licensing agreements with local firms.[1] In most cases the decision to manufacture locally or to grant a manufacturing licence was forced upon British firms as the result of very stringent import controls in the Dominions. In the case of South Africa at least, local manufacturing costs were higher than in the United Kingdom and the majority of firms would clearly have preferred to satisfy the market by direct exports from the home country.

The knitting industry's best overseas selling range in the nineteen-fifties was knitted woollen outerwear, and in 1959 the United States and Canada were respectively the industry's best and second-best customers for this type of knitted garment. This was especially true of pullovers, cardigans and men's socks. After about 1956 occurred, however, very heavy sales promotion of man-made fibre outwear by United States manufacturers, both in their own market and Canada, and this had an adverse effect upon U.K. sales of outerwear. Nevertheless, by 1960, there were signs of a distinct revival of interest in British woollens in both the United States and Canada.

The North American market absorbed a substantial quantity of knitwear manufactured on hand machines, and for this type of product the U.K. was, at least up to 1959, a long way ahead of Japan. However, the Italian challenge in men's sweaters and cardigans was more serious

[1] The royalties derived from these agreements are very low—usually about 5%.

O

especially after 1956 and British firms were conscious of the fact that in styling and colouring the Italians had gained an advantage over them. The Italians were at pains to make the American market Italian fashion conscious and they spent large sums of money in so doing.

ITALIAN COMPETITION

One of the most remarkable features of world fashion trends since the war has been the resurgence of the Italian fashion goods, especially knitwear and beachwear. This movement was associated with the rapid rise of Rome as a centre of high fashion—a rise which was hastened in the nineteen-fifties by the convening of many international fashion congresses and the development of a film industry in the city. Italian styles and colours became popular all over the western world; these styles are less sophisticated than the French, but not quite as 'sporting' as the American. They had considerable appeal in Great Britain and western Europe as well as in the United States.

In regard to the growth of Italian influence, it is interesting to note that the great success achieved by Italian exports followed closely on a revival of interest in clothes among the Italians themselves. This revival occurred quite suddenly after 1955. In that year, to take one index, cotton consumption per head was 2½ kilos. In 1956 it was 3½ kilos per head; this considerable increase in *per capita* consumption was but one aspect of a remarkable change in social habits in regard to clothing. It is probably true to say that the average Italian in all classes of society cares more about clothes than almost any other people in the world. This dress consciousness is shared equally by men and women and has shown itself in the attention manufacturers have devoted to the appearance of their fabrics. Whereas manufacturers in other countries try to make natural fibres as tough as the synthetics, the Italians are concentrating on making all their fibres (man-made as well as natural) look like real silk. Colour is one of the leading selling points of Italian garments. It has, however, been alleged that although Italian colours have often stolen the field from the U.K. the standard of the actual dyeing in the garment industry in general, as in ladies' stockings, was superior in the U.K. British dyeing firms were able to secure much greater uniformity of colour for a large output than their Italian counterparts.

One advantage which the Italians had over the United Kingdom was their ability and willingness to supply very small quantities of particular styles and colours of knitted and other garments. This advantage they derived from the small-scale nature of their knitting industry. An Italian retailer could readily obtain from one of the small manufacturing units—or sometimes even from a cottage worker—a single consignment of, say, a dozen articles made to a specified colour and pattern. The existence of a multitude of small retail shops in Italy and the comparative absence of large stores, even in Rome and Florence, encouraged the manufacturer to think always in terms of small specialist deliveries rather than in large uniform consignments. Thus the structure and atmosphere of the Italian knitwear industry put it into an ideal position for satisfying the import needs of a very large number of diverse country markets. This was strengthened by the fact that 90% of Italian clothing exports were sold as the result of the representatives of foreign buying houses themselves visiting Italy and making their detailed requirements known in person to the manufacturers.

In contrast to the Italian industry, British manufacturers were generally reluctant to supply special orders; indeed the U.K. knitwear industry is generally carried out in larger scale units than on the Continent. Naturally the large scale U.K. firms are reluctant to accept small orders, either for the home or for the overseas market; a manufacturer turning out 20,000 dozen articles a week is hardly likely to be interested in a request for a dozen in a particular shade.

In this connexion it is interesting to note that in regard to the size of producing unit, the U.K. hosiery and knitwear industry as a whole lies somewhere between the small scale so common in Italy and the very large manufacturing concerns of the U.S.A. Thus while the U.K. industry was during our period reluctant to supply the very small consignments which the Italians were happy to deal in, neither could it compete with the mass-production methods so common in the U.S.A. Hence the particular role of the U.K. might well be to supply goods which are required in substantial quantities, but not tailored to such a uniform pattern as the typical products of U.S. industry. Manufacturing on a large scale the Americans have exceptionally low marginal costs and although exports generally account for only a tiny fraction of total output, their relatively low prices, together with the distinctive American style which is so acceptable for casual wear in the warmer Dominions, create serious difficulties for British exporters to countries like South Africa and Australia.

JAPAN AND OTHER EXPORTING COUNTRIES

As regards competition from countries other than the U.S. and Italy, Japan undoubtedly provided the most serious threat to Britain's position after 1955, especially in the Far East. The full force of Japanese competition was felt in Australia where, following the removal of discriminatory restrictions on the import of Japanese goods into that country, there was a marked switch of demand from British to Japanese knitwear products.

It would be quite wrong to disparage the quality of Japanese clothing. In knitwear, Japanese products were in 1959 only slightly inferior to British goods, and their quality was gradually improving. While the dubious trading practices engaged in by the Japanese have long since stopped, they are adept at copying ideas and designs from other nations and incorporating them into their own products. It has been said that in the garment field a Japanese manufacturer can copy and reproduce an American design in as short a period as eight weeks. In some cases the Americans themselves actually own and control Japanese plant, thus combining the advantages of American know-how and Japanese cheap labour.

So far as one can see, British manufacturers were in 1959 less worried about exports from Hong Kong than from Japan. If anything, costs in Hong Kong were lower even than in Japan. Nevertheless Hong Kong's clothing exports were often of very poor quality indeed and seldom approached Japanese or British goods in style and finish.

In Commonwealth markets competition from European countries other than Italy was not very serious, but after about 1954 there was a growing threat from western Germany, which began to export mass-produced clothing in large quantities. Another country which came into the field was Sweden, which manufactures all kinds of clothing. The Swedes concentrated on ready-made clothing—in 1954, 47,000 out of 53,000 garment workers were employed in ready-made clothing. The Swedish Government have been very active in encouraging exports and Sweden has a sound reputation in many parts of the world. It was however in Europe, and to a lesser extent in North America, that the main force of competition from Germany and Sweden was felt by the United Kingdom.

The French and Swiss, unlike the Swedes and Germans, never wholly adopted ready-made manufacture, and especially in women's outer-wear small-scale specialist production continued to predominate. Both countries had a substantial export trade in knitted lingerie, and the French (like the Italians) in gloves as well.

BRITISH EXPORT DIFFICULTIES

On the general subject of hosiery and knitwear exports, we found that the great majority of British exporters regarded the satisfying of the home market as their first objective. Even those who had outstandingly good export achievements to their credit insisted that a thriving home market was absolutely essential for a successful export effort. This is partly because of the high risks entailed in exporting clothing—a change in fashions can leave large quantities of stocks unsold—and partly be-cause import requirements differ so widely between countries. One very well-known firm pointed out that the cost of holding adequate stocks to satisfy repeat-orders from overseas was quite prohibitive, and in many lines the ability to meet these repeat orders was essential to export success.

Protection

One of the first steps taken by a country desirous of establishing local manufacturing industries and providing employment is to set up a textile and clothing industry. This is almost always followed by the granting of protection to the infant industry by very high import duties and/or severe import restrictions, if not outright prohibition. Local industries which grow up under the shelter of these protective measures are almost always able to persuade their Governments to maintain high import duties, even when quantitative trade controls have been removed. Moreover, when overseas Commonwealth countries have felt it necessary to impose import restrictions in the interest of the balance of payments, clothing imports have invariably been among the first to be restricted. Thus imports of some types of clothing into New Zealand were completely forbidden in 1958. Even within Europe, where there were in general no quantitative restrictions on imports of clothing, United Kingdom exporters encountered serious tariff difficulties.

Most E.E.C. countries' import duties on clothing tended throughout our period to be high (incidentally, most knitwear manufacturers with whom we discussed the subject were in favour of the U.K. joining the Common Market). Additionally, there were certain institutional difficulties in selling to Europe. One such difficulty was said to be the lack of agents. Since the amount of business available to British exporters in the past had been relatively small, few really first-class agents thought it worth their while to take on an agency for a British firm. Another difficulty was the fact that selling margins were higher on the Continent than in the U.K. and thus the tariff handicap under which British firms worked was magnified.[1]

In some countries, e.g. Switzerland and the Netherlands, clothing tends to be sold in large departmental stores rather than in specialist shops. Since prices in these large stores are generally lower than those which can be obtained in specialist garment shops, British exporters of high quality specialist lines found it relatively difficult to sell in such countries.

The U.K. Home Market

A further factor which might be thought to have militated against exporting is the ownership of retail shops in the United Kingdom by some of the large knitwear manufacturers. Inevitably, such organisations regard the satisfying of their own retailer's demands as a first call on their resources. At the same time it is only fair to add that among firms who manufacture and sell in their own shops are some of the most export-conscious companies in the industry. The very closeness of such firms to the final purchaser keeps them well abreast of consumer preferences—they were, for example, particularly conscious of the effect of the 'Italian line' upon the British woman shopper and took vigorous steps to counter this.

Another point which should not be forgotten is that manufacturers with domestic retail outlets make substantial sales through their shops to visitors to the U.K. In the case of one firm these sales were in 1959

[1] This applies also to the U.S.A. and to Canada, where the retailer's mark-up is 40% as against 33⅓% in the U.K.

equivalent in value to about 8% of its total direct exports and were in fact greater in value than its exports to either Australia or the Union of South Africa.

Although the licensing and local manufacturing arrangements we discussed above are very much 'second best' devices, designed to secure some share rather than none of a country's market, the contribution of the knitwear industry to Britain's invisible trading account should not be minimised. One firm with whom we discussed this question conducted two-thirds of its wholesale turnover in overseas countries; and two-thirds of that turnover was in North America.

There is, however, no denying the fact that during the period we have reviewed the home market exercised a very strong pull on the average producer's output, and most firms regarded this market as very much more attractive and certainly more profitable than markets overseas. At the same time domestic disinflationary measures in the U.K. have had relatively little effect upon sales. In the economic and social climate of the nineteen-fifties and nineteen-sixties only a very drastic reduction in internal purchasing power would seem adequate to deflect a substantial part of output into exports, and in view of our discussion of the kind of competition faced by the U.K. it seems very doubtful whether the goods released would in fact have been saleable abroad. This was especially true of some of the United Kingdom's most promising markets (e.g. Canada) which would themselves have suffered serious repercussions from any substantial deflation in the U.K.

On the other hand, it might be argued that if the expansionist policy we have pleaded for in other parts of this Study had been implemented in 1955–58, the proportion of clothing output exported would have been even lower than it was. In practice this is unlikely to have been the case, for a rapid growth of home demand for clothing would almost certainly have encouraged long-term expansion and plant-renewal in the industry. This might well have enabled the industry to provide both variety of styles and colours (which it did well in the latter nineteen-fifties), and low-priced garments (which it did not do as well). There can be no doubt either that a rapid rate of internal growth creates an atmosphere in which both consumers and producers are highly sensitive to new ideas and it is in this atmosphere that exports of fashion goods are most likely to grow. This was certainly the case in Italy and might well have been so in the United Kingdom. There is, however, one problem which a rapidly growing hosiery and knitwear industry might have to face in the U.K. but which was absent in Italy— a chronic shortage of (a) skilled labour and (b) building space. The latter problem is likely to be more easily solved than the former. There is a serious lack of building space in the traditional centres of the hosiery industry, e.g. Leicester, but more and more firms have found it worth their while to move to Northern Ireland and South and Central Wales. No doubt this trend will continue.

CHAPTER XIII

POTTERY

POTTERY exports provide a useful case study in the effect of Japanese competition upon British export performance. The share of the United Kingdom in the world market for pottery fell from 32·1% in 1953 to 26·9% in 1958 and 24·6% in 1959. The share of western Germany was more or less stationary (at about 24%) while that of Japan rose from 26·1% in 1953 to 36·6% in 1959.

As Appendix Table W shows, in 1959 about three-quarters by value of United Kingdom exports of pottery was shipped to a handful of countries—Canada (by far the largest market for the United Kingdom), the United States of America, Australia, the Union of South Africa and New Zealand. The Table shows that in each of these countries the U.K. share of the respective import markets fell; with the exception of South Africa (where western Germany made substantial gains), the Japanese secured a larger share of each.

Towards the end of the period, the Italians made significant advances in the pottery field. Although in the industry as a whole Italy was still only a relatively small exporter, in some items and in certain country markets by 1959 the Italians were offering a serious challenge to older-established exporting nations. An example of this is in ceramics where, in better quality wall and floor tiles, Italy became the leading overseas supplier of the United States market. For cheaper tiles (and these provide the bulk of the value of tile imports into the United States) Italy was still behind Japan, but in 1957 and 1958 about one-fifth by value of these cheaper tiles imported into the U.S. were of Italian manufacture. In general, however, we can safely discount competition from continental countries, and in this case study concentrate our attention upon Japan as an exporter.

UNITED KINGDOM MARKETS

Japan's most striking success of all was in the United States, where by 1959 she was supplying well over half the import market.

Table W shows that the U.S.A. was, next to Canada, the most important oversea market for the British pottery industry. The decline in the U.K. share of this very substantial import market between 1953 and 1959 was, however, quite considerable—falling from 22·7% to 16·5%. Japan's share rose from 42·4% to 58·9% over the same period.

The North American Market

In a number of items the United Kingdom share of the United States market was by 1959 quite small. In household china it was well under

3%—Japan holding over four-fifths of the market. The only other substantial exporter of household china to the United States was western
Germany. The U.K. share in the U.S. import market in electrical
porcelain ware was little more than 1%. Only in better quality earthenware was the share of the U.K. significant; in earthenware plates, cups
and saucers the United Kingdom supplied in 1958 over one-third of
the United States import market. But even here the share of Japan
was rising and by 1959 over one-fifth of the value of imports of table-
ware were supplied by Japan. In sanitary ware and in china ornaments,
the U.K. share was less than 5%.

The United Kingdom supplied only a tiny fraction of United States
imports of mosaic tiles, but in glazed tiles, especially the more expensive
ones, the U.K. maintained a substantial share of the market.

In Canada, perhaps because of Imperial Preference, the gains of
Japan were much less spectacular, the United Kingdom being still by
far the largest supplier.

Table 13.1 gives some idea of the measure of Japanese competition
in some of the important categories of pottery which were imported into
Canada. It will be seen that from 1956 Japan supplied over one-half by
value of Canadian imports of tiles and blocks for mosaic flooring. By
1959, Japan had secured one-third of the import market in porcelain
electrical insulators and was well on the way to obtaining a similar
share of the stoneware market.

In porcelain insulators, Japan gained at the expense of the U.S.; the
U.K. share being more than maintained. But in most other categories
it was the United Kingdom which suffered the full impact of Japanese
competition. In tiles, the U.K. share fell steadily; this applies also to
stoneware. The one field where the decline in the U.K. share was
much less pronounced was the quantitatively very important sector of
tableware. Here the United Kingdom managed to retain four-fifths of
the import market. Nevertheless, even in this sector there took place
some switch in demand away from British products and in the later nineteen-fifties the U.K. share showed no sign of reaching the 85% to 86%
of the import market obtained in 1952–53.

Western Europe

The import market for pottery on the continent of Europe is a limited
one, but in the more important importing markets (Belgium-Luxembourg, the Netherlands, and Italy), Japan gained at the expense of the
United Kingdom. Western Germany remained easily the largest supplier of the Common Market countries, but imports from Japan exceeded those from any other non-member country, including the
United Kingdom. Tariffs on china-ware imports into E.E.C. countries
were throughout the period high—but an even more serious hindrance
to U.K. exports was the high transport cost of most pottery products.

THE GROWTH OF JAPANESE EXPORTS

At the end of the war, the Japanese pottery industry was an obvious candidate for rapid development. Most pottery factories were in the scattered country districts and had thus escaped the devastation rained upon the industrial centres: raw materials were available locally, and since for Japan pottery products in general have a very low import content, the net foreign exchange earnings from exports were relatively high. What is more, the expansion of the pottery industry offered an immediate prospect of providing work for demobilised Japanese servicemen, and for the rapidly increasing working population.[1] Although modernisation was to be effected in subsequent years, pottery products (of which in 1945 and 1946 there was a world shortage) can if necessary be made with a minimum of machinery.

In Japan there was a rapid expansion of production of a very wide range of pottery products, the volume of domestic production and export of which is given in Table 13.2. Eating utensils, internal wall tiles, and ornamental ware accounted for much of the value of Japanese export of pottery. Japanese competition was particularly severe in earthenware and table ware, exports of electrical and sanitary ware being relatively unimportant.

Owing to wide variations in quality, it is extremely difficult to make a sensible comparison of price differentials between British and Japanese export goods. Generally speaking, Japanese quality is lower than British, and often products from these two countries do not compete at all closely with one another. Certainly, the unit value of United Kingdom table-ware sold in the United States is considerably higher than that of Japan. One large manufacturer told us in 1960 that as a rule of thumb he found that in Australia Japanese goods *retailed* at about the same price as the landed costs of similar British goods. British firms, however, generally aim at selling higher grade products in the United States than do the Japanese; accordingly Mintons and Josiah Wedgwood, for example, who concentrate on the production of high quality bone china table-ware, have probably not felt the direct force of Japanese competition. On the other hand British manufacturers admit that there have been some very fine quality Japanese dinner-ware exported which, we were informed by one, 'could not be faulted'.

Apart altogether from the direct impact of higher British prices for comparable goods, the fact that British prices were so much higher gave Japan an advantage in selling to countries where there were only limited currency quotas available for the importation of pottery; and in the early nineteen-fifties this meant practically all the United Kingdom's major markets, with the exception of Canada and the United States. Where the importer had only a small licence available, he tended

[1] See *Financial Times* supplement on Japan, 26th July 1954, "Modernisation in the Pottery Industry'.

to use it for importing a larger quantity of cheaper goods rather than a small quantity of more expensive ones.

The reason why Japanese pottery was so much cheaper than that of the United Kingdom is not hard to find. In the Japanese industry, labour costs account for nearly half the total costs of china and earthenware. Although an exact comparison between wage costs in the two countries is impossible, it is clear that throughout the nineteen-fifties British labour costs were significantly higher than those of Japan. The British Pottery Manufacturers' Federation have suggested that in, say, one hundred of the largest producing factories in Japan, earnings in 1959 might well have been about 25 % less than in the United Kingdom.

As we noted in chapter VII one problem in making this kind of comparison is the difficulty in determining 'standard' wage rates or earnings in Japan. Whereas in the United Kingdom there are fairly clearly laid down rates for the job, in Japanese pottery firms there are enormous variations in the rates of remuneration received by workers undertaking similar tasks. There are different rates for workers of varying ages, and there are also substantial differentials as between factories. Employees also receive an annual bonus, which is equivalent to about one month's pay, but which itself varies from firm to firm. Another difficulty in obtaining reliable figures is that in Japan workers are divided into 'regular' and 'casual' groups. The regular workers, who form the majority of operatives in the pottery industry, are often members of, or have some connexion with, the employer's family, and are paid rather more than casual workers.

As pointed out in our general discussion on wage rates in Japan, fringe benefits are important in the case of larger firms, and this applies to pottery as well as to textiles.[1] On the other hand a very substantial number of factories in the pottery industry are extremely small—of a total of 4,395 firms in the industry in 1958, 3,857 employed less than twenty operatives, and of these by far the greater number employed five or fewer workers. Only the very large firms provide good hostels, canteens, and medical services, the benefits which are so often quoted as the answer to the 'cheap labour' charge levied against the Japanese industry. Officially the average working week in 1958–59 was forty-eight hours, but this figure should be treated with reserve. Most workers appeared to put in a considerably greater number of hours than this. In many of the smaller rural potteries, on the other hand, workers combine their factory work with the cultivation of a small holding which is generally inadequate to provide a living for the average peasant family. This division of interest makes difficult an assessment of hours worked in factories.

Regarding raw material costs, Japan cannot have much of an advantage over the United Kingdom. In both countries the principal raw

---

[1] I am particularly grateful to Mr. S. H. Jerrett, Director of the British Pottery Manufacturers' Federation, for providing much of the data upon which this and the following paragraphs are based.

material (kaolin) is indigenous, but of course Japanese labour costs of extraction are lower than the British.

As regards relative efficiency, as we have seen, in 1959 there were a very large number of extremely small 'factories' in Japan, most of which were hardly worthy of the description. In these, and indeed in all except the very largest plants, mechanisation was a long way behind the United Kingdom. Electrical firing of kilns had not yet been introduced; some of the kilns were of the type which were in use some 1,000 years ago! However, it is the large firms which produce the bulk of Japanese pottery exports, while small concerns concentrate upon cheaper goods for the domestic market.[1]

Some of the large units in Japan are said to be very efficient. One of the largest concerns is the Nortake group which consists of a number of very large and very modern factories. The group's factory at Nagoya produces porcelain table-ware and employs 3,000 operatives. At Nagoya, too, is located the Associated Nipon Gaishi Plant, employing over 1,500 people, and the largest producer of insulators in Japan. There is a sanitary-ware plant at Kokura, where over 2,500 people are employed; 75% of the production of this plant is exported. Incidentally the strong competitive position of this firm is enhanced by the fact that it is staffed almost entirely by female labour. In 1959, the average monthly wage for regular male workers in potteries was the equivalent of £14 2s. 3d., but for females it was less than half this—£6 7s. 6d. Any organisation therefore which can employ a high proportion of women clearly has this strong competitive advantage.

One branch of Japan's pottery exports which expanded particularly rapidly since the war was ceramic tiles—especially in the North American and Australian markets. Although hand presses were still being used in 1959, many factories making tiles were employing fully automatic modern plants and some of these were extremely up to date. One factory, employing 200 girls, was reputed to turn out one million one-inch by one-inch mosaic pieces a day. These and similar tiles have been described as being of 'disturbingly good quality'.

Whereas in Japan there is a concentration of export output in a few very large firms (the rest of the industry being made up of a very great number of small ones), in Great Britain the bulk of output for both domestic and foreign consumption comes from medium-sized companies—those employing between 200 and 500 operatives. In Great Britain there were, according to the 1954 Census, only 331 pottery companies. This can be compared with Japan where there were about 3,900 different firms. Probably British firms which engaged in export were a little smaller in terms of output than Japanese exporting firms, but technically this should not have made the Japanese industry much

[1] Even in the United Kingdom substantial export sales are generally achieved only by a relatively few—but large—firms. The industry as a whole exports about 60 of its table-ware output, but in the case of some of the largest organisations the proportion might well be higher than this. A significant number of small firms export little or nothing.

more efficient than the British pottery industry. Certainly the great British exporting firms (Lawleys, Minton and Wedgwood, for example) have since the war engaged in rapid technical advance, particularly in the change from coal-fired bottle ovens to those fired by gas, electricity and oil. The modern tunnel oven is cleaner and its thermal efficiency greater than that of the coal oven.

The conclusion we must draw from this case study is that in the export sector of the pottery industry, Japan was probably not much more, and perhaps a little less, technically efficient than the United Kingdom. The very best exporting units were probably not far behind those of the United Kingdom in technical efficiency; but the combination of reasonable efficiency and a very low wage rate placed Japan in an extremely strong position in the world market. No doubt there was still scope for improvement in the British industry, but in view of the unavoidably high labour content of pottery manufactures in both countries, it seems unlikely that British manufacturers will in the future be able to offer great opposition to Japan, except in the very best quality ware where the standard of craftsmanship of the 'Five Towns' is likely to continue to be well ahead of that of Japan. As world standards of living improve it might well be that there will be a growing demand for the relatively high quality British goods.

But to sell these products United Kingdom exporters will have to look increasingly to those markets which are growing most rapidly and where Japanese influence is least felt. There is no doubt that these are in western Europe and it is perhaps here that the industry will do well to concentrate its efforts in the 'sixties—although the markets of the Commonwealth—particularly Canada—should not be neglected.

Table 13.1. *Imports of pottery into Canada*

£000

Item	1952	1953	1954	1955	1956	1957	1958	1959
Tiles and blocks for mosaic flooring								
Value of imports	122	87	109	128	136	104	147	216
U.K. %	36·7	29·2	18·3	13·4	12·1	16·2	9·7	6·3
U.S.A. %	42·8	37·0	42·8	25·1	27·4	19·6	12·8	16·2
Japan %	4·4	23·0	32·7	49·3	52·4	50·9	58·8	53·6
Tiles, earthenware								
Value of imports	458	457	464	600	719	468	673	621
U.K. %	74·6	62·0	53·2	49·1	52·2	60·8	60·1	56·6
U.S.A. %	16·4	19·4	18·6	13·9	10·1	14·9	11·2	8·0
Japan %	2·0	3·8	2·9	4·8	8·5	4·3	13·5	17·5
Tableware of china and porcelain, not teapots, jugs, etc.								
Value of imports	4444	4594	4588	4754	4958	4605	5052	4950
U.K. %	85·4	86·7	84·9	82·1	82·0	77·4	78·6	81·4
U.S.A. %	8·3	7·0	7·8	10·0	8·9	10·6	12·3	8·9
Japan %	3·7	3·9	3·7	4·3	5·9	7·4	6·5	6·4
Stoneware—Rockingham earthenware nop.								
Value of imports	538	627	632	690	745	786	790	870
U.K. %	25·7	22·0	19·9	18·8	15·5	13·6	16·0	15·2
U.S.A. %	48·4	49·8	48·9	46·6	47·6	48·2	37·7	38·0
Japan %	16·6	17·2	18·1	18·4	19·6	21·3	27·6	27·2
Insulators: electric porcelain								
Value of imports	200	185	179	170	406	341	263	227
U.K. %	5·9	5·8	21·9	6·9	11·9	7·9	24·4	11·3
U.S.A. %	91·1	88·4	74·3	82·1	72·8	66·8	51·1	49·8
Japan %	0·0	0·0	0·0	6·5	12·6	22·0	17·4	31·8

Source: Trade of Canada, Vol. III.

Table 13.2. *Production and exports of pottery from Japan*

Tons 1958

Category	Production	Exports
Electrical ware	56,393	11,358
Industrial porcelain	12,128	41
Chemical porcelain	2,083	4
Kitchen utensils and table-ware	212,778	88,053
Toys and ornamental ware	46,205	38,538
Sanitary ware	28,171	1,907
Tiles (other than mosaic)	76,047	22,961
Tiles (mosaic)	53,038	17,696
Miscellaneous	45,383	26

Source: British Pottery Federation.

CHAPTER XIV

CONCLUSIONS AND PROSPECTS

THE first conclusion to be drawn from our Study is surely the fact that both in terms of absolute level of market shares and of changes in those shares there were in the vital years 1953–59 substantial differences in export performance as between country markets and between export commodities. With a few notable exceptions the U.K. share of world trade in most commodity groups declined after 1953, but the decline was by no means uniform. In textiles (including clothing), non-motorised transport equipment and pottery the decline was much more marked than in most branches of engineering and in chemicals. On the subject of comparative export performance a great deal of work needs to done, perhaps elaborating with the aid of more refined techniques case studies of the kind we have attempted in this book. Undoubtedly the establishment of overseas manufacture by United Kingdom firms played some part in the decline in the British share in certain industries—but this was hardly true of the industries in which the United Kingdom share declined most steeply. In these—and other cases—the plain truth seems to be that in varying degrees U.K. goods were no longer as competitive as they used to be in relation to those of other competitors. Generally the reason for this lack of competitiveness was the inability or unwillingness of British exporters to quote attractive prices, but quite often the failure of British exports was due to lack of appropriate styling, finish, and salesmanship. In the earlier post-war years this did not matter so much—the world was a sellers' market for manufactures. But as supplies became more plentiful, markets were increasingly competitive and overseas buyers turned to those suppliers who were prepared to pay very careful attention to the requirements of particular importers. Where careful attention was paid to these factors export sales were well maintained, in sectors as wide apart as high quality woollen goods, specialist paints, and high performance motor cars. In many of these sectors the U.K. share in world trade was held or even increased, in spite of prices which were often somewhat on the high side. More generally, however, U.K. export prices were such that over a wide field of manufactures ground was lost to exporting countries like Germany, Japan and Italy, whose export prices did not rise as rapidly as those asked by British exporters for comparable products.

When we come to ask why U.K. export prices rose faster than those of other competing countries, it is not easy to give a clear-cut answer. Money wages in Japan clearly rose less rapidly than those in the United Kingdom, as did the labour costs borne by the Japanese manufacture after due account is taken of fringe benefits, payments in kind and social charges (p. 92). But this was true to only a limited extent in the case of Germany, where between 1953 and 1959 money wage rates, adjusted for social charges, actually rose more rapidly than in the United Kingdom (p. 74). Broadly speaking, it is not possible to explain the failure of United Kingdom products to hold their own in so many markets simply by the fact that labour costs rose more quickly in Britain than elsewhere. The truth is rather that whereas in the U.K. higher rates of productivity did not keep pace with advances in money wages, increased productivity absorbed the wage increases granted on the Continent.

Now if it were politically possible to maintain a wages and profits pause in the United Kingdom this would undoubtedly act as a dampener upon further price increases, and might well make United Kingdom export prices more competitive with those of other manufacturing countries. But such a policy would go only part of the way towards improving the long-term prospects of British exports. For it would not bring about any increase in *productivity*. It is in productivity that the Germans and in some cases the Italians, Japanese and French advanced faster than the United Kingdom; and it is on improved productivity that the United Kingdom must concentrate in the future. Otherwise there is no practicable alternative to a steady deterioration in the U.K. external position, culminating in devaluation forced upon a reluctant Government as a crisis measure—and almost certainly preceded by Canute-like attempts by the authorities to avoid the inevitable devaluation by successive bouts of domestic deflation.

It has been our contention in this Study that far too little attention has been paid by the Government and people to the harmful effects of neglecting the importance of productivity. After 1954–55 considerable attention was paid to speculative changes in the gold reserves. Obviously the reserves cannot and should not be neglected, but it is well to remember that Britain's real prosperity in the long run rests not upon what Zürich bankers think of the immediate prospects of sterling, but upon what is happening in the factories, mines and sales offices of the country. Accordingly we plead that for the future priority should be given to policy measures which will increase productivity throughout British industry.

There is no simple panacea which will magically increase productivity, but rather a number of fronts upon which advance could well be made. Perhaps the French have something to teach the U.K. with their Four-Year Plans (see p. 110). Perhaps from the Germans the British Government could learn that investment, if it is to help exports, must be in appropriate industries (see p. 75). Perhaps from Italians and Japanese the United Kingdom can learn something which is not easy to grasp but which has real significance in aiding progress—that is a 'philosophy of growth', a desire to see one's output and factory expand, and to see one's products on sale throughout the world. It is, however, difficult to see such a philosophy being embraced by British businessmen in present conditions. The atmosphere of industry is still over a very wide field much too restrictive. In remedying this state of affairs, the Government can make a great contribution to a reorientation of thinking about output and exports.

Firstly, the Government must avoid policies which act as a deterrent to progress and expansion. This means that it must adopt a clear-cut 'growth-policy' and frame budgetary and financial policies accordingly. Stagnation cannot be afforded and is much too high a price to pay for any given exchange rate, especially when, as its long-term result, the slowing down in the rate of growth of the domestic economy has adverse international economic repercussions (e.g. on the import capacity of the overseas Sterling Area).

Secondly, ministers would do well to pay more attention to productivity, modernisation and capital development in their public pronouncements. It is probably true to say that if British industry were really competitive—if it were 'growth-minded'—the pound could to a considerable extent look after itself. Perhaps the mistake made in official quarters after 1954–55 was to think and talk as if the be-all and end-all of policy was to safeguard for all time a predetermined rate of exchange, as if in some way the economy would continue to develop along the right lines and British goods remain competitive, provided only that the pound was held at $2.80. Experience has shown that some quite definite reorientation of official thinking and policy-making in this respect is required.

Thirdly, the Government can do much to make British industry more competitive by giving its whole-hearted support to greater freedom of international trade. The effect upon competitive efficiency of trade liberalisation has been discussed above in the case of both Germany (p. 81) and France (p. 109). In these countries the effect of greater freedom of importation was to sharpen the edge of competition and thereby put hitherto sheltered industries very much more on their toes. Indeed, the exposure of British industry to direct competition from the Common Market might in the long run provide the most valid justification for Britain in due course again attempting to join the E.E.C. Certainly it was the knowledge that they would have to face vigorous competition from their E.E.C. partners that made both French and Italian manufacturers improve their methods and cut their costs in 1957 and 1958. Moreover, if eventually the United Kingdom is in the E.E.C. as a full member, it is to be hoped that her influence will be used to keep down the level of the common tariff *vis-à-vis* the outside world.

Now it might be agreed that the long-term policy we have advocated —one of capital development, freer trade, freedom from discriminatory domestic restrictions, and a very restrained use of bank rate—might well achieve worth-while results, provided the reserves are not exhausted and the country made bankrupt in the process.

Clearly, no responsible Government would throw away what weapons it has against balance-of-payments disequilibrium without making sure that some alternative was at hand. In the case of the United Kingdom, some short-term cushion must be provided to enable the overhaul of the economy which we have advocated to take place. Almost certainly the present resources of the I.M.F. are inadequate for this purpose. It is therefore to be hoped that a radical reform of the machinery of the Fund will be urged by H.M. Government, in order to fit the Fund for doing the job it was established to do—that is to avoid precisely the adoption of the kind of restrictive policies which have been pursued in the U.K. and other countries in recent years.

In the second place, a more enlightened view should be taken of the relationship between the 'reserves' and Britain's long-term portfolio and direct investments overseas. Too often an inflow of foreign funds into the reserves which is matched by the creation of a short-term liability to some overseas holder is regarded as in some way a more real asset than an investment by a British firm in a productive manufacturing enterprise in a developing country. In fact, the scale of U.K. investment, both direct and portfolio, has since the war been of massive proportions. It is often forgotten that this investment does in fact represent real national wealth. There is no reason why an international credit-creating organisation like a reformed I.M.F. should not accept a claim on some of these investments as collateral against a substantial loan. The sale of British interests in Trinidad oil in 1959, and the disposal of the British interest in Ford's at Dagenham 1960 show that such international investments are not as illiquid as is sometimes thought.

Finally, and this is perhaps the most controversial suggestion of all, the time has surely come when a fresh look ought to be taken at the whole question of the exchange rate. Our Study has shown that U.K. prices have tended to get out of line with those of other countries. Provided productivity in Britain increases more rapidly than it does elsewhere this disequilibrium will eventually be corrected, but in the short run there is probably a case for allowing a much wider margin within which the pound is allowed to fluctuate. Alternatively it might be necessary to devalue the pound as a matter of deliberate policy without waiting for an exchange crisis. If the aid from the I.M.F. which we regard as desirable is not forthcoming some revision of exchange rate policy might indeed be necessary. Certainly if the choice is between the present system of a long-term tardy rate of growth, punctuated by recurrent crises, or the revision of the rate of exchange, behind which the Government carries out desirable internal economic reforms, then it is to be hoped that the country will opt for the exchange rate adjustment.

P

APPENDIX TABLES

NOTES ON THE TABLES IN APPENDIX

(1) The Tables show the share of the import market in selected
S.I.T.C. groups held by the United Kingdom, the United States of
America, western Germany and certain other major supplying countries
in the years 1953, 1955, 1957 and 1959. The change in the share held
by these countries between 1953 and 1959 is shown in the last column.

(2) By share of market is meant the share of an import market held
by an exporting country of exports from the eleven leading manufacturing countries. The eleven countries are as follows: the United
Kingdom, the United States of America, western Germany, France, the
Belgium-Luxembourg Economic Union, Canada and Japan.

(3) A bracket round a set of percentage figures indicates that the
total value of imports of the commodity group into a country from all
eleven supplying countries amounted to less than 0·2% of exports of
the commodity to the world.

(4) U.S. Special Category exports are included.

Source: United Nations Commodity Trade Statistics, Series D; for
Switzerland Statistique Annuelle du Commerce Extérieur de la Suisse.

Table A. Inorganic chemicals (S.I.T.C. 511)*

Import Market	U.K. Exports 1959 $m.	1953 U.K.	1953 W.G.	1953 U.S.A.	1957 U.K.	1957 W.G.	1957 U.S.A.	1959 U.K.	1959 W.G.	1959 U.S.A.	1953–59 U.K.	1953–59 W.G.	1953–59 U.S.A.
Belgium-Luxembourg	1·5	13·7	38·6	9·0	6·0	31·7	4·4	6·0	27·8	8·2	− 7·7	−10·8	− 0·8
Denmark	1·8	28·9	36·6	1·7	16·0	43·1	1·9	14·5	40·1	4·5	−14·4	+ 3·5	+ 2·8
Finland	1·2	48·1	8·7	2·0	18·7	33·4	1·4	14·5	34·3	3·3	−33·6	+25·6	+ 1·3
France	1·7	20·8	27·9	15·2	17·5	51·9	14·7	7·3	26·3	21·1	−13·5	− 1·6	+ 5·9
West Germany	3·5	20·9	—	17·8	13·2	—	20·7	14·4	—	30·8	− 6·5	—	+13·0
Italy	4·4	27·9	25·3	7·6	15·1	43·8	24·3	22·5	40·9	23·6	− 5·4	+15·6	+16·0
Netherlands	3·4	12·8	39·2	5·8	9·2	45·5	5·2	9·4	46·4	10·6	− 3·4	+ 7·2	+ 4·8
Norway	4·0	27·5	35·6	1·6	21·1	53·8	10·8	20·6	50·1	6·9	− 6·9	+14·5	+ 5·3
Sweden	3·4	19·2	39·6	4·4	13·5	45·3	6·2	14·9	45·4	8·1	− 4·3	+ 5·8	+ 3·7
Australia	5·9	61·1	13·0	12·3	57·6	10·6	12·1	49·9	9·3	23·2	−11·3	− 3·7	+10·9
British East Africa	0·7	(88·7)	9·0	0·0	(71·7)	25·7	0·0	37·3	17·5	0·0	−51·4	+ 8·5	0·0
Ceylon	0·7	(74·4)	2·3	3·2	(67·5)	12·0	0·0	(66·2)	5·0	1·4	− 8·2	+ 2·7	—
Ghana	0·4	(83·9)	0·0	0·0	(90·6)	0·0	0·0	(85·7)	3·9	0·0	+ 1·8	+ 3·9	− 1·8
India	13·7	71·0	8·6	3·7	65·1	14·6	5·6	64·5	10·6	4·8	− 6·5	+ 2·0	+ 1·1
Malaya	1·9	(94·7)	0·0	3·0	68·8	14·8	0·3	47·8	18·2	3·4	−46·9	+18·2	+ 0·4
New Zealand	2·2	87·7	7·5	3·9	62·0	17·0	5·2	61·3	16·9	10·6	−26·4	+ 9·4	+ 6·7
Nigeria	1·0	(96·8)	3·2	0·0	82·9	5·4	0·0	(73·9)	15·8	(2·5)	−22·9	+12·6	+ 2·5
Pakistan	1·7	(66·7)	9·7	4·4	38·0	44·5	2·9	53·0	26·3	0·0	−13·7	+ 6·6	− 4·4
Rhodesia and Nyasaland	0·8	(99·7)	0·0	0·0	70·8	6·5	5·6	39·2	4·2	33·8	−60·5	+ 4·2	+33·8
Union of South Africa	3·1	66·3	8·3	13·1	48·2	15·4	19·1	35·1	14·6	28·7	−31·2	+ 6·3	+15·6
Iran	1·6	(20·7)	31·6	(46·7)	52·0	20·7	14·1	50·6	14·2	16·0	+29·9	−17·4	−30·7
Iraq	0·4	(86·2)	13·8	0·0	(60·5)	22·5	5·5	(39·3)	26·2	26·1	−46·9	+12·4	+26·1
Argentine	2·6	13·3	13·0	49·5	37·2	12·6	24·6	26·7	15·6	34·5	+13·4	+ 2·6	−15·0
Brazil	2·7	0·8	16·5	25·8	23·3	16·9	33·9	20·1	19·3	35·0	+19·3	+ 2·8	+ 9·2
Colombia	0·1	16·8	14·6	58·5	12·3	20·1	52·4	2·6	0·0	87·8	−14·2	−14·6	+29·3
Peru	0·7	37·4	14·2	39·5	0·0	20·5	56·7	22·8	10·5	59·0	−14·6	−14·2	+19·5
Venezuela	0·9	22·4	10·3	59·2	0·0	18·0	65·4	7·8	6·6	74·6	−14·6	+ 0·2	+15·4
Mexico	0·7	14·3	0·0	81·9	3·9	3·9	87·6	3·5	2·1	85·1	−10·8	+ 6·6	+ 3·2
Canada	4·2	18·1	2·5	79·0	11·6	4·0	78·6	7·9	8·2	83·0	−10·2	− 0·4	+ 4·0
U.S.A.	6·6	5·7	11·6	—	7·3	12·0	—	8·6	—	—	+ 2·9	+ 3·4	—
W. Europe Sample	25·0	20·8	30·7	7·8	13·4	36·4	10·2	13·0	34·3	14·2	− 7·8	+ 3·6	+ 6·4
E.E.C.	14·6	18·2	28·6	10·3	11·6	31·4	12·3	11·3	29·4	17·9	− 6·9	+ 0·8	+ 7·6
S. Com'wealth Sample	32·0	72·2	8·9	6·8	59·6	16·0	8·1	54·1	12·6	12·7	−18·1	+ 3·7	+ 5·9
World	108·1	19·7	18·6	18·6	17·7	23·9	21·9	16·1	20·1	26·4	− 3·6	+ 1·5	+ 7·8

* Inorganic acids and anhydrides (e.g. nitric, sulphuric and hydrochloric acids), copper sulphate, sodium carbonates, sodium hydroxide, inorganic compounds.

Table B. *Organic chemicals (S.I.T.C. 512)**

Import Market	U.K. Exports 1959 $m.	1953			1957			1959			1953-59		
		U.K.	W.G.	U.S.A.	U.K.	W.G.	U.S.A.	U.K.	W.G.	U.S.A.	U.K.	W.G.	U.S.A.
Belgium-Luxembourg	2·8	11·9	38·1	27·4	8·0	23·4	52·3	7·5	24·9	46·5	−4·4	−13·2	+19·1
Denmark	2·1	27·6	46·6	1·9	13·3	43·5	12·5	17·1	45·0	7·5	−10·5	−1·6	+5·6
Finland	0·6	33·9	27·6	7·1	19·6	38·3	5·7	13·4	46·0	4·8	−20·5	+18·4	−2·3
France	2·5	16·9	46·6	14·6	8·6	38·1	26·8	5·6	39·8	25·2	−11·3	−6·8	+10·6
West Germany	5·6	12·8	—	35·6	16·2	—	38·3	10·7	—	26·9	−2·1	—	−8·7
Italy	5·4	13·3	38·7	26·8	8·0	32·2	37·4	9·3	44·0	19·7	−4·0	+5·3	−7·1
Netherlands	7·2	36·3	39·1	10·2	10·2	32·9	40·8	11·9	31·2	41·2	−24·4	−7·9	+31·0
Norway	0·7	30·1	41·3	9·9	14·0	39·8	12·5	13·6	50·2	7·3	−16·5	+8·9	−2·6
Sweden	3·2	30·2	48·8	11·4	16·6	50·1	16·6	17·3	44·8	13·7	−12·9	−4·0	+2·3
Australia	7·6	49·5	26·8	17·4	44·4	28·2	8·4	39·4	29·1	16·2	−10·1	+2·3	−1·2
British East Africa	0·3	(75·6)	24·4	0·0	(37·2)	46·9	8·2	(41·5)	27·5	6·1	−34·1	+3·1	+6·1
Ceylon	0·3	(46·2)	17·5	10·3	(48·0)	19·0	8·9	(38·7)	11·7	10·5	−7·5	−5·8	+0·2
Ghana	0·2	(86·4)	0·0	10·6	(56·6)	8·9	34·4	(15·8)	74·8	7·9	−70·6	+74·8	−2·7
India	7·5	35·9	37·0	8·2	31·0	26·5	5·9	37·8	26·0	7·2	+1·9	−11·0	−1·0
Malaya	1·3	63·7	15·4	10·1	46·1	16·0	12·0	50·7	16·0	5·1	−13·0	+0·6	−5·0
New Zealand	1·2	65·8	19·7	5·0	43·2	19·7	18·9	35·8	28·1	16·0	−30·0	+8·4	+11·0
Nigeria	0·5	(88·9)	2·4	8·6	(67·0)	8·8	11·3	(62·6)	11·6	15·4	−26·3	+9·2	+6·8
Pakistan	0·7	(45·4)	25·6	11·5	23·3	38·7	7·9	29·8	41·6	7·7	−15·6	+16·0	−3·8
Rhodesia and Nyasaland	0·4	35·6	0·0	64·4	15·3	23·1	34·5	16·5	36·6	14·6	−19·1	+36·6	−49·8
Union of South Africa	2·8	56·6	8·6	30·6	35·3	22·0	25·1	23·7	21·3	24·6	−32·9	+12·7	−6·0
Iran	0·4	(12·8)	46·0	28·2	40·1	19·7	24·9	21·5	29·3	10·7	+8·7	−16·7	−17·5
Iraq	0·3	(68·0)	5·3	15·4	(31·7)	14·1	(36·7)	(31·3)	31·8	21·5	−36·7	+26·5	+6·1
Argentine	2·4	17·3	28·2	35·2	12·9	22·4	27·9	14·5	33·8	17·4	−2·8	+5·6	−17·8
Brazil	0·9	1·4	31·4	28·6	5·2	32·9	39·9	4·6	26·2	31·4	+3·2	−5·2	+2·8
Colombia	0·1	1·4	18·1	77·2	1·6	22·1	68·3	3·4	39·8	41·8	+2·0	+21·7	−35·4
Peru	0·2	5·4	14·1	74·9	6·4	18·5	62·9	6·4	22·7	55·7	+1·0	+8·6	−19·2
Venezuela	0·7	6·4	1·6	89·9	4·0	2·8	89·5	11·6	10·3	67·4	+5·2	+8·7	−22·5
Mexico	0·7	0·8	3·8	93·8	2·3	10·6	78·8	2·9	10·9	75·1	+2·1	+7·1	−18·7
Canada	4·1	3·2	1·8	93·4	6·0	2·7	88·5	7·1	3·8	84·6	+3·9	+2·0	−8·8
U.S.A.	6·2	25·6	38·7	—	13·7	41·0	—	15·6	38·1	—	−10·0	−0·6	—
W. Europe Sample	30·1	21·0	36·8	19·0	10·9	28·1	35·1	10·3	30·7	28·3	−10·7	−6·1	+9·3
E.E.C.	23·4	18·9	34·7	21·6	10·1	26·2	38·9	9·3	28·3	31·2	−9·6	−6·4	+9·6
S. Com'wealth Sample	22·6	48·8	24·4	16·1	36·9	25·5	12·8	35·1	27·2	13·8	−13·7	+2·8	−2·3
World	88·9	14·8	27·5	39·0	11·2	27·0	38·0	11·0	29·3	30·4	−3·8	+1·8	−8·6

* Aliphatic and other organic acids and anhydrides (e.g. acetic acid), alcohol, glycerine, spirits of turpentine, organic compounds.

Table C. Paints, dyes, varnishes, etc. (S.I.T.C. 53)*

Import Market	U.K. Exports 1959 $m.	1953 U.K.	1953 W.G.	1953 U.S.A.	1957 U.K.	1957 W.G.	1957 U.S.A.	1959 U.K.	1959 W.G.	1959 U.S.A.	1953–59 U.K.	1953–59 W.G.	1953–59 U.S.A.
Belgium-Luxembourg	1·9	13·8	26·5	26·4	14·7	30·6	21·5	13·5	33·8	19·7	−0·3	+7·3	−6·7
Denmark	1·3	26·4	33·7	5·9	26·8	35·5	7·6	25·9	38·0	8·1	−0·5	+4·3	+2·2
Finland	1·1	34·3	20·1	10·9	30·4	35·0	4·8	27·8	39·2	3·8	−6·5	+19·1	−7·1
France	2·1	10·4	16·2	34·1	9·7	21·5	34·7	12·3	26·8	28·6	+1·9	+10·6	−5·5
West Germany	1·1	4·1	—	4·6	8·7	—	17·2	11·0	—	17·1	+6·9	—	+12·5
Italy	2·2	12·5	31·9	34·9	12·4	27·3	26·9	11·6	31·3	23·6	−0·9	−0·6	−11·3
Netherlands	3·8	27·9	27·4	9·9	28·4	30·5	15·2	28·3	35·9	13·6	+0·4	+8·5	+3·7
Norway	1·5	23·5	24·1	23·2	30·6	24·5	14·9	36·1	26·0	12·1	+12·6	+1·9	−11·1
Sweden	2·3	24·4	34·8	18·7	23·2	40·5	15·9	21·1	43·4	15·7	−3·3	+8·6	−3·0
Australia	3·5	51·5	4·6	32·7	55·2	8·2	21·2	57·9	6·7	17·9	+6·4	+2·1	−14·8
British East Africa	3·0	98·5	0·7	0·0	87·8	5·3	0·0	94·5	1·4	0·3	−4·0	+0·7	+0·3
Ceylon	1·7	96·2	1·5	1·9	92·4	2·0	3·9	92·4	3·4	3·3	−3·8	+1·9	+1·4
Ghana	1·7	97·5	0·0	0·0	90·5	6·3	9·9	95·0	0·9	0·0	−2·5	+0·9	0·0
India	0·8	36·5	26·9	13·5	34·3	27·1	9·9	32·2	29·5	13·4	−4·3	+2·6	−0·1
Malaya	3·3	87·3	3·5	4·9	82·3	3·8	9·3	82·6	1·7	9·3	−4·7	−1·8	+4·4
New Zealand	1·4	70·5	2·1	21·7	75·0	3·7	15·7	72·6	3·1	16·8	+2·1	+1·0	−4·9
Nigeria	3·0	89·1	4·4	0·0	88·7	5·5	0·0	88·3	9·1	0·3	−0·8	+4·7	+0·3
Pakistan	0·9	49·5	23·3	10·9	31·4	34·7	7·6	36·4	36·0	1·0	−13·1	+12·7	−9·9
Rhodesia and Nyasaland	0·6	100·0	0·0	(0·0)	94·3	2·9	1·5	89·4	1·6	5·0	−10·6	+1·6	+5·0
Union of South Africa	3·5	52·7	4·1	41·9	53·1	5·3	32·3	52·3	4·6	33·6	−0·4	+0·5	−8·3
Iran	1·0	11·3	45·8	21·8	28·8	28·5	10·6	20·3	33·3	7·7	+9·0	−12·5	−14·1
Iraq	0·8	70·7	10·7	3·4	63·8	11·7	5·3	51·6	16·2	5·3	−19·1	+5·5	+1·9
Argentine	0·2	19·6	33·9	20·4	16·4	17·4	36·6	19·2	17·6	35·4	−0·4	−16·3	+15·0
Brazil	0·4	0·1	22·3	40·1	3·8	25·0	33·1	10·1	27·6	24·9	+10·0	+5·3	−15·2
Colombia	0·1	3·1	15·5	71·8	3·4	21·9	57·4	5·5	25·3	44·7	+2·4	+9·8	−27·1
Peru	0·2	14·3	12·0	54·2	11·4	18·4	47·5	13·7	25·6	32·7	−0·6	+13·6	−21·5
Venezuela	0·5	7·6	9·9	72·7	11·2	12·9	65·0	10·2	16·0	57·3	+2·6	+6·1	−15·4
Mexico	0·5	3·6	7·3	79·0	6·3	17·0	56·0	10·2	19·1	48·0	+6·6	+11·8	−31·0
Canada	6·4	16·9	1·0	78·3	23·5	2·5	69·4	25·4	3·9	65·4	+8·5	+2·9	−12·9
U.S.A.	2·5	20·2	13·3	—	19·6	23·4	—	20·0	26·1	—	−0·2	+12·8	—
W. Europe Sample	17·2	16·1	22·5	22·5	16·9	25·9	22·2	17·2	28·9	19·1	+1·1	+6·4	−3·4
E.E.C.	11·1	13·6	20·4	24·3	14·5	23·3	24·8	14·9	26·2	21·2	+1·3	+5·8	−3·1
S. Com'wealth Sample	23·4	54·6	14·2	17·9	54·3	14·9	14·1	59·3	12·4	14·2	+4·7	−1·8	−3·7
World	73·8	20·0	18·9	29·7	20·7	22·3	27·4	20·4	24·6	24·0	+0·4	+5·7	−5·7

* Dyestuffs, dyeing and tanning extracts, colouring materials, printers' ink, prepared paints, enamels, varnishes, etc.

Table D. Drugs and pharmaceuticals (S.I.T.C. 54)*

Import Market	U.K. Exports 1959 $m	1953				1957				1959				1953–59			
		U.K.	W.G.	U.S.A.	Switz.	U.K.	W.G.	U.S.A.	Switz.	U.K.	W.G.	U.S.A.	Switz.	U.K.	W.G.	U.S.A.	Switz.
Belgium-Luxembourg	2·0	5·9	9·0	39·3	19·2	9·0	10·8	37·9	18·5	5·9	11·0	36·6	18·8	0·0	+2·0	−2·7	+0·4
Denmark	1·6	27·8	15·7	11·0	22·8	20·2	11·2	16·0	28·7	14·1	14·1	11·2	29·3	−13·7	+1·6	+0·2	+6·5
Finland	1·5	32·4	16·4	13·0	6·2	17·9	20·3	12·3	22·3	16·5	24·4	5·9	24·1	−15·9	+8·0	−7·1	+17·9
France	1·0	7·0	6·7	50·6	25·9	9·2	16·2	20·3	28·3	5·4	15·3	23·9	30·2	−1·6	+8·6	−26·7	+4·3
West Germany	1·6	4·9	—	13·2	52·8	3·8	—	22·7	45·2	5·5	—	16·9	50·2	+0·6	—	+3·7	+2·6
Italy	2·2	10·2	13·3	29·6	33·9	7·2	15·8	31·1	28·7	6·3	16·7	34·0	24·2	−3·9	+3·4	+4·4	+9·7
Netherlands	1·4	23·1	18·7	7·2	27·1	9·6	20·8	25·7	16·6	8·0	19·9	25·3	19·0	−15·1	+1·2	+18·1	−8·1
Norway	0·9	23·4	17·8	31·1	9·1	21·2	15·3	20·5	14·3	20·5	12·9	16·5	14·5	−2·9	+4·9	−14·6	+5·4
Sweden	2·1	22·6	19·8	18·5	20·1	15·4	18·0	15·1	29·6	14·1	21·8	13·2	27·7	−8·5	+2·0	−5·3	+7·6
Australia	12·2	71·7	5·6	11·7	9·6	63·7	6·6	0·8	14·1	58·6	6·8	15·2	16·8	−13·1	+1·2	+3·5	+7·2
British East Africa	5·0	97·6	1·6	0·0	0·1	82·0	3·8	0·8	3·8	87·7	5·2	1·3	3·7	−9·9	+3·6	+1·3	+3·7
Ceylon	2·4	55·4	4·6	31·7	0·1	56·1	10·3	13·8	9·0	55·9	15·9	8·9	11·0	+0·5	+11·3	−22·8	+10·9
Ghana	3·4	97·2	2·8	0·0	0·0	93·4	0·0	0·4	0·5	78·7	14·9	0·9	2·7	−18·5	+12·1	+0·9	+2·7
India	4·3	38·7	5·5	42·4	6·5	32·1	10·0	25·6	17·4	26·1	8·3	31·2	21·7	−12·6	+2·8	−11·2	+15·2
Malaya	3·8	77·6	3·3	14·0	0·0	69·3	5·6	12·0	1·3	66·6	7·6	13·0	0·0	−11·0	+4·3	−1·0	0·0
New Zealand	5·8	91·9	1·4	3·4	2·2	92·4	2·4	2·3	1·7	87·4	4·1	3·2	4·0	−4·5	+2·7	−0·2	+1·8
Nigeria	7·6	98·1	0·8	1·0	0·0	90·3	6·1	0·3	0·2	88·8	9·3	0·2	0·2	−9·3	+8·5	−0·8	+0·2
Pakistan	3·8	65·4	9·7	16·2	0·1	46·2	10·6	16·4	10·5	44·1	12·7	14·3	15·4	−21·3	+3·0	−1·9	+15·3
Rhodesia and Nyasaland	1·4	(92·3)	0·0	7·7	(0·0)	86·2	0·9	8·9	1·1	77·6	6·6	11·0	2·1	−14·7	+6·6	+3·3	+2·1
Union of South Africa	4·6	48·9	1·7	48·4	0·0	43·3	4·6	37·5	8·1	35·3	9·8	39·4	10·1	−13·6	+8·1	−9·0	+10·1
Iran	1·5	11·6	19·3	42·1	0·6	13·7	16·0	28·9	22·9	9·5	21·3	26·4	21·0	−2·1	+2·0	−15·7	+20·4
Iraq	1·7	40·9	8·9	36·2	0·0	37·9	11·4	22·4	14·3	31·1	17·2	23·0	17·2	−9·8	+8·3	−13·2	+17·2
Argentine	0·7	5·8	6·0	70·8	16·2	4·9	3·6	61·4	22·7	7·0	12·9	42·9	25·6	+1·2	+6·9	−27·9	+9·4
Brazil	0·6	0·3	7·6	73·1	4·3	1·9	6·1	65·7	12·3	4·7	9·0	55·8	19·9	+4·4	+1·4	−17·3	+15·6
Colombia	0·2	2·2	7·1	79·9	0·6	1·7	16·5	68·0	9·5	1·7	12·2	66·2	15·2	+0·5	+5·1	−13·7	+14·6
Peru	0·2	4·9	7·1	68·4	15·9	4·4	15·5	52·3	18·2	3·0	21·4	45·2	18·3	−1·9	+14·3	−23·2	+2·4
Venezuela	0·8	3·2	6·1	86·7	2·3	2·6	13·5	64·7	12·7	2·5	15·3	58·4	16·5	−0·7	+9·2	−28·3	+14·2
Mexico	0·6	1·6	1·3	89·8	3·8	1·9	4·7	75·5	8·1	2·0	0·0	75·9	12·3	+0·4	+1·3	−13·9	+8·5
Canada	4·2	8·6	0·5	88·7	1·7	10·6	1·9	79·7	5·1	13·5	2·4	72·5	8·9	+4·9	+1·9	−16·2	+7·2
U.S.A.	3·5	9·5	19·4	—	13·8	13·2	20·2	—	14·0	13·5	17·2	—	31·2	+4·0	−2·2	—	+17·4
W. Europe Sample	14·3	12·1	10·5	27·1	29·1	10·0	12·8	25·9	27·3	8·2	13·5	24·4	28·1	−3·9	+3·0	−2·7	−1·0
E.E.C.	8·3	8·8	8·9	29·7	31·8	6·1	11·8	29·0	27·7	6·1	11·8	28·3	28·7	−2·7	+2·9	−1·4	+3·1
S. Com'wealth Sample	54·4	61·7	4·2	26·5	3·7	56·3	6·9	17·7	10·0	56·6	8·8	17·0	11·3	−5·1	+4·6	−9·5	+7·6
World	120·3	16·2	6·1	42·0	13·1	15·1	10·8	36·4	14·3	14·3	12·1	34·0	16·1	−1·9	+4·2	−8·0	+3·0

* Vitamins and vitamin preparations, sera, vaccines, penicillin, streptomycin, other antibiotics; opium alkaloids, cocaine, caffein, quinine and their derivatives, aspirin, dressings, etc.

Table E. Soaps and cosmetics (S.I.T.C. 552)*

Import Market	U.K. Exports 1959 $m	1953 U.K.	1953 W.G.	1953 U.S.A.	1953 France	1957 U.K.	1957 W.G.	1957 U.S.A.	1957 France	1959 U.K.	1959 W.G.	1959 U.S.A.	1959 France	1953–1959 U.K.	1953–1959 W.G.	1953–1959 U.S.A.	1953–1959 France
Belgium-Luxembourg	1.5	28.3	9.9	8.6	11.1	16.6	21.4	9.6	15.5	15.8	23.1	6.9	15.5	−12.5	+13.2	−1.7	+4.4
Denmark	0.9	29.2	16.8	3.2	1.1	36.8	22.0	1.8	5.8	22.5	36.6	2.8	8.0	−6.7	+19.8	−0.4	+8.0
Finland	0.3	(28.8)	30.3	0.0	(0.0)	15.4	20.0	4.0	23.5	17.4	32.6	3.3	16.8	−11.4	+2.3	+3.3	+16.8
France	0.4	13.8	21.5	11.2	—	11.1	48.8	9.9	—	10.8	41.2	12.4	—	−3.0	+19.7	+1.2	—
West Germany	3.2	45.3	—	1.8	41.1	33.7	—	6.3	27.1	27.9	—	10.3	30.1	−17.4	—	+8.5	−11.0
Italy	1.7	18.7	17.9	13.3	22.6	58.1	15.0	4.2	11.5	20.4	26.7	11.5	19.7	+1.7	+8.8	+1.8	−2.9
Netherlands	1.7	22.0	21.2	4.9	9.1	19.0	18.5	5.7	8.0	15.3	19.3	7.4	8.6	−6.7	+1.9	−2.5	−0.5
Norway	0.4	33.3	35.4	0.0	0.0	23.1	25.0	9.0	11.2	26.0	26.1	6.7	12.7	−7.3	+9.3	+6.7	+12.7
Sweden	2.6	27.4	24.8	2.4	13.9	38.6	21.3	8.7	13.0	39.9	20.3	9.7	11.6	+12.5	+4.5	+7.3	+2.3
Australia	1.9	77.2	12.8	5.7	0.0	62.7	13.6	11.5	5.4	56.8	12.1	18.5	6.4	−20.4	+0.7	+12.8	+6.4
British East Africa	4.2	99.2	0.0	0.0	0.0	95.5	1.7	0.0	0.0	91.1	3.2	0.4	3.2	−8.1	+3.2	+0.4	+3.2
Ceylon	1.6	94.2	3.7	0.0	0.0	91.1	4.8	0.0	0.0	91.7	4.2	0.0	1.1	−2.5	+0.5	0.0	+1.1
Ghana	6.8	98.8	0.4	0.0	0.0	96.4	1.5	0.3	1.2	96.2	1.2	0.6	0.9	−2.6	+0.8	+0.6	+0.9
India	0.3	78.4	2.7	2.3	0.0	58.7	13.2	2.1	1.7	26.3	19.2	7.7	4.6	−52.1	+16.5	+5.4	+4.6
Malaya	5.1	83.6	2.9	6.1	5.7	73.2	2.7	17.1	4.8	64.5	3.0	23.7	4.8	−19.1	+0.1	+17.6	+0.9
New Zealand	0.4	89.1	0.0	10.9	0.0	88.5	3.4	3.9	0.6	59.2	3.8	22.4	0.0	−29.9	+3.8	+11.5	0.0
Nigeria	2.8	99.3	0.7	0.0	0.0	92.8	1.5	0.0	0.0	90.8	2.0	0.0	1.7	−8.5	+1.3	0.0	+1.7
Pakistan	0.6	93.4	2.2	0.0	0.0	63.7	12.6	10.0	1.6	63.8	9.2	8.0	3.2	−29.6	+7.0	+8.0	+3.2
Rhodesia and Nyasaland	1.6	100.0	0.0	0.0	0.0	97.2	4.5	0.0	0.0	93.3	0.0	3.6	2.0	−6.7	0.0	+3.6	+2.0
Union of South Africa	1.3	68.9	1.5	22.4	0.0	50.0	4.5	25.8	7.3	52.6	9.9	23.1	6.1	−16.3	+8.4	+0.7	+6.1
Iran	0.4	8.9	29.2	50.0	0.0	30.5	12.0	40.2	11.9	20.5	17.3	43.7	11.0	+11.6	−11.9	−6.3	+11.0
Iraq	2.1	89.9	2.4	4.6	0.0	71.5	10.2	3.7	3.1	69.8	21.0	0.0	0.0	−20.1	+18.6	−3.1	0.0
Argentine	0.1	(6.3)	29.0	61.4	(0.0)	12.6	4.4	25.3	15.5	22.4	15.0	23.5	23.3	+16.1	−14.0	−37.9	+23.3
Brazil	0.1	7.5	14.7	74.7	0.0	4.2	31.3	24.4	36.1	6.5	20.8	30.2	31.7	−1.0	+6.1	−44.5	+31.7
Colombia	0.1	8.2	3.7	79.4	0.0	3.7	18.7	75.0	0.0	10.5	28.8	43.6	8.8	+2.3	+25.1	−35.8	+8.8
Peru	0.0	18.1	5.7	72.5	0.0	9.9	9.4	71.9	3.9	4.5	17.3	61.8	11.4	−13.6	+11.6	−10.7	+11.4
Venezuela	0.9	8.9	2.0	87.3	0.0	16.0	4.5	66.8	7.7	18.3	6.5	58.0	13.8	+9.4	+4.5	−29.3	+13.8
Mexico	0.1	4.7	2.9	78.3	0.0	3.2	9.6	65.4	9.2	4.7	10.8	60.2	11.8	0.0	+7.9	−18.1	+11.8
Canada	0.8	4.4	1.2	89.8	4.0	5.6	2.5	86.0	4.6	6.2	2.7	85.3	4.1	+1.8	+1.5	−4.5	+0.1
U.S.A.	0.7	12.4	3.3	—	66.8	11.2	6.7	—	63.2	7.7	7.8	—	57.7	+4.7	+4.5	—	−9.1
W. Europe Sample	12.8	27.9	14.5	6.5	15.7	33.2	18.7	6.5	12.9	21.8	20.6	8.6	15.6	−6.1	+6.1	+2.1	−0.1
E.E.C.	8.6	27.7	12.4	7.5	17.5	32.9	17.9	6.5	13.2	19.1	18.6	9.3	16.9	−8.6	+6.2	+1.8	−0.6
S. Com'wealth Sample	26.5	89.8	2.1	3.7	1.5	80.9	4.1	7.4	2.8	76.8	4.5	10.1	3.3	−13.0	+2.4	+6.4	+1.8
World	73.6	33.9	5.5	23.9	23.6	33.7	8.6	24.0	21.4	28.0	10.6	23.8	22.3	−5.9	+5.1	−0.1	+1.3

* Perfumery, cosmetics, dentifrices, soaps, cleansing preparations, waxes and polishes.

Table F. Yarn thread (S.I.T.C. 651)*

Import Market	U.K. Exports 1959 $m	1953 U.K.	1953 W.G.	1953 U.S.A.	1953 Japan	1957 U.K.	1957 W.G.	1957 U.S.A.	1957 Japan	1959 U.K.	1959 W.G.	1959 U.S.A.	1959 Japan	1953–59 U.K.	1953–59 W.G.	1953–59 U.S.A.	1953–59 Japan
Belgium-Luxembourg	1·7	8·9	3·8	4·2	1·5	11·9	7·7	1·5	0·2	5·4	9·6	3·0	0·1	−3·5	+5·8	−1·2	+1·4
Denmark	4·7	34·8	12·1	2·0	0·0	23·9	18·2	2·6	3·5	18·8	19·6	2·4	1·5	−16·0	+7·5	+0·4	+1·5
Finland	3·0	32·2	1·3	0·1	0·0	27·0	9·6	0·0	0·0	20·6	17·7	0·1	0·3	−11·6	+16·4	0·0	+0·3
France	3·0	8·8	13·3	33·7	4·9	17·2	22·5	1·2	0·0	20·4	19·2	7·0	0·0	+11·6	+5·9	−26·7	+4·9
West Germany	20·9	16·6	—	0·1	1·5	19·1	0·0	4·5	1·1	14·8	—	8·0	0·6	−1·8	—	+7·9	+0·9
Italy	2·1	25·3	16·5	3·0	0·9	38·5	27·7	1·9	0·4	25·2	20·3	1·1	0·0	−0·1	+3·8	+1·9	+0·9
Netherlands	4·4	8·3	4·4	1·8	0·5	8·0	8·0	1·1	0·1	5·7	11·6	0·0	0·2	−2·6	+7·2	−1·2	−0·3
Norway	3·9	29·5	7·9	2·5	0·2	27·4	11·6	2·1	1·6	23·3	11·7	2·2	0·3	−6·2	+3·8	−0·3	+0·1
Sweden	6·7	21·4	18·8	5·6	0·7	21·6	20·4	2·8	6·4	20·3	17·6	5·1	2·8	−1·1	+1·2	−0·5	+2·1
Australia	18·7	73·4	0·9	1·8	1·3	83·2	1·6	0·4	0·6	71·9	1·4	6·6	3·8	−1·5	+0·5	+4·8	+2·5
British East Africa	0·9	77·1	5·8	0·0	0·0	(75·7)	7·9	0·0	0·0	(74·1)	3·8	0·0	9·7	−3·0	+2·0	0·0	+9·7
Ceylon	2·3	12·9	0·0	0·0	86·9	90·5	1·4	1·7	3·3	93·7	1·7	1·7	1·5	+80·8	+10·7	+1·7	−85·4
Ghana	0·9	63·5	0·0	0·0	35·5	(88·8)	4·8	0·0	0·0	(75·8)	10·7	0·0	0·0	+12·3	+16·5	+1·8	−35·5
India	6·3	26·2	6·0	0·0	1·9	32·2	16·7	0·7	13·1	25·9	22·5	1·8	17·4	−0·3	+15·5	+1·8	+15·5
Malaya	1·0	61·7	2·5	0·0	0·6	74·2	3·0	0·0	10·2	(64·4)	6·9	0·7	12·9	+2·7	+4·4	+0·7	+12·3
New Zealand	10·4	96·6	1·3	0·0	1·0	94·6	0·8	1·5	0·0	87·3	0·5	9·0	0·1	−9·3	+0·8	+9·0	0·0
Nigeria	1·5	49·2	1·1	0·0	39·9	85·5	1·1	0·0	0·7	75·2	1·1	0·0	3·6	+26·0	0·0	0·0	−36·3
Pakistan	0·7	12·3	0·5	0·0	36·8	26·3	2·2	0·0	48·8	14·1	5·0	0·0	56·9	+1·8	+4·5	0·0	+20·1
Rhodesia and Nyasaland	0·8	81·8	0·0	0·0	0·0	(82·3)	1·3	0·0	0·0	(70·8)	1·9	0·0	0·0	−11·0	+1·9	0·0	0·0
Union of South Africa	10·4	62·7	4·1	0·9	0·1	55·2	9·7	12·2	0·5	46·7	10·8	21·8	1·2	−16·0	+6·7	+20·9	+1·1
Iran	0·3	11·7	13·8	1·3	9·9	6·1	13·5	4·7	50·1	3·5	13·1	0·0	42·6	−8·2	−0·7	+1·3	+32·7
Iraq	0·4	50·9	11·0	0·0	1·6	(23·9)	9·2	0·9	6·5	(40·3)	26·7	2·9	13·9	−10·6	+15·7	+2·9	+12·3
Argentine	0·2	(26·0)	14·5	5·9	(0·0)	28·1	6·1	26·3	12·7	3·2	21·8	45·3	1·9	−22·8	+7·3	+39·4	+1·9
Brazil	0·1	18·7	0·7	18·9	0·6	13·8	5·2	7·8	21·6	(26·6)	0·0	7·1	7·1	+7·9	+0·7	−11·8	+6·5
Colombia	0·1	20·0	7·5	31·1	1·6	14·1	3·7	30·2	34·1	2·5	5·2	78·0	2·5	−17·5	+2·3	+46·9	+0·9
Peru	0·2	32·3	4·8	35·6	0·0	31·9	6·7	29·0	0·9	8·5	10·2	62·2	0·0	−23·8	+5·4	+22·6	0·0
Venezuela	1·2	16·2	1·6	38·9	0·0	11·8	1·6	59·2	8·1	9·4	3·1	57·2	6·2	−6·8	+1·5	+18·3	+6·2
Mexico	0·2	26·8	1·0	70·1	0·0	24·7	2·2	58·4	0·4	1·6	1·1	76·6	0·1	−25·2	+0·1	+6·5	+0·1
Canada	8·6	53·0	0·4	37·4	3·3	50·5	1·7	42·2	0·0	40·2	1·8	47·6	1·9	−12·8	+1·4	+10·2	+1·4
U.S.A.	4·1	12·6	10·5	—	22·4	24·0	14·9	—	21·3	14·2	14·9	—	20·6	+1·6	+4·4	—	+1·8
W. Europe Sample	50·4	18·1	6·9	3·7	1·0	17·5	8·0	2·6	1·4	13·9	8·7	4·5	0·7	−4·2	+1·8	+0·8	+0·3
E.E.C.	32·1	12·7	3·8	4·0	1·4	15·0	5·2	2·8	0·6	11·8	6·0	5·1	0·4	−0·9	+2·2	+1·1	+1·0
S. Com'wealth Sample	53·7	51·3	2·5	0·7	12·4	62·5	7·3	2·6	6·5	54·6	9·0	8·2	8·7	+3·3	+6·5	+7·5	+3·7
World	155·1	24·3	5·4	8·1	7·1	21·8	8·1	7·4	10·4	17·7	9·6	9·8	8·1	−6·6	+4·2	+1·7	+1·0

* Silk, wool and hair yarn; yarn and thread of flax, hemp and ramie, yarn and thread of synthetic fibres and spun glass.

Table G. Cotton fabrics (S.I.T.C. 652)*

Import Market	U.K. Exports 1959 $m.	1953				1957				1959				1953–59			
		U.K.	W.G.	U.S.A.	Japan	U.K.	W.G.	U.S.A.	Japan	U.K.	W.G.	U.S.A.	Japan	U.K.	W.G.	U.S.A.	Japan
Belgium-Luxembourg	0·7	9·0	18·0	2·0	0·1	4·6	12·2	0·2	8·5	3·0	14·0	1·9	2·4	− 6·0	− 4·0	− 0·1	+ 2·3
Denmark	1·9	27·4	38·3	0·0	0·0	16·5	40·4	0·2	12·0	10·8	36·1	0·3	14·0	−16·6	− 2·2	+ 0·3	+14·0
Finland	0·8	36·9	2·5	8·1	10·9	31·7	16·1	0·0	16·1	11·6	36·6	0·0	2·1	−25·3	+34·1	+ 8·1	− 8·8
France	0·5	8·0	16·9	5·8	0·0	10·4	36·9	2·4	0·8	8·8	18·4	7·0	0·0	+ 0·8	+ 1·5	+ 1·2	0·0
West Germany	0·9	4·0	—	0·2	2·5	6·2	—	5·8	42·1	2·6	—	1·7	4·6	− 1·4	—	+ 1·5	+ 2·1
Italy	0·6	23·4	6·1	5·8	0·1	10·2	11·8	2·8	5·9	10·4	18·6	3·5	0·7	−13·0	+12·5	+ 2·3	+ 0·6
Netherlands	0·5	10·2	19·5	0·7	12·1	2·1	15·7	2·6	31·1	1·7	21·8	3·0	12·6	− 8·5	+ 2·3	+ 2·3	+ 0·5
Norway	2·5	34·5	22·5	3·0	1·6	22·4	28·2	5·0	3·1	17·5	28·4	2·1	7·9	−17·0	+ 5·9	+ 0·9	+ 6·3
Sweden	1·8	13·6	36·1	0·4	8·0	13·0	36·1	0·7	22·3	8·4	35·3	2·1	19·1	− 5·2	− 0·8	+ 1·7	+11·1
Australia	16·5	70·5	3·5	0·3	10·2	40·9	7·2	0·5	38·4	24·1	6·8	1·5	52·8	−46·4	+ 3·3	+ 1·2	+42·6
British East Africa	6·1	88·7	3·1	0·1	0·1	69·1	3·6	0·1	22·2	44·0	1·8	0·7	44·4	−44·7	+ 1·3	+ 0·6	+44·4
Ceylon	2·0	77·8	0·3	0·4	20·6	22·7	2·2	0·2	75·4	0·8	0·8	0·0	78·0	−57·8	+ 0·5	+ 0·6	+57·4
Ghana	6·9	54·3	1·1	0·0	14·7	60·9	2·2	0·0	36·4	52·7	1·1	0·6	39·5	− 1·6	0·0	0·0	+24·8
India	1·4	94·0	0·7	0·0	1·3	69·3	4·7	0·0	23·0	61·7	11·0	0·6	22·8	−32·3	+10·3	+ 0·6	+21·5
Malaya	1·9	45·8	3·0	4·5	40·2	13·4	1·8	2·4	79·9	12·5	2·1	2·1	80·4	−33·3	− 0·9	+ 2·4	+40·2
New Zealand	11·7	91·2	1·2	0·0	0·0	73·8	3·2	3·8	13·4	59·3	4·7	2·7	23·5	−31·9	+ 3·5	+ 2·7	+23·5
Nigeria	9·1	68·6	12·1	0·0	7·1	52·3	2·4	0·0	42·7	42·8	1·6	0·1	54·4	−25·8	−10·5	+ 0·1	+47·3
Pakistan	0·1	(74·3	2·4	0·0	7·7)	(25·4	17·3	0·0	42·2)	(11·6	2·6	0·0	85·0)	−62·7	+ 0·2	0·0	+77·3
Rhodesia and Nyasaland	7·4	99·3	0·0	0·0	0·1	90·5	0·7	0·8	5·3	66·5	3·9	2·1	16·9	−32·8	+ 3·9	+ 2·1	+16·8
Union of South Africa	13·5	52·6	2·2	12·5	16·5	35·0	4·3	26·5	17·5	30·4	6·3	19·3	23·3	−22·2	+ 4·1	+ 6·8	+ 6·8
Iran	0·8	7·8	2·9	7·5	73·1	12·0	5·3	10·5	67·2	7·2	7·3	5·4	73·1	− 0·6	+ 4·4	− 2·1	0·0
Iraq	0·3	25·2	5·0	2·8	44·8	14·2	2·8	2·8	68·1	7·2	9·6	4·0	72·9	−18·0	+ 4·6	+ 1·2	+28·1
Argentine	0·1	(11·0	0·0	69·0	0·0)	64·8	0·0	18·8	4·6)	(35·2	0·0	51·5	0·0)	+24·2	0·0	−17·5	0·0
Brazil	0·0	0·0	0·0	5·4	36·4)	100·0	0·0	0·0	0·0	(8·6	0·0	0·0	0·0)	+ 6·7	0·0	− 5·4	−36·4
Colombia	0·0	5·3	1·7	89·3	0·2	0·0	0·0	100·0	0·0	(12·2	0·0	60·8	0·0)	+ 6·9	+ 1·7	−28·5	− 0·2
Peru	0·0	17·1	2·1	46·7	24·3	2·7	5·1	21·4	57·7	4·4	5·0	52·7	25·3)	−12·7	+ 2·9	+ 6·0	+ 1·0
Venezuela	0·2	7·4	0·7	82·6	0·0	1·1	1·2	45·3	48·1	1·2	2·7	38·6	44·0	− 6·2	+ 2·0	−44·0	+ 6·0
Mexico	0·0	(3·3	3·9	80·6	0·0)	(1·4	—	84·3	2·3)	(3·8	0·0	54·4	21·8)	+ 0·5	+ 2·0	−26·2	+21·8
Canada	3·7	11·5	1·7	81·4	0·5	11·4	2·1	7·3	7·3	5·9	2·2	74·8	11·5	− 5·6	+ 0·5	− 6·6	+11·0
U.S.A.	4·8	29·0	3·4	—	23·1	16·5	6·4	76·5	56·8	10·7	6·7	—	51·7	−18·3	+ 3·3	—	+28·6
W. Europe Sample	10·2	16·5	21·9	1·5	4·4	10·0	21·6	2·3	19·7	6·4	20·2	2·1	8·6	−10·1	+ 1·7	+ 0·6	+ 4·2
E.E.C.	3·2	9·0	11·7	1·8	4·9	4·8	13·3	2·7	23·7	3·2	11·9	2·5	5·9	− 5·8	+ 0·2	+ 0·7	+ 1·0
S. Com'wealth Sample	76·5	66·0	3·7	3·5	12·7	45·1	4·1	7·3	34·4	34·8	4·6	4·9	44·1	−31·2	+ 0·9	+ 1·4	+31·4
World	129·6	24·4	6·5	18·9	17·6	17·1	7·5	17·5	31·8	13·7	8·5	16·1	30·7	−10·7	+ 2·0	− 2·8	+13·1

* Cottón fabrics, grey and other than grey; unbleached and bleached, dyed, mercerised, printed or otherwise finished.

Table H. Non-cotton fabrics (S.I.T.C. 653)*

Import Market	U.K. Exports 1959 $m.	1953 U.K.	1953 W.G.	1953 U.S.A.	1953 Japan	1957 U.K.	1957 W.G.	1957 U.S.A.	1957 Japan	1959 U.K.	1959 W.G.	1959 U.S.A.	1959 Japan	1953–59 U.K.	1953–59 W.G.	1953–59 U.S.A.	1953–59 Japan
Belgium-Luxembourg	4·5	10·4	12·2	3·7	1·1	11·2	16·3	3·2	6·1	9·5	17·7	6·7	3·0	− 0·9	+ 5·5	+ 3·0	+ 1·9
Denmark	7·3	33·2	33·0	0·1	0·0	29·8	26·7	0·4	6·6	26·1	24·4	1·1	8·1	− 7·1	− 8·6	+ 1·1	+ 8·1
Finland	1·3	29·5	3·4	0·0	15·6	24·6	19·7	2·3	5·3	15·5	30·6	0·3	0·6	−14·0	+27·2	+ 0·3	+15·0
France	4·7	29·9	12·5	5·0	7·1	28·3	10·8	0·0	4·5	30·6	10·3	0·9	7·1	+ 0·7	− 2·2	+ 4·1	0·0
West Germany	21·5	19·4	—	0·2	2·3	21·7	—	1·7	9·5	17·0	—	1·2	4·1	− 2·4	—	+ 1·0	+ 1·8
Italy	6·4	58·5	6·6	4·0	0·7	47·1	10·5	1·6	12·2	39·4	9·7	0·9	6·1	−19·1	+ 3·1	+ 3·1	+ 5·4
Netherlands	4·9	11·2	15·5	2·7	1·0	8·4	14·1	2·0	6·5	9·2	17·2	2·4	3·3	− 2·0	+ 1·7	+ 0·3	+ 2·3
Norway	3·3	29·7	29·5	0·3	0·2	21·3	34·9	4·7	0·1	20·1	31·4	9·0	1·4	− 9·6	+ 1·9	+ 8·7	+ 1·2
Sweden	8·3	25·1	24·7	2·5	0·7	22·3	29·1	10·8	3·7	23·9	28·8	8·0	3·8	− 1·2	+ 4·1	+ 5·5	+ 3·1
Australia	11·1	65·4	5·1	0·6	1·3	57·4	11·9	3·8	9·3	43·7	9·9	3·2	22·3	−21·7	+ 4·8	+ 2·6	+21·0
British East Africa	1·6	73·1	11·2	0·0	0·3	8·0	4·1	0·0	84·8	10·2	2·3	0·4	84·1	−62·9	+ 8·9	+ 0·4	+83·8
Ceylon	0·7	20·1	0·2	1·5	78·0	12·8	6·0	6·0	74·0	9·1	1·9	7·0	78·9	−11·0	+ 1·7	+ 5·5	+ 0·9
Ghana	0·6	65·3	18·7	0·0	15·3	5·7	6·5	0·1	84·7	6·7	8·8	0·3	81·4	−58·6	+ 9·9	+ 0·3	+66·1
India	0·7	49·5	2·2	23·6	10·6	28·9	20·7	1·2	34·5	17·5	40·8	9·6	27·5	−32·1	+38·6	+ 9·6	+16·9
Malaya	1·0	29·0	2·4	0·1	34·4	6·5	6·6	10·9	72·3	4·2	5·2	9·4	78·9	−24·8	+ 2·8	−14·2	+44·5
New Zealand	14·0	90·7	2·1	0·0	0·3	79·3	5·0	5·7	1·6	73·5	5·7	3·8	9·5	−17·2	+ 3·6	+ 3·7	+ 9·2
Nigeria	1·6	25·9	30·8	0·0	10·8	6·1	8·0	0·0	83·8	7·4	7·5	0·1	81·6	−18·5	−23·3	+ 0·1	+70·8
Pakistan	0·2	(60·0	9·7	0·9	11·0)	(32·0	3·5	15·9	43·0)	(17·4	36·5	13·6	29·6)	−42·4	+26·8	+12·7	+18·6
Rhodesia and Nyasaland	2·8	99·5	0·0	0·0	0·1	72·4	4·2	1·4	15·1	51·1	11·7	0·8	22·4	−48·4	+11·7	+ 0·8	+22·3
Union of South Africa	10·6	39·7	2·8	13·4	17·5	25·2	6·5	18·4	35·8	22·1	6·6	17·1	33·2	−17·6	+ 3·7	+ 3·7	+15·7
Iran	4·5	20·1	38·3	7·0	13·9	16·7	16·1	3·3	48·8	15·3	14·6	3·2	48·9	− 4·8	−23·7	+ 3·8	+35·0
Iraq	1·9	18·8	2·8	0·6	58·2	16·3	3·0	0·2	72·3	14·4	3·6	1·1	78·9	− 4·4	+ 0·8	+ 0·5	+20·7
Argentine	0·1	(7·3	1·2	19·7	2·8)	(19·6	0·7	59·8	0·6)	2·1	5·7	28·9	1·7	− 5·2	+ 4·5	+ 9·2	+ 1·1
Brazil	0·6	76·1	0·3	9·2	0·2	76·4	1·2	14·5	0·9	(64·6	2·2	6·9	0·0)	−11·5	+ 1·9	− 2·3	− 0·2
Colombia	0·0	0·0	5·6	85·2	1·3	2·7	5·0	90·4	0·4	32·2	0·0	38·9	0·0	+32·2	+ 5·6	−46·3	+ 1·3
Peru	0·3	40·9	1·6	55·6	0·7	29·5	3·5	41·7	19·8	(32·3	32·6	17·2	6·3)	− 8·6	+31·0	−38·4	+ 5·6
Venezuela	5·3	38·7	0·7	48·9	1·5	37·6	4·3	42·6	2·7	38·7	6·1	23·7	12·1	0·0	+ 5·4	−25·2	+10·6
Mexico	0·1	7·3	6·4	63·2	15·8	11·7	1·4	68·2	7·3	(9·5	1·3	32·9	37·7)	+ 2·2	+ 5·1	−30·3	+21·9
Canada	32·2	61·0	0·9	30·7	0·8	55·8	3·2	23·2	5·1	52·0	2·9	27·7	6·1	− 9·0	+ 2·0	− 3·0	+ 5·3
U.S.A.	41·4	52·7	5·5	—	4·9	33·7	3·7	—	32·5	24·0	3·1	—	42·9	−28·7	− 2·4	—	+38·0
W. Europe Sample	62·2	23·6	16·0	1·8	1·6	20·5	13·5	2·9	6·9	18·0	13·1	3·1	4·1	− 5·6	− 2·9	+ 1·3	+ 2·5
E.E.C.	42·0	19·9	7·9	2·3	2·0	19·0	7·8	1·9	7·9	16·3	8·0	2·4	4·0	− 3·6	+ 0·1	+ 0·1	+ 2·0
S. Com'wealth Sample	44·9	51·6	7·0	6·6	13·3	29·1	7·0	7·7	48·1	24·9	7·5	7·3	49·2	−26·7	+ 0·5	+ 0·7	+35·9
World	252·5	34·3	8·4	12·5	9·9	23·3	8·7	9·3	25·2	20·4	9·2	8·2	23·9	−13·9	+ 0·8	+ 4·3	+14·0

* Silk, woollen and worsted fabrics; linen, hemp and jute fabrics; of synthetic fibres and spun glass, of textile fibres mixed with metal, and fabrics of coarse hair and paper yarns.

Table I. *Made-up textiles (non-clothing) (S.I.T.C. 656)**

Import Market	U.K. Exports 1959 $m.	1953 U.K.	1953 W.G.	1953 U.S.A.	1953 Japan	1957 U.K.	1957 W.G.	1957 U.S.A.	1957 Japan	1959 U.K.	1959 W.G.	1959 U.S.A.	1959 Japan	1953–59 U.K.	1953–59 W.G.	1953–59 U.S.A.	1953–59 Japan
Belgium-Luxembourg	0.3	14.7	3.8	12.6	0.5	7.0	7.5	8.1	1.4	4.0	6.9	7.4	0.2	−10.7	+3.1	−5.2	−0.3
Denmark	0.9	36.3	29.1	0.0	0.0	30.1	25.1	2.0	14.4	28.3	30.7	3.1	10.7	−8.0	+1.6	+3.1	+10.7
Finland	0.0	(52.0)	0.0	16.3	(0.0)	(45.3)	0.0	0.0	0.0	7.6	12.2	52.6	0.0	−44.4	+12.2	+36.3	0.0
France	0.4	16.5	14.5	7.7	0.0	7.0	10.3	0.0	0.0	12.0	14.4	11.6	0.0	−4.4	−0.1	+7.7	0.0
West Germany	1.1	22.6	—	3.0	0.0	9.5	—	4.6	20.9	6.9	—	11.6	0.7	−15.7	—	+8.6	+0.7
Italy	0.4	31.8	11.2	37.8	0.0	32.0	19.9	15.8	0.2	23.5	24.6	6.3	1.1	−8.3	+13.4	−31.5	+1.1
Netherlands	0.7	19.8	4.5	12.9	0.1	11.2	17.6	4.8	0.1	6.1	14.9	12.4	0.7	−13.7	+10.4	−0.5	+0.6
Norway	0.3	23.6	33.1	1.8	0.0	14.5	42.9	5.9	0.0	15.2	35.4	4.7	0.5	−8.4	+2.3	+2.9	+0.5
Sweden	0.2	16.8	21.5	4.4	0.1	10.1	42.2	10.7	2.4	6.6	36.0	24.7	7.7	−10.2	+14.5	+20.3	+7.6
Australia	2.8	84.9	1.5	1.8	5.4	66.0	3.6	1.5	23.9	60.5	3.7	5.6	23.3	−24.4	+2.2	+3.8	+17.9
British East Africa	1.3	44.0	0.5	0.0	10.9	33.6	0.9	0.0	26.1	31.5	1.5	0.3	36.2	−12.5	+1.0	+0.3	+36.2
Ceylon	0.3	(86.4)	0.0	0.0	12.4	44.5	3.0	0.0	15.9	47.1	5.7	1.7	45.5	−39.3	+5.7	+1.7	+33.1
Ghana	1.0	67.8	0.7	5.8	21.5	50.7	3.0	2.0	36.0	50.5	5.7	5.3	35.4	−17.3	+5.0	−0.5	+13.9
India	0.1	37.0	0.0	5.8	0.2	(37.5)	3.0	3.0	6.0	30.0	5.3	0.0	0.0	−7.0	+5.3	−5.8	−0.2
Malaya	0.5	45.9	1.0	5.6	11.0	27.4	1.2	5.1	47.1	29.9	1.3	3.1	11.5	−16.0	+0.3	−2.5	+0.5
New Zealand	3.1	99.0	0.0	0.0	0.0	88.3	5.1	3.1	0.0	80.0	3.4	10.7	44.8	−19.0	+3.4	+10.7	+44.8
Nigeria	1.0	58.6	2.4	0.0	0.0	42.8	3.6	0.0	0.0	33.7	1.5	17.0	0.0	−24.9	−0.9	+17.0	0.0
Pakistan	0.1	43.1	24.0	0.0	5.4	88.4	2.1	7.4	37.5	9.2	10.7	0.5	44.8	−33.9	−13.3	+0.5	+39.4
Rhodesia and Nyasaland	1.9	94.8	0.4	0.0	10.9	91.5	0.6	1.0	0.0	94.0	0.6	0.5	0.0	−0.8	+0.2	+0.5	−10.9
Union of South Africa	1.6	52.7	0.4	25.6	7.2	36.7	1.7	39.5	12.9	31.6	4.2	36.3	17.8	−21.1	+3.8	+10.7	+10.6
Iran	0.3	0.0	0.0	0.0	0.5	(76.1)	9.6	17.3	39.5	45.1	6.4	29.8	0.0	+45.1	+6.4	+23.1	−0.5
Iraq	0.3	24.6	2.7	6.7	8.1	46.3	2.2	3.9	11.1	46.9	11.6	8.8	19.8	+22.3	+8.9	+2.0	+11.7
Argentine	neg.	(0.0)	0.0	52.7	(0.0)	(0.0)	0.0	82.7	0.0	0.0	0.0	100.0	0.0	0.0	0.0	−43.9	0.0
Brazil	neg.	(12.7)	0.0	57.7	21.2	0.0	0.0	74.6	21.2	(0.0)	0.0	—	0.0	−12.7	0.0	+100.0	−21.2
Colombia	neg.	2.1	0.0	95.0	0.3	3.9	22.0	69.2	0.0	6.0	24.8	36.4	0.0	+3.9	+24.8	−21.3	−0.3
Peru	neg.	8.1	1.9	67.6	11.4	5.7	7.8	54.3	2.3	6.1	2.6	77.8	0.0	−2.0	+0.7	−17.2	−11.4
Venezuela	0.1	3.5	1.0	90.0		2.2	4.8	78.4	9.0	2.8	16.2	72.3	0.0	−0.7	+14.3	+4.7	0.0
Mexico	neg.	0.0	0.0	64.4	34.9	0.8	0.0	88.9	6.9	0.0	2.9	73.3	14.2	0.0	+2.9	−16.7	−20.7
Canada	2.2	11.9	0.7	81.0	3.6	11.9	1.0	71.0	9.7	9.2	3.7	78.9	13.9	−2.7	+3.0	+14.5	+10.3
U.S.A.	4.7	34.4	2.6	—	35.7	24.7	4.1	—	47.1	26.5	4.0	—	50.3	−7.9	+1.4	—	+14.6
W. Europe Sample	4.5	21.2	11.8	8.8	0.1	11.8	14.1	5.4	4.2	9.1	13.0	10.8	0.4	−12.1	+1.2	+2.0	+0.3
E.E.C.	2.9	19.3	5.2	11.6	0.1	10.2	9.5	5.3	3.7	8.1	8.1	13.2	1.7	−11.9	+2.9	+1.6	+1.6
S. Com'wealth Sample	13.7	65.0	1.2	5.4	5.5	55.3	2.1	7.7	19.9	48.9	4.1	10.0	25.8	−16.1	+2.9	+4.6	+20.3
World	34.8	21.7	3.1	30.2	8.5	17.8	5.2	25.9	12.8	15.2	5.6	27.5	14.0	−6.5	+2.5	+2.7	+5.5

* Bags and sacks, tarpaulins, tents, blankets, travelling rugs, bed and table linen, towels, made-up curtains, cases made of textile materials.

Table J. Clothing (S.I.T.C. 84)*

Import Market	U.K. Exports 1959 $m	1953					1957					1959					1953–59				
		U.K.	W.G.	U.S.A.	Japan	Italy	U.K.	W.G.	U.S.A.	Japan	Italy	U.K.	W.G.	U.S.A.	Japan	Italy	U.K.	W.G.	U.S.A.	Japan	Italy
Belgium-Luxembourg	1.4	3.0	6.2	8.0	1.1	7.5	5.2	10.8	3.9	4.1	8.7	4.1	10.2	2.3	5.6	11.7	+1.1	+4.0	−5.7	+4.5	+4.2
Denmark	1.1	20.4	25.7	4.2	0.3	17.5	11.2	32.9	12.5	1.1	15.6	7.7	27.8	3.4	17.6	20.7	−12.7	+2.1	−0.8	+17.3	+3.2
Finland	0.2	(53.1)	0.0	0.0	0.0	24.3	(17.0)	24.8	0.0	0.0	(25.6)	10.5	29.2	1.8	0.0	25.1	−42.6	+29.2	+1.8	0.0	+0.8
France	1.5	32.0	21.5	3.7	0.2	14.7	25.2	19.8	1.2	0.0	27.5	13.8	14.2	1.8	4.7	57.9	−18.2	−7.3	−1.9	+4.5	+43.2
West Germany	6.6	14.0	—	1.3	0.3	23.9	15.9	—	4.4	1.6	27.9	9.4	—	4.1	4.2	35.2	−4.6	—	+2.8	+3.9	+11.3
Italy	1.4	17.1	18.3	11.3	0.3	—	21.2	44.6	1.6	3.4	—	20.0	44.0	1.3	4.2	—	+2.9	+25.7	−10.0	+3.9	—
Netherlands	3.0	8.0	9.3	8.4	0.4	3.6	5.8	16.3	3.8	0.2	8.2	5.1	17.2	12.6	1.6	10.5	−2.9	+7.9	+4.2	+1.2	+6.9
Norway	2.1	34.7	25.9	0.6	0.3	11.8	16.3	47.4	1.4	0.0	6.0	13.0	41.5	5.0	0.0	8.8	−21.7	+15.6	+4.4	−0.3	−3.0
Sweden	5.6	35.9	27.0	0.6	1.1	13.5	18.4	39.4	0.8	0.8	6.7	18.7	35.6	0.9	3.2	21.0	−17.2	+8.6	+0.3	+2.1	+7.5
Australia	4.8	71.8	3.6	0.0	0.1	22.1	64.5	7.8	0.0	7.1	11.7	60.1	6.5	1.8	15.0	9.1	−11.7	+2.9	+1.8	+14.9	−13.0
British East Africa	1.4	68.5	9.5	0.6	0.0	0.0	10.2	4.1	0.0	83.4	1.1	17.2	4.0	0.7	73.7	0.8	−51.3	−5.5	+0.1	+73.7	+0.8
Ceylon	0.4	32.1	1.2	6.7	59.9	0.0	(28.2)	4.4	4.4	63.1	0.0	(43.3)	5.6	7.1	40.1	0.0	+11.2	+4.4	+0.4	−19.8	0.0
Ghana	1.2	38.7	0.9	0.0	58.9	0.0	25.1	6.4	0.9	62.1	1.5	18.8	5.6	0.8	69.8	1.7	−19.9	+4.7	+0.8	+10.9	+1.7
India	0.0	74.2	0.0	0.0	9.5	11.3	74.2	0.0	8.0	5.0	7.3	(76.8)	0.0	16.0	0.0	0.0	+2.6	0.0	+16.0	−9.5	−11.3
Malaya	1.6	39.9	1.2	31.2	26.1	0.6	26.6	3.2	18.0	49.2	0.4	16.5	1.7	62.3	11.7	0.8	−23.4	+0.5	+31.1	−14.4	+0.2
New Zealand	1.8	94.2	2.3	0.0	0.0	2.8	92.3	3.2	0.2	0.2	0.4	79.8	9.9	0.0	2.4	2.0	−14.4	+7.6	0.0	+2.4	−0.8
Nigeria	1.8	28.9	3.2	0.0	56.9	7.9	17.7	3.8	0.0	69.0	2.9	19.3	4.8	0.3	67.9	2.9	−9.6	+1.6	+0.3	+11.0	−5.0
Pakistan	0.3	(67.5)	0.0	0.0	12.3	14.4	(48.1)	19.8	0.0	32.1	0.0	(54.3)	13.7	0.0	31.7	0.0	−13.2	+13.7	0.0	+19.4	−14.4
Rhodesia and Nyasaland	1.8	99.8	0.0	0.0	0.0	0.0	81.1	2.4	0.0	0.0	1.5	72.5	10.5	0.0	0.0	0.0	−27.3	+10.5	0.0	0.0	0.0
Union of South Africa	4.3	50.1	1.7	38.1	3.0	4.2	29.6	3.9	34.5	12.8	7.2	29.1	5.8	22.8	13.6	12.2	−21.0	+4.1	−15.3	+10.6	+8.0
Iran	0.7	(0.0)	14.8	34.7	3.2	45.4	6.3	32.6	2.6	6.3	10.8	23.5	39.9	5.2	3.8	9.5	+23.5	+25.1	−29.5	+0.6	−35.9
Iraq	0.4	39.5	2.0	15.4	8.8	22.3	16.2	14.0	0.6	56.6	9.5	20.8	28.0	8.0	34.3	0.9	−18.7	+26.0	−7.4	+25.5	−21.4
Argentine	0.0	0.0	54.2	0.0	0.0	0.0	(1.8)	3.5	87.4	0.6	1.5	(1.8)	4.0	81.7	2.8	2.3	+1.8	−50.2	+81.7	+2.8	+2.3
Brazil	0.0	7.5	0.0	33.8	31.9	0.0	(1.2)	1.9	69.3	0.0	3.0	(4.0)	11.0	19.3	0.0	12.0	−3.5	+11.0	−14.5	−31.9	+12.0
Colombia	0.0	5.1	15.2	72.6	0.1	6.7	(1.2)	8.1	59.7	0.0	3.3	(0.0)	8.1	84.1	1.5	4.7	−5.1	−7.1	+11.5	+1.4	−2.0
Peru	0.0	3.6	5.9	85.2	1.6	2.7	(4.8)	8.1	33.1	6.7	4.8	(6.2)	15.9	46.1	8.7	8.1	+2.6	+10.0	−39.1	+7.1	+5.4
Venezuela	0.3	3.2	1.8	85.3	0.0	7.0	0.6	4.4	47.1	8.1	5.1	4.7	8.0	53.3	9.0	12.8	+1.5	+6.2	−32.0	+9.0	+5.8
Mexico	0.0	0.6	1.4	92.1	0.0	1.0	0.6	3.9	75.2	24.5	5.1	0.0	2.8	60.7	29.9	5.1	−0.6	+1.4	−31.4	+29.9	+4.1
Canada	8.2	32.2	2.1	54.0	5.2	2.1	29.3	3.9	24.5	32.9	3.7	35.2	7.3	36.6	0.1	7.7	+3.0	+5.2	−17.4	−5.1	+5.6
U.S.A.	16.8	30.9	3.4	—	30.3	12.7	12.3	5.6	—	60.8	9.6	9.5	5.7	—	63.2	10.7	−21.4	+2.3	—	+32.9	−2.0
W. Europe Sample	22.9	19.2	13.7	4.1	0.6	12.8	11.9	20.8	2.7	3.1	13.0	9.4	16.5	3.3	4.0	21.4	−9.8	+2.8	−0.8	+3.4	+8.6
E.E.C.	13.9	11.6	6.4	5.7	0.5	12.0	10.1	13.4	3.3	1.9	13.2	7.6	10.1	3.6	3.5	22.6	−4.0	+3.7	−2.1	+3.0	+10.6
S. Com'wealth Sample	18.3	57.6	2.4	17.5	12.8	6.6	36.9	4.6	12.3	34.9	4.8	32.0	5.5	7.9	41.2	5.6	−25.6	+3.1	−9.6	+28.4	+1.0
World	84.8	22.7	6.8	23.5	8.9	8.8	13.9	11.7	13.1	20.9	9.3	10.2	10.2	10.5	24.8	12.6	−12.5	+3.4	−13.0	+15.9	+3.8

* Underwear, outerwear, leather, plastic and rubberised clothing, headgear, gloves, shawls. The group does not include rubber gloves, or any kind of footwear.

Table K. Iron and steel (S.I.T.C. 681)*†

Import Market	U.K. Exports 1959 $m	1953 U.K.	1953 W.G.	1953 U.S.A.	1953 Japan	1953 France	1953 B-Lux	1957 U.K.	1957 W.G.	1957 U.S.A.	1957 Japan	1957 France	1957 B-Lux
Belgium-Luxembourg	5·5	8·3	30·8	13·0	1·0	33·4	—	7·1	35·5	10·0	0·1	31·9	—
Denmark	17·7	29·8	21·3	3·7	0·0	5·9	27·6	20·2	27·5	4·8	0·0	13·6	23·2
Finland	7·7	24·8	13·0	2·9	2·7	30·6	16·8	27·1	25·8	0·8	0·0	19·3	14·4
France	1·9	9·2	15·6	20·1	5·8	—	22·9	1·6	30·5	3·4	1·9	—	47·0
West Germany	13·2	0·9	—	1·3	3·7	43·5	40·0	0·7	—	12·8	2·5	45·6	25·0
Italy	8·2	15·3	16·8	14·7	0·9	28·7	15·7	5·9	28·6	6·3	0·0	23·9	10·8
Netherlands	18·8	12·2	26·6	8·0	0·1	7·7	42·7	5·9	39·4	7·6	0·1	5·8	39·0
Norway	15·3	21·2	20·8	9·0	1·9	14·1	18·1	19·2	28·0	8·3	0·0	10·7	18·5
Sweden	23·6	16·3	27·8	8·1	4·3	8·9	28·6	12·5	36·9	8·3	1·6	9·4	25·9
Australia	22·4	69·1	2·2	17·8	1·4	6·0	0·7	76·2	1·1	13·8	0·4	1·7	1·0
British East Africa	10·6	76·7	4·0	0·5	0·7	2·4	15·2	65·0	6·5	0·7	8·7	0·0	16·2
Ceylon	6·0	(63·0)	3·1	1·0	2·8	11·9	18·2	(56·3)	2·5	0·3	0·8	20·9	19·1
Ghana	5·2	71·3	0·5	0·2	21·4	0·0	6·6	(63·8)	4·4	0·4	14·8	4·3	12·2
India	35·6	30·2	8·5	11·6	22·1	13·7	9·1	17·2	18·0	12·2	25·2	8·1	9·1
Malaya	5·8	32·8	8·0	5·3	33·1	8·7	11·4	37·0	8·1	6·7	21·2	9·9	16·0
New Zealand	20·0	90·6	0·1	7·9	0·0	0·0	1·2	87·3	1·5	4·4	0·0	2·1	2·6
Nigeria	14·2	82·9	0·8	1·6	0·0	0·0	14·2	53·9	5·5	2·4	20·6	2·0	8·3
Pakistan	6·0	30·4	11·8	2·6	12·0	23·5	16·8	23·3	16·1	8·8	3·9	21·7	15·5
Rhodesia and Nyasaland	3·6	95·9	0·7	0·6	0·1	0·0	2·7	72·6	2·8	1·9	0·0	5·1	15·5
Union of South Africa	11·5	35·1	3·9	26·3	0·6	17·1	14·0	32·2	9·9	18·4	1·3	14·8	18·0
Iran	6·3	6·2	49·3	12·2	14·3	6·0	10·5	24·7	36·8	7·0	3·3	12·6	8·0
Iraq	13·7	44·9	10·8	3·4	2·0	18·2	15·3	29·2	16·8	5·2	0·2	7·1	36·7
Argentine	33·6	5·7	27·2	18·6	19·6	19·3	4·9	15·8	14·6	12·6	1·3	6·6	30·4
Brazil	5·0	0·9	11·4	37·7	13·4	25·9	0·8	3·5	7·0	53·5	8·5	9·8	5·5
Colombia	1·2	5·2	9·2	52·7	0·9	17·5	13·0	5·8	13·8	58·1	0·6	8·3	8·3
Peru	0·6	8·4	6·1	52·2	0·2	7·1	23·9	10·1	6·7	55·2	1·4	11·5	12·3
Venezuela	12·5	12·5	6·1	52·0	0·0	11·9	13·3	9·1	17·8	52·9	0·4	5·8	8·6
Mexico	1·5	0·8	5·6	82·1	0·0	5·9	13·3	1·0	7·0	56·7	0·2	4·7	1·6
Canada	42·2	13·9	0·4	80·0	0·6	1·0	3·4	13·2	1·6	77·5	1·9	4·1	4·1
U.S.A.	39·8	6·1	13·6	—	5·6	14·6	26·9	5·5	21·7	—	5·5	15·7	23·5
W. Europe Sample	111·9	13·1	18·6	7·9	1·9	20·3	29·0	7·7	26·0	7·1	1·0	18·9	27·1
E.E.C.	47·5	8·9	16·9	8·5	1·7	24·1	31·3	3·6	24·0	7·5	1·2	21·6	29·2
S. Com'wealth Sample	141·0	53·9	4·7	11·1	9·2	9·5	9·4	39·2	11·2	10·4	13·3	8·5	10·5
World	536·2	14·6	13·0	19·9	5·4	18·5	19·3	12·2	19·2	22·7	4·3	14·6	16·7

* Pig iron, ferro-alloys, ingots, blooms, slabs, billets, sheet bars, tinplate bars, joints, girders, angles, shapes, sections, railway rails, wire rods, tubes, castings, forgings.
† Excluding exports from Switzerland.

Table K. Iron and steel (S.I.T.C. 681)*†

Import Market	1959						1953–59					
	U.K.	W.G.	U.S.A.	Japan	France	B-Lux.	U.K.	W.G.	U.S.A.	Japan	France	B-Lux.
Belgium-Luxembourg	6·6	31·0	5·2	0·0	36·0	—	—1·7	+0·2	—7·8	—1·0	+2·6	—
Denmark	18·2	31·5	0·3	0·0	14·8	19·7	—11·6	+10·2	—3·4	0·0	+8·9	—7·9
Finland	15·7	27·5	0·5	0·1	20·7	15·6	+9·1	+14·5	—2·4	—2·6	—9·9	—1·2
France	1·0	51·1	0·5	0·0	—	34·6	—8·2	+35·5	—19·6	—5·8	—	+11·7
West Germany	3·2	—	3·2	0·1	44·6	30·7	+2·3	—	+1·9	—3·6	+1·1	—9·3
Italy	6·5	26·3	5·0	0·1	39·1	14·9	—8·8	+9·5	—9·7	—0·8	+10·4	—0·8
Netherlands	7·7	43·2	3·6	0·1	7·8	35·0	—4·5	+16·6	—4·4	0·0	+0·1	—7·7
Norway	22·8	21·0	2·1	1·0	17·1	18·0	+1·6	+0·7	—8·4	—0·9	+3·0	—0·1
Sweden	18·2	26·4	7·4	0·1	13·5	22·6	+1·9	—1·4	—0·7	—4·2	+4·6	—6·0
Australia	66·7	2·5	7·6	2·3	5·3	3·2	—2·4	+0·3	—10·2	+0·9	+0·7	+2·5
British East Africa	49·4	7·5	0·9	15·9	7·6	17·4	—27·3	+3·5	+0·4	+15·2	+5·2	+2·2
Ceylon	(71·0	2·9	0·9	3·6	5·8	15·6)	+8·0	+6·1	+0·1	+0·8	+6·1	+2·6
Ghana	(62·5	4·3	0·0	9·9	1·7	19·8)	—8·8	+3·8	—0·2	—11·5	+1·7	+13·2
India	35·1	15·5	3·9	16·5	10·1	5·6	+4·9	+7·0	+7·7	+5·6	+3·6	+3·5
Malaya	23·9	6·5	5·0	42·1	7·7	12·8	—8·9	+1·5	—0·3	+9·0	+1·0	+1·4
New Zealand	92·4	1·2	1·7	0·1	0·5	2·0	+1·8	+1·1	—6·2	+0·1	+0·5	+0·8
Nigeria	62·7	3·9	0·3	16·1	1·4	14·4	—20·2	+3·1	+1·3	+16·1	+8·6	+0·2
Pakistan	22·1	17·7	9·4	14·7	14·9	14·3	—8·3	+5·9	+6·8	+2·7	+3·8	+2·5
Rhodesia and Nyasaland	(76·3	4·5	1·9	0·0	3·8	4·5)	—19·6	+3·8	+1·3	+0·1	+3·8	+1·8
Union of South Africa	46·9	8·8	5·3	0·6	8·3	12·5	+11·8	+4·9	—21·0	0·0	+8·8	+1·5
Iran	13·3	34·6	6·8	3·5	21·3	11·4	+7·1	—14·7	—5·4	—10·8	+15·3	+0·9
Iraq	41·2	24·9	4·2	1·0	4·0	20·6	—3·7	+14·1	+0·8	+1·0	—14·2	+5·3
Argentine	18·5	32·9	7·2	3·6	9·3	12·7	+12·8	+5·7	—11·4	—16·0	—10·0	+7·8
Brazil	7·5	7·5	21·4	27·3	18·8	2·3	+6·6	+3·9	—16·3	+13·9	+7·1	+1·5
Colombia	5·2	11·4	49·2	16·9	5·6	8·0	0·0	+2·2	—3·5	+16·0	—11·9	+5·0
Peru	4·0	12·3	41·8	5·1	7·2	23·1	—4·4	+6·2	—10·4	+4·9	+0·1	+0·8
Venezuela	12·1	15·0	36·1	2·6	10·1	18·8	—0·4	+8·9	—15·9	+2·6	+1·8	+5·5
Mexico	5·5	13·2	52·9	5·3	12·1	1·3	+4·7	+7·6	—29·2	+5·3	+6·2	+1·7
Canada	19·4	4·8	63·2	3·8	1·6	6·1	+5·5	+4·4	—16·8	+3·2	+0·6	+2·7
U.S.A.	7·2	17·2	—	13·8	12·7	23·3	+1·1	+3·6	—	+8·2	+1·9	+3·6
W. Europe Sample	8·0	25·5	3·2	0·1	23·8	26·1	—5·1	+6·9	—4·7	+1·8	+3·5	—2·9
E.E.C.	4·5	25·0	3·1	0·1	26·5	28·1	—4·4	+8·1	—5·4	+1·6	+2·4	—3·2
S. Com'wealth Sample	47·3	9·6	4·2	13·5	7·7	9·2	—6·6	+4·9	—6·9	+4·3	+1·8	—0·2
World	12·6	21·7	9·6	5·9	19·0	17·6	—2·0	+8·7	—10·3	+0·5	+0·5	+1·7

* Pig iron, ferro-alloys, ingots, blooms, slabs, billets, sheet bars, tinplate bars, joints, girders, angles, shapes, sections, railway rails, wire rods, tubes, castings, forgings.

† Excluding exports from Switzerland.

Table L. Power machinery (S.I.T.C. 711)*

Import Market	U.K. Exports 1959 $m.	1953 U.K.	1953 W.G.	1953 U.S.A.	1957 U.K.	1957 W.G.	1957 U.S.A.	1959 U.K.	1959 W.G.	1959 U.S.A.	1953–59 U.K.	1953–59 W.G.	1953–59 U.S.A.
Belgium-Luxembourg	6·0	25·5	27·3	11·8	46·9	17·1	8·4	14·7	24·1	11·4	−10·8	−3·2	−0·4
Denmark	3·1	28·0	47·1	2·8	45·8	27·3	3·5	21·0	32·5	21·2	−7·0	−14·6	+18·4
Finland	3·6	13·7	32·7	24·1	21·6	37·9	7·6	16·1	36·9	14·1	+2·4	+4·2	−10·0
France	21·8	32·2	25·3	14·7	33·9	37·7	7·7	38·7	35·7	4·0	+6·5	+10·4	−10·7
West Germany	13·0	17·8	—	12·8	29·4	—	13·2	27·0	—	8·9	+9·2	—	−3·9
Italy	16·6	23·8	41·6	21·9	23·1	43·5	15·0	42·5	28·5	12·1	+18·7	−13·1	−9·8
Netherlands	18·2	22·1	37·7	7·5	19·8	31·2	6·4	26·9	28·9	5·9	+4·8	−8·8	−1·6
Norway	4·5	19·3	29·1	7·4	15·3	25·8	5·9	22·1	20·7	8·4	+2·8	−8·4	+1·0
Sweden	14·5	16·3	58·8	6·5	44·4	35·4	5·6	37·8	30·6	19·7	+21·5	−28·2	+13·2
Australia	28·6	83·6	1·4	11·5	83·0	1·1	10·7	75·7	2·3	18·2	−7·9	+0·9	+6·7
British East Africa	7·1	94·1	2·9	0·0	82·3	6·6	1·6	89·1	3·0	2·5	−5·0	+0·1	+2·5
Ceylon	2·6	(59·7)	16·2	(6·4)	(77·7)	3·1	(5·5)	86·6	2·8	3·6	+26·9	−13·4	−2·8
Ghana	2·0	91·3	2·3	6·4	92·6	3·0	2·1	(88·3)	4·8	(3·7)	−3·0	+2·5	−2·7
India	35·0	59·7	24·4	7·8	57·7	20·0	3·1	61·5	20·8	3·7	+1·8	−3·6	−4·1
Malaya	7·7	73·8	6·1	10·1	66·8	8·7	8·3	70·0	6·1	7·5	−3·8	0·0	−2·6
New Zealand	5·3	93·3	0·5	3·7	74·6	1·0	7·4	68·1	0·3	13·5	−25·2	−0·2	+9·8
Nigeria	5·9	90·7	3·4	2·6	84·3	4·8	4·2	88·8	2·4	4·5	−1·9	−1·0	+1·9
Pakistan	7·5	53·6	29·7	9·8	45·1	15·6	17·1	64·5	18·5	12·4	+10·9	−11·2	+2·6
Rhodesia and Nyasaland	4·7	98·6	0·0	1·2	91·1	0·9	5·3	92·4	0·5	3·4	−6·2	+0·5	+2·2
Union of South Africa	16·4	72·3	3·1	22·7	77·3	4·9	8·4	67·9	7·4	13·0	−4·4	+4·3	−9·7
Iran	8·6	13·3	66·7	15·9	49·2	24·4	10·7	53·3	26·9	7·2	+40·0	−39·8	−8·7
Iraq	4·4	79·1	9·8	9·0	72·9	15·4	6·0	61·5	25·6	6·8	−17·6	+15·8	−2·2
Argentine	9·4	9·6	36·4	21·8	14·5	19·6	19·5	20·6	19·1	24·5	+11·0	−17·3	+2·7
Brazil	1·6	6·3	18·2	32·4	6·1	15·7	25·9	4·8	12·2	47·7	−1·5	−6·0	+15·3
Colombia	1·5	9·6	5·9	61·3	9·7	11·3	60·2	14·5	10·8	50·0	+4·9	+4·9	−11·3
Peru	1·5	9·5	8·5	59·4	18·0	19·8	51·8	16·4	21·9	50·7	+6·9	+13·4	−8·7
Venezuela	4·8	8·4	2·4	80·5	11·3	7·2	67·5	15·1	5·7	64·4	+6·7	+3·3	−16·1
Mexico	3·4	2·8	5·9	85·9	4·0	3·0	78·0	12·4	7·8	67·0	+9·6	+1·9	−18·9
Canada	33·0	25·8	0·2	72·9	18·6	0·6	77·2	31·6	1·1	65·2	+5·8	+0·9	−7·7
U.S.A.	50·5	26·4	7·2	—	23·4	6·6	—	48·7	4·2	—	+22·3	−3·0	—
W. Europe Sample	101·2	23·2	35·0	11·7	31·3	29·4	8·1	29·1	25·8	10·2	+5·9	−9·2	−1·5
E.E.C.	75·5	25·4	31·0	12·7	30·5	28·4	9·0	30·0	24·1	7·9	+4·6	−6·9	−4·8
S. Com'wealth Sample	123·0	75·1	8·6	11·9	70·3	9·4	7·2	70·5	10·3	9·4	−4·6	+1·7	−2·5
World	439·5	31·1	17·4	27·2	30·1	16·6	27·2	33·3	15·8	22·9	+2·2	−1·6	−4·3

* Steam generating boilers, boiler-house plant, steam engines, aircraft engines, internal combustion engines, water and gas turbines.

Table M. Agricultural machinery (S.I.T.C. 712)*

Import Market	U.K. Exports 1959 $m.	1953 U.K.	1953 W.G.	1953 U.S.A.	1957 U.K.	1957 W.G.	1957 U.S.A.	1959 U.K.	1959 W.G.	1959 U.S.A.	1953–59 U.K.	1953–59 W.G.	1953–59 U.S.A.
Belgium-Luxembourg	1·1	16·2	45·3	5·9	12·0	58·3	6·8	11·9	60·4	4·7	− 4·3	+15·1	− 1·2
Denmark	1·1	19·8	32·3	0·8	14·7	47·8	0·8	10·9	57·3	0·9	− 8·9	+25·0	+ 0·1
Finland	0·5	(62·9)	4·8	0·0	40·2	21·1	0·0	12·6	43·8	0·0	−50·3	+39·0	0·0
France	1·9	29·3	29·7	11·7	16·7	50·6	9·8	6·6	63·9	9·4	−22·7	+34·2	− 2·3
West Germany	1·6	35·4	—	1·9	25·6	—	15·4	20·2	—	28·0	−15·2	—	+26·1
Italy	1·5	14·4	49·1	8·2	10·9	59·3	5·9	16·9	55·5	4·6	+ 2·5	+ 6·4	− 3·6
Netherlands	2·1	20·4	50·6	3·0	15·5	52·8	4·7	17·4	51·6	7·3	− 3·0	+ 1·0	+ 4·3
Norway	0·5	18·2	18·4	2·9	15·8	25·8	3·7	14·3	38·7	3·1	− 3·9	+20·3	+ 0·2
Sweden	0·7	47·4	42·1	6·9	33·1	26·4	32·5	25·8	40·6	12·6	−21·6	+ 1·5	+ 5·7
Australia	4·5	58·8	2·7	34·1	59·8	6·0	21·5	47·4	6·2	34·8	−11·4	+ 3·5	+ 0·7
British East Africa	1·3	(44·7)	26·0	0·0	60·9	16·4	14·9	71·7	1·8	17·2	+27·0	−24·2	+17·2
Ceylon	0·3	(73·6)	0·0	8·2	93·9	0·0	1·8	(74·8)	0·0	(7·3)	+ 1·2	0·0	0·9
Ghana	0·2	80·3	0·0	0·0	(90·5)	0·0	9·5	(94·1)	0·0	5·4	+13·8	0·0	− 5·4
India	0·5	44·8	1·9	38·5	43·1	11·8	34·8	51·6	4·5	20·9	+ 6·8	+ 2·6	−17·6
Malaya	0·3	(84·5)	0·0	13·0	(82·5)	0·0	10·8	(68·2)	2·6	14·0	−16·3	+ 2·6	+ 1·0
New Zealand	1·4	60·2	2·7	29·4	54·3	6·1	29·2	47·2	10·4	31·3	−13·0	+ 7·7	− 1·9
Nigeria	0·4	(72·8)	0·0	27·2	(88·9)	4·2	6·9	(93·4)	3·3	3·0	+20·6	+ 3·3	−24·2
Pakistan	0·2	(26·2)	2·6	55·5	10·6	3·2	84·8	44·7	4·2	49·6	+18·5	+ 1·6	− 5·9
Rhodesia and Nyasaland	0·8	71·0	0·0	23·9	70·7	0·0	26·3	77·5	0·0	18·8	+ 6·5	0·0	− 5·1
Union of South Africa	1·7	27·8	6·4	46·1	25·5	8·2	45·4	31·3	9·6	36·4	+ 3·5	+ 3·2	− 9·7
Iran	1·1	3·4	4·3	55·3	31·7	20·7	39·5	31·9	26·8	33·8	+28·5	+22·5	−21·5
Iraq	0·1	32·9	8·5	54·2	17·6	9·8	59·6	27·4	9·0	60·7	+ 5·5	+ 0·5	+ 6·5
Argentine	0·1	1·9	14·5	57·7	4·5	31·9	36·0	12·1	17·3	57·0	+10·2	+ 2·8	0·7
Brazil	0·2	3·6	21·1	55·8	6·8	6·7	68·8	7·4	1·8	21·4	+ 3·8	−19·3	−34·4
Colombia	0·3	3·1	2·5	76·4	6·0	1·1	77·1	6·8	3·7	72·0	+ 3·7	+ 1·2	− 4·4
Peru	0·1	3·6	2·5	84·1	(6·5)	2·2	80·0	(22·5)	7·1	68·0	+18·9	+ 4·6	−16·1
Venezuela	0·5	2·6	2·1	82·6	4·9	4·0	84·9	9·5	2·9	81·4	+ 6·9	+ 0·8	+ 1·2
Mexico	0·9	1·9	1·2	85·5	5·0	1·5	79·5	9·2	1·1	79·0	+ 7·3	+ 0·1	− 6·5
Canada	1·1	1·7	0·2	97·5	1·7	0·7	96·9	1·3	0·4	97·3	+ 0·4	+ 0·2	+ 0·2
U.S.A.	2·7	3·1	0·1	—	3·0	1·0	—	2·3	0·6	—	+ 0·8	+ 0·5	—
W. Europe Sample	10·9	24·2	35·7	6·8	17·1	46·6	8·5	12·7	51·6	8·3	−11·5	+15·9	+ 1·5
E.E.C.	8·1	23·0	38·2	8·3	15·6	50·0	8·4	12·3	52·3	10·0	−10·7	+14·1	+ 1·7
S. Com'wealth Sample	11·6	49·8	3·7	35·9	51·7	6·4	29·7	49·2	6·5	30·6	− 0·6	+ 2·8	− 5·3
World	44·5	12·2	8·7	39·7	13·6	17·9	37·7	10·3	17·8	33·4	− 1·9	+ 9·1	− 6·3

* Machinery for preparing and cultivating the soil, harvesting, threshing and sorting; milking machines, cream separators; poultry brooders, cake and seed crushers, etc.

Table N. Office machinery (S.I.T.C. 714)*

Import Market	U.K. Exports 1959 $m.	1953				1957				1959				1953–59			
		U.K.	W.G.	U.S.A.	Italy	U.K.	W.G.	U.S.A.	Italy	U.K.	W.G.	U.S.A.	Italy	U.K.	W.G.	U.S.A.	Italy
Belgium-Luxembourg	1.4	9.1	21.7	37.0	9.3	8.1	23.8	23.9	12.9	11.4	24.3	18.3	12.0	+ 2.3	+ 2.6	− 18.7	+ 2.7
Denmark	0.8	17.5	29.3	8.6	4.6	10.7	33.7	11.7	9.5	10.5	33.4	13.2	7.8	− 7.0	+ 4.1	+ 4.6	+ 3.2
Finland	0.2	6.7	10.0	28.8	25.3	9.9	23.2	4.6	22.3	4.8	33.9	6.6	11.3	− 1.9	+ 23.9	− 22.2	− 14.0
France	4.3	9.8	17.0	39.3	15.6	10.2	24.6	27.5	18.3	12.3	25.2	24.7	20.1	+ 2.5	+ 8.2	− 14.6	+ 4.5
West Germany	3.4	6.8	—	35.6	12.0	8.8	—	27.4	18.7	7.8	—	27.9	17.2	+ 1.0	—	− 7.7	+ 5.2
Italy	1.0	8.6	17.7	39.2	—	6.9	22.0	28.7	—	5.9	23.0	33.0	—	− 2.7	+ 5.3	− 6.2	—
Netherlands	2.1	14.8	24.9	22.4	14.9	7.9	28.1	26.7	8.6	8.8	27.1	23.0	6.5	− 6.0	+ 2.2	+ 0.6	− 8.4
Norway	0.6	33.4	17.2	19.7	3.8	17.6	26.1	13.2	6.7	10.2	25.6	16.1	5.6	− 23.2	+ 8.4	− 3.6	+ 1.8
Sweden	2.0	14.9	30.6	28.9	4.1	14.6	22.7	17.6	8.5	17.9	28.3	22.1	7.4	+ 3.0	− 2.3	− 6.8	+ 3.3
Australia	10.0	62.6	4.9	22.0	0.8	60.3	9.3	14.6	1.4	53.6	10.7	17.0	1.8	− 9.0	+ 5.8	− 5.0	+ 1.0
British East Africa	0.7	82.7	3.9	0.0	1.5	64.7	8.8	1.3	12.6	59.9	8.9	5.9	15.6	− 22.8	+ 5.0	+ 5.9	+ 14.1
Ceylon	0.2	(45.5)	8.2	29.1	0.0	(37.8)	21.6	18.2	4.9	(36.9)	25.7	16.1	7.6	− 8.6	+ 17.5	− 13.0	+ 7.6
Ghana	0.4	(82.4)	13.4	0.0	0.0	(63.9)	16.4	0.0	6.5	(64.9)	13.4	8.4	3.0	− 17.5	0.0	+ 8.4	+ 3.0
India	0.9	54.0	7.0	48.2	1.6	53.9	6.5	21.0	2.8	51.1	12.6	16.7	0.0	− 2.9	+ 5.6	− 31.5	− 1.6
Malaya	0.7	24.9	6.2	59.1	0.0	30.4	11.8	31.3	7.2	38.2	9.9	20.2	6.2	+ 13.3	+ 3.7	− 38.9	+ 6.2
New Zealand	2.0	54.0	1.1	37.2	0.0	63.0	6.0	22.4	1.2	74.0	5.7	13.2	0.0	+ 20.0	+ 4.6	− 24.0	0.0
Nigeria	0.8	(83.3)	8.7	3.3	0.0	80.2	6.4	1.4	2.9	73.0	8.7	6.9	2.9	− 10.3	0.0	+ 3.6	+ 2.9
Pakistan	0.3	44.1	5.6	38.1	0.0	41.5	6.4	40.7	4.2	(33.3)	11.7	32.1	3.0	− 10.8	+ 6.1	− 6.0	+ 3.0
Rhodesia and Nyasaland	0.7	87.6	0.0	6.8	0.0	81.3	5.2	4.2	1.7	69.9	10.1	6.5	4.0	− 17.7	+ 10.1	− 0.3	+ 4.0
Union of South Africa	5.3	36.4	2.9	47.7	6.5	57.4	8.6	15.6	8.1	57.1	8.8	11.5	9.6	+ 20.7	+ 5.9	− 36.2	+ 3.1
Iran	0.2	(0.0)	26.5	52.0	0.0	21.1	8.1	63.2	2.3	16.0	24.7	28.0	6.5	+ 16.0	− 1.8	− 24.0	+ 6.5
Iraq	0.1	(61.9)	4.4	25.9	1.1	(35.4)	14.7	32.3	3.0	(50.4)	12.9	18.5	0.0	− 11.5	+ 8.5	− 7.4	0.0
Argentine	0.2	0.0	1.5	54.1	42.2	6.7	5.2	69.0	10.5	5.6	4.2	63.4	13.3	+ 5.6	+ 2.7	+ 9.3	− 28.9
Brazil	0.4	0.5	22.5	41.7	2.4	4.2	14.5	44.1	15.8	5.1	14.1	36.3	23.0	+ 4.6	− 8.4	− 5.4	+ 20.6
Colombia	0.2	1.1	10.4	67.2	6.7	7.7	9.0	54.6	10.7	9.6	9.7	48.6	14.0	+ 8.5	− 0.7	− 18.6	+ 7.3
Peru	0.3	1.4	18.9	56.8	6.1	7.3	20.6	37.9	10.5	12.8	22.2	29.3	12.6	+ 11.4	+ 3.3	− 27.5	+ 6.5
Venezuela	1.1	2.0	17.0	57.4	3.5	7.8	14.4	39.5	16.3	10.1	20.0	33.2	14.6	+ 8.1	+ 3.0	− 24.2	+ 11.1
Mexico	1.1	1.1	6.9	71.3	7.9	10.2	16.1	51.5	0.0	10.0	13.4	38.5	15.0	+ 8.9	+ 6.5	− 32.8	+ 7.1
Canada	4.0	8.9	1.0	87.8	0.8	10.9	3.0	82.6	3.0	8.7	3.4	80.0	3.3	− 0.2	+ 2.4	− 7.8	+ 2.5
U.S.A.	5.4	22.8	11.9	—	14.8	9.7	30.4	—	13.8	8.9	34.1	—	18.9	− 13.9	+ 22.2	—	+ 4.1
W. Europe Sample	15.8	11.8	17.4	32.3	10.0	9.8	19.5	24.2	12.8	9.9	19.3	24.1	12.3	− 1.9	+ 1.9	− 8.2	+ 2.3
E.E.C.	12.1	9.6	15.4	35.6	11.1	8.7	17.8	27.1	13.5	9.3	16.9	25.9	13.4	− 0.3	+ 1.5	− 9.7	+ 2.3
S. Com'wealth Sample	22.0	51.6	4.4	33.2	2.3	58.5	8.5	16.4	4.0	55.6	10.1	14.9	4.3	+ 4.0	+ 5.7	− 18.3	+ 2.0
World	60.4	14.6	12.4	43.2	7.1	13.3	17.1	34.6	10.2	12.3	18.9	32.0	10.2	− 2.3	+ 6.5	− 11.2	+ 3.1

* Typewriters, accounting, book-keeping, calculating and other office machinery, including cash registers and dictaphones.

Table O. Metal-working machinery (S.I.T.C. 715)*

Import Market	U.K. Exports 1959 $m.	1953			1957			1959			1953–59		
		U.K.	W.G.	U.S.A.	U.K.	W.G.	U.S.A.	U.K.	W.G.	U.S.A.	U.K.	W.G.	U.S.A.
Belgium-Luxembourg	1·7	9·4	49·9	19·6	10·1	54·1	14·4	8·1	58·8	10·7	− 1·3	+ 8·9	− 8·9
Denmark	1·3	12·7	52·7	8·8	9·6	61·5	3·1	10·0	63·5	4·3	− 2·7	+10·8	− 4·5
Finland	0·3	10·6	56·1	3·3	9·9	43·4	13·0	4·8	57·3	6·2	− 5·8	+ 1·2	+ 2·9
France	8·5	8·0	30·3	43·2	8·0	37·5	33·6	10·9	46·9	16·9	+ 2·9	+16·6	−26·3
West Germany	2·9	13·2	—	27·0	10·0	—	36·9	5·6	—	45·1	+ 7·6	—	+18·1
Italy	3·0	6·8	40·0	41·6	10·6	44·3	32·1	10·2	51·9	17·0	+ 3·4	+11·9	−24·6
Netherlands	1·9	10·3	50·3	18·8	12·0	55·4	16·4	9·1	52·7	16·1	+ 1·2	+ 2·4	− 2·7
Norway	0·8	32·2	43·6	9·6	19·8	46·5	4·9	16·9	44·6	3·9	−15·3	+ 2·9	− 5·7
Sweden	1·3	18·7	56·8	13·4	17·2	58·6	11·8	4·5	66·1	9·0	−14·2	+ 9·3	− 4·4
Australia	14·7	69·0	4·6	21·8	52·1	13·7	28·3	49·9	20·5	18·9	−19·1	+15·9	− 2·9
British East Africa	0·6	(84·5)	10·8	4·6	(83·4)	9·6	2·4	(76·0)	17·2	5·3	− 8·5	+ 6·4	+ 0·7
Ceylon	0·5	(74·1)	21·4	4·6	(82·7)	12·4	0·0	(75·8)	13·6	5·0	+ 1·7	+ 7·8	+ 0·4
Ghana	0·4	(90·7)	9·3	0·0	(69·9)	9·1	0·0	(86·3)	10·9	0·0	− 4·4	+ 1·6	0·0
India	30·1	59·4	25·2	8·3	20·4	61·6	9·2	36·5	50·6	9·2	−22·9	+25·4	+ 0·9
Malaya	1·3	(82·8)	8·2	8·4	(70·6)	10·1	4·7	(49·2)	23·2	5·3	−33·6	+15·0	+ 3·1
New Zealand	0·9	83·7	3·2	11·7	62·6	17·6	10·9	68·0	16·1	10·4	−15·7	+12·9	+ 1·3
Nigeria	0·6	(90·4)	5·7	0·0	(86·5)	10·3	0·0	(80·4)	14·6	1·7	−10·0	+ 8·9	+ 1·7
Pakistan	0·9	51·6	30·4	14·5	29·8	43·5	16·7	30·3	34·0	15·6	−21·3	+ 3·6	+ 1·1
Rhodesia and Nyasaland	1·4	(69·4)	7·7	20·5	(11·9)	10·1	11·1	71·9	10·0	8·3	+ 2·5	+ 2·3	−12·2
Union of South Africa	4·5	48·0	19·1	28·1	44·0	25·9	17·6	16·8	43·5	34·5	−31·2	+24·4	+ 6·4
Iran	0·5	(9·9)	61·3	9·0	(23·1)	27·2	43·8	14·8	58·2	14·3	+ 4·9	− 3·1	+ 5·3
Iraq	0·2	(70·8)	7·3	19·3	(32·7)	46·3	8·7	(40·4)	24·4	32·1	−30·4	+17·1	+12·8
Argentine	0·5	7·8	42·7	16·4	11·2	25·5	32·7	1·7	13·6	68·4	− 6·1	−29·1	+52·0
Brazil	2·4	4·8	28·0	48·3	2·8	24·6	60·7	3·1	33·1	51·8	− 1·7	+ 5·1	+ 3·5
Colombia	0·2	1·7	3·5	24·2	1·6	24·2	47·3	7·3	5·8	63·4	+ 5·6	+ 2·3	+39·2
Peru	0·0	8·9	20·6	37·6	4·2	18·2	63·7	(2·1)	20·2	55·2	− 6·8	+ 0·4	+17·6
Venezuela	0·1	3·7	6·6	79·4	1·7	16·2	42·6	0·7	18·2	58·9	− 3·0	+11·6	−20·5
Mexico	0·5	2·2	15·0	66·2	3·5	19·0	62·8	2·1	9·8	82·7	− 0·1	− 5·2	+16·5
Canada	5·6	11·7	2·7	82·8	9·3	5·0	83·9	1·6	4·2	83·3	− 1·1	+ 1·5	+ 0·5
U.S.A.	7·1	10·9	31·8	—	19·9	31·0	—	18·8	39·2	—	+ 7·9	+ 7·4	—
W. Europe Sample	21·5	10·2	38·0	32·1	10·4	40·1	26·6	8·6	42·6	20·1	− 1·6	+ 4·6	−12·0
E.E.C.	17·9	8·5	35·4	35·9	7·0	27·3	21·4	9·0	37·6	23·4	+ 0·5	+ 2·2	−12·5
S. Com'wealth Sample	55·4	61·2	15·2	18·7	38·8	39·1	16·0	37·3	41·3	15·7	−23·9	+26·1	− 3·0
World	110·0	12·0	27·3	39·2	11·9	34·8	34·0	11·9	36·2	32·2	− 0·1	+ 8·9	− 7·0

* Machine tools for working metals, and metal working machinery other than machine tools—e.g. rolling mills, forging, wire drawing, bending and forming machinery, foundry equipment.

Table 1. *Mining, constructional and other specified machinery* (S.I.T.C. 715) *

Import Market	U.K. Exports 1959 $m.	1953 U.K.	1953 W.G.	1953 U.S.A.	1957 U.K.	1957 W.G.	1957 U.S.A.	1959 U.K.	1959 W.G.	1959 U.S.A.	1953–59 U.K.	1953–59 W.G.	1953–59 U.S.A.
Belgium-Luxembourg	17·3	18·6	39·7	17·4	14·9	45·7	14·0	12·9	15·1	13·8	− 5·7	+ 5·4	− 3·6
Denmark	11·0	22·6	44·3	10·0	20·9	47·5	8·4	19·1	46·4	7·0	− 3·5	+ 2·1	− 3·0
Finland	9·8	20·7	38·4	21·0	16·1	37·5	19·3	16·0	33·7	23·2	− 4·7	− 4·7	+ 2·2
France	26·3	19·8	30·2	33·6	13·3	43·4	24·7	13·2	50·3	17·5	− 6·6	+20·1	−16·1
West Germany	33·5	27·0	—	28·1	23·0	—	29·1	22·2	—	23·9	− 4·8	—	− 4·2
Italy	26·2	24·1	44·7	20·9	16·6	50·4	21·1	15·4	54·7	15·9	− 8·7	+10·0	− 5·0
Netherlands	31·1	24·4	45·1	12·1	19·2	50·2	12·6	18·9	51·7	10·0	− 5·5	+ 6·6	− 2·1
Norway	12·5	27·8	29·1	13·8	23·6	32·1	13·0	22·3	30·9	12·8	− 5·5	+ 1·8	− 1·0
Sweden	24·0	29·9	43·6	19·5	21·7	46·1	24·2	21·9	47·6	21·1	− 8·0	+ 4·0	+ 1·6
Australia	58·6	60·0	11·5	23·0	58·4	7·4	27·1	47·3	14·6	28·8	−13·5	+ 3·1	+ 5·8
British East Africa	13·7	75·6	8·3	13·3	70·7	11·6	10·2	70·4	8·2	13·6	− 5·2	− 0·1	+ 0·3
Ceylon	6·7	74·6	6·2	15·7	(56·9)	7·3	18·3	(72·6)	5·2	(13·4)	− 2·0	− 1·0	− 2·3
Ghana	9·5	80·3	2·4	16·1	(74·8)	8·3	13·3	64·7	7·4	15·6	−15·6	+ 5·0	− 0·5
India	83·4	57·1	12·1	23·4	38·3	29·7	18·2	48·7	17·8	16·8	− 8·4	+ 5·7	+ 1·3
Malaya	10·3	58·9	6·9	26·6	54·6	5·1	23·0	48·6	8·0	27·9	−10·3	+ 1·1	+ 3·9
New Zealand	20·0	72·5	3·8	16·4	65·7	6·1	20·9	60·2	7·2	20·3	−12·3	+ 3·4	+ 2·0
Nigeria	16·3	82·9	2·9	12·2	0·0	0·0	82·4	74·2	6·3	14·2	− 8·7	+ 3·4	+ 5·9
Pakistan	10·7	52·1	15·4	16·1	41·0	19·7	28·9	29·0	13·7	22·0	−23·1	− 1·7	− 6·7
Rhodesia and Nyasaland	10·7	74·7	1·2	21·4	(0·0)	10·6	65·5	68·5	8·8	14·7	− 6·2	+ 7·6	− 1·0
Union of South Africa	42·6	45·6	25·3	25·3	45·3	12·1	31·5	44·0	17·8	24·3	− 1·6	− 7·5	+ 2·6
Iran	19·4	10·3	42·2	29·2	35·5	18·1	30·6	27·5	22·2	31·8	+17·2	−20·0	+ 5·4
Iraq	11·1	54·0	7·5	34·7	35·2	21·9	33·5	52·8	12·7	29·3	− 1·2	+ 5·2	− 5·4
Argentine	11·8	8·8	27·8	44·5	8·7	12·9	58·3	10·8	13·9	49·4	+ 2·0	−13·9	+ 4·9
Brazil	5·2	11·8	18·0	40·8	5·4	15·3	59·0	5·1	16·5	62·0	− 6·7	− 1·5	+21·2
Colombia	2·3	3·8	7·5	70·3	5·9	10·9	71·3	6·0	13·8	68·7	+ 2·2	+ 6·3	− 1·6
Peru	2·4	8·5	7·9	68·0	8·1	11·1	65·9	10·4	0·0	67·6	+ 1·9	− 7·9	− 0·4
Venezuela	7·7	8·6	22·0	64·1	7·0	5·3	80·4	5·3	9·9	72·1	− 3·3	−12·1	+ 8·0
Mexico	5·8	4·4	10·7	78·3	0·0	9·1	80·4	4·4	10·3	76·0	0·0	− 0·4	− 2·3
Canada	35·7	6·4	5·3	86·1	7·0	1·4	89·7	7·3	2·4	87·9	+ 0·9	− 2·9	+ 1·8
U.S.A.	30·4	30·5	5·6	—	18·0	31·1	—	16·8	31·4	—	−13·7	+25·8	—
W. Europe Sample	191·8	23·2	36·6	20·8	17·7	41·0	19·4	17·4	41·3	16·5	− 5·8	+ 4·7	− 4·3
E.E.C.	134·5	22·1	36·0	22·4	16·8	40·9	20·0	16·4	41·3	16·2	− 5·7	+ 5·3	− 6·2
S. Com'wealth Sample	281·8	58·4	13·6	21·8	47·1	16·9	24·5	50·1	14·3	21·3	− 8·3	+ 0·7	+ 0·5
World	846·0	22·2	19·7	40·6	17·3	22·2	42·2	18·1	24·7	35·7	− 4·1	+ 5·0	− 4·9

* Pumps, conveying, hoisting, excavating, road construction and mining machinery; wood working, paper mill and pulp machinery; printing, bookbinding, textile and air-conditioning machinery, roller bearings, sewing machines (industrial and household), pneumatic tools.

† Exports from Switzerland not included.

Table Q. Electrical machinery and equipment (S.I.T.C. 72)*

Import Market	U.K. Exports 1959 $m.	1953 U.K.	1953 W.G.	1953 U.S.A.	1953 Neths.	1957 U.K.	1957 W.G.	1957 U.S.A.	1957 Neths.	1959 U.K.	1959 W.G.	1959 U.S.A.	1959 Neths.	1953–59 U.K.	1953–59 W.G.	1953–59 U.S.A.	1953–59 Neths.
Belgium-Luxembourg	9·6	14·2	27·4	12·6	25·8	9·1	40·9	7·1	27·9	8·2	32·9	9·3	34·3	− 6·0	+ 5·5	− 3·3	+ 8·5
Denmark	8·1	16·2	28·6	4·6	22·1	19·6	35·8	4·2	18·5	16·0	37·8	5·9	20·5	− 0·2	+ 9·2	+ 1·3	+ 1·6
Finland	3·9	14·7	34·9	4·8	8·3	17·2	40·4	1·9	6·9	10·3	53·8	2·4	10·4	− 4·4	+ 18·9	− 2·4	+ 2·1
France	8·6	13·3	22·3	29·4	11·6	14·4	41·4	15·3	12·1	11·3	40·5	16·8	12·2	− 2·0	+ 18·2	− 12·6	+ 0·6
West Germany	17·1	12·2	—	5·9	48·5	15·6	—	13·1	34·2	16·2	—	15·5	35·1	+ 4·0	—	+ 9·6	− 13·4
Italy	10·3	12·6	36·3	13·9	6·8	12·8	45·3	21·2	8·1	10·5	44·6	20·4	9·7	− 2·1	+ 8·3	+ 6·5	+ 2·9
Netherlands	20·7	18·9	32·3	6·0	—	13·5	41·8	3·5	—	11·8	41·6	3·3	—	− 7·1	+ 9·3	− 2·7	—
Norway	7·0	22·5	36·6	8·0	5·7	18·0	40·5	7·6	7·2	16·8	40·5	4·2	10·4	− 5·7	+ 3·9	− 3·8	+ 4·7
Sweden	15·4	24·7	43·7	4·6	16·1	14·0	54·4	7·3	14·8	11·3	55·4	5·6	18·0	− 13·4	+ 11·7	− 1·0	+ 1·9
Australia	55·7	80·0	3·8	10·3	1·6	69·5	6·5	13·5	3·9	63·4	9·1	12·5	5·1	− 16·6	+ 5·3	+ 2·2	+ 3·5
British East Africa	12·2	92·9	3·1	0·0	3·1	83·2	9·1	0·5	4·5	79·1	9·6	0·4	6·5	− 13·8	+ 6·5	+ 0·4	+ 3·4
Ceylon	6·3	85·2	5·0	3·8	4·3	58·1	7·8	1·3	7·6	67·9	8·8	1·3	13·0	− 17·3	+ 3·8	− 2·5	+ 8·7
Ghana	7·7	(94·0)	3·3	1·4	1·2	(85·5)	7·6	0·5	5·5	82·7	8·7	0·9	3·6	− 11·3	+ 5·4	− 0·5	+ 2·4
India	57·9	71·4	8·1	8·6	3·3	51·8	19·1	12·0	3·2	46·5	30·6	3·8	1·8	− 24·9	+ 22·5	− 4·8	+ 1·5
Malaya	15·3	84·6	3·3	3·4	2·1	75·0	7·9	2·5	7·2	58·5	8·7	3·2	10·0	− 26·1	+ 5·4	− 0·2	+ 2·8
New Zealand	26·5	90·8	0·5	1·5	4·9	84·8	1·9	2·5	2·5	77·1	1·6	3·3	4·5	− 13·7	+ 1·1	+ 1·8	+ 2·4
Nigeria	15·7	93·4	0·8	0·9	2·9	83·9	7·7	0·9	5·3	84·5	5·3	0·7	5·8	− 8·9	+ 4·5	− 0·2	+ 0·9
Pakistan	8·0	60·9	21·0	5·6	1·4	37·1	27·3	15·4	2·5	29·9	30·5	19·5	3·0	− 31·0	+ 9·5	+ 13·9	+ 0·1
Rhodesia and Nyasaland	21·1	93·8	0·2	3·4	2·0	87·1	3·7	2·7	3·7	89·2	2·1	2·1	2·1	− 4·6	+ 1·9	− 1·3	+ 0·7
Union of South Africa	53·4	78·4	4·9	10·7	2·6	65·1	12·4	11·1	4·3	60·5	19·6	7·3	2·6	− 17·9	+ 14·7	− 3·4	+ 0·6
Iran	10·2	10·7	50·5	27·5	2·6	38·8	34·8	9·6	5·4	21·1	40·2	11·8	5·4	+ 10·4	− 10·3	− 15·7	+ 2·8
Iraq	9·0	73·8	7·3	7·5	5·3	47·9	20·3	12·1	8·1	47·2	19·1	6·0	11·2	− 26·6	+ 11·8	+ 1·5	+ 5·9
Argentine	6·6	10·1	24·4	34·8	4·9	11·1	35·1	35·5	5·0	14·7	16·4	43·7	4·7	+ 4·6	− 8·0	+ 8·9	+ 0·2
Brazil	2·5	5·6	19·5	44·9	3·8	6·7	16·7	43·4	3·2	4·1	15·6	53·7	3·2	− 1·5	− 3·9	+ 8·8	+ 2·6
Colombia	1·2	4·9	8·4	61·6	7·8	6·8	12·0	41·5	8·3	4·7	18·5	42·2	6·4	− 0·2	+ 10·1	− 19·4	+ 4·0
Peru	1·1	7·9	10·6	60·0	2·5	8·2	19·2	41·0	7·3	5·9	19·9	38·8	11·8	− 2·0	+ 9·3	− 21·2	+ 4·0
Venezuela	12·9	9·4	7·6	69·3	3·0	11·7	11·7	56·1	4·0	12·6	14·9	47·4	3·1	+ 3·2	+ 7·3	− 21·9	+ 0·6
Mexico	1·7	1·9	3·8	73·0	0·6	2·6	11·0	65·8	3·0	2·9	9·7	63·4	3·7	+ 1·0	+ 5·9	− 9·6	+ 0·7
Canada	37·5	11·3	0·2	87·1		14·8	2·0	79·3	2·1	14·9	4·1	74·5	1·4	+ 3·6	+ 3·9	− 12·6	+ 0·8
U.S.A.	41·2	16·3	7·7	—	10·7	28·6	23·8	—	6·8	21·7	15·0	—	7·9	+ 5·4	+ 7·3	—	− 2·8
W. Europe Sample	100·8	16·8	30·3	13·3	13·7	13·7	40·5	9·1	13·0	12·0	37·9	9·4	16·6	− 4·8	+ 7·6	− 3·9	+ 2·9
E.E.C.	66·3	14·8	27·1	16·7	14·0	12·7	38·0	10·3	13·1	11·6	32·5	11·5	16·8	− 3·2	+ 5·4	− 5·2	+ 2·8
S.Com'wealth Sample	279·7	79·7	5·4	7·3	2·7	65·6	11·9	9·3	3·7	60·3	17·0	6·5	3·9	− 19·4	+ 11·6	− 0·8	+ 1·2
World	648·6	26·0	14·9	30·5	5·9	22·6	22·8	26·5	6·8	19·2	24·3	22·5	8·4	− 6·8	+ 9·4	− 8·0	+ 2·5

Table R. Railway vehicles (S.I.T.C. 731)*

Import Market	U.K. Exports 1959 $m.	1953 U.K.	1953 W.G.	1953 U.S.A.	1957 U.K.	1957 W.G.	1957 U.S.A.	1959 U.K.	1959 W.G.	1959 U.S.A.	1953–59 U.K.	1953–59 W.G.	1953–59 U.S.A.
Belgium-Luxembourg	0·2	28·5	40·2	10·2	37·6	17·7	2·9	3·7	26·8	5·0	−24·8	−13·4	−5·2
Denmark	0·1	(15·6)	60·2	0·0	2·5	15·5	0·0	7·6	77·1	0·7	−8·0	+16·9	+0·7
Finland	0·2	4·6	92·8	0·0	(36·5)	38·6	0·0	15·3	35·8	0·0	+10·7	−57·0	0·0
France	0·0	19·2	20·5	1·1	23·8	62·5	0·7	0·4	62·9	5·2	−18·8	+42·4	+4·1
West Germany	0·7	46·5	—	1·2	21·8	—	0·0	17·1	—	4·8	−29·4	—	+3·6
Italy	0·1	11·2	22·5	41·2	—	26·8	49·5	6·2	65·6	3·0	−5·0	+43·1	−36·4
Netherlands	0·2	34·7	29·5	0·0	50·5	21·8	7·4	3·9	49·2	0·0	−30·8	+19·7	+1·8
Norway	0·1	17·0	47·9	4·8	7·6	25·7	0·1	(20·8)	57·8	3·1	+3·8	+9·9	−1·7
Sweden	0·2	4·5	57·2	12·3	11·7	84·0	2·3	12·1	81·9	1·3	+7·6	+24·7	−11·0
Australia	1·1	81·9	6·6	4·8	88·4	6·1	5·4	52·2	24·3	22·2	−29·7	+17·7	+17·4
British East Africa	2·0	96·9	0·3	0·0	80·9	6·6	1·6	96·7	0·0	0·5	−0·2	−0·3	+0·5
Ceylon	0·7	82·6	17·4	0·0	(96·6)	0·0	0·0	25·6	51·8	1·4	−57·0	+34·4	+1·4
Ghana	1·5	(95·3)	0·0	2·9	99·3	0·0	0·7	21·4	78·6	0·0	−73·9	+78·6	+2·9
India	10·5	38·1	24·5	1·2	23·5	13·4	10·8	39·5	17·2	17·3	+1·4	−7·3	+16·1
Malaya	0·4	99·2	0·0	0·0	88·1	0·4	0·0	(85·9)	7·4	0·0	−13·3	+7·4	0·0
New Zealand	2·9	99·7	0·0	0·3	94·7	16·2	0·8	96·6	0·0	0·5	−3·1	0·0	+0·2
Nigeria	5·4	98·2	1·8	0·0	65·3	3·1	0·0	82·6	9·7	0·2	−15·6	+7·9	+0·2
Pakistan	10·0	11·7	2·2	26·0	63·4	2·0	23·7	32·5	37·9	14·4	+20·8	+35·7	−11·6
Rhodesia and Nyasaland	7·8	94·2	1·2	4·3	88·8	3·1	0·5	98·2	0·0	0·0	+4·0	−1·2	+3·7
Union of South Africa	23·5	37·0	40·5	8·0	74·6	11·2	3·1	69·9	9·1	15·2	+32·9	−31·4	+7·2
Iran	0·0	56·6	0·6	1·2	5·2	58·0	32·7	0·2	42·1	56·1	−56·4	+41·5	+54·9
Iraq	0·2	100·0	0·0	0·0	34·4	51·3	2·1	17·0	41·8	0·0	−83·0	+41·8	0·0
Argentine	8·7	9·7	4·9	22·2	2·3	0·4	53·1	24·4	6·6	38·0	+14·7	+1·7	+15·8
Brazil	1·2	4·2	13·4	61·9	19·9	3·5	61·7	7·4	7·3	81·3	+3·2	−6·1	+19·4
Colombia	0·0	2·7	7·4	47·8	0·0	7·7	56·6	1·3	3·9	29·1	−1·4	−3·5	−18·7
Peru	0·3	70·2	4·5	16·3	23·9	9·4	44·8	10·1	1·7	84·9	−60·1	−2·8	+68·6
Venezuela	0·0	2·4	0·4	96·9	0·0	0·9	96·0	0·0	2·0	75·6	−2·4	+1·6	−21·3
Mexico	0·6	0·0	0·0	65·3	0·0	0·9	97·2	4·3	3·8	84·3	+4·3	+3·8	+19·0
Canada	4·2	23·3	0·0	76·7	24·7	0·3	75·0	37·0	2·6	60·4	+13·7	+2·6	−16·3
U.S.A.	0·2	1·0	1·3	—	0·0	9·7	—	5·4	14·3	—	+4·4	+13·0	—
W. Europe Sample	1·8	22·4	38·9	10·3	19·0	29·7	6·1	6·9	44·1	3·0	−15·5	+5·2	−7·3
E.E.C.	1·2	31·3	24·1	11·9	22·2	22·3	7·4	5·6	38·8	3·5	−25·7	+14·7	−8·4
S. Com'wealth Sample	65·7	55·8	18·9	6·3	52·9	10·0	7·5	53·5	22·3	12·0	−2·3	+3·4	+5·7
World	95·1	28·0	14·2	25·2	25·2	13·3	31·0	27·3	22·1	23·9	−0·7	+7·9	−1·3

* Railway locomotives, self-propelled railway cars, carriages, freight cars, parts (non-electrical).

Table S. Road motor vehicles (S.I.T.C. 732)*

Import Market	U.K. Exports 1959 $m.	1953			1957			1959			1953–59		
		U.K.	W.G.	U.S.A.	U.K.	W.G.	U.S.A.	U.K.	W.G.	U.S.A.	U.K.	W.G.	U.S.A.
Belgium-Luxembourg	23·3	20·8	26·1	24·7	14·5	37·7	18·3	12·2	38·9	10·7	− 8·6	+ 12·8	− 14·0
Denmark	27·1	41·3	38·8	5·6	28·5	45·5	9·5	26·4	48·3	3·3	− 14·9	+ 9·5	− 2·3
Finland	16·3	53·5	5·5	15·1	32·3	34·0	5·4	34·2	29·8	3·4	− 19·3	+ 24·3	− 11·7
France	7·2	31·9	24·1	23·6	20·6	44·2	20·2	15·5	55·6	9·4	− 16·4	+ 31·5	− 14·2
West Germany	8·9	28·6	—	3·8	15·4	—	6·3	6·6	—	2·3	− 22·0	—	− 1·5
Italy	4·5	29·2	27·8	12·6	17·9	47·9	11·7	13·2	41·6	7·8	− 16·0	+ 13·8	− 4·8
Netherlands	20·9	28·6	34·5	10·0	15·0	33·5	4·2	13·7	29·3	2·7	− 14·9	− 5·2	− 7·3
Norway	7·5	32·1	32·1	9·2	22·5	41·5	4·3	18·6	43·5	2·7	− 13·5	+ 11·4	− 6·5
Sweden	39·2	40·2	26·5	17·0	23·9	55·9	9·1	23·2	57·1	9·6	− 17·0	+ 30·6	− 7·4
Australia	93·0	76·9	0·3	7·0	71·2	9·2	9·3	63·7	12·9	10·0	− 13·2	+ 12·6	+ 3·0
British East Africa	21·0	87·1	5·0	2·0	68·3	15·7	2·0	60·7	19·9	1·6	− 26·4	+ 14·9	− 0·4
Ceylon	14·5	84·4	5·0	7·4	71·1	16·5	5·0	71·4	15·4	4·5	− 13·0	+ 10·4	− 2·9
Ghana	12·0	90·3	7·3	2·3	72·0	18·1	1·2	56·9	29·7	3·1	− 33·4	+ 22·4	+ 0·8
India	25·4	45·9	0·5	38·5	33·4	29·0	28·8	38·5	27·7	25·9	− 7·4	+ 27·2	− 12·6
Malaya	16·8	92·7	0·9	3·0	76·3	10·5	2·8	61·8	18·0	2·2	− 30·9	+ 17·1	− 0·8
New Zealand	36·1	95·8	0·2	1·7	86·6	5·2	2·6	89·7	3·5	1·9	− 6·1	+ 3·3	+ 0·2
Nigeria	19·3	81·7	6·1	9·9	64·1	24·7	3·1	61·6	26·3	2·7	− 20·1	+ 20·2	− 7·2
Pakistan	6·4	41·7	2·6	27·3	34·4	11·4	45·0	36·5	10·1	44·2	− 5·2	+ 7·5	+ 16·9
Rhodesia and Nyasaland	19·1	96·3	0·1	2·2	88·5	3·7	3·6	78·2	11·2	1·3	− 18·1	+ 11·1	− 0·9
Union of South Africa	52·9	44·6	4·9	29·6	39·9	18·0	26·5	37·5	28·2	16·7	− 7·1	+ 23·3	− 12·9
Iran	12·2	(15·3)	15·9	(66·8)	20·7	24·7	48·6	20·4	30·1	38·5	+ 5·1	+ 14·2	− 28·3
Iraq	5·1	48·9	7·9	42·7	20·4	19·6	53·7	42·4	13·9	36·5	− 6·5	+ 6·0	− 6·2
Argentine	1·5	7·7	69·3	18·0	11·3	13·0	62·0	3·4	15·7	61·1	− 4·3	− 53·6	+ 43·1
Brazil	0·4	5·6	11·2	61·9	1·8	22·1	65·8	0·4	35·3	55·0	− 5·2	+ 24·1	− 6·9
Colombia	0·8	4·3	3·8	89·8	2·0	6·2	88·7	2·2	2·8	92·0	− 2·1	− 1·0	+ 2·2
Peru	0·8	1·7	1·3	86·5	2·5	5·3	87·8	4·2	8·8	77·9	+ 2·5	+ 7·5	− 8·6
Venezuela	11·8	5·9	2·0	82·9	4·1	7·6	78·0	8·1	12·8	67·4	+ 2·2	+ 10·8	− 15·5
Mexico	6·6	1·2	0·7	86·3	1·8	3·0	91·2	5·5	11·4	75·7	+ 4·3	+ 10·7	− 10·6
Canada	100·0	11·7	0·7	87·6	10·3	6·6	83·0	19·8	8·2	67·5	+ 8·1	+ 7·5	− 20·1
U.S.A.	266·4	73·9	9·1	—	35·5	39·9	—	31·1	34·7	—	− 42·8	+ 25·6	—
W. Europe Sample	154·8	31·3	27·9	16·2	21·0	30·7	27·9	16·9	36·7	6·2	− 14·4	+ 8·8	− 10·0
E.E.C.	64·7	24·8	26·5	19·0	15·4	33·1	12·3	11·6	28·4	6·2	− 13·2	+ 1·9	− 12·8
S. Com'wealth Sample	316·6	70·9	2·4	14·0	58·5	15·0	15·5	55·6	19·7	11·9	− 15·3	+ 17·3	− 2·1
World	1069·0	23·4	9·1	51·9	22·5	21·2	37·1	23·8	24·4	25·8	+ 0·4	+ 15·3	− 26·1

* Passenger and commercial road motor vehicles, including chassis and parts; buses, trucks, lorries and parts; motor cycles and parts.

Table T. Non-motorised road vehicles (S.I.T.C. 733)*

Import Market	U.K. Exports 1959 $m.	1953 U.K.	1953 W.G.	1953 U.S.A.	1957 U.K.	1957 W.G.	1957 U.S.A.	1959 U.K.	1959 W.G.	1959 U.S.A.	1953–59 U.K.	1953–59 W.G.	1953–59 U.S.A.
Belgium-Luxembourg	1·0	26·8	22·4	0·0	24·3	37·4	1·2	19·1	36·4	1·6	− 7·7	+ 14·0	+ 1·6
Denmark	0·5	23·4	53·0	0·0	17·7	63·0	0·0	14·3	62·5	0·0	− 9·1	+ 9·5	0·0
Finland	0·1	8·0	1·1	0·0	14·4	15·9	2·0	4·5	37·5	0·0	− 3·5	+ 36·4	0·0
France	0·3	38·0	40·4	1·5	27·5	47·7	0·7	21·2	46·3	2·9	− 16·8	+ 5·9	+ 1·4
West Germany	0·7	33·8	—	1·4	23·8	—	1·6	17·3	—	0·6	− 16·5	—	− 0·8
Italy	0·1	25·6	49·1	12·6	7·8	83·5	4·8	15·2	66·4	8·4	− 10·4	+ 17·3	− 4·2
Netherlands	2·5	25·4	39·7	0·0	22·3	48·4	0·4	21·1	52·9	0·7	− 4·3	+ 13·2	+ 0·7
Norway	0·1	19·1	32·6	1·6	12·4	63·2	1·9	9·4	48·3	0·0	− 9·7	+ 15·7	− 1·6
Sweden	0·2	18·3	73·6	0·0	9·7	81·9	1·2	9·4	81·4	5·2	− 8·9	+ 7·8	+ 5·2
Australia	0·9	94·5	2·9	0·0	73·9	5·8	7·8	58·4	10·4	19·2	− 36·1	+ 7·5	+ 19·2
British East Africa	2·5	97·4	1·9	0·0	88·2	7·3	0·5	73·5	4·7	0·0	− 23·9	+ 2·8	0·0
Ceylon	1·6	97·8	1·3	0·0	92·1	4·0	0·0	88·4	2·5	0·0	− 9·4	+ 1·2	0·0
Ghana	1·3	93·4	5·3	3·1	82·1	11·9	0·0	80·7	7·7	1·5	− 12·7	+ 2·4	− 1·6
India	1·7	90·5	3·8	0·3	77·9	6·9	1·2	89·5	3·6	0·6	− 1·0	− 0·2	+ 0·3
Malaya	3·3	92·2	0·0	0·0	82·8	5·8	0·0	67·0	3·4	0·3	− 25·2	+ 3·4	+ 0·3
New Zealand	1·2	99·1	0·0	0·0	97·1	1·0	0·5	92·3	4·7	0·0	− 6·8	+ 4·7	0·0
Nigeria	4·7	96·6	2·6	0·0	85·6	8·2	3·9	80·4	6·7	0·2	− 16·2	+ 4·1	+ 0·2
Pakistan	0·7	73·5	17·2	9·3	64·0	9·9	12·3	63·1	6·3	0·0	− 10·4	− 10·9	− 9·3
Rhodesia and Nyasaland	3·4	100·0	0·0	0·0	95·7	3·2	0·0	96·2	2·8	0·0	− 3·8	+ 2·8	0·0
Union of South Africa	1·1	85·4	7·6	2·7	67·5	21·8	2·6	57·9	17·8	11·5	− 27·5	+ 10·2	+ 8·8
Iran	3·4	83·6	8·2	0·0	77·2	3·4	8·0	68·7	8·4	7·4	− 14·9	+ 0·2	+ 7·4
Iraq	1·2	85·5	3·8	9·7	80·1	6·4	5·9	71·6	2·4	10·9	− 13·9	− 1·4	+ 1·2
Argentine	0·1	(20·3)	57·0	0·0	1·6	12·5	7·1	6·2	1·3	82·4	− 14·1	− 55·7	+ 82·4
Brazil	0·0	18·7	24·9	32·5	3·1	34·4	21·8	(11·8)	13·6	29·0	− 6·9	− 11·3	− 3·5
Colombia	0·0	48·0	4·5	35·5	9·5	15·4	38·9	(15·0)	37·1	25·2	− 33·0	+ 32·6	− 10·3
Peru	0·3	50·6	6·0	36·4	49·0	10·6	22·3	33·0	11·6	41·5	− 17·6	+ 5·6	+ 5·1
Venezuela	2·2	45·6	1·7	45·3	12·5	4·0	50·9	49·6	4·4	25·4	+ 4·0	+ 2·7	− 19·9
Mexico	0·3	46·8	5·7	42·8	15·8	11·1	53·1	14·7	11·8	51·1	− 32·1	+ 6·1	+ 8·3
Canada	3·0	18·4	0·8	80·4	17·9	2·1	79·2	15·7	2·1	78·3	− 2·7	+ 1·3	− 2·1
U.S.A.	8·4	68·5	12·7	—	44·2	37·1	—	34·7	36·2	—	− 33·8	+ 23·5	—
W. Europe Sample	5·5	24·8	36·0	0·6	21·3	46·3	0·9	17·1	45·2	1·3	− 7·7	+ 9·2	+ 0·7
E.E.C.	4·6	27·7	32·6	0·7	23·3	42·8	0·8	19·8	39·8	1·3	− 7·9	+ 7·2	+ 0·6
S. Com'wealth Sample	22·4	94·3	2·6	0·8	83·9	7·3	1·6	77·6	5·8	2·0	− 16·7	+ 3·2	+ 1·2
World	61·6	48·0	11·2	13·2	37·5	18·8	16·4	33·7	20·3	15·7	− 14·3	+ 9·1	+ 2·5

* Bicycles and other cycles, not motorised, and parts (not including tyres and electric parts); other non-motorised vehicles and parts——e.g. caravans, carts, wheel chairs, trailers, wheelbarrows. Children's tricycles, etc, are not included.

Table U. Rubber manufactures (S.I.T.C. 62)*

Import Market	U.K. Exports 1959 $m.	1953 U.K.	1953 W.G.	1953 U.S.A.	1953 Neths.	1957 U.K.	1957 W.G.	1957 U.S.A.	1957 Neths.	1959 U.K.	1959 W.G.	1959 U.S.A.	1959 Neths.	1953-59 U.K.	1953-59 W.G.	1953-59 U.S.A.	1953-59 Neths.
Belgium-Luxembourg	2·0	17·6	16·7	10·9	27·2	13·5	23·6	9·4	34·5	9·7	22·0	7·5	41·9	− 7·9	+ 5·3	− 3·4	+14·7
Denmark	6·4	52·3	14·6	0·7	1·4	41·8	20·7	2·0	3·9	37·9	24·0	2·0	3·1	−14·4	+ 9·4	+ 1·3	+ 1·7
Finland	2·0	67·2	4·4	7·0	4·0	36·3	15·2	1·0	4·2	24·8	26·0	1·2	2·2	−42·4	+21·6	− 5·8	− 1·8
France	1·4	28·0	20·2	18·7	2·8	18·7	30·9	13·9	1·4	14·7	38·8	15·2	1·9	−13·3	+18·6	+ 3·5	+ 0·9
West Germany	3·8	20·9	—	4·6	8·5	19·2	—	12·2	11·0	16·2	—	6·9	12·3	− 4·7	—	+ 2·3	+ 3·8
Italy	2·9	41·5	34·7	7·1	0·4	33·4	41·3	0·3	1·7	30·0	34·2	9·6	2·2	−11·5	+ 0·5	+ 2·5	+ 1·8
Netherlands	2·6	20·1	23·1	2·0	—	34·5	34·5	5·6	—	14·7	39·9	9·0	—	− 5·4	+16·8	+ 4·0	—
Norway	2·4	46·4	22·6	5·5	0·7	30·4	25·7	5·5	1·7	28·7	26·0	4·7	26·2	−17·7	−22·3	+ 0·8	+25·5
Sweden	3·7	42·0	23·8	5·8	1·2	25·2	41·7	11·6	1·5	27·2	42·1	9·1	3·5	−14·8	+18·3	+ 3·3	+ 2·3
Australia	3·0	78·4	0·4	14·8	0·0	56·8	8·4	18·5	0·0	54·9	4·2	19·6	0·0	−23·5	+ 3·8	+ 4·8	0·0
British East Africa	4·9	70·6	3·8	0·9	2·9	69·1	17·0	0·4	3·2	64·8	12·7	0·2	1·6	− 5·8	+ 8·9	+ 0·7	+ 1·3
Ceylon	2·9	83·3	2·4	0·0	0·0	67·9	5·8	1·4	0·0	63·4	8·3	1·3	0·6	−19·9	+ 5·9	+ 1·2	+ 0·6
Ghana	3·0	82·3	1·7	0·8	1·0	69·5	12·2	0·0	0·0	57·5	18·3	1·3	5·2	−24·8	+16·6	+ 0·5	+ 4·2
India	2·1	61·9	2·0	32·0	0·0	52·4	6·7	11·5	0·3	59·0	8·9	12·9	0·0	− 2·9	+ 6·9	−19·1	0·0
Malaya	5·2	85·3	7·8	1·3	3·4	63·7	10·7	1·7	1·2	65·5	11·8	1·6	0·9	−19·8	+ 4·5	+ 0·3	+ 2·5
New Zealand	2·4	90·7	2·1	5·1	0·0	68·0	17·6	7·1	0·0	67·3	15·5	8·8	0·0	−23·4	+13·4	+ 3·7	0·0
Nigeria	5·1	24·1	8·6	0·0	28·6	69·9	17·2	0·2	2·9	64·9	13·3	0·2	0·8	+40·8	+ 4·7	+ 0·2	−27·8
Pakistan	2·7	79·6	9·6	1·8	0·7	50·5	7·6	15·8	0·5	52·8	9·5	11·9	0·0	−26·8	− 0·1	+10·1	+ 0·7
Rhodesia and Nyasaland	1·4	98·7	0·0	0·0	0·0	79·2	3·7	2·2	5·8	78·1	5·7	6·4	4·3	−20·6	+ 5·7	+ 6·4	+ 4·3
Union of South Africa	2·3	51·7	3·9	41·7	0·0	40·4	14·3	37·1	0·4	43·1	18·8	25·0	1·9	− 8·6	+14·9	−16·7	+ 1·9
Iran	3·8	71·8	28·1	37·3	0·6	15·8	5·6	61·9	2·7	21·0	5·8	53·0	2·2	+ 3·2	−22·3	+15·7	+ 1·6
Iraq	1·4	71·3	4·6	9·7	2·7	26·4	10·1	39·2	0·8	28·4	15·1	39·2	3·2	−42·9	+10·5	+29·5	+ 0·5
Argentine	0·5	13·8	26·2	21·4	0·0	19·5	7·4	39·4	0·0	11·8	13·0	46·3	0·0	− 2·0	+13·2	+24·9	0·0
Brazil	0·1	(5·6	9·7	71·1	0·0)	2·9	8·6	90·9	0·0	(12·1)	6·0	77·6	(0·0)	+ 6·5	− 3·7	−11·3	0·0
Colombia	0·2	7·0	5·2	67·7	0·0	4·8	16·4	64·3	0·0	7·4	19·1	56·4	0·0	+ 0·4	+13·9	−11·3	0·0
Peru	0·3	18·6	8·6	63·7	3·5	11·9	8·2	67·8	0·0	9·5	7·0	73·9	0·0	+ 9·1	+ 1·6	+10·2	+ 3·5
Venezuela	0·7	8·2	3·3	73·7	0·4	8·6	7·3	74·8	1·0	9·8	10·7	68·8	1·7	+ 1·6	+ 7·4	− 4·9	+ 1·0
Mexico	0·1	2·9	5·6	86·4	0·2	2·2	6·3	80·9	0·4	2·2	7·1	79·0	0·0	− 0·7	+ 1·5	− 7·4	+ 0·4
Canada	2·9	4·1	0·6	92·0	—	8·1	1·6	85·2	0·6	10·0	2·5	80·0	1·2	+ 5·9	+ 1·9	−12·0	+ 1·0
U.S.A.	3·9	14·5	4·4	—	0·5	12·0	19·4	—	1·2	12·6	12·4	—	2·9	− 1·9	+ 8·0	—	+ 2·4
W. Europe Sample	27·3	32·1	19·0	6·7	6·7	24·1	26·7	7·8	8·3	21·3	23·9	6·8	12·0	−10·8	+ 4·9	+ 0·1	+ 5·3
E.E.C.	12·7	22·7	19·0	8·4	9·8	18·5	25·6	8·9	11·9	15·7	23·1	8·2	14·8	− 7·0	+ 4·1	− 0·2	+ 5·0
S. Com'wealth Sample	34·9	75·4	4·2	9·1	2·0	61·4	11·3	9·2	1·2	60·3	12·0	7·2	1·2	−15·1	+ 7·8	+ 1·9	+ 0·8
World	111·1	24·7	8·4	34·0	2·4	20·8	13·2	31·7	3·0	20·7	5·2	26·7	14·8	− 4·0	+ 3·2	− 7·3	+12·4

* Rubber fabricated materials (e.g. plates, sheets, pastes, tubes), tyres, medical and surgical goods of rubber; rubber bands, gloves, mats, pillows, etc.

Table V. Glass and glassware (S.I.T.C. 664 and 665)*

Import Market	U.K. Exports 1959 $m.	1953 U.K.	1953 W.G.	1953 U.S.A.	1953 B-Lux.	1957 U.K.	1957 W.G.	1957 U.S.A.	1957 B-Lux.	1959 U.K.	1959 W.G.	1959 U.S.A.	1959 B-Lux.	1953-59 U.K.	1953-59 W.G.	1953-59 U.S.A.	1953-59 B-Lux.
Belgium-Luxembourg	0·4	3·0	24·7	7·6	—	4·2	34·7	5·9	—	3·4	31·9	3·7	—	+ 0·4	+ 7·2	− 3·9	+ 1·4
Denmark	1·0	27·6	20·8	2·5	20·2	16·8	29·6	4·5	16·5	15·2	29·4	4·7	21·6	− 12·4	+ 8·6	+ 2·2	+ 1·4
Finland	0·3	60·3	0·0	6·7	0·0	38·9	14·8	8·5	13·7	29·7	28·8	2·2	13·7	− 30·6	+ 28·8	− 4·5	+ 13·7
France	0·4	8·5	12·7	19·5	37·7	9·3	40·2	7·6	26·2	5·4	37·6	8·4	20·8	+ 0·8	+ 24·9	− 17·2	+ 1·6
West Germany	0·7	6·2	—	25·9	3·5	5·9	—	12·6	9·3	5·4	—	6·6	34·3	+ 0·3	—	− 17·5	+ 17·3
Italy	0·7	3·2	20·5	5·5	42·4	4·3	35·4	6·5	35·8	3·5	26·9	2·8	58·3	+ 0·3	+ 6·4	+ 1·1	− 8·1
Netherlands	1·5	6·1	16·8	6·6	69·6	5·9	26·5	4·5	53·8	4·9	27·5	1·6	35·8	− 1·2	+ 10·7	− 3·8	− 11·3
Norway	0·7	24·6	13·0	2·2	27·7	18·2	18·5	1·3	34·4	15·0	19·8	1·6	33·8	− 9·6	+ 6·8	− 0·6	− 8·1
Sweden	1·4	18·6	18·2	11·6	38·4	15·4	34·6	11·3	27·4	12·5	32·0	10·1	33·8	− 6·1	+ 13·8	− 1·5	+ 4·6
Australia	7·2	53·4	2·6	1·7	39·1	43·8	6·6	12·0	24·7	37·9	7·9	15·0	25·8	− 15·5	+ 5·3	+ 13·3	− 13·3
British East Africa	0·7	67·5	17·1	0·0	4·7	22·5	34·1	0·0	17·1	48·8	11·2	0·0	9·7	− 18·7	− 5·9	0·0	− 5·0
Ceylon	0·3	54·3	8·4	6·4	5·9	49·1	3·5	0·0	11·3	(42·9)	2·9	0·0	(14·3)	− 11·4	− 5·5	− 6·4	+ 8·4
Ghana	0·6	80·1	5·7	0·0	10·4	45·7	4·5	0·0	25·6	44·6	7·9	5·9	23·7	− 35·5	+ 2·2	0·0	+ 13·3
India	0·6	46·4	3·1	3·4	30·2	36·3	7·1	4·8	23·5	26·3	9·7	1·5	11·6	− 15·4	+ 6·6	+ 2·5	− 18·6
Malaya	0·5	41·7	4·2	26·2	13·4	39·7	7·4	2·6	21·5	55·9	7·1	2·1	19·8	+ 15·4	+ 2·9	− 24·7	+ 6·4
New Zealand	2·3	80·3	0·6	0·0	18·6	68·9	5·3	0·7	21·2	57·2	7·1	2·1	28·9	− 24·4	+ 6·5	+ 2·1	+ 10·3
Nigeria	0·9	53·4	7·7	0·0	6·5	57·1	13·3	0·0	7·2	57·2	12·2	0·0	4·5	+ 3·8	+ 4·5	0·0	− 2·0
Pakistan	0·5	29·1	17·7	4·2	22·4	36·5	20·3	5·2	7·5	42·0	8·1	4·4	11·2	+ 12·9	− 9·6	+ 0·2	− 11·2
Rhodesia and Nyasaland	0·7	100·0	0·0	0·0	—	78·7	1·7	4·1	7·3	83·6	3·0	3·4	2·1	− 16·4	+ 3·0	+ 3·4	+ 2·1
Union of South Africa	5·1	65·5	2·5	18·7	5·1	65·4	7·8	10·8	5·8	67·7	6·2	7·9	7·5	+ 2·2	+ 3·7	− 10·8	+ 2·4
Iran	0·3	0·0	7·0	45·3	37·4	11·7	20·4	13·1	23·5	9·8	13·0	12·4	11·3	+ 9·8	+ 6·0	− 32·9	− 26·1
Iraq	0·3	26·7	6·4	15·6	17·7	16·6	16·8	8·3	16·7	20·0	13·7	7·9	16·2	− 6·7	+ 7·3	− 7·7	− 1·5
Argentine	0·4	14·2	49·4	9·4	0·0	21·4	10·6	18·0	18·4	13·7	17·7	14·8	21·0	− 0·5	− 31·7	+ 5·4	+ 21·0
Brazil	0·5	0·0	13·6	34·6	2·7	10·1	10·0	33·9	17·9	15·0	11·4	19·5	23·9	+ 15·0	+ 2·2	− 15·1	+ 21·2
Colombia	0·2	4·7	6·7	80·8	5·8	9·6	13·6	45·2	23·0	8·3	15·8	39·0	25·0	+ 3·6	+ 9·1	− 41·8	+ 19·2
Peru	0·0	4·2	15·9	58·3	17·9	4·7	17·9	38·9	20·1	1·8	16·8	36·3	23·3	+ 2·4	+ 0·9	− 22·0	+ 5·4
Venezuela	0·0	1·2	4·7	84·9	5·4	3·7	11·2	61·4	14·4	1·6	12·0	55·1	21·5	+ 0·4	+ 7·3	− 29·8	+ 16·1
Mexico	0·1	0·4	6·5	73·1	13·3	2·6	5·6	67·9	11·0	2·9	6·3	73·8	6·9	+ 2·5	+ 0·2	+ 0·7	− 6·4
Canada	7·5	2·2	2·6	83·0	9·0	14·4	23·8	0·0	8·8	12·5	6·6	61·5	12·7	+ 10·3	+ 4·0	− 21·5	+ 3·7
U.S.A.	8·6	1·3	27·4	—	35·7	8·7	—	6·5	32·4	10·6	9·6	—	33·8	+ 9·3	+ 7·8	—	+ 1·9
W. Europe Sample	7·1	9·2	17·5	8·5	39·3	8·2	28·5	6·4	31·8	6·7	25·3	5·2	35·0	− 2·5	+ 7·8	− 3·3	− 4·3
E.E.C.	3·7	5·0	17·5	9·1	42·2	5·6	28·4	6·4	33·6	4·5	24·3	4·7	36·4	− 0·5	+ 6·8	− 4·4	− 5·8
S. Com'wealth Sample	19·2	59·0	3·7	7·1	21·7	51·4	7·9	7·7	17·9	47·3	7·6	9·2	19·3	− 11·7	+ 3·9	+ 2·1	− 2·4
World	52·8	13·6	13·0	32·4	18·3	13·5	17·7	22·9	21·0	12·3	17·2	19·3	24·4	+ 1·3	+ 4·2	− 13·1	+ 6·1

* Sheet and plate glass, bottles, flasks, glass table-ware, etc.

Table W. Pottery (S.I.T.C. 666)*

Import Market	U.K. Exports 1959 $m	1953			1957			1959			1953–59		
		U.K.	W.G.	Japan	U.K.	W.G.	Japan	U.K.	W.G.	Japan	U.K.	W.G.	Japan
Belgium-Luxembourg	0·1	3·7	47·6	5·0	1·6	49·0	9·7	2·1	42·5	8·9	− 1·6	− 5·1	+ 3·9
Denmark	0·1	21·3	67·8	0·0	18·5	55·1	2·4	7·8	57·6	16·2	− 13·5	− 10·2	+ 16·2
Finland	0·0	(0·0	0·0	0·0)	(0·0	65·0	0·0)	(0·0	97·0	0·0)	0·0	+ 97·0	0·0
France	0·2	11·5	61·8	4·1	12·6	65·0	0·0	9·3	71·8	2·2	− 2·2	+ 10·0	− 1·9
West Germany	0·6	50·4	—	27·9	24·3	—	28·6	19·4	—	27·1	− 31·0	—	− 0·8
Italy	0·7	2·8	94·1	2·1	6·9	83·1	6·3	7·2	81·3	7·2	+ 4·4	− 12·8	+ 5·1
Netherlands	0·3	5·8	75·9	12·4	4·8	75·4	11·1	6·3	67·3	10·9	+ 0·5	− 8·6	− 1·5
Norway	0·1	29·6	14·1	42·1	30·3	22·7	5·5	12·5	63·1	0·0	− 17·1	+ 49·0	− 42·1
Sweden	0·3	12·0	74·9	6·3	8·1	69·4	16·7	10·7	58·7	23·4	− 1·3	− 16·2	+ 17·1
Australia	5·2	97·2	1·9	0·3	70·2	6·7	19·5	63·5	3·6	31·2	− 33·7	+ 1·7	+ 30·9
British East Africa	0·2	62·5	13·8	23·7	38·2	4·8	57·0	38·9	0·0	58·1	− 23·6	− 13·8	+ 34·4
Ceylon	0·1	41·8	0·0	58·2	34·5	0·0	65·5	43·6	0·0	56·4	+ 1·8	0·0	− 1·8
Ghana	0·0	(48·1)	16·9	35·1	(39·4)	13·8	31·3	(51·5)	12·3	18·1	+ 3·4	− 4·6	− 17·0
India	0·2	(29·1)	0·0	69·8	(37·7)	5·9	55·5	(90·3)	0·0	0·0	+ 61·2	0·0	− 69·8
Malaya	1·5	17·4	6·0	82·6	17·9	0·9	81·3	18·2	1·1	80·3	+ 0·8	− 4·9	− 2·3
New Zealand	0·2	91·3	30·1	0·0	89·1	6·5	2·0	75·4	6·4	17·4	− 15·9	− 23·7	+ 17·4
Nigeria	0·1	49·0	0·0	0·0	30·9	5·4	51·8	45·5	8·9	33·8	− 3·5	+ 8·9	+ 33·8
Pakistan	0·6	(63·0)	0·0	34·8	18·0	0·0	82·0	12·1	0·0	87·9	− 50·9	0·0	+ 53·1
Rhodesia and Nyasaland	0·6	100·0	0·0	0·0	95·4	4·6	0·0	96·0	4·0	0·0	− 4·0	+ 4·0	0·0
Union of South Africa	2·0	64·1	2·7	29·2	52·9	8·3	30·0	60·5	9·8	22·2	− 3·6	+ 7·1	− 7·0
Iran	0·0	0·0	0·0	100·0	1·5	7·3	90·9	1·6	9·3	89·0	+ 1·6	+ 9·3	− 11·0
Iraq	0·0	5·6	0·0	94·4	6·6	6·1	86·9	5·6	7·5	86·9	0·0	+ 7·5	− 7·5
Argentine	0·0	(43·6)	53·8	1·6	(25·7)	49·7	7·3	(12·3)	67·9	0·0	− 31·3	+ 14·1	0·0
Brazil	0·0	10·2	85·0	0·0	5·9	61·6	7·4	0·0	47·8	18·8	− 10·2	− 37·2	+ 17·2
Colombia	0·0	11·0	58·2	15·3	0·0	69·7	30·3	0·0	84·7	15·3	− 11·0	+ 26·5	0·0
Peru	0·0	36·3	43·2	16·3	22·7	20·1	44·2	(38·1)	42·9	19·0	+ 1·8	− 0·3	+ 2·7
Venezuela	0·3	33·4	35·5	0·0	15·6	24·4	38·8	11·9	20·0	47·3	− 21·5	− 15·5	+ 47·3
Mexico	0·0	5·3	53·3	0·0	3·1	35·9	40·9	(4·3)	33·4	34·4	− 1·0	− 19·9	+ 34·4
Canada	13·1	77·5	2·0	6·9	69·9	4·4	11·9	72·9	3·8	11·9	− 4·6	+ 1·8	+ 5·0
U.S.A.	9·8	22·7	16·4	42·4	16·5	14·4	57·8	16·5	14·5	58·9	− 6·2	− 1·9	+ 16·5
W. Europe Sample	2·4	8·0	71·2	6·4	8·1	63·3	10·0	8·1	58·4	11·7	+ 0·1	− 12·8	+ 5·3
E.E.C.	1·9	5·3	72·7	5·4	7·3	63·6	9·5	7·7	58·2	10·5	+ 2·4	− 14·5	+ 5·1
S. Com'wealth Sample	10·4	77·3	3·4	17·9	61·0	6·1	28·7	58·4	4·8	33·8	− 18·9	+ 1·4	+ 15·9
World	39·4	32·1	23·0	26·1	24·7	24·7	34·9	24·6	23·6	36·6	− 7·5	+ 0·6	+ 10·5

* Table and other household articles of ordinary baked clay, stoneware, chinaware and porcelain.

Table X. Scientific instruments (S.I.T.C. 861)*

Import Market	U.K. Exports 1959 $m.	1953				1957				1959				1953–59			
		U.K.	W.G.	U.S.A.	Japan	U.K.	W.G.	U.S.A.	Japan	U.K.	W.G.	U.S.A.	Japan	U.K.	W.G.	U.S.A.	Japan
Belgium-Luxembourg	1·6	11·6	36·4	20·4	0·3	10·2	42·4	15·0	3·9	6·7	30·6	11·1	5·1	− 4·9	− 5·8	− 9·3	+ 4·8
Denmark	1·4	16·7	55·5	9·9	0·5	12·9	44·7	8·1	3·1	12·4	53·1	9·4	5·3	− 4·3	− 2·4	− 0·5	+ 4·8
Finland	0·6	26·7	30·5	7·7	0·4	10·1	56·5	3·1	2·2	10·6	51·2	8·8	6·4	− 16·1	+ 20·7	+ 1·1	+ 6·0
France	3·5	20·4	26·3	17·5	0·0	17·1	33·8	20·8	0·2	14·9	36·1	22·2	0·5	− 5·5	+ 9·8	+ 4·7	+ 0·5
West Germany	3·9	9·9	—	20·7	0·1	12·8	—	36·0	2·0	12·0	—	24·0	8·5	+ 2·1	—	+ 3·3	+ 8·4
Italy	3·0	11·2	49·4	19·3	0·0	12·8	50·5	16·4	0·3	12·1	46·0	19·8	3·3	+ 0·9	− 3·4	+ 0·5	+ 3·3
Netherlands	3·9	20·1	48·5	5·4	0·3	15·5	55·5	7·4	4·3	15·7	50·0	12·8	6·7	− 4·4	+ 1·5	+ 7·4	+ 6·4
Norway	1·0	19·8	41·6	10·7	0·8	18·3	49·3	6·2	2·4	13·0	49·2	9·3	6·4	− 6·8	+ 7·6	+ 1·4	+ 5·6
Sweden	2·7	11·3	53·3	7·0	2·8	9·2	45·5	10·6	5·9	10·1	50·9	11·5	13·4	− 1·2	+ 2·4	+ 4·5	+ 10·6
Australia	8·3	63·5	18·8	7·2	0·5	45·5	24·1	11·0	7·3	38·6	24·4	12·9	15·5	− 24·9	+ 5·6	+ 5·7	+ 15·0
British East Africa	1·3	64·1	16·4	0·0	1·5	52·8	26·8	3·9	6·4	59·0	20·4	2·8	9·0	− 5·1	+ 4·0	+ 2·8	+ 7·5
Ceylon	0·5	62·0	12·3	18·3	4·9	62·1	19·7	8·8	5·1	(47·1)	18·2	14·0	9·9	− 14·9	+ 5·9	− 4·3	+ 5·0
Ghana	0·6	(77·9)	19·6	0·0	2·5	(58·1)	28·3	1·4	1·8	(62·4)	21·4	6·7	6·3	− 15·5	+ 1·8	+ 6·7	+ 3·8
India	5·1	44·0	24·3	20·0	4·1	35·1	24·8	20·6	7·2	44·3	18·4	21·2	4·3	+ 0·3	+ 5·9	+ 1·2	+ 0·2
Malaya	1·5	48·8	25·7	21·1	4·0	29·2	43·6	7·5	17·5	33·3	27·3	7·2	29·8	− 15·5	+ 1·6	− 13·9	+ 25·8
New Zealand	1·9	67·0	18·8	9·4	0·8	42·7	33·8	8·7	9·3	46·1	24·5	12·3	8·2	− 20·9	+ 5·7	+ 2·9	+ 7·4
Nigeria	1·1	77·0	11·1	0·0	8·9	61·9	16·8	0·0	9·3	58·7	15·1	3·0	10·1	− 18·3	+ 4·0	+ 3·0	+ 1·2
Pakistan	1·1	51·8	22·0	12·9	4·9	38·0	16·7	35·2	2·7	32·1	16·5	34·4	6·1	− 19·7	+ 5·5	+ 21·5	+ 1·2
Rhodesia and Nyasaland	0·8	85·8	14·1	0·0	0·0	50·4	25·1	18·1	0·0	49·7	29·5	9·0	0·0	− 36·1	+ 15·4	+ 9·0	+ 0·0
Union of South Africa	3·3	48·0	21·6	26·5	1·9	30·0	25·9	25·2	8·9	26·8	29·7	20·8	11·7	− 21·2	+ 8·1	+ 5·7	+ 9·8
Iran	1·5	5·9	36·8	42·7	7·0	27·4	40·4	13·0	4·8	29·9	34·9	20·2	4·5	+ 24·0	− 1·9	− 22·5	− 2·5
Iraq	0·7	60·0	15·2	9·7	4·6	48·6	26·2	11·6	2·5	49·0	24·9	9·6	8·4	− 11·0	+ 9·7	+ 0·1	+ 3·8
Argentine	0·3	9·8	47·1	17·2	4·3	7·1	34·7	16·8	7·9	5·6	29·7	28·9	3·8	− 4·2	− 17·4	+ 11·7	+ 0·5
Brazil	0·3	3·4	28·6	37·7	2·4	5·6	33·5	33·8	8·1	4·1	36·3	34·5	6·2	+ 0·7	+ 7·7	− 3·2	+ 3·8
Colombia	0·2	4·2	24·6	58·1	2·8	2·4	29·2	56·9	2·4	6·9	34·8	46·8	6·8	+ 2·7	+ 5·3	− 11·3	+ 4·0
Peru	0·1	2·7	27·4	57·4	3·0	2·8	36·9	30·1	10·7	2·4	34·8	42·2	12·7	− 0·3	+ 7·4	− 15·2	+ 9·7
Venezuela	0·5	7·3	20·0	61·9	2·4	4·6	21·4	60·7	3·3	3·6	26·2	52·7	6·7	− 3·7	+ 6·2	− 9·2	+ 4·3
Mexico	0·2	1·6	22·1	65·4	4·8	2·0	30·5	50·6	5·0	2·5	24·3	62·0	5·4	+ 0·9	+ 2·2	+ 3·4	+ 0·6
Canada	2·8	7·3	8·3	80·6	1·8	4·8	12·2	71·8	7·2	4·5	24·3	75·4	7·9	− 2·8	+ 0·0	− 5·2	+ 6·1
U.S.A.	4·0	4·9	61·4	—	15·5	3·8	41·0	—	29·7	4·1	38·4	20·8	33·0	− 0·8	− 23·0	—	+ 17·5
W. Europe Sample	21·6	15·1	40·8	13·7	0·7	13·0	40·5	15·4	2·9	12·0	36·5	16·1	6·4	− 3·1	− 4·3	+ 2·4	+ 5·7
E.E.C.	15·9	15·1	36·3	16·2	0·2	13·9	37·2	18·8	2·1	12·3	30·7	18·3	5·1	− 2·8	− 5·6	+ 2·1	+ 4·9
S. Com'wealth Sample	25·5	56·1	20·7	14·6	2·4	39·4	26·9	15·6	8·3	39·2	23·7	15·8	11·8	− 16·9	+ 3·0	+ 1·2	+ 9·4
World	74·1	14·2	34·8	25·5	5·6	11·8	33·1	28·2	8·6	10·6	30·0	28·9	10·6	− 3·6	− 4·8	+ 3·4	+ 5·0

* Optical instruments and appliances; photographic and cinematograph apparatus; surgical, medical and dental appliances (not electric); measuring and controlling instruments.

INDEX